AF531072

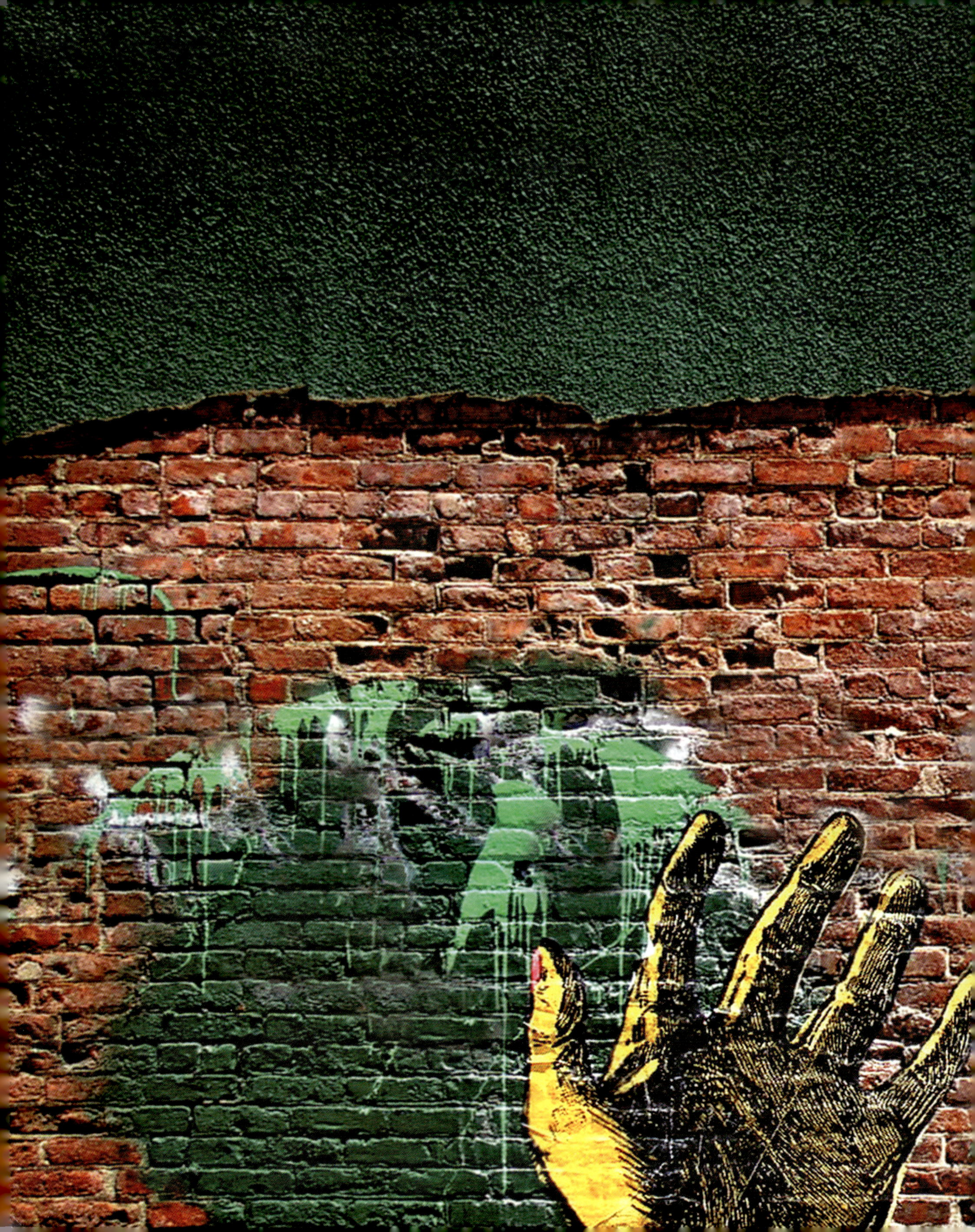

STREET ART NEW YORK

JAIME ROJO AND STEVEN P. HARRINGTON

WITH A FOREWORD BY CAROLINA A. MIRANDA

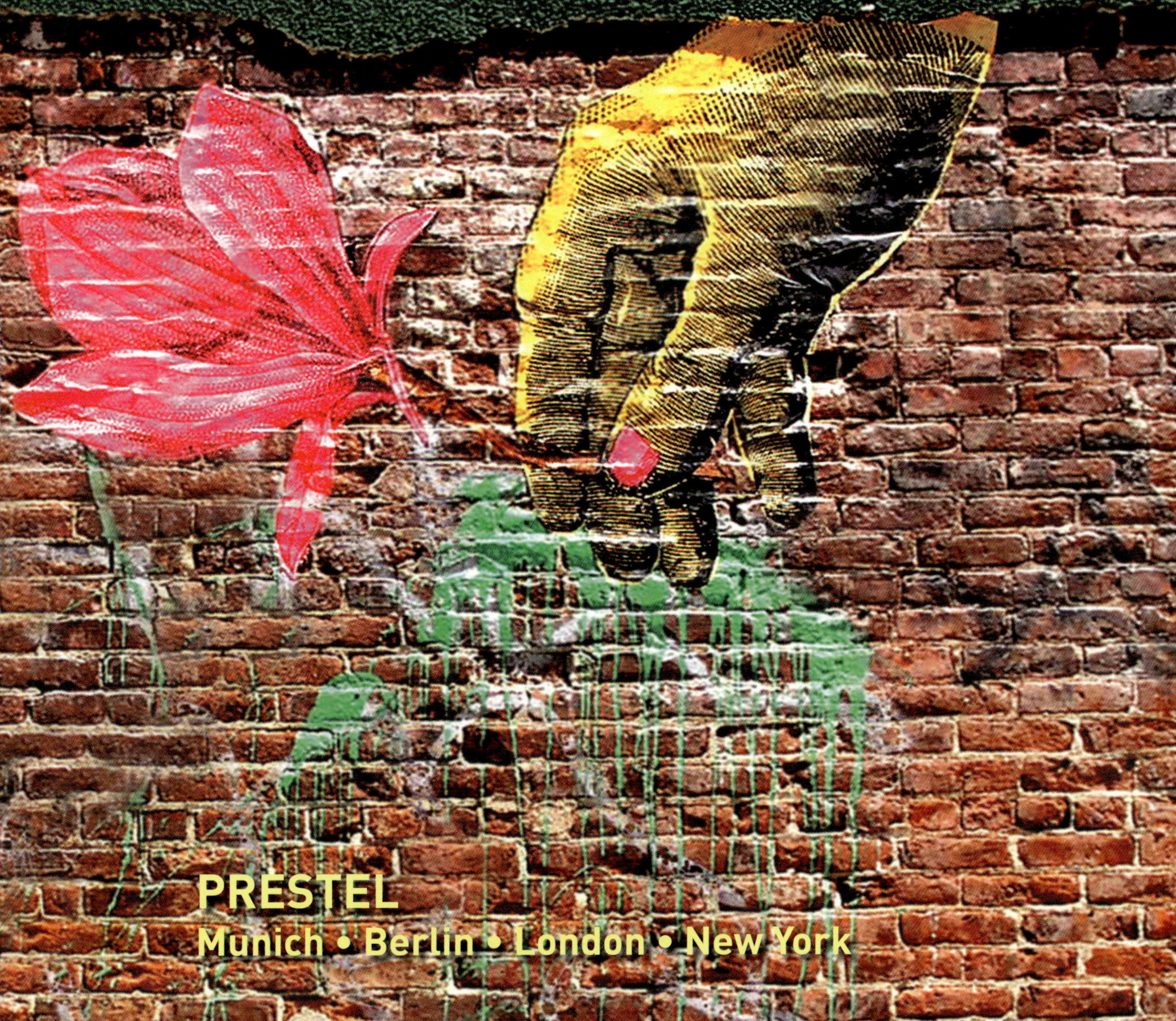

PRESTEL
Munich • Berlin • London • New York

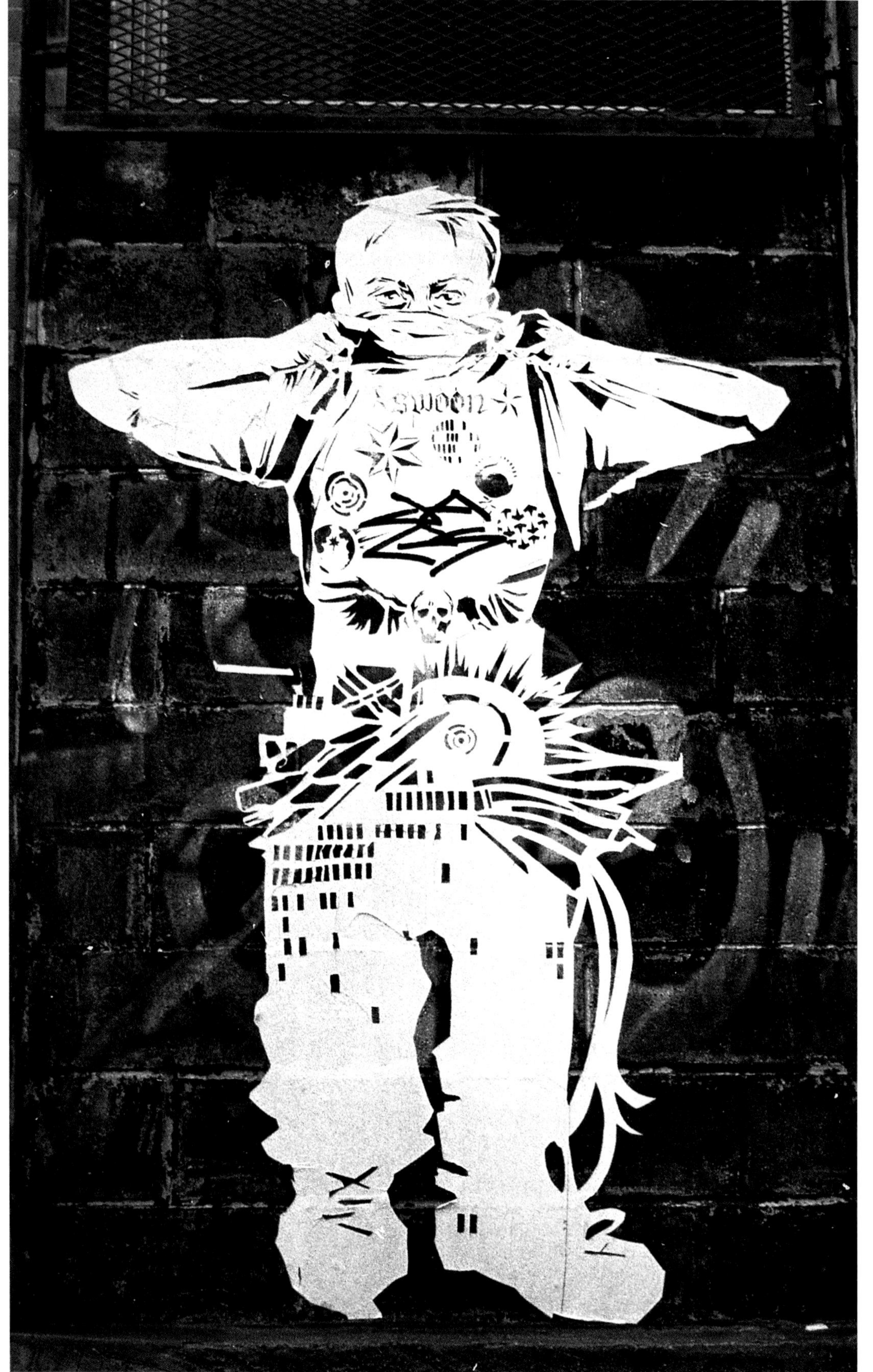
swoon

As far as works of art go, this one was technically crude: an unlawful doodle of a robot in blue ink, one metallic arm held up as if saying hello. He resided on the side of a fire department call box somewhere on the downtown end of Lexington Avenue—about a foot tall, with a hasty, crooked smile and a pair of sleepy eyes that suggested he might be stoned. For years I saw him almost daily as I made my way around the neighborhood. (I lived in the area then.) And, everyday, without fail, he would dutifully greet me with a wave of his wrench-shaped hand. There were days I felt compelled to wave back.

This funny little creature wasn't the most eye-popping piece of street art I'd ever seen. It was neither elaborate, nor drenched with layers of socio-political meaning. It was a simple gesture, by an anonymous artist, yet it had the power to draw my attention on a daily basis, to turn a slab of dull municipal furniture into a dynamic piece of sculpture. In recent years, as street art has gone mainstream—assiduously documented in all manner of media, showcased in galleries, and acquired by museums—it can be easy to forget about the visceral reaction that comes from simply stumbling upon a piece of art on the street. Mummies and men made of sticks crowd doorways and alleys and the infinite nooks and crannies of New York City's grimy infrastructure, ready to greet and surprise during the course of an average, lost-in-thought day. In some spots, it's as if the city's walls are engaged in constant conversation with its citizens.

If street art has the power to induce reaction with its puking monsters, floating slugs, and silly sayings (*Fuck No Evil*), it also has the power to transform. A rusty metal panel becomes a textured backdrop to an oversized woodblock print by Swoon. A dingy brick wall highlights the nuclear colors of Judith Supine's hallucinogenic collages. The abstract works of artists such as MOMO and Aakash Nihalani highlight the city's boxy forms. And all of the overlooked elements of urban life—electrical pipes and garbage cans—are scrambled and reinterpreted by the brothers Skewville, whose three-dimensional sculptures have been found illicitly bolted, drilled, and nailed to urban walls.

These pieces, along with the many others featured in this book, remind us to open our eyes to the architecture we've stopped perceiving. New York City is a jumble of concrete and bricks and aluminum siding. Spend enough time here and it's as if the structures begin to fade into the background.

Old brownstones, graceful Beaux-Arts apartment buildings, and humble row houses all disappear as the eye becomes trained on more immediate concerns, like doggie doo, errant cyclists, and any signage advertising a two-for-one beer special.

Absent-mindedly round a corner, however, and come face to face with a well-placed, wildly colorful piece of graffiti and all of a sudden you're forced to really examine the city: the color of the walls, the texture of the bricks, the shape of the buildings, and the color of the sky around them. Even the most inane scrawl—a giant claw reaching along the entire side of a structure—can turn a monotonous row of concrete warehouses into a fantastical oversized comic book. Vandalism is often equated with the destruction of architecture. I'd like to argue that it can give it new life.

Ultimately, it's this energy that Jaime Rojo and Steven P. Harrington are celebrating in this book. The images you see before you have been culled from Rojo's personal archive of more than 12,000 film and digital photographs, taken throughout New York City over the course of seven years. Interestingly, it is a project that has its roots in another. Rojo, a devout photographer, was in the midst of shooting a series on abandoned furniture (a subject that still interests him as an artist), when he came across a small stencil of a man with a horse's head on a surfboard, done by the Brooklyn-based collective Faile. It was, he recalls, a moment of discovery. This was art that was all around him, yet he had never really taken it in. From that moment on, he chronicled what he found on the street: graffiti tags, paste-ups of giant wrestlers, mosaics of alien invaders, stickers of suggestive ladies, and even delicate trompe l'oeil paintings. In many cases, he had no idea who the artists were, only the visual evidence that they had been there.

Street Art New York is a record of these discoveries, the little moments when a piece of art peers at you from a wall and says *Look*. The works are big and small, by artists well-known and not. There are paintings and photographs, collages and stencils. Some have long since been destroyed, others, as I write this, are still living. It's an ongoing dialogue between an observer and the street. To listen, all you have to do is look.

Carolina A. Miranda
C-Monster.net

Carolina A. Miranda is a New York–based cultural journalist whose work has appeared in publications including TIME Magazine, ARTnews, *and on* NYTimes.com. *She also runs the arts and culture blog* C-Monster.net.

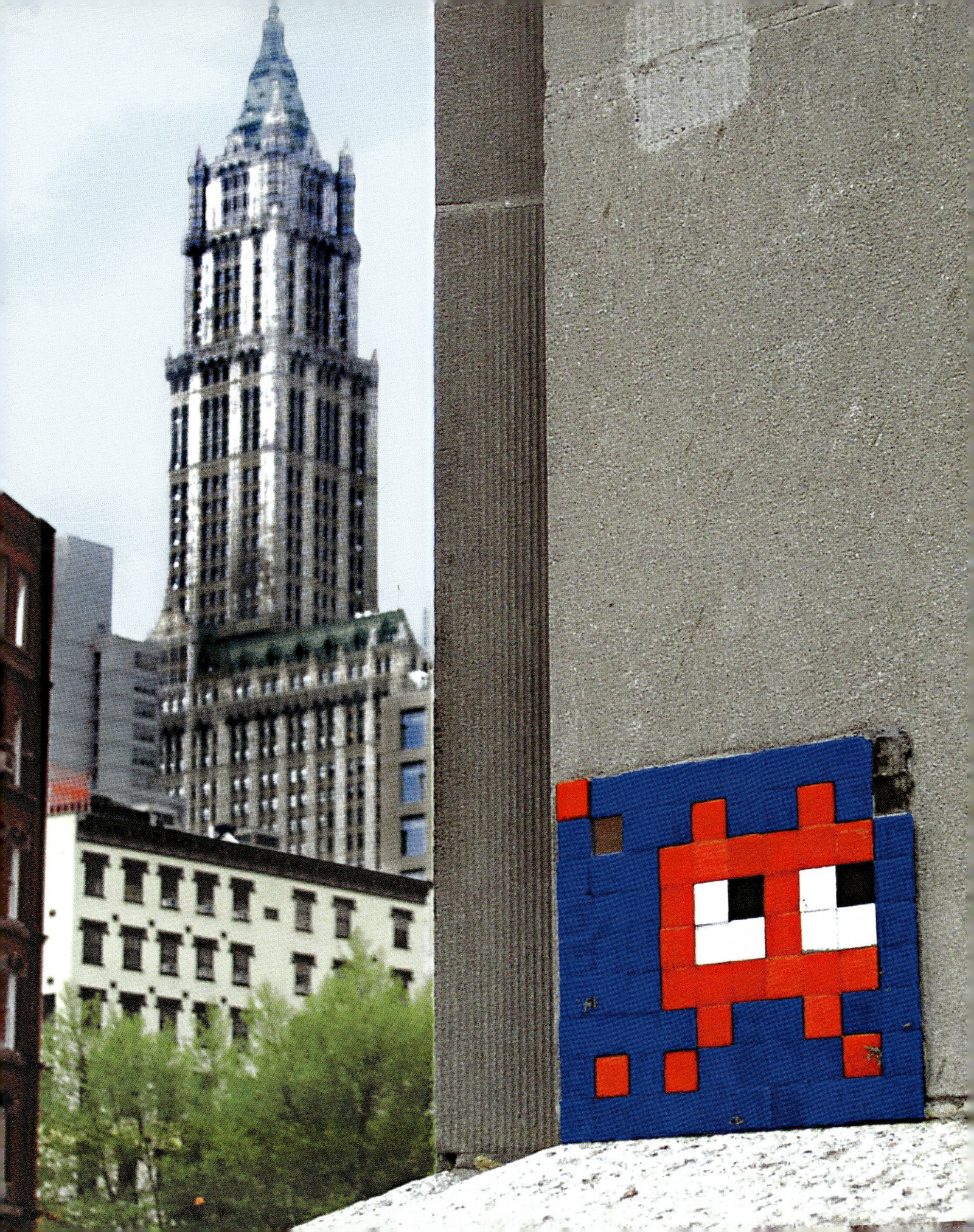

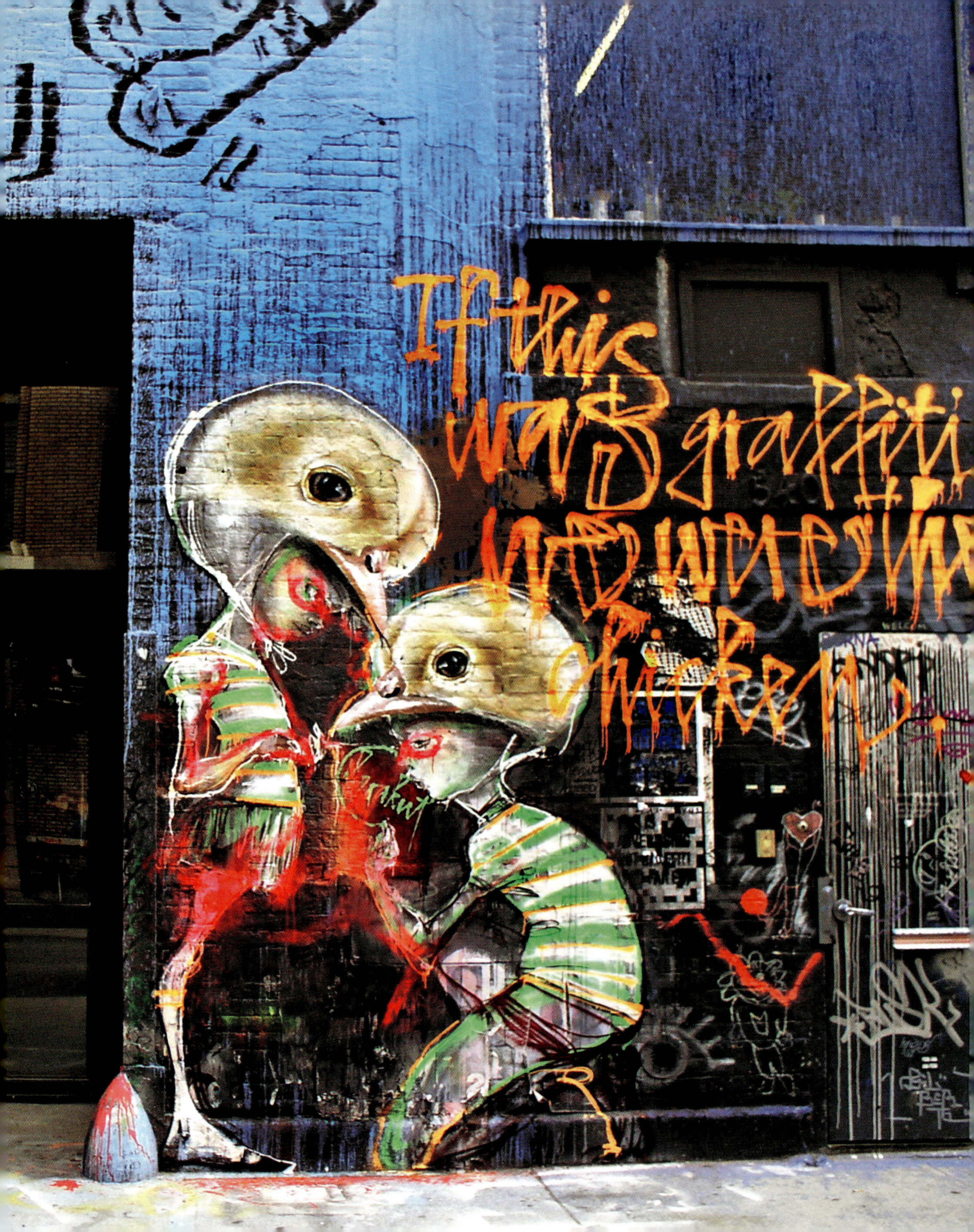
If this
was graffiti
chicken

LUCKY IN NEW YORK

We've been fortunate to witness the explosion of street art in New York.

If Walt Whitman were alive today, maybe he would be a photographer or street artist, capturing or being captured in images. The great American poet would wander the city, as we have, without a destination. It was during such an aimless walk, camera in hand, that Jaime first took photos of the new conversation on the streets by a population of artists who were no longer looking for a gallery but intent on creating one of their own. With roots in graffiti and inspired by 1980s artists including Keith Haring, Jean-Michel Basquiat, Jenny Holzer, and Richard Hambleton, this evolution of contemporary art broadened and began to take shape as "Street Art."

New York has always been a magnet for artists of all disciplines. With D.I.Y. spirit in full effect this past decade, many young artists simply took it upon themselves to rewrite the rules and make their art for the street. The resulting body of work bucks the lettering tradition of graffiti and the established gallery system at the same time by placing fine art in the "gallery of the street," in whatever style or school, under whatever influence, in any material and by any technique desired.

Jaime's collection of images began to grow in the autumn of 2001. Photographing discarded chairs left outdoors for a show at a Brooklyn gallery, he started to see curious visual traces left by anonymous artists. These were pasted, glued, bolted, or painted in hidden places and obvious ones. It was as though the street had started talking. (Whitman surely would have captured the words.) As a photographer, Jaime captured images, including the ones in this book.

In the years since then, it feels like one explosion has followed another, and the artists have taken their very personal messages to the street to meet and challenge viewers, including ourselves. We experience the art in a very personal way. We hope you are moved too, that you are inspired by the art presented here and this celebration of the creative spirit alive and well on the street. May you be as lucky in New York.

Steven P. Harrington and Jaime Rojo

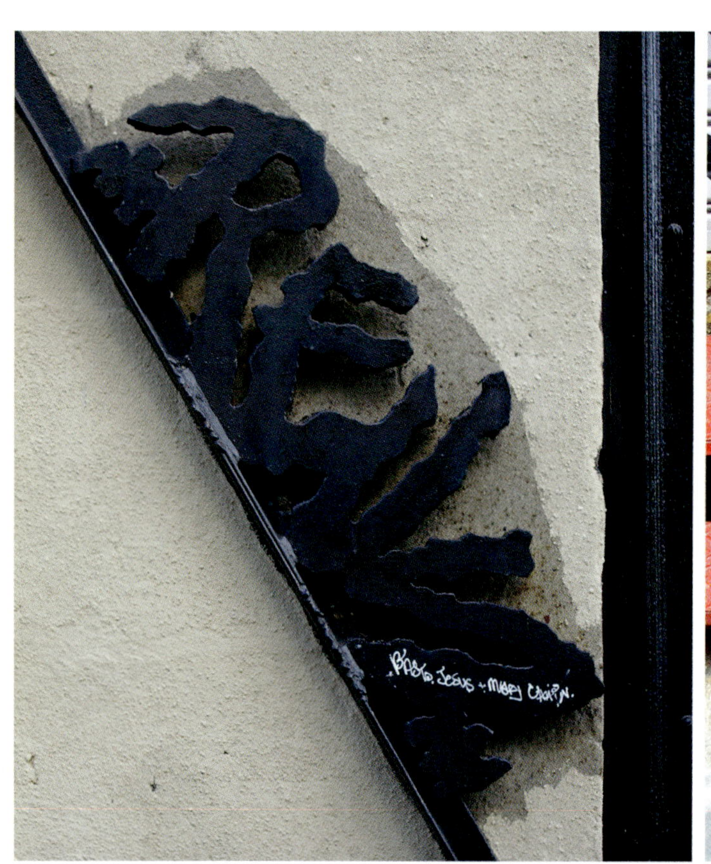
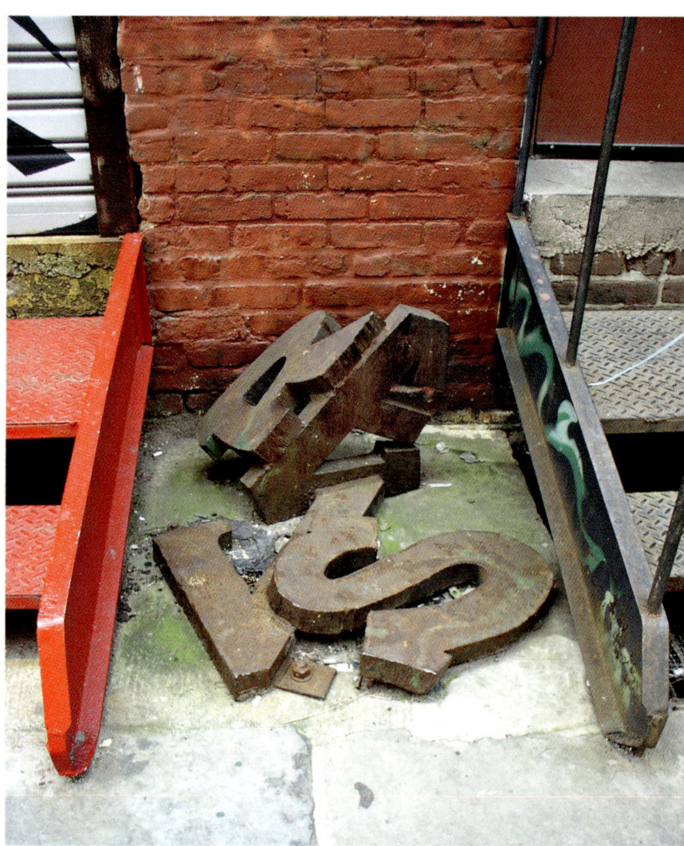
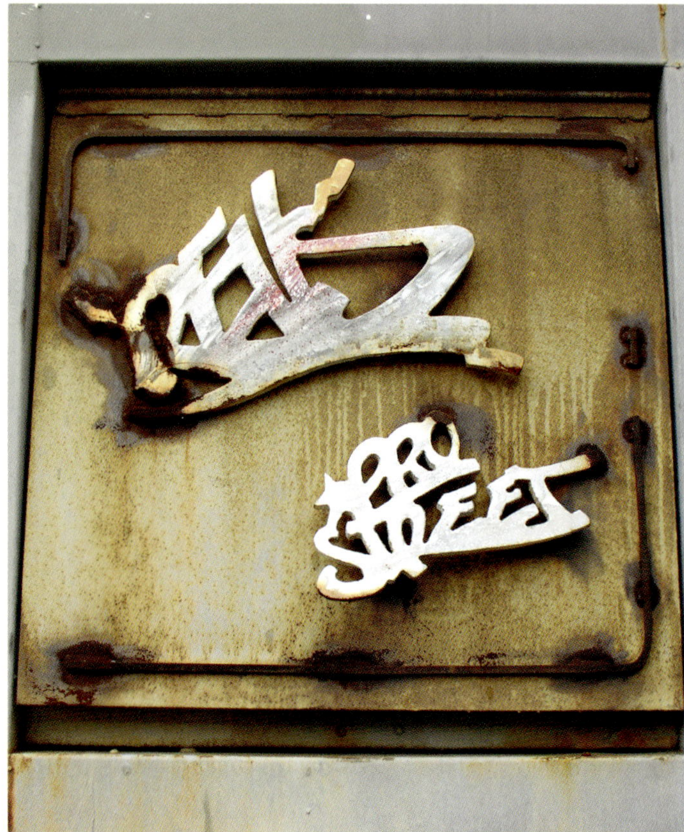
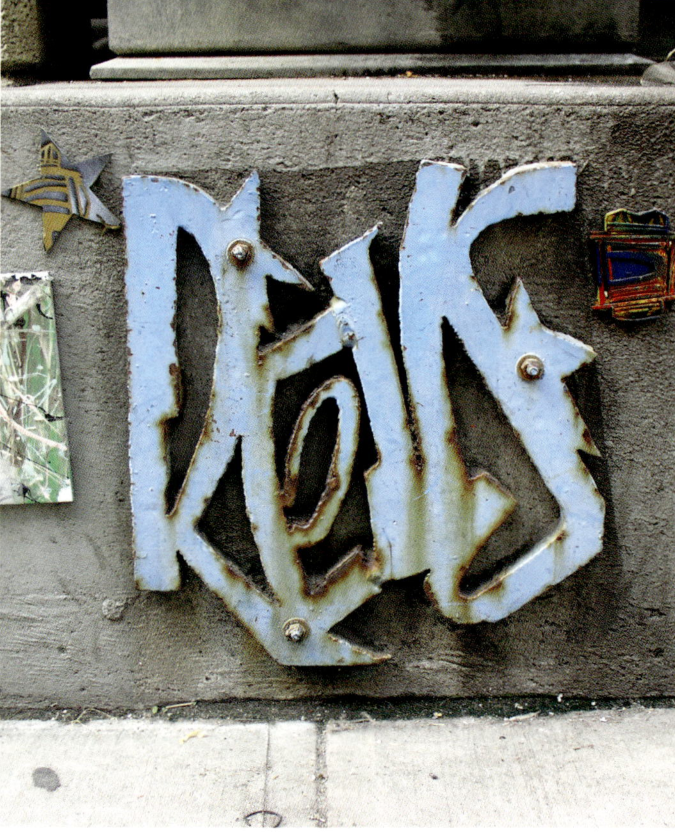

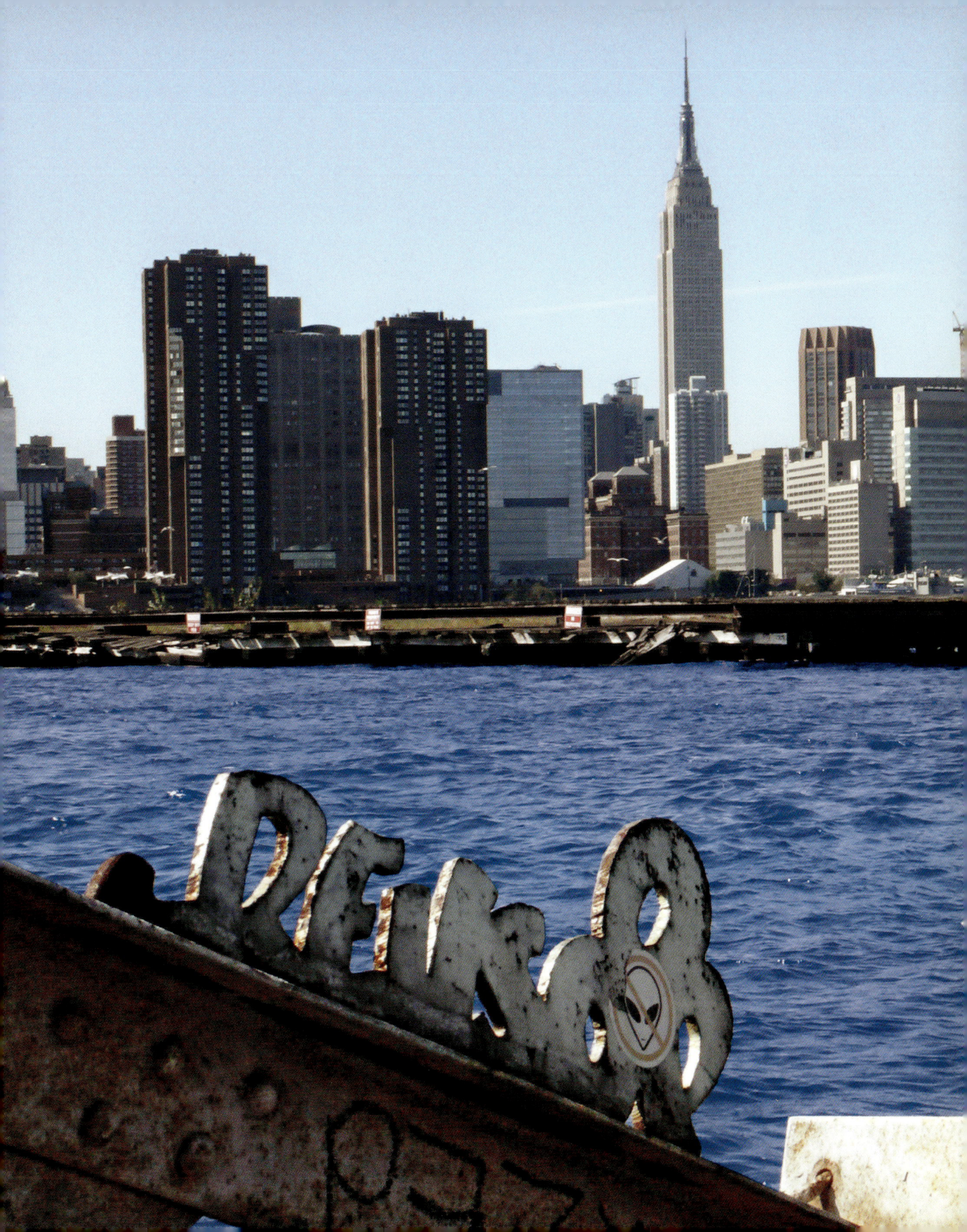

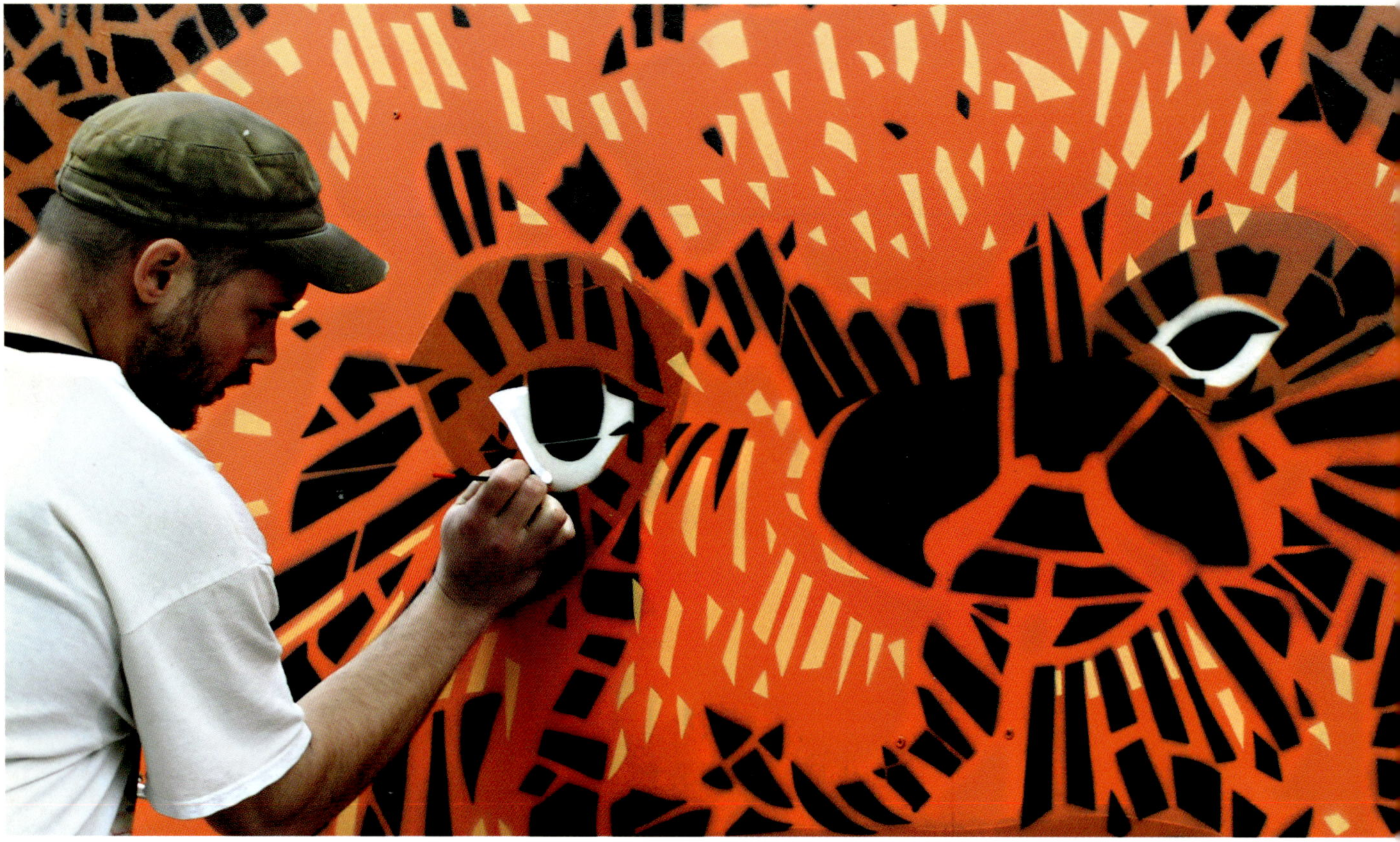

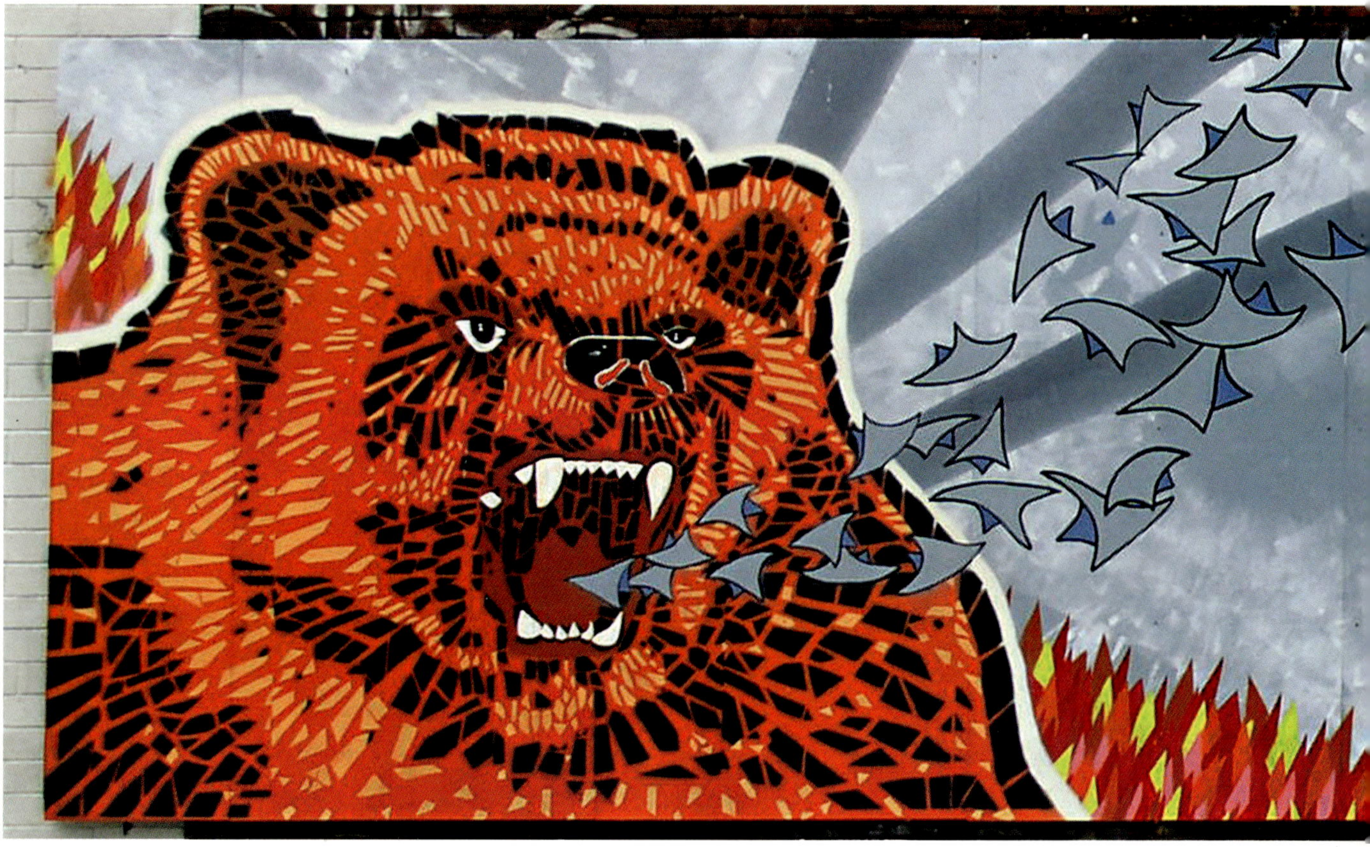

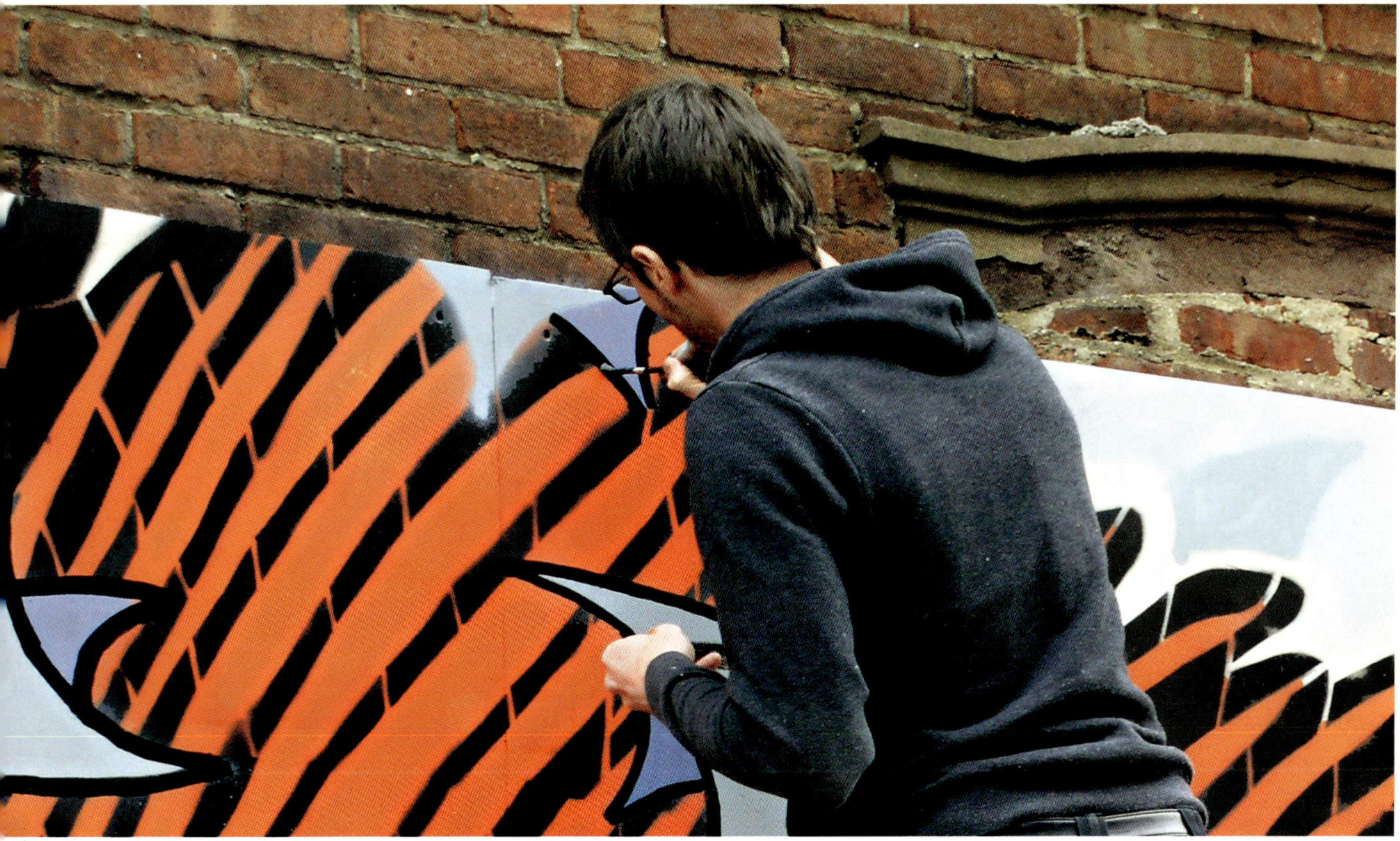

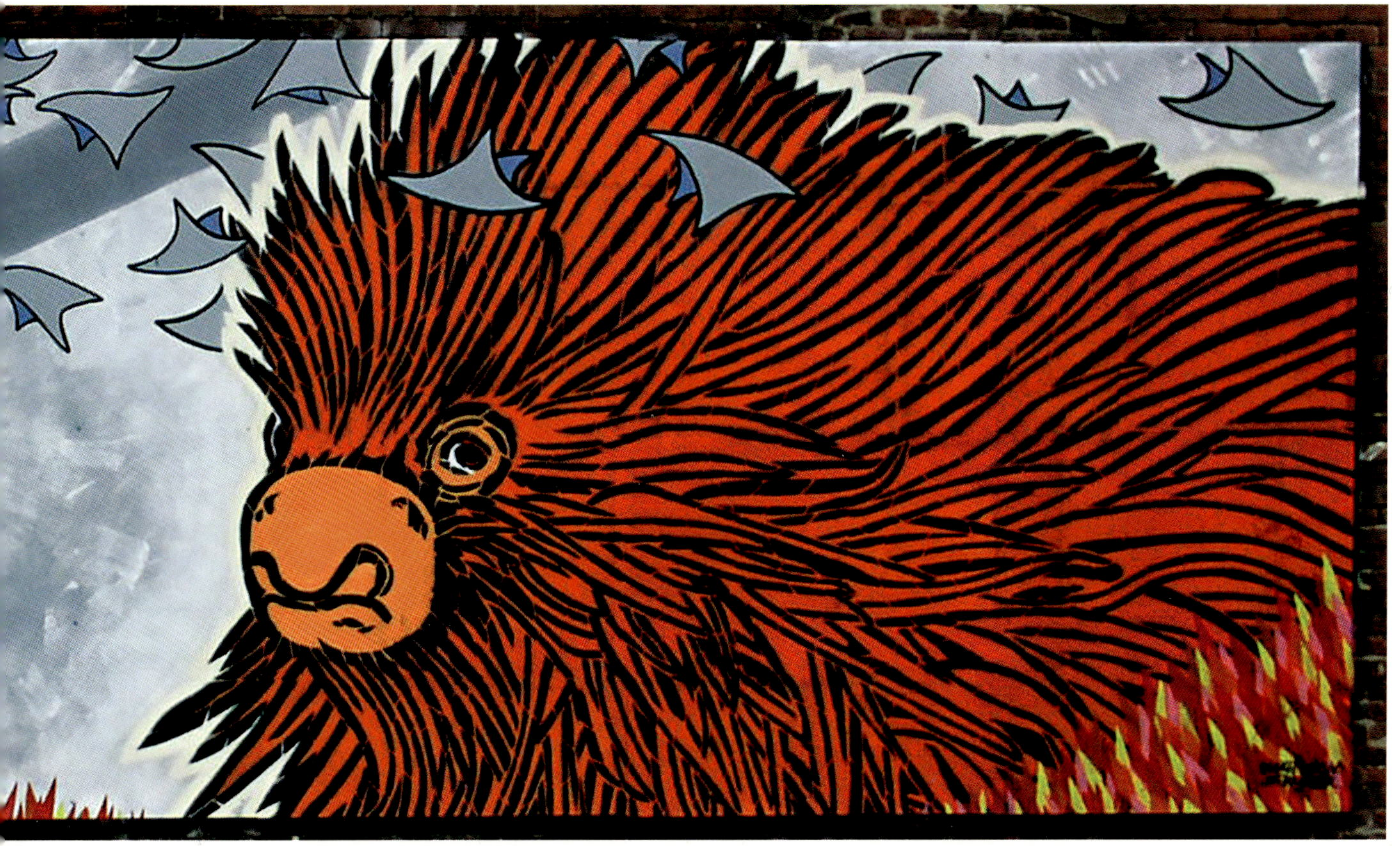

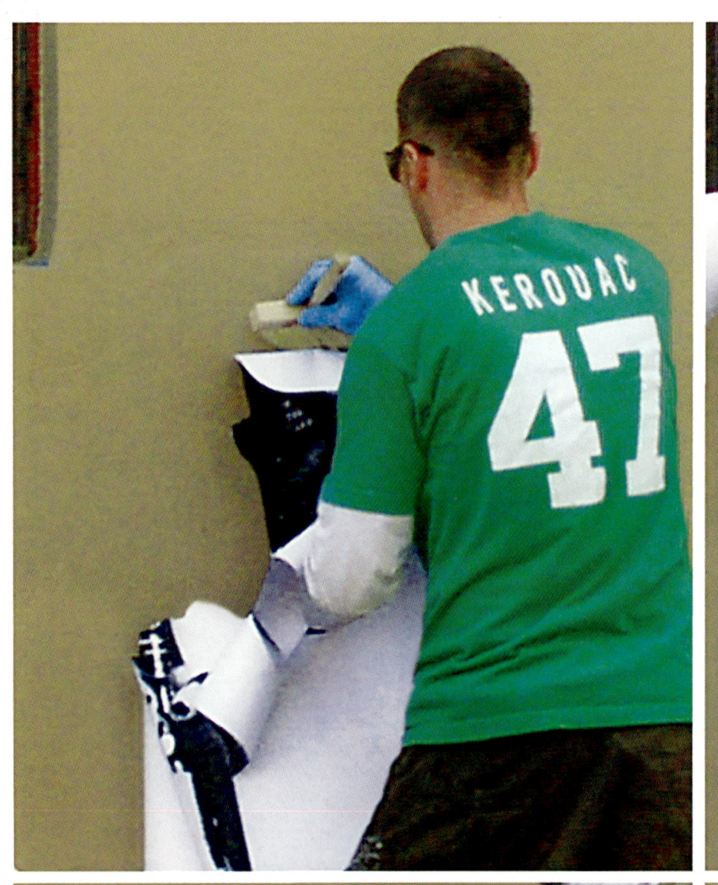
KEROUAC
47

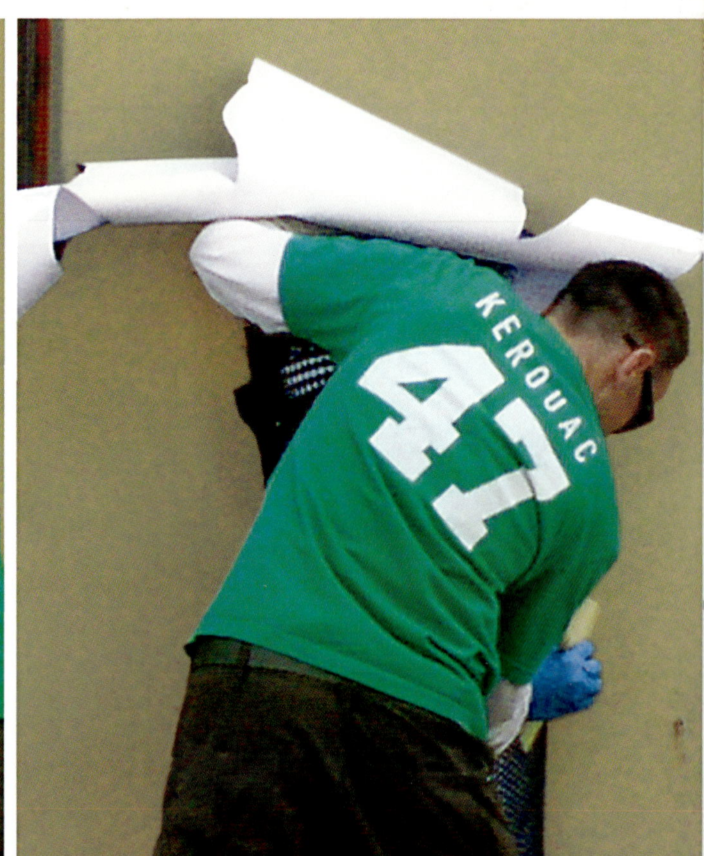
KEROUAC
47

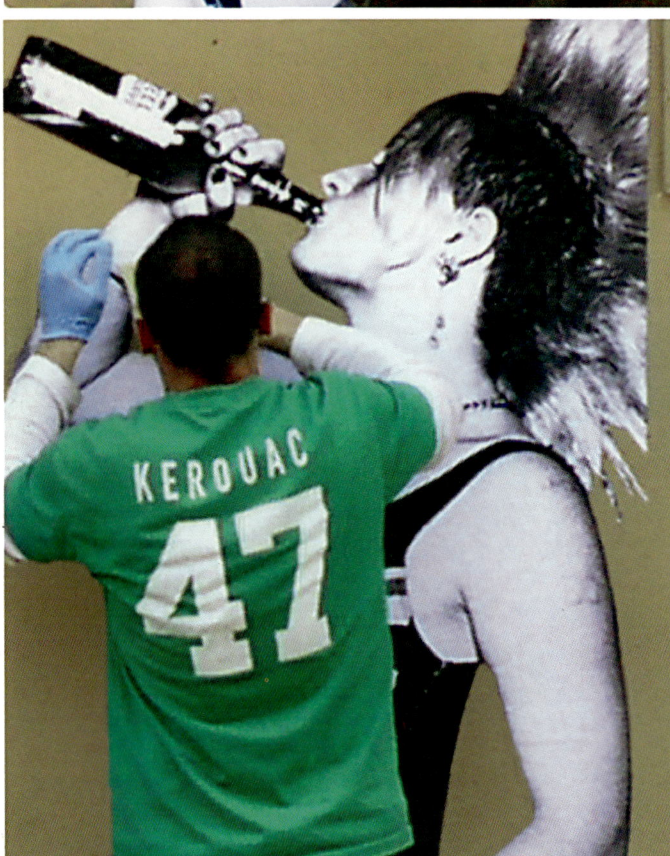
KEROUAC
47

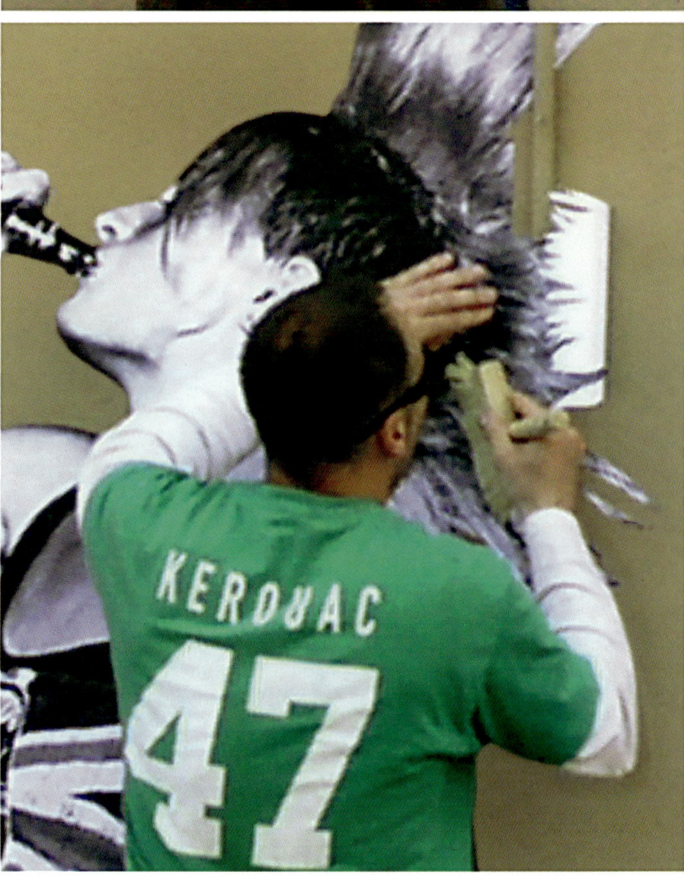
KEROUAC
47

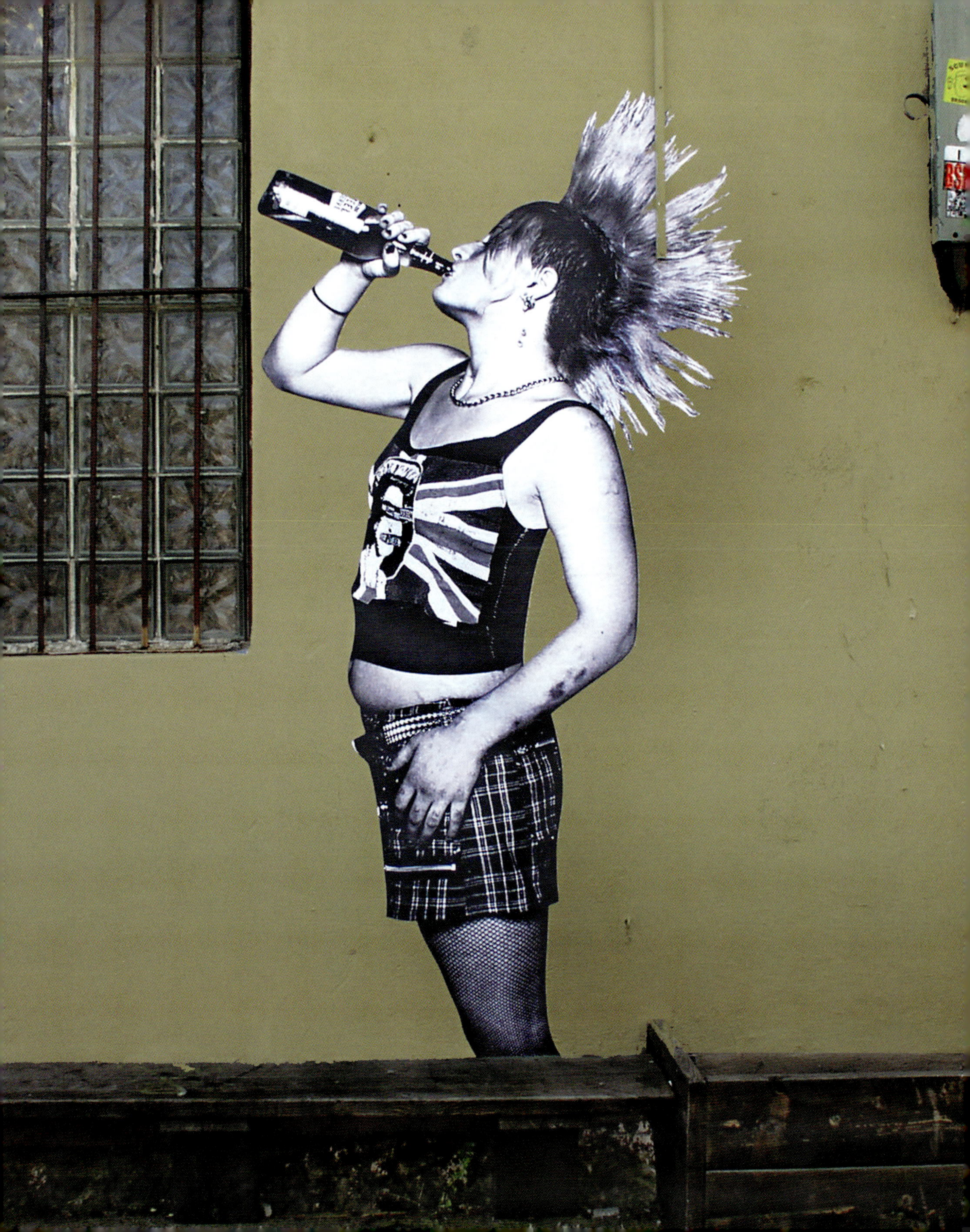

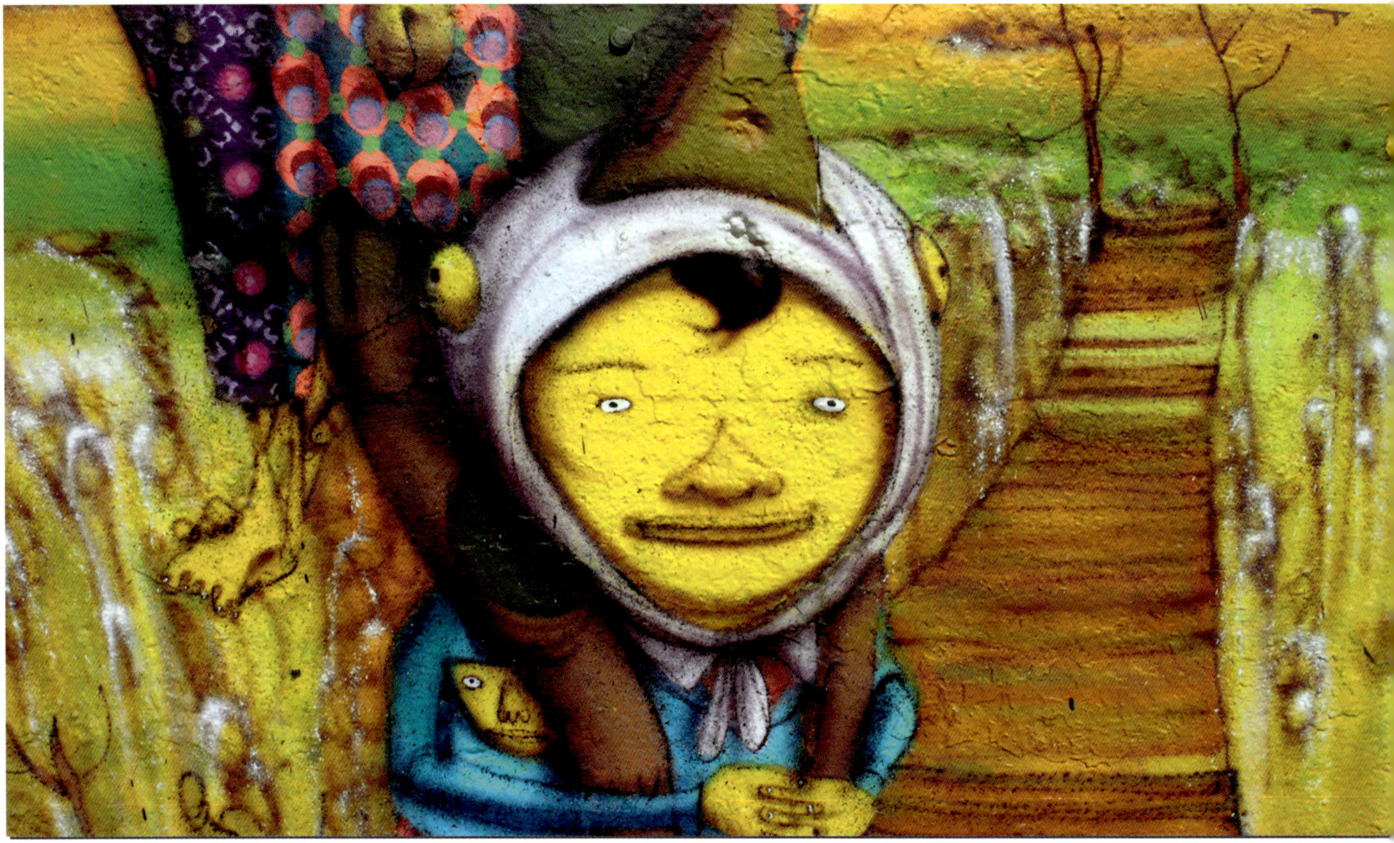

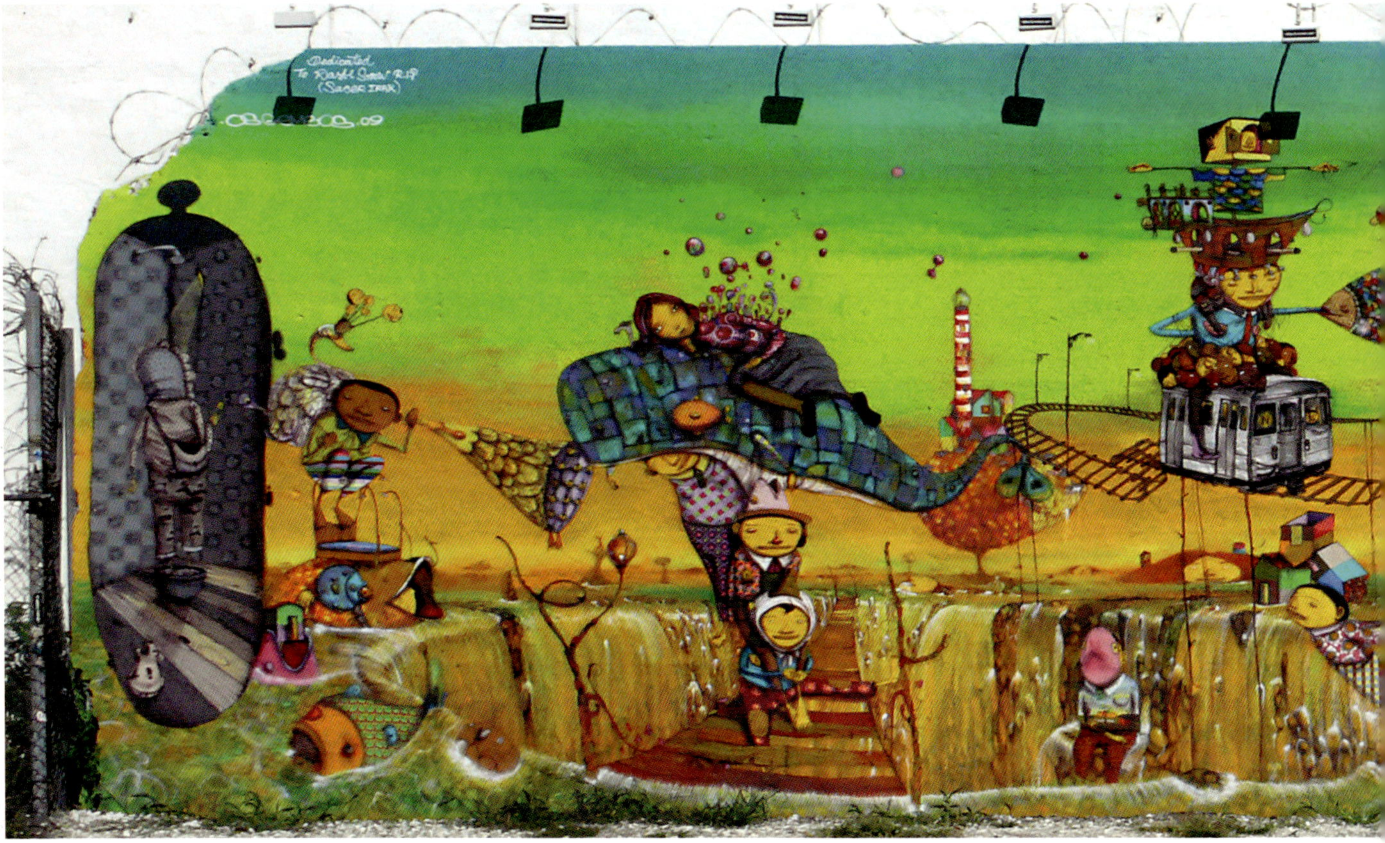

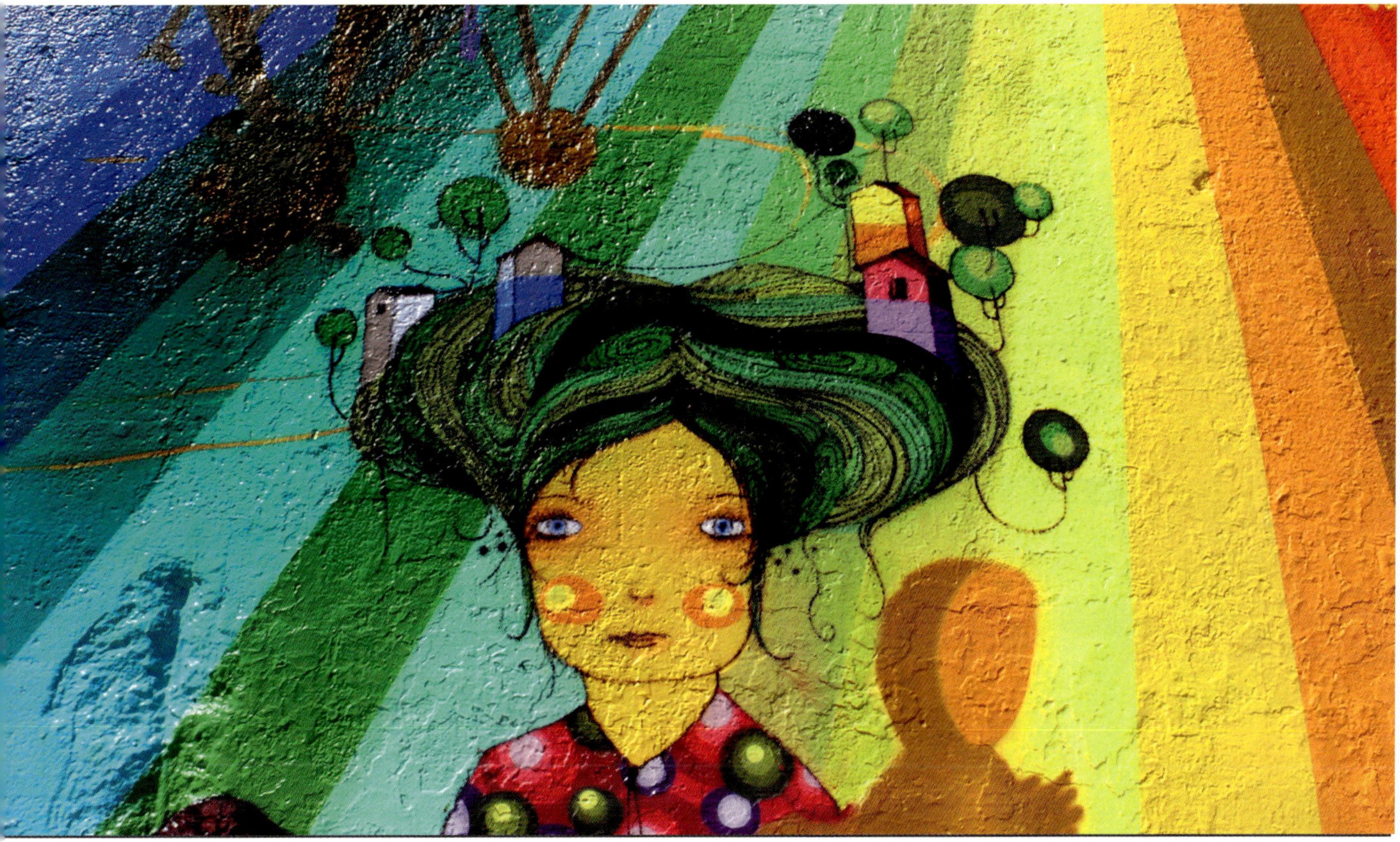

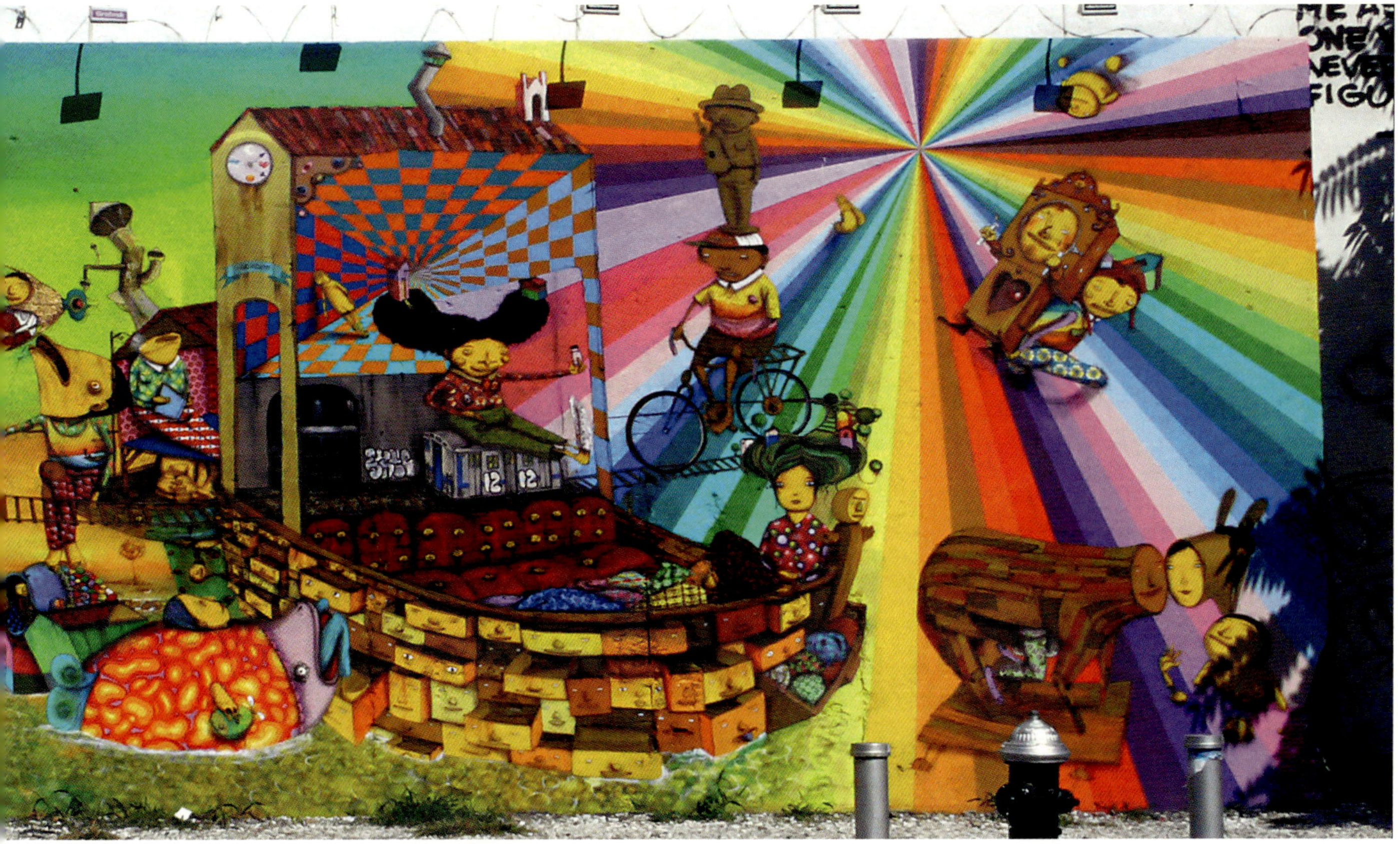

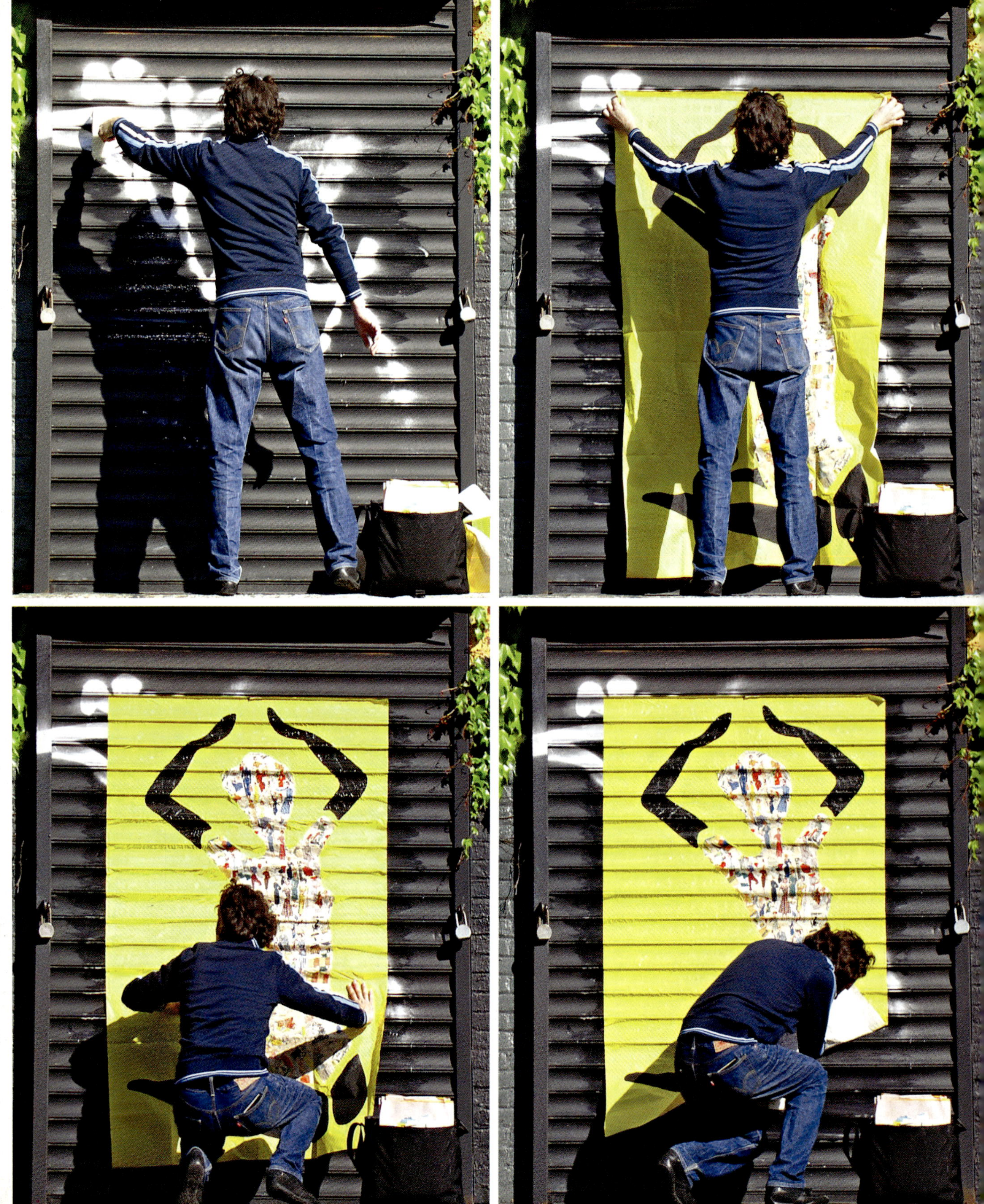

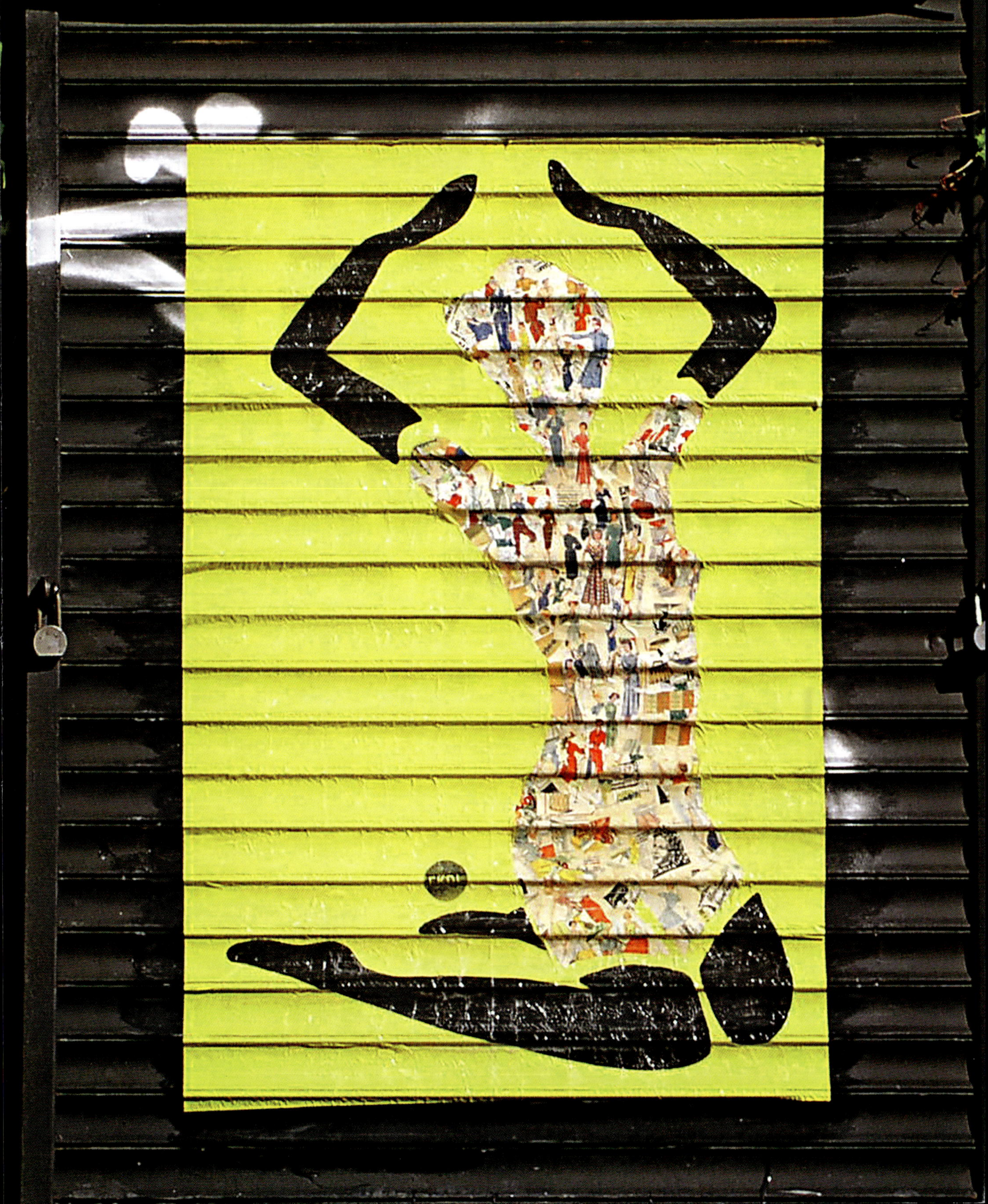

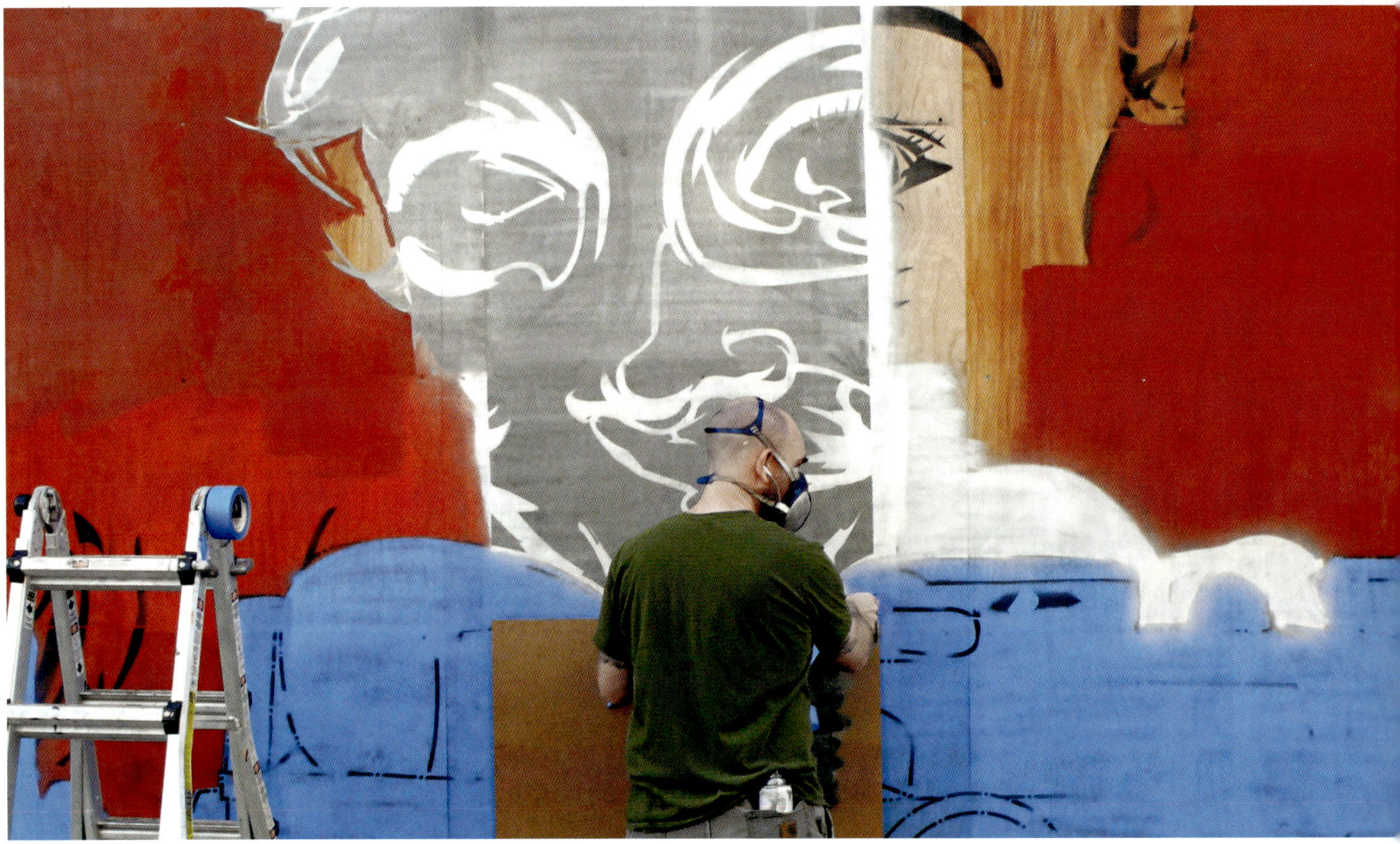

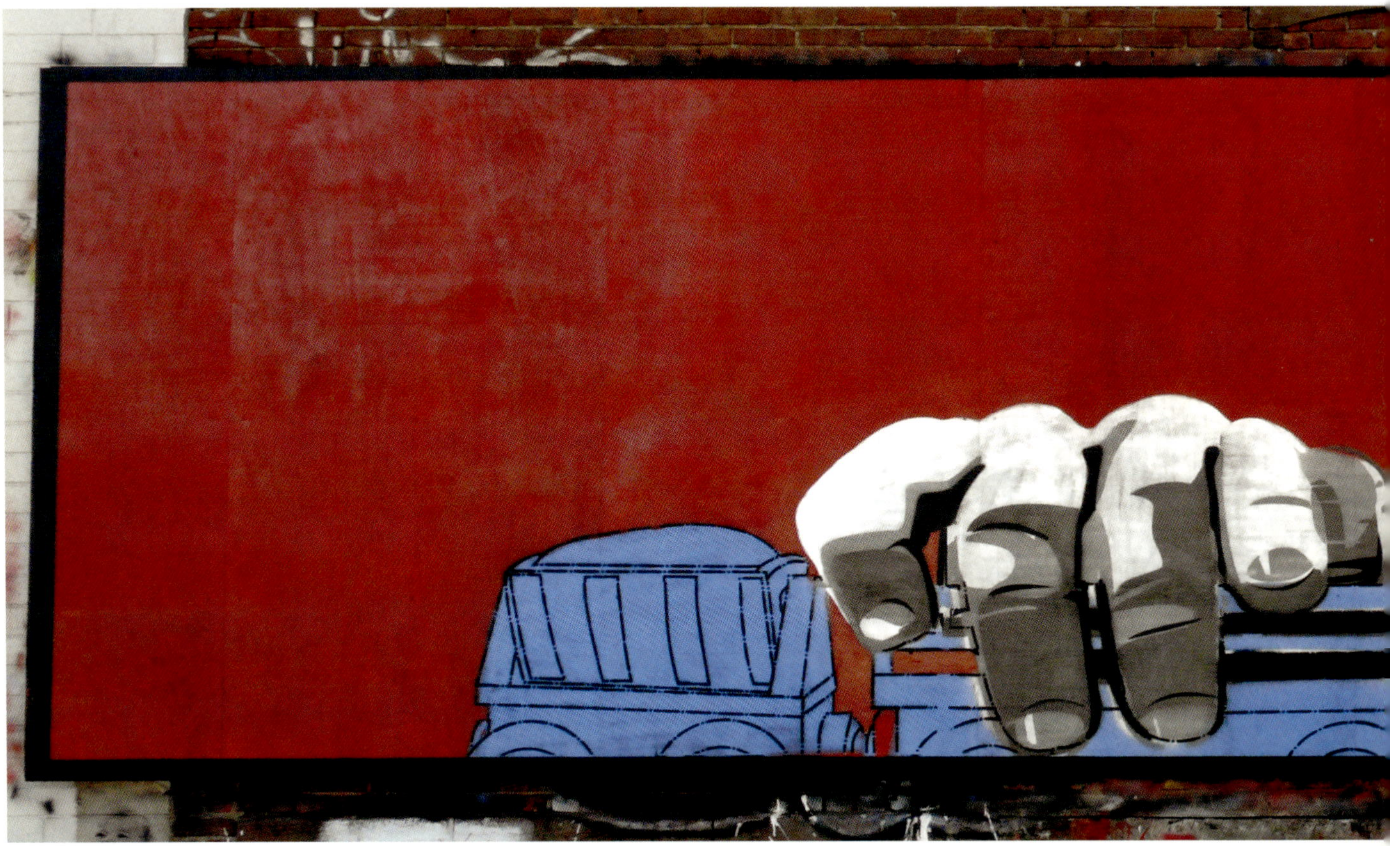

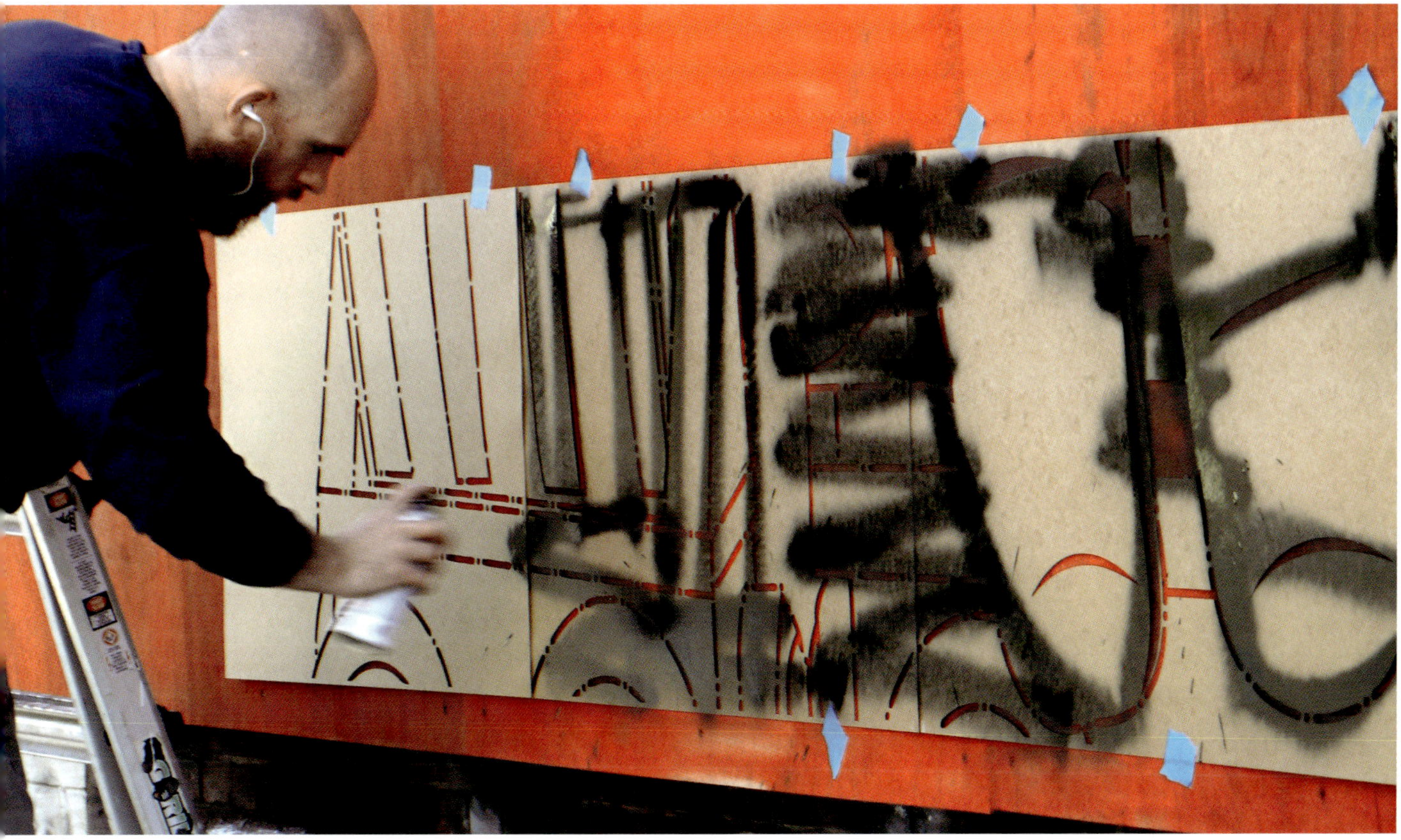

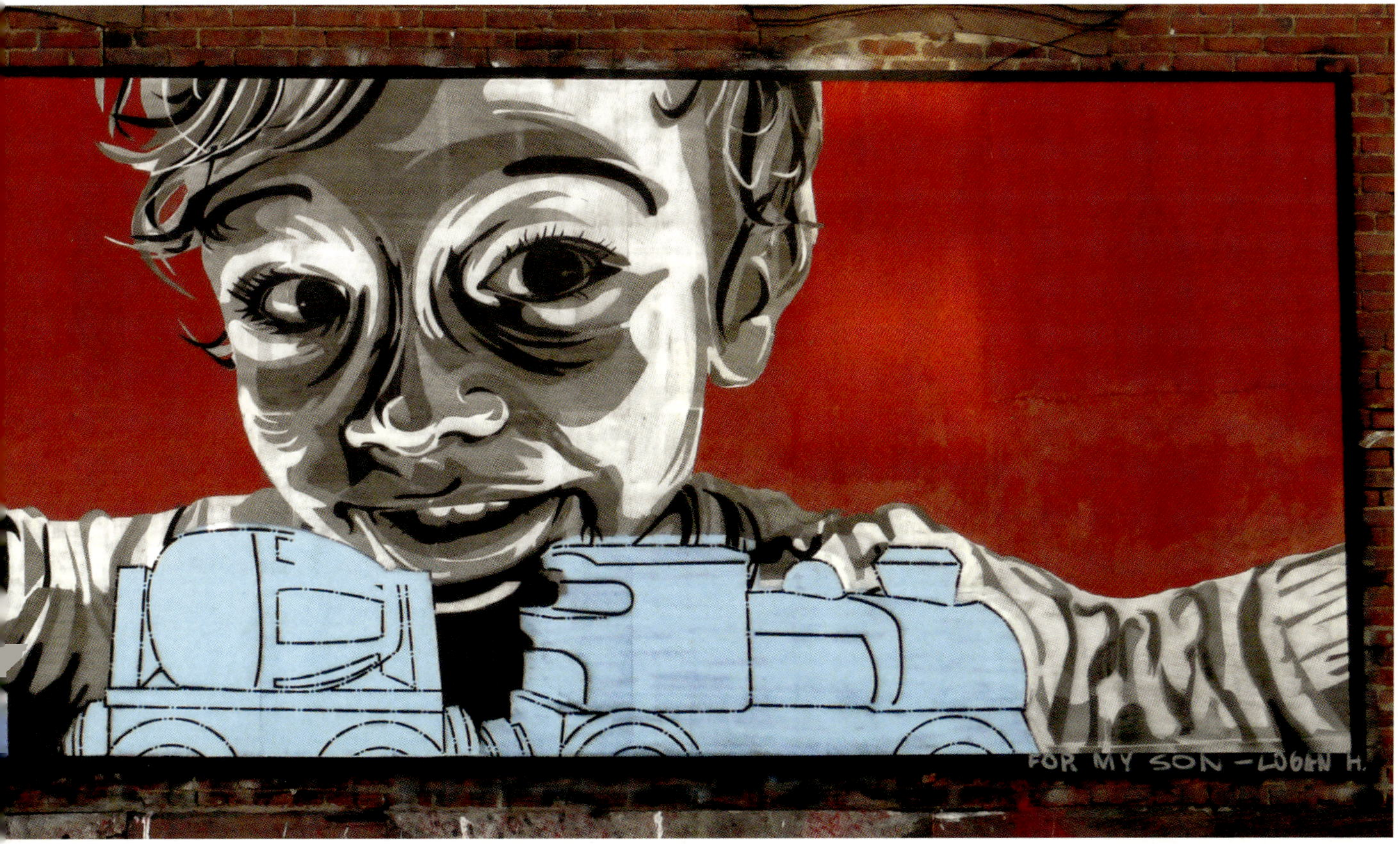

FOR MY SON - LOGEN H.

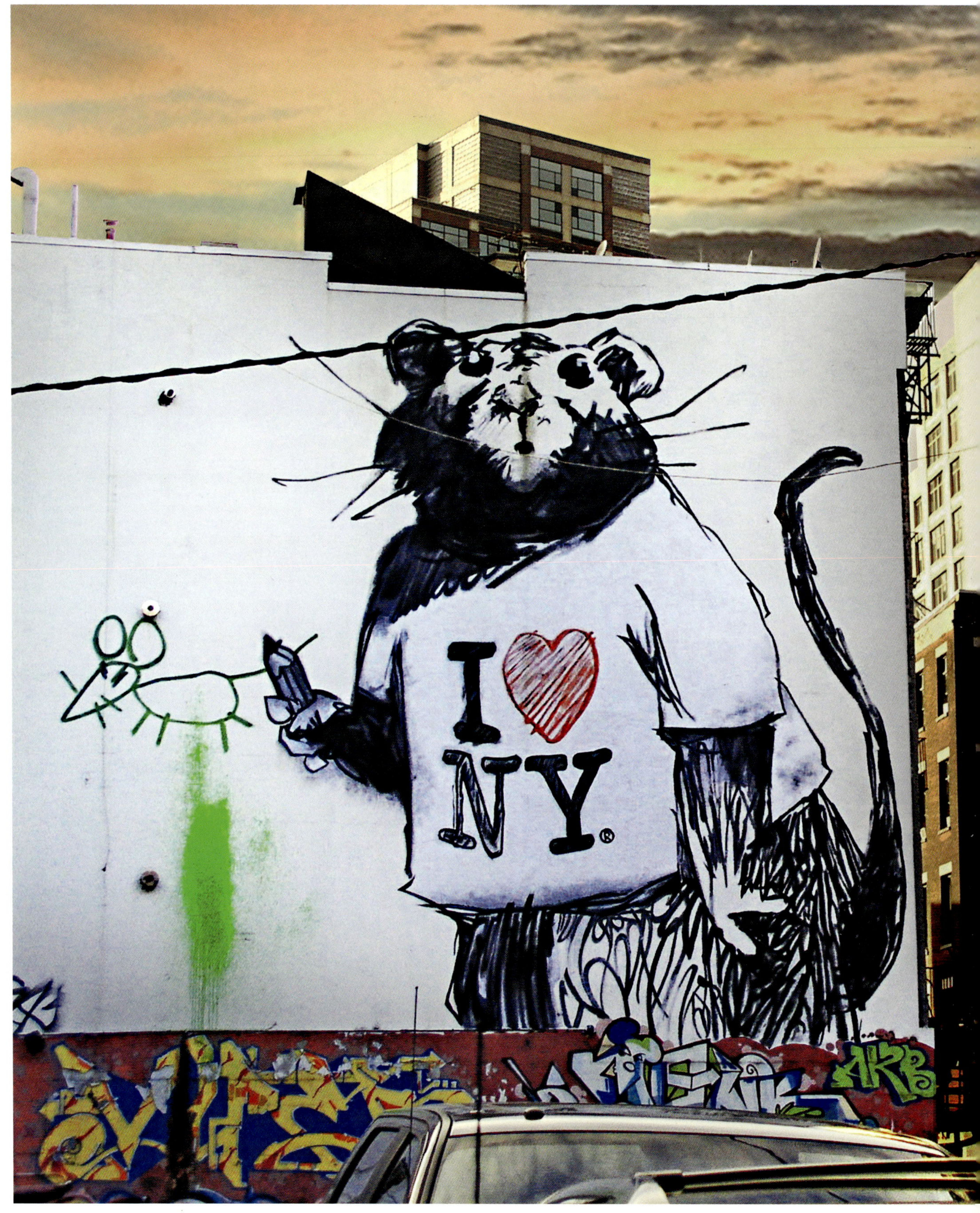
I ♥ NY

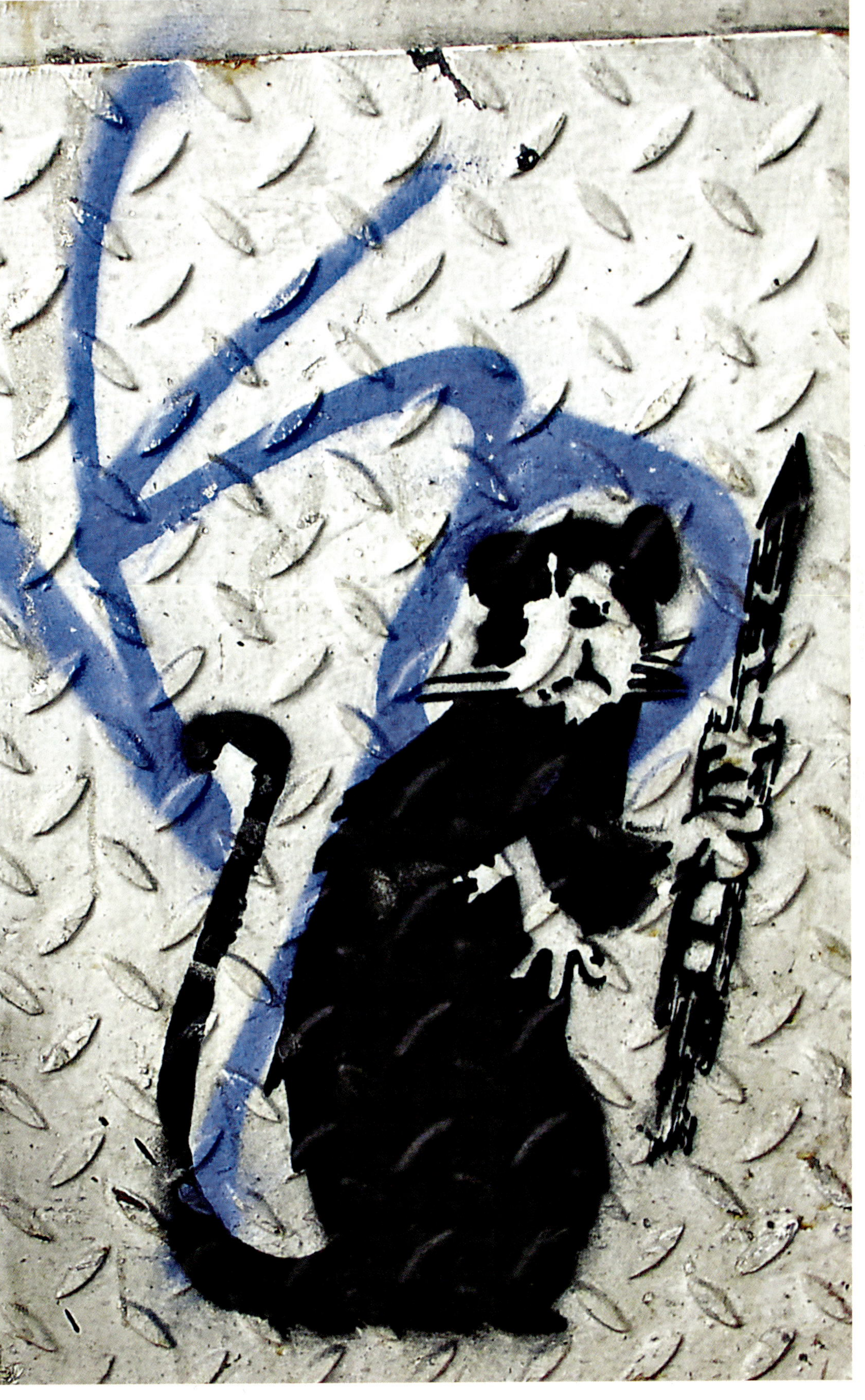

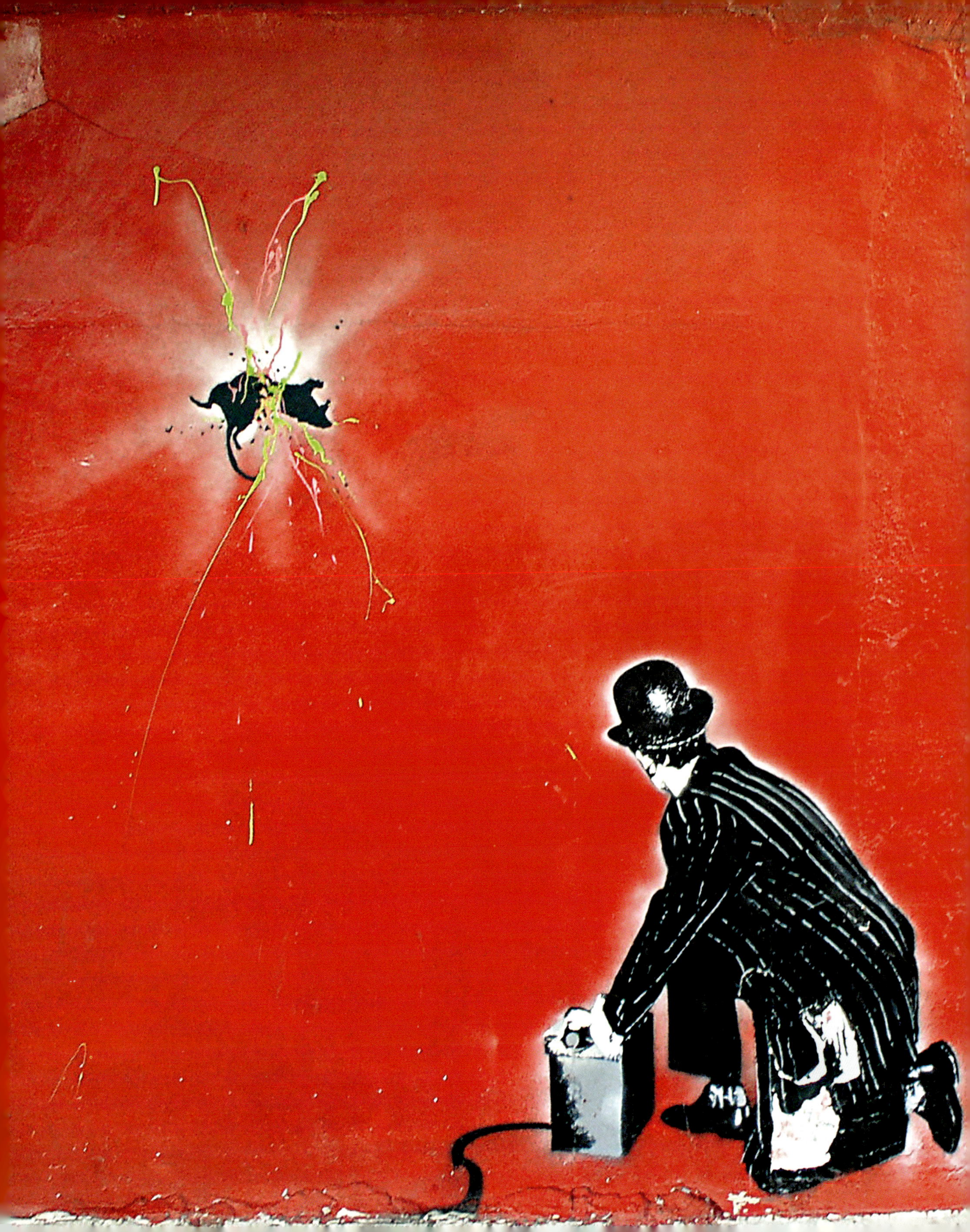

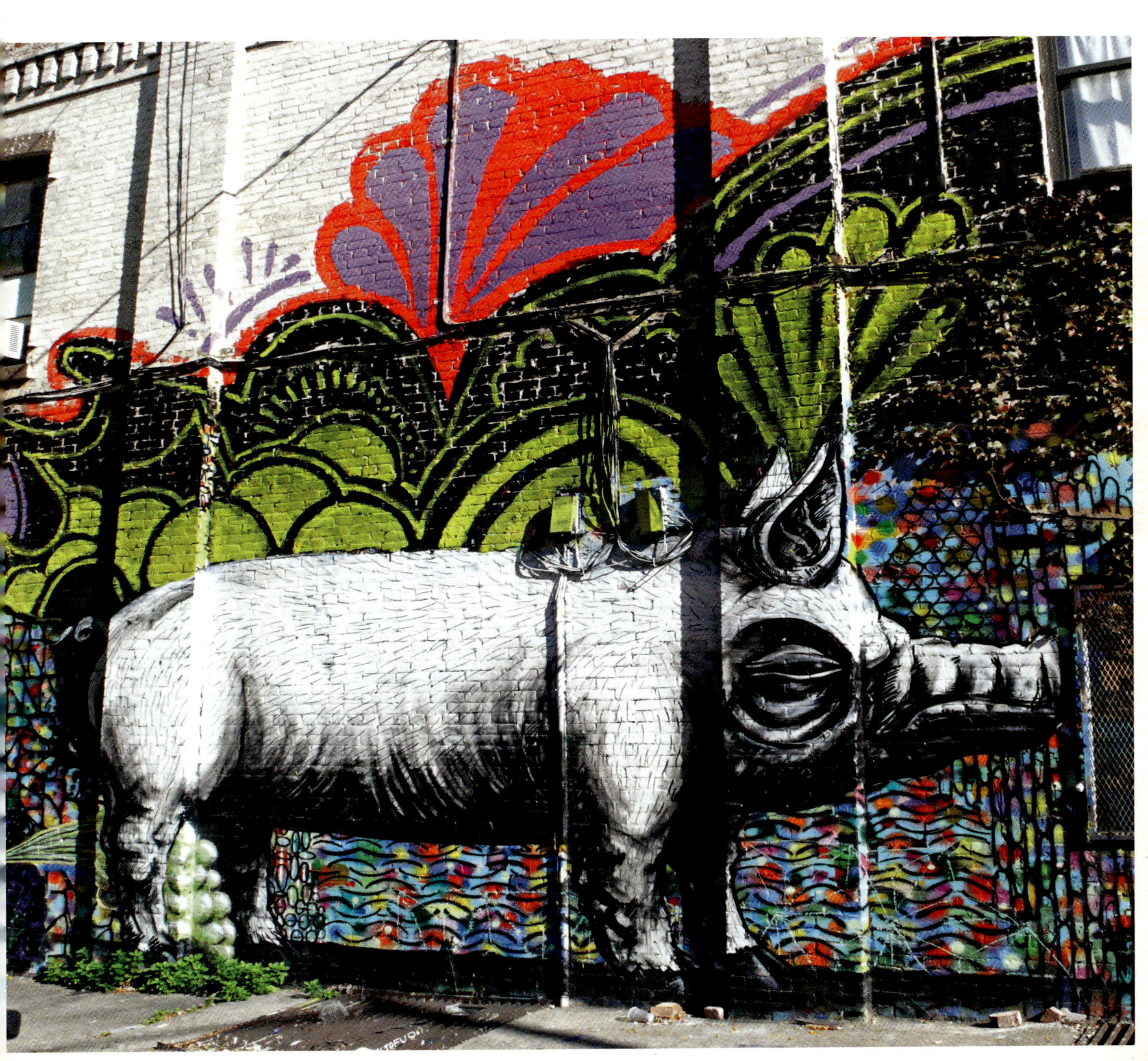

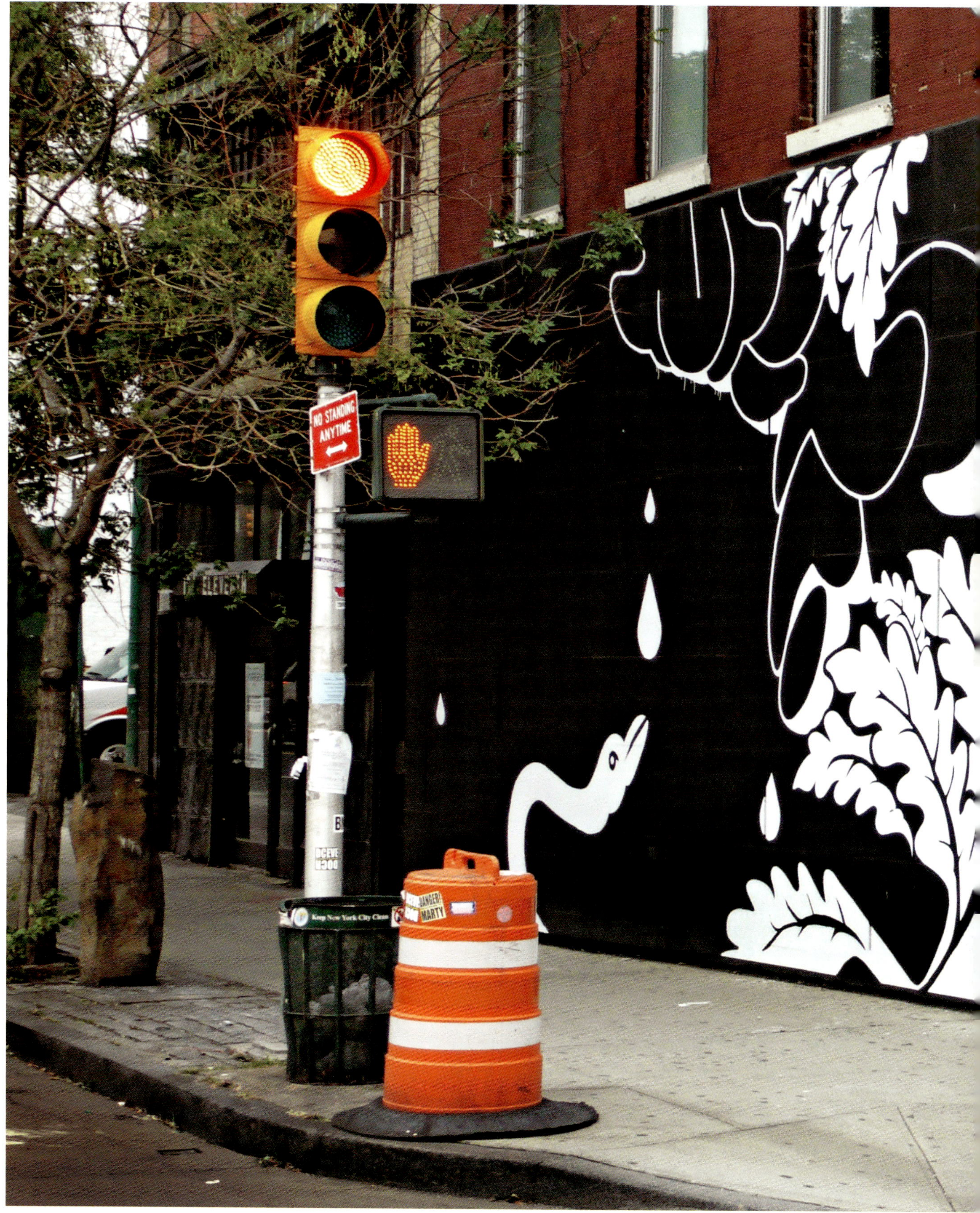
NO STANDING ANYTIME
Keep New York City Clean
DANGER! MARTY
DCEVE

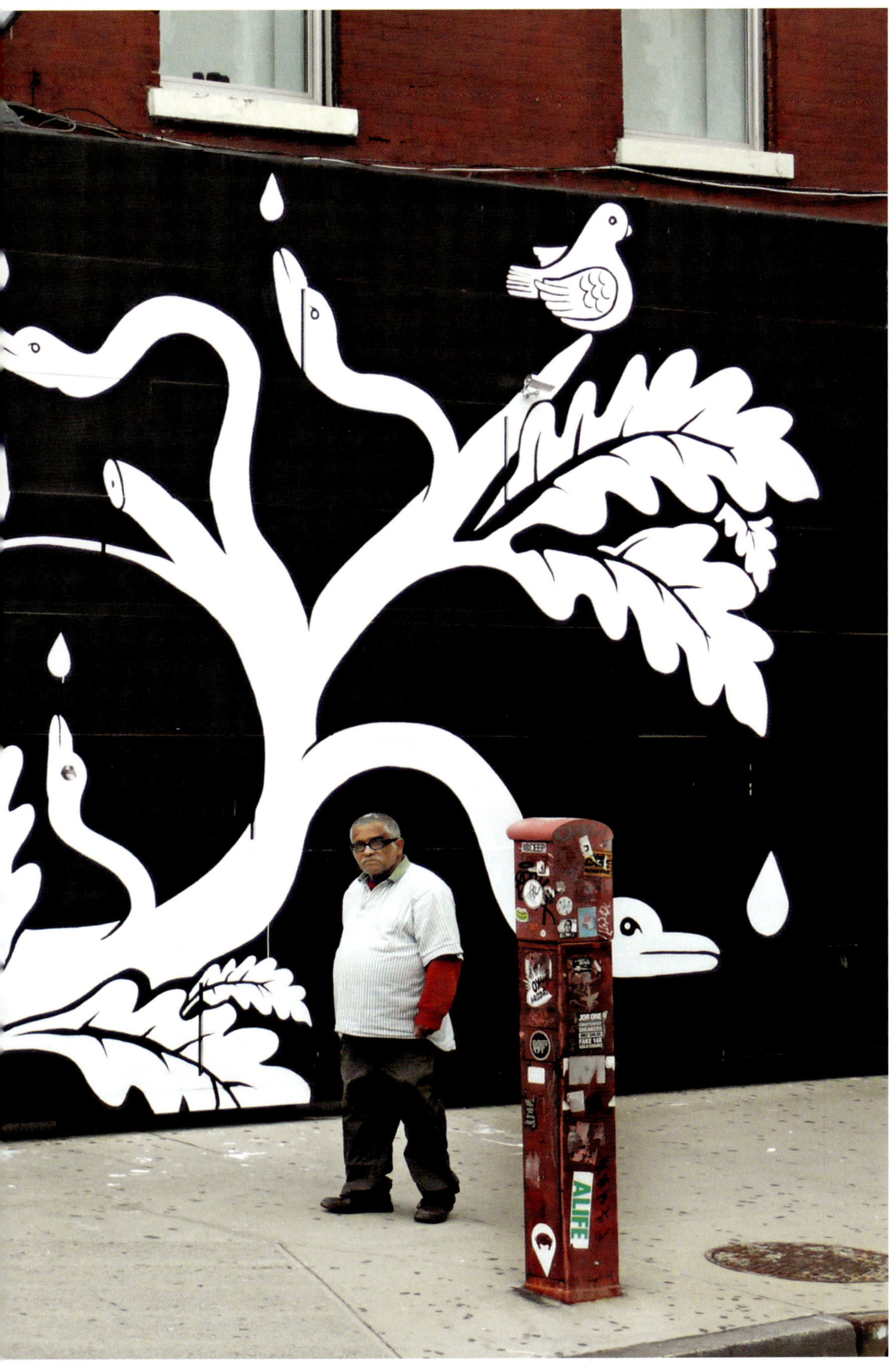
JOR ONE
SNEAKERS
FAKE 14K
ALIFE

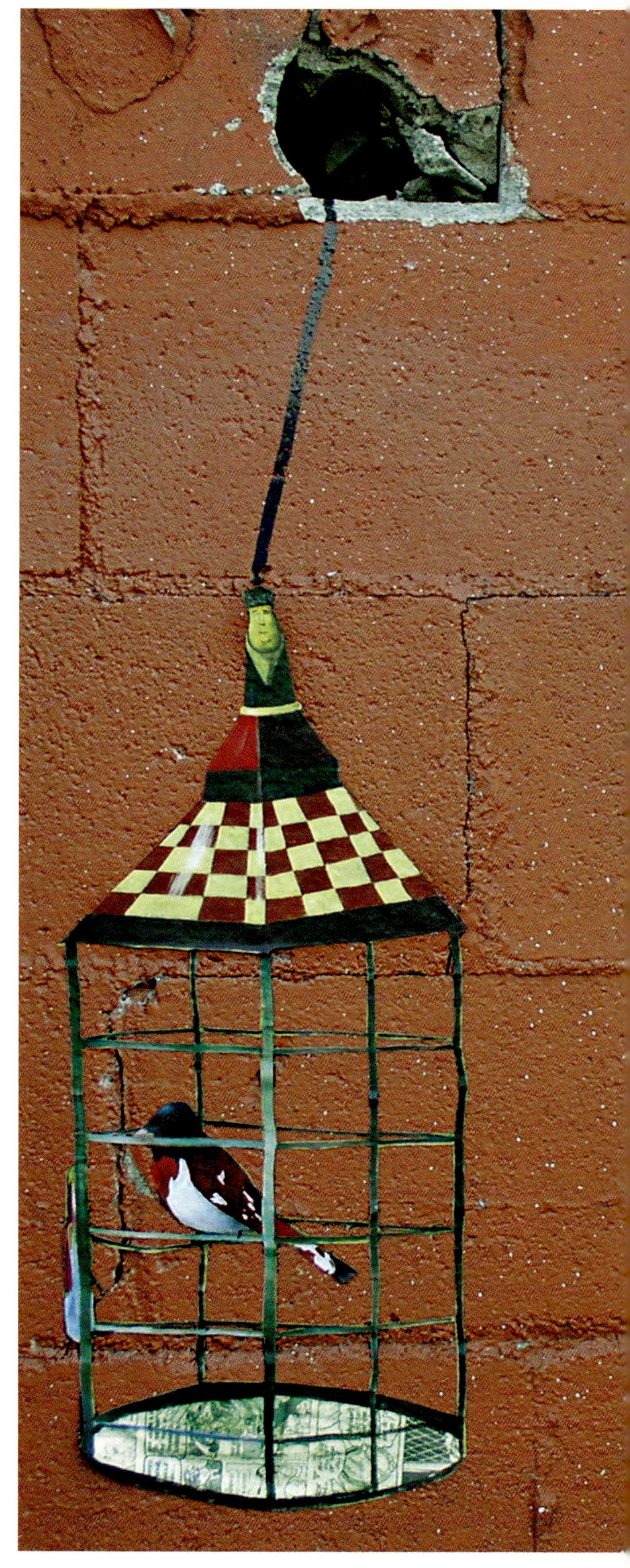

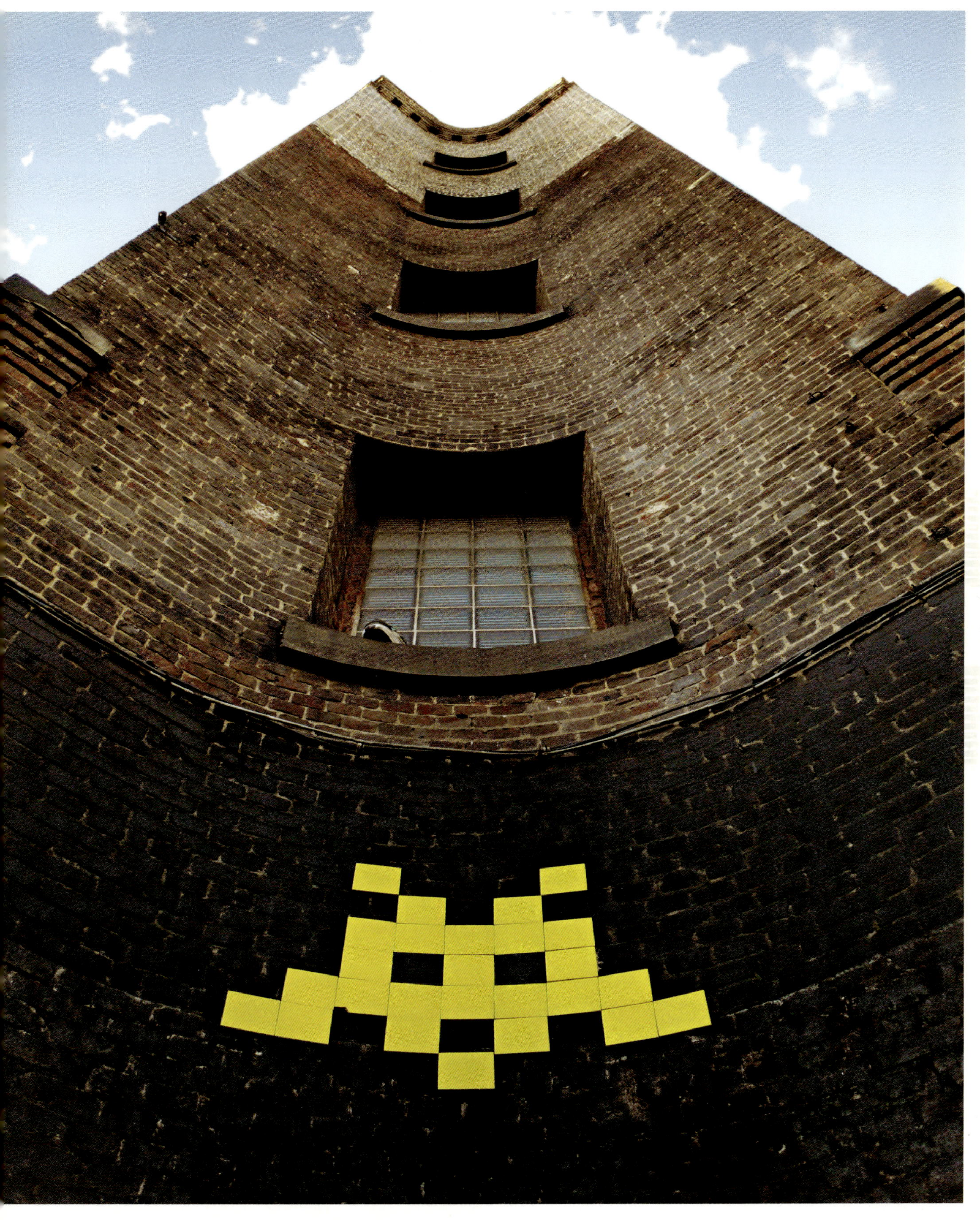

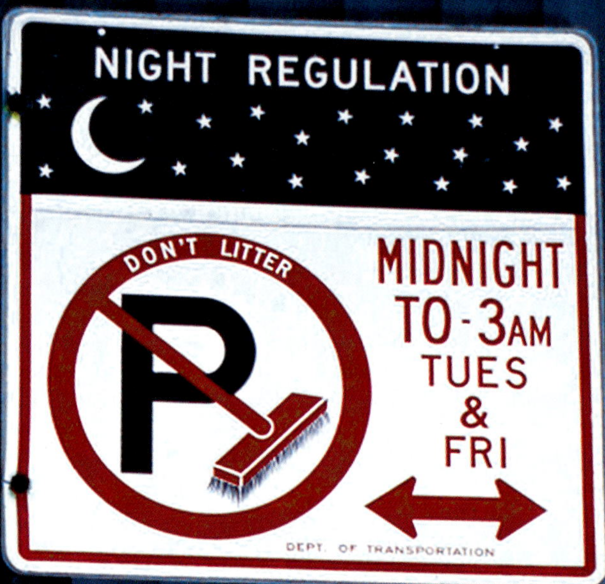
NIGHT REGULATION
DON'T LITTER
MIDNIGHT
TO - 3AM
TUES
&
FRI
DEPT. OF TRANSPORTATION

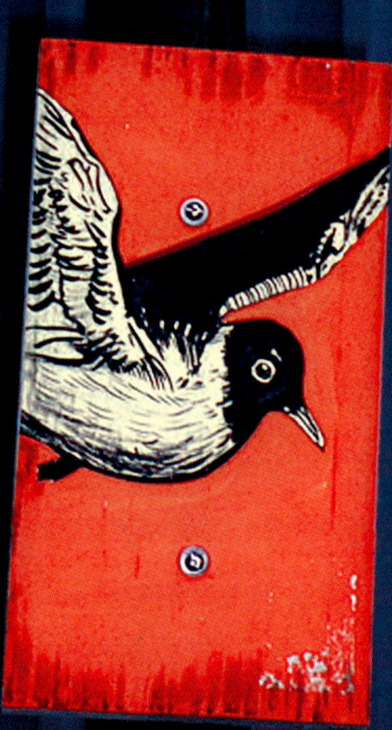

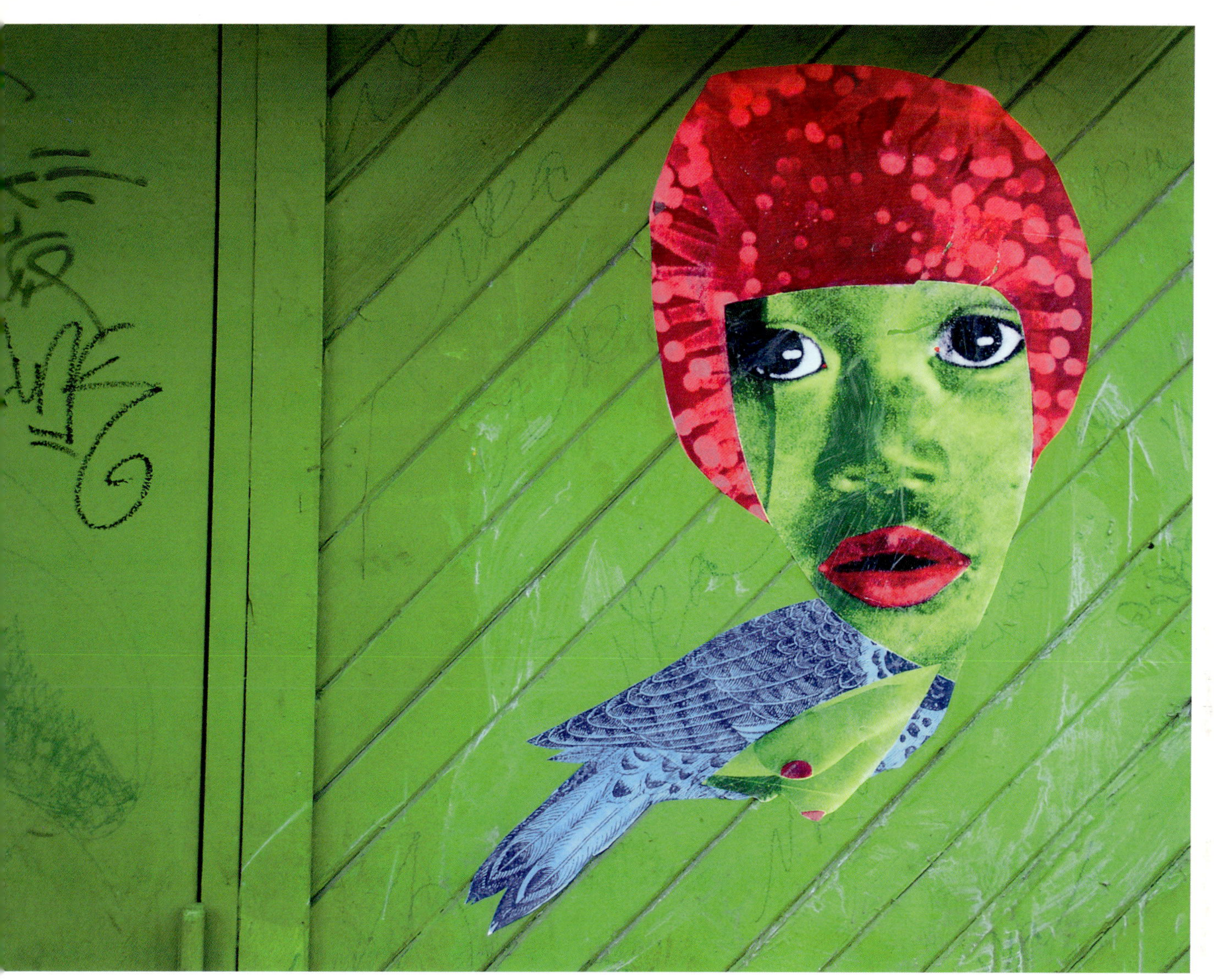

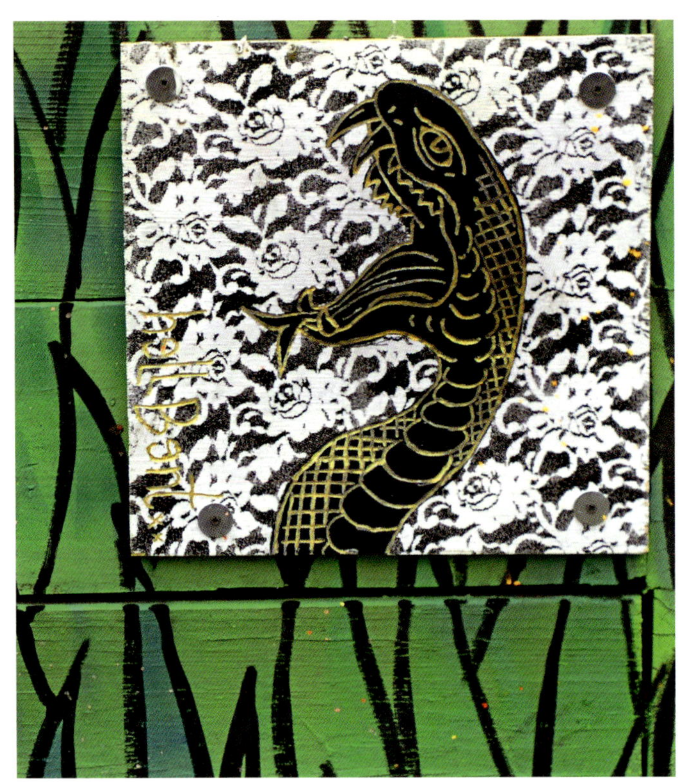
hellbent

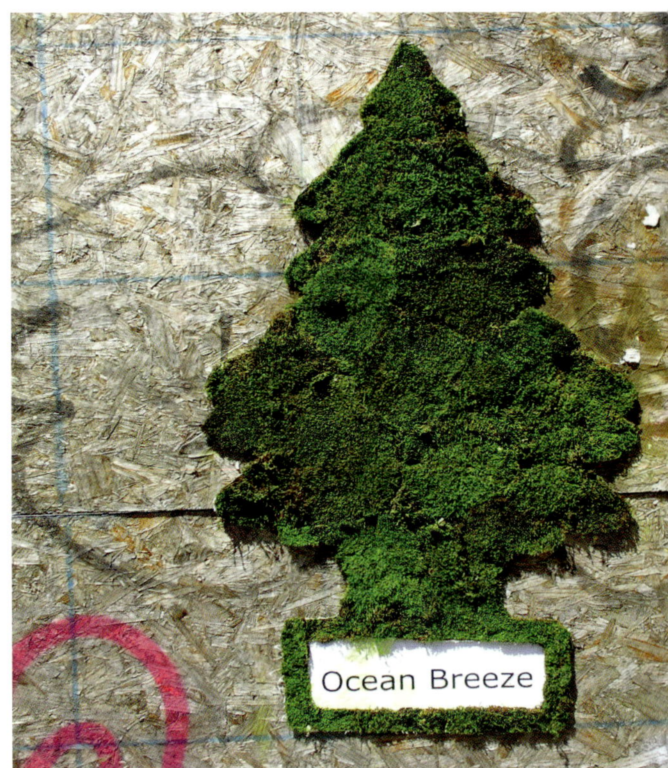
Ocean Breeze

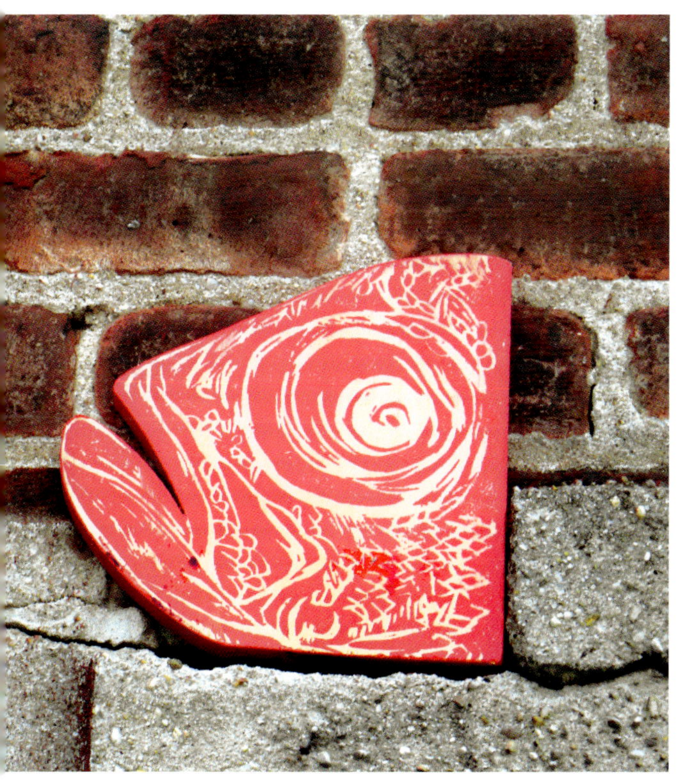

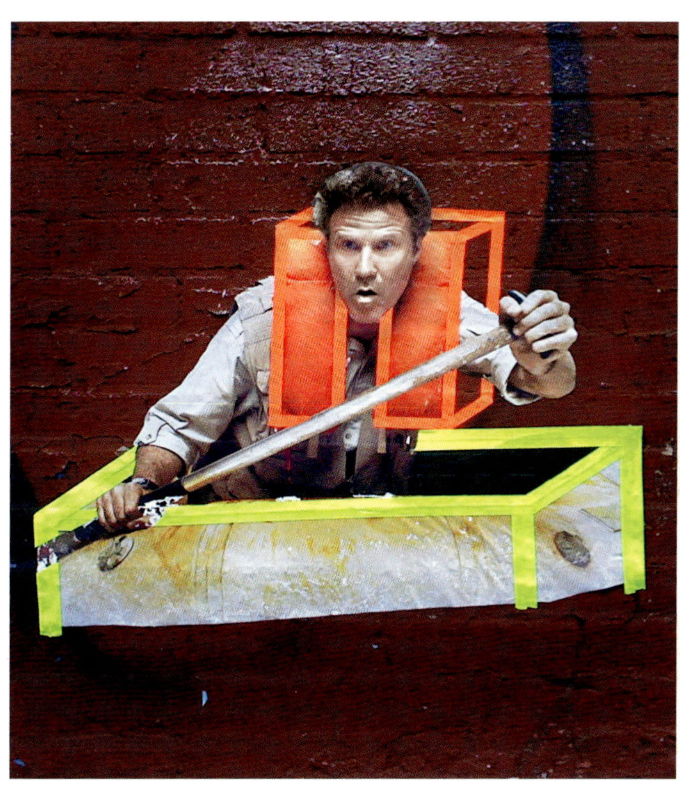

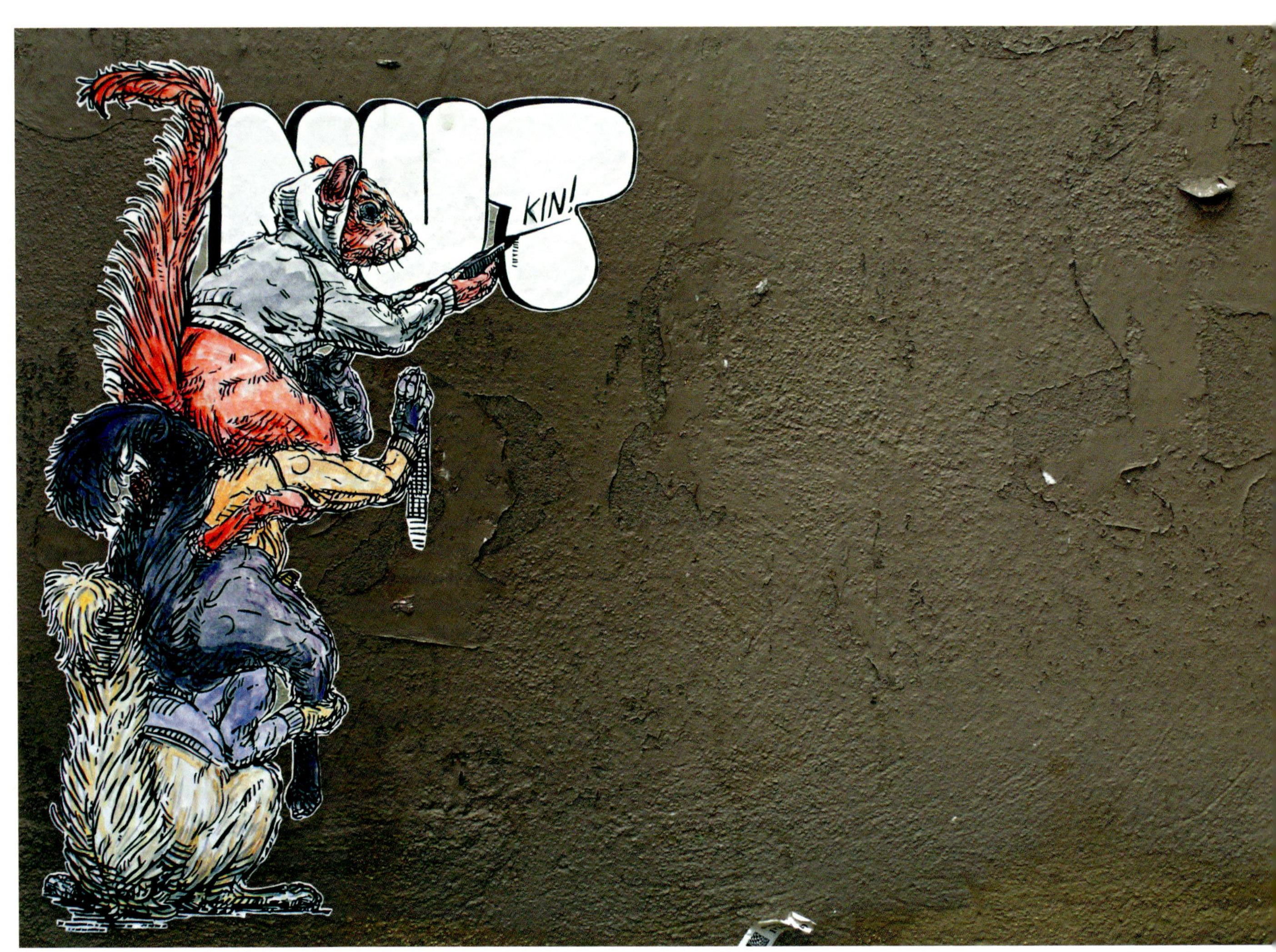
KIN!

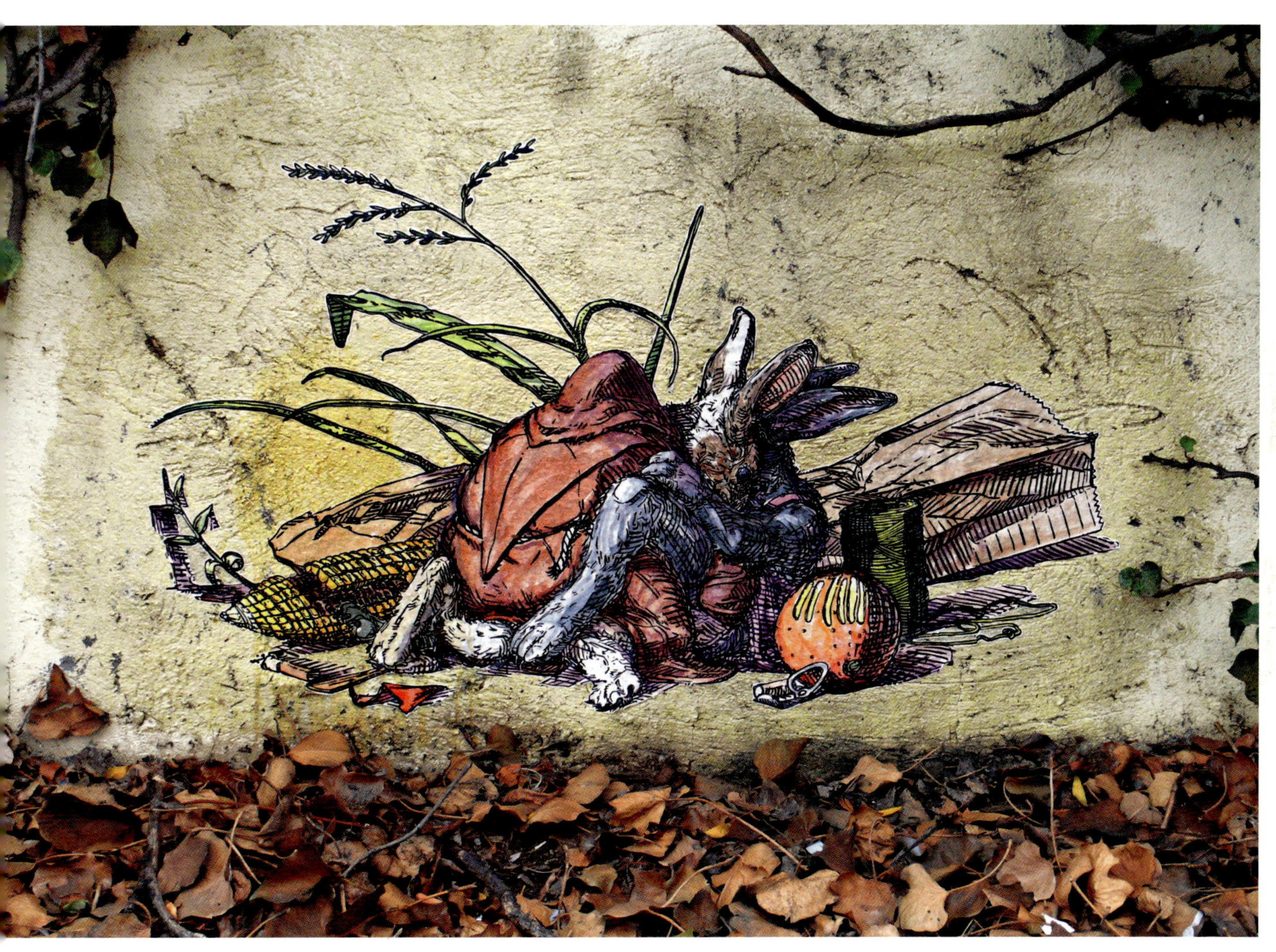

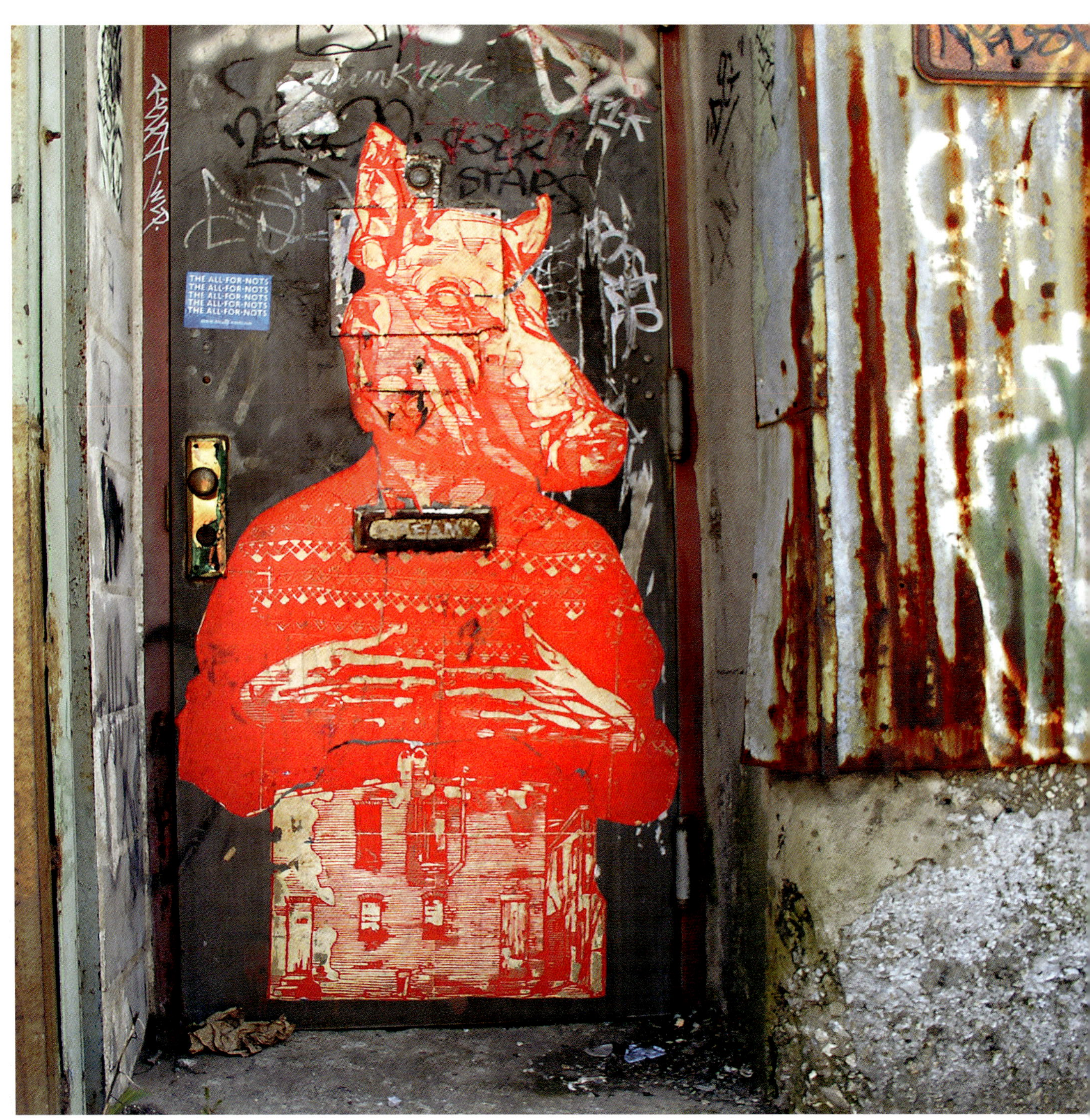
THE ALL-FOR-NOTS
THE ALL-FOR-NOTS
THE ALL-FOR-NOTS
THE ALL-FOR-NOTS
THE ALL-FOR-NOTS

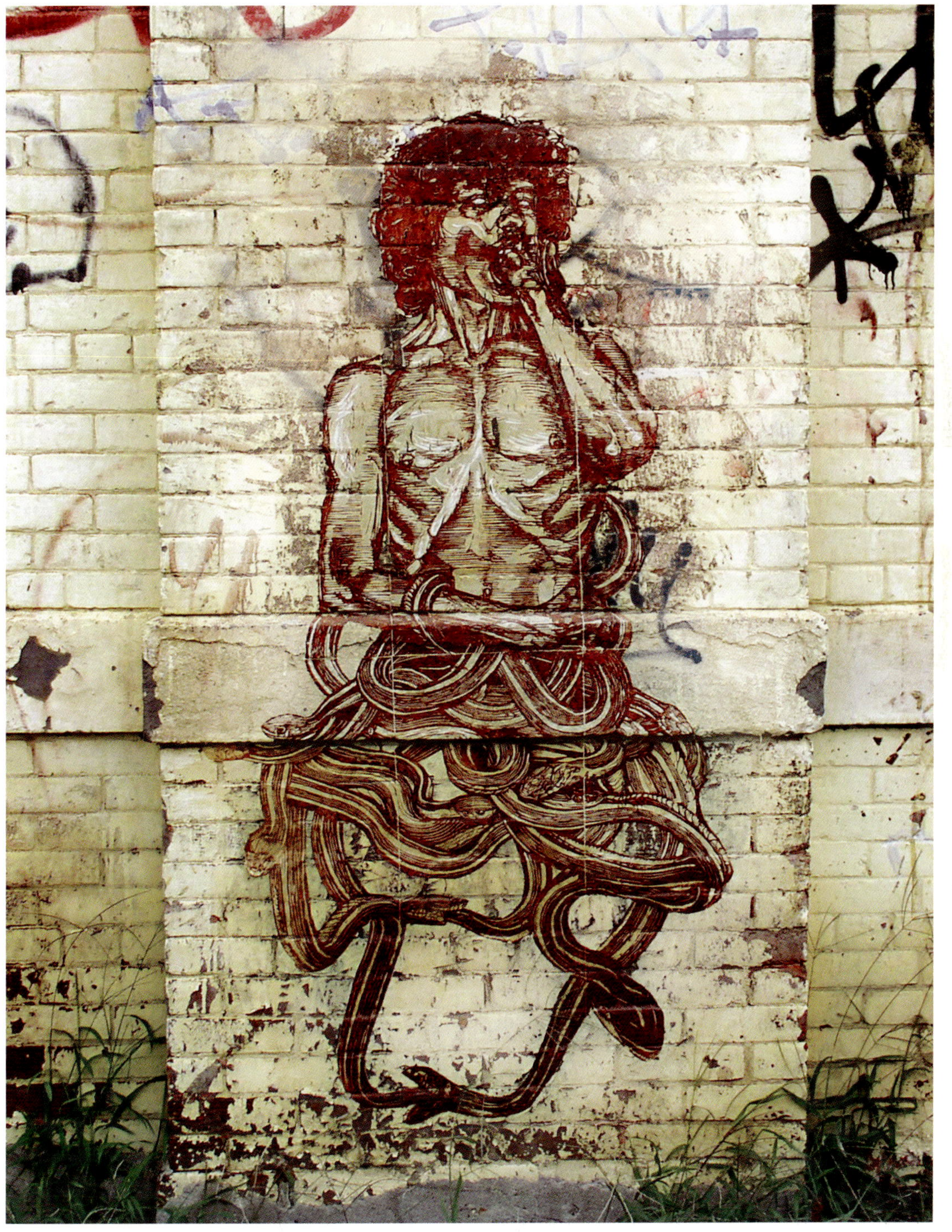

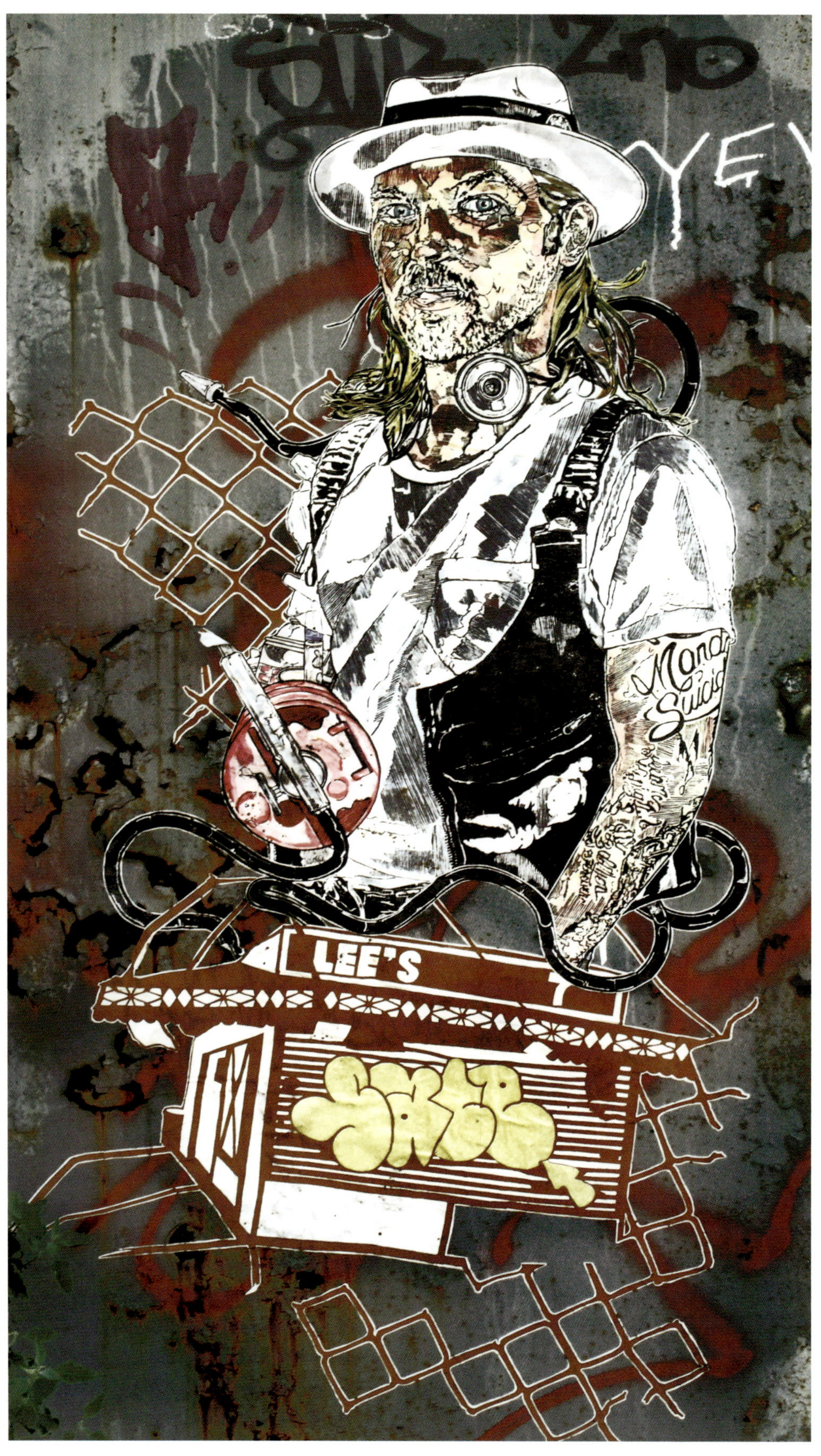
LEE'S

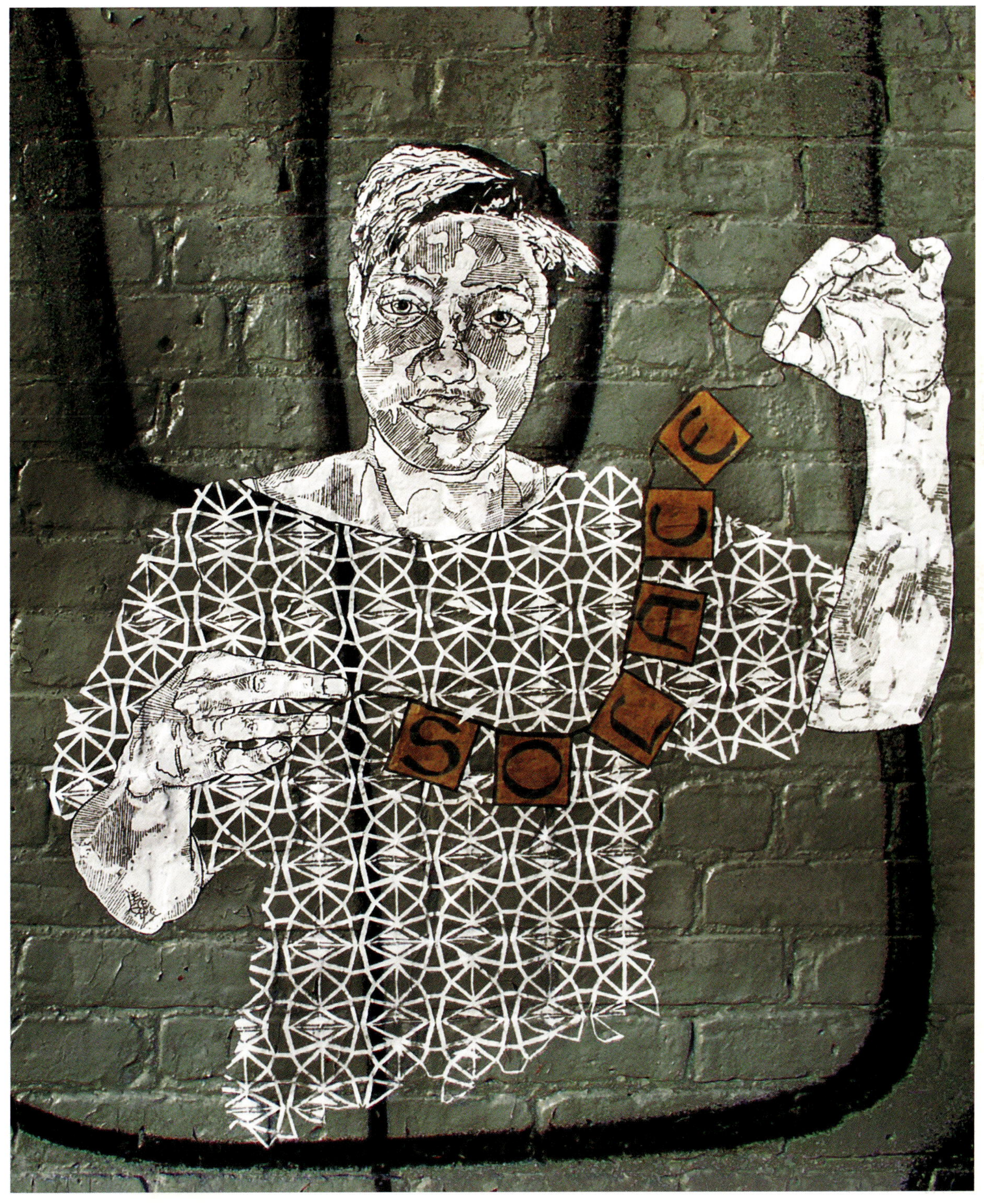
SOLACE

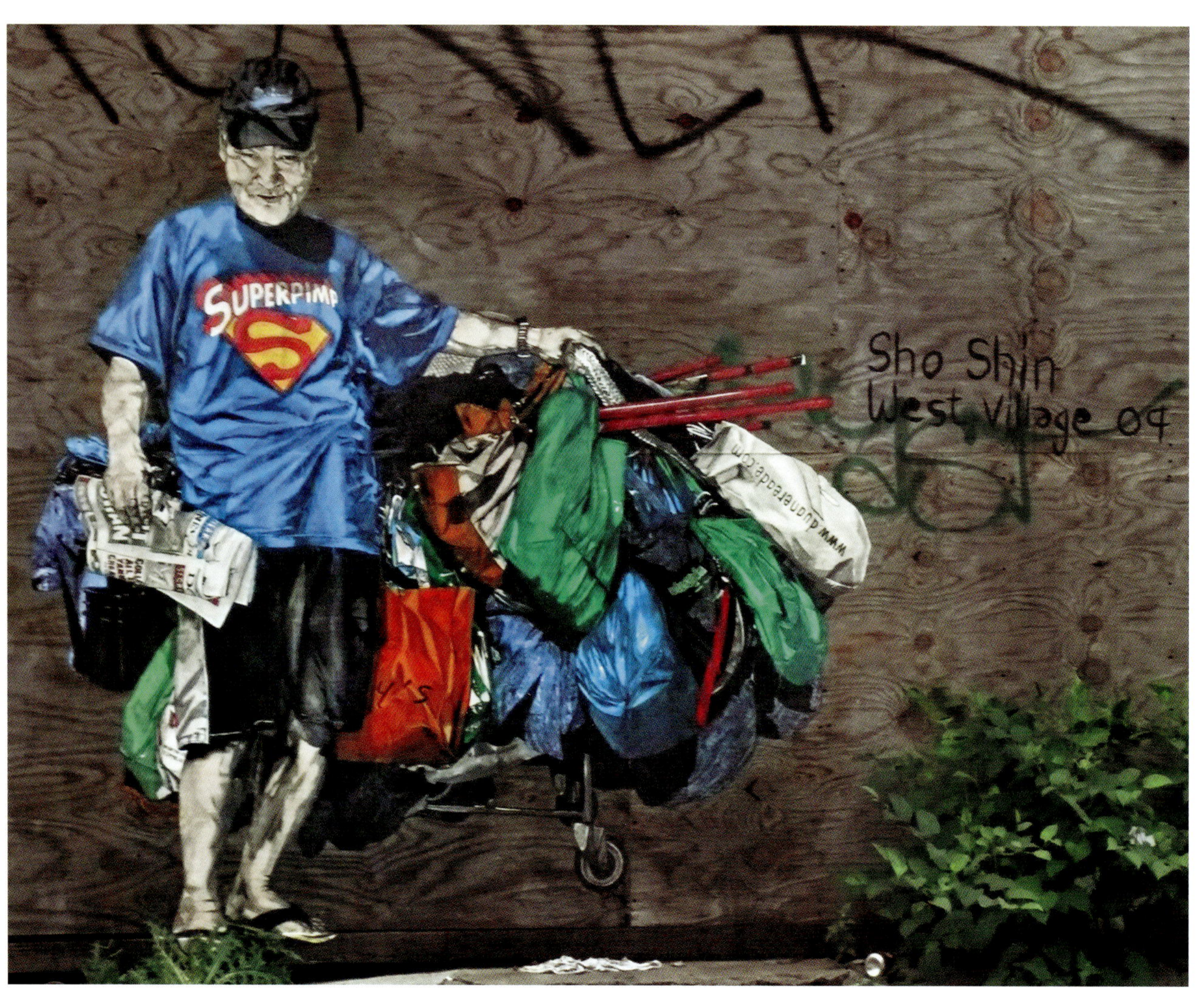
SUPERPIMP
Sho Shin
West Village 04
www.duanereade.com

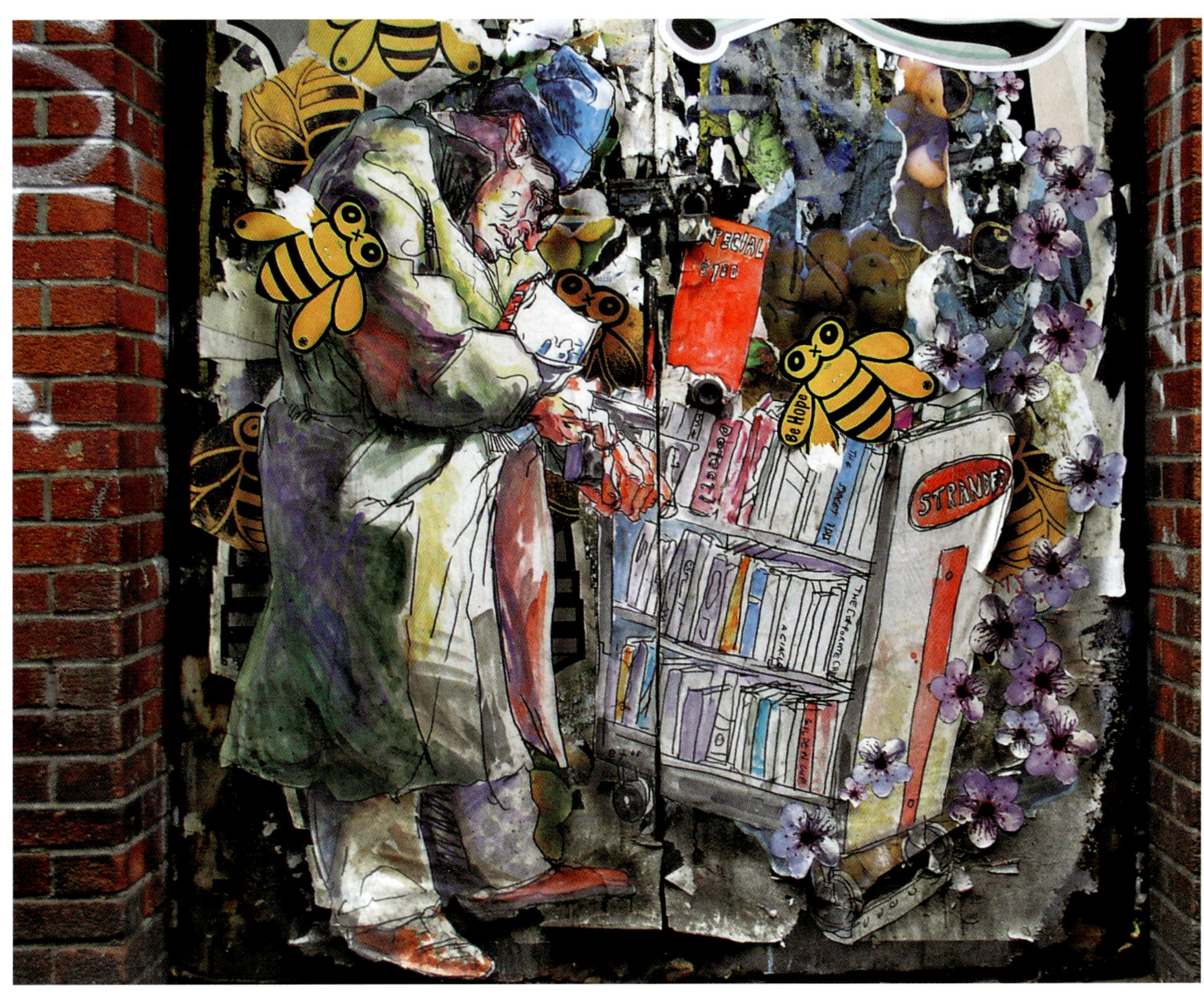
Be Hope

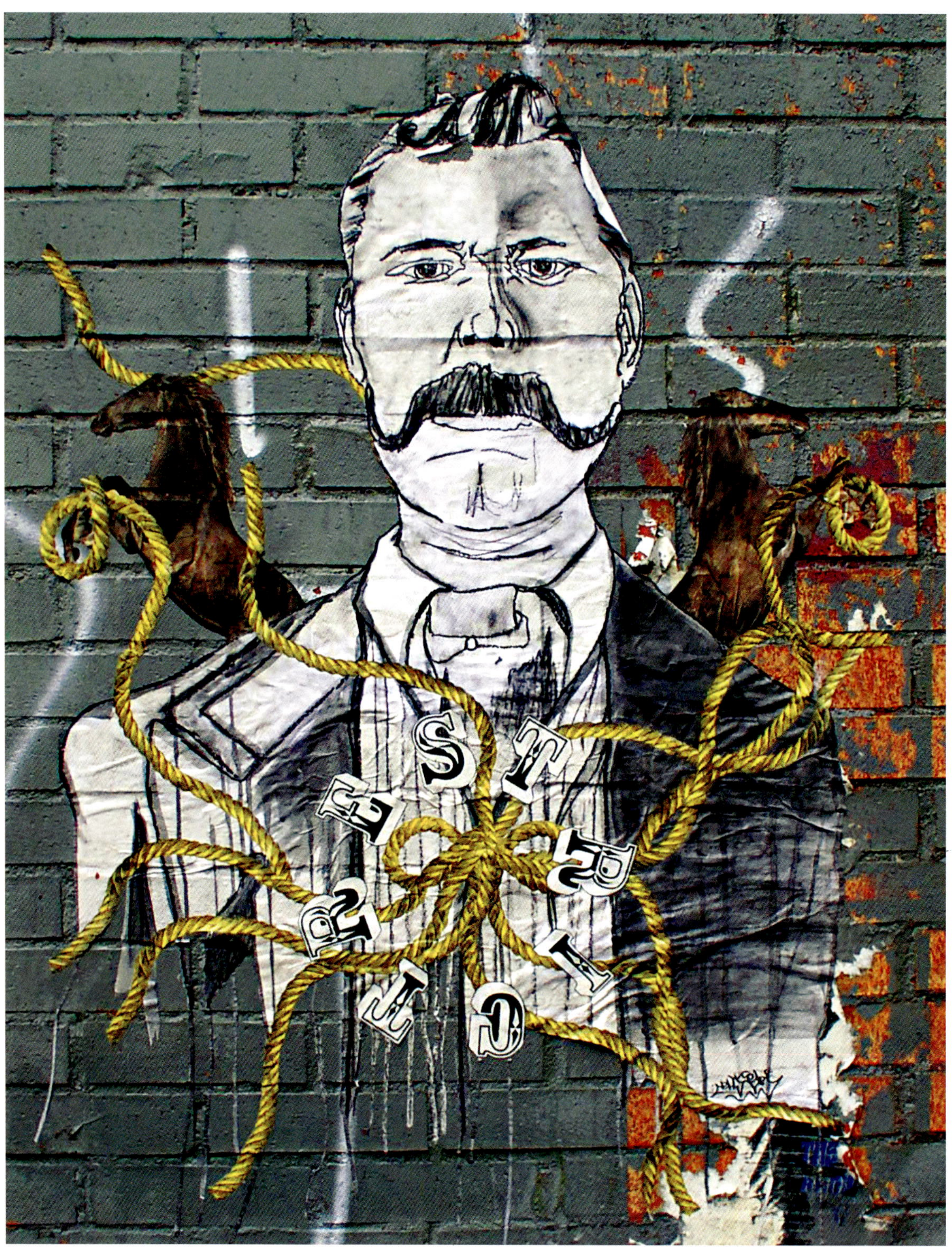

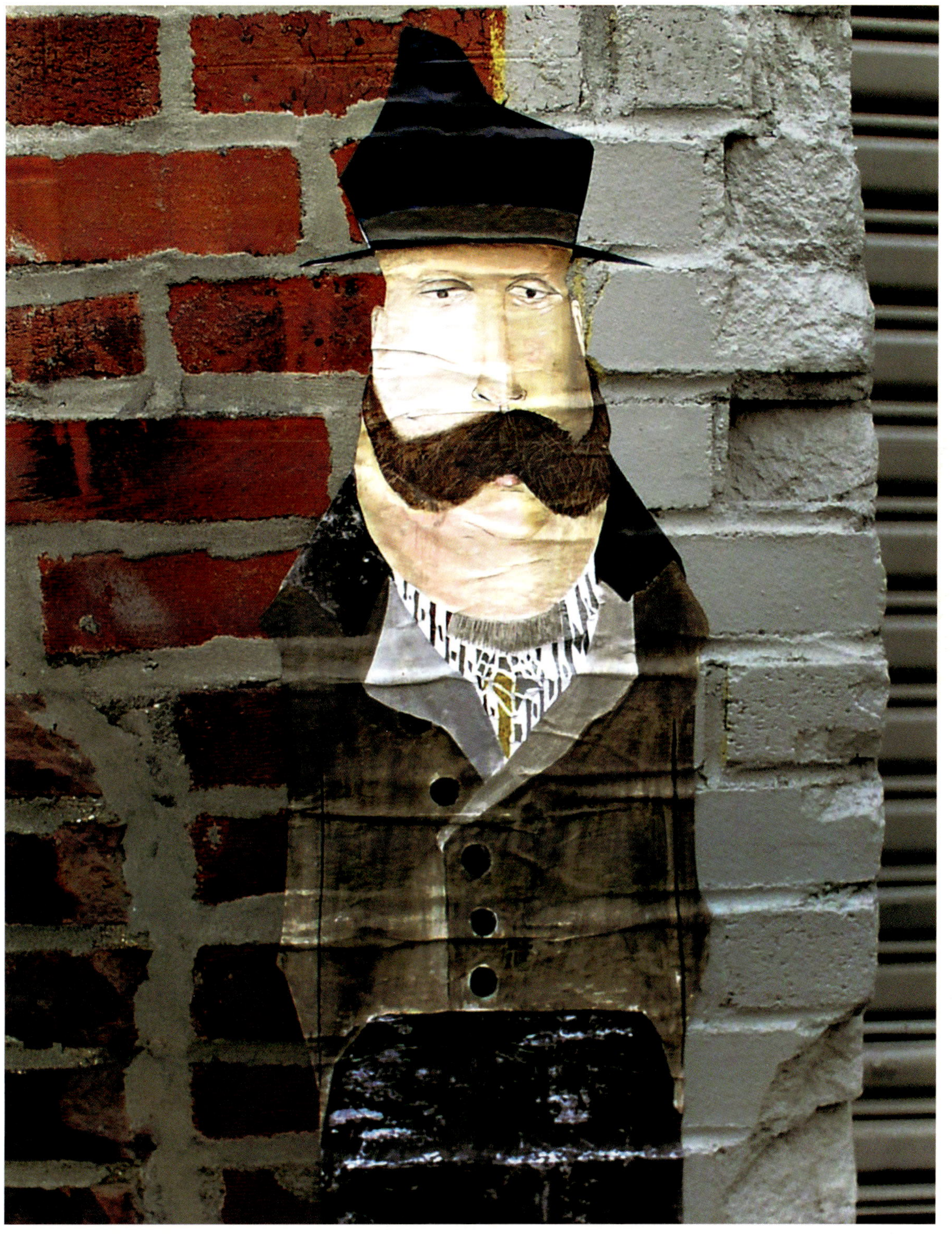

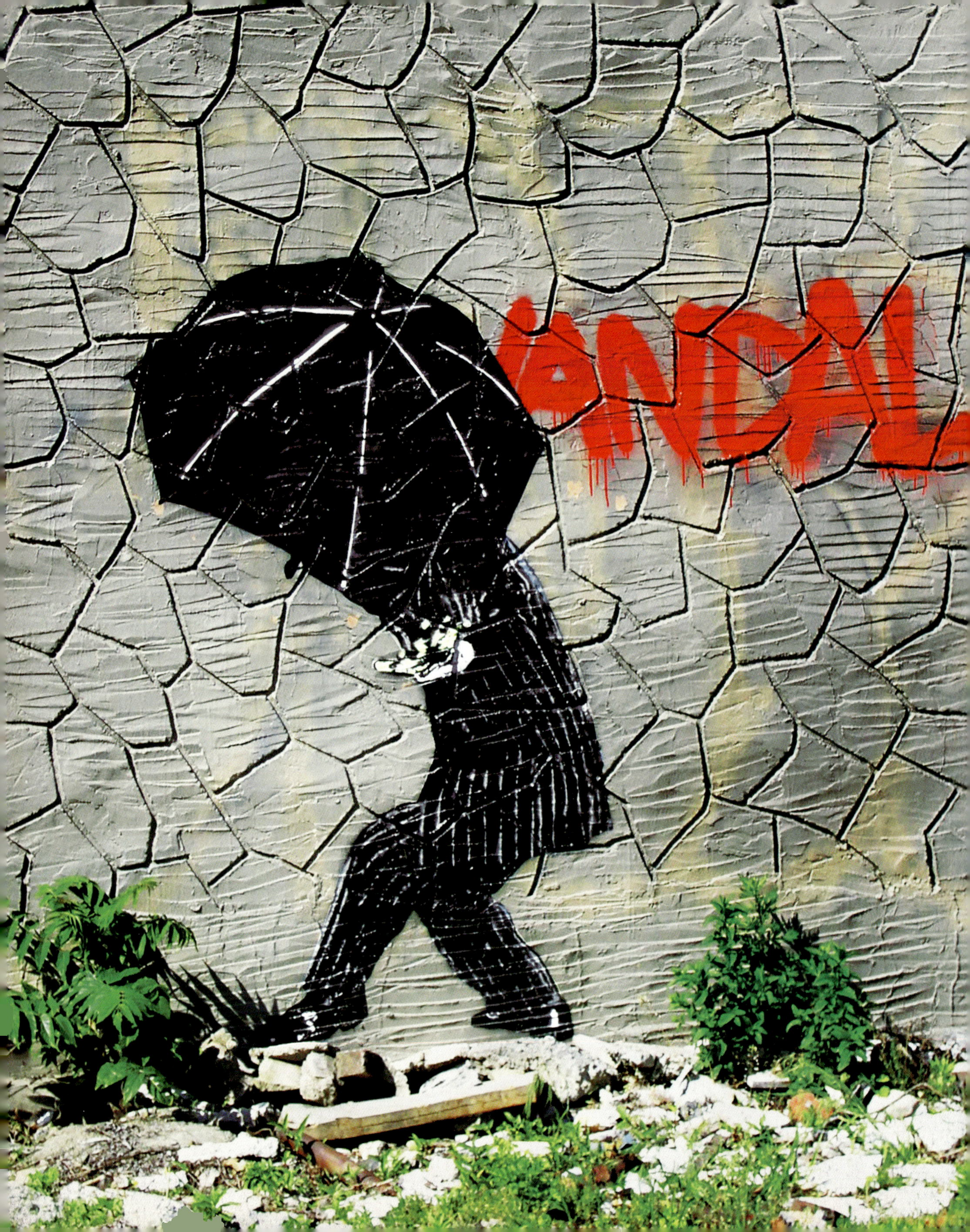
ANDAL

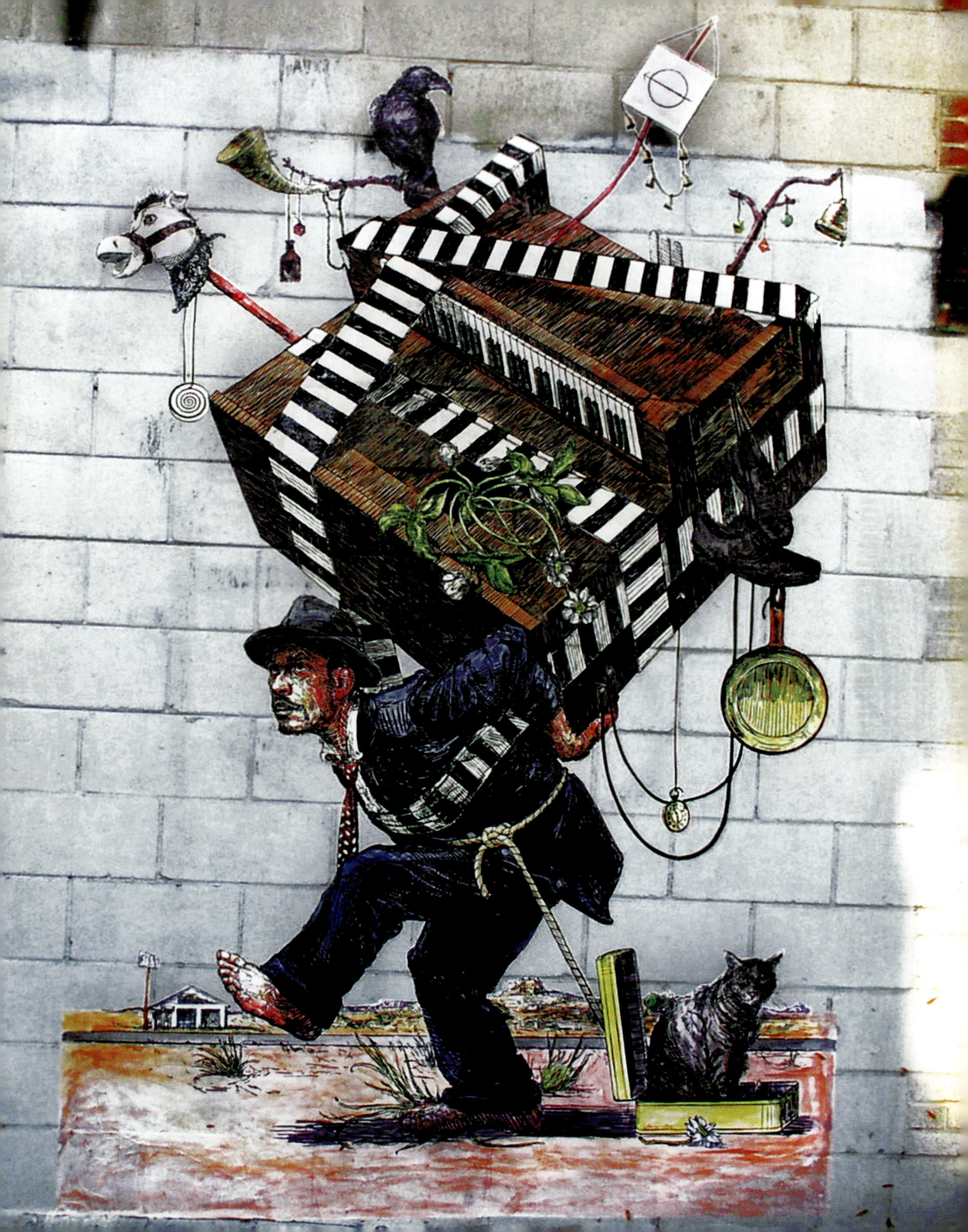

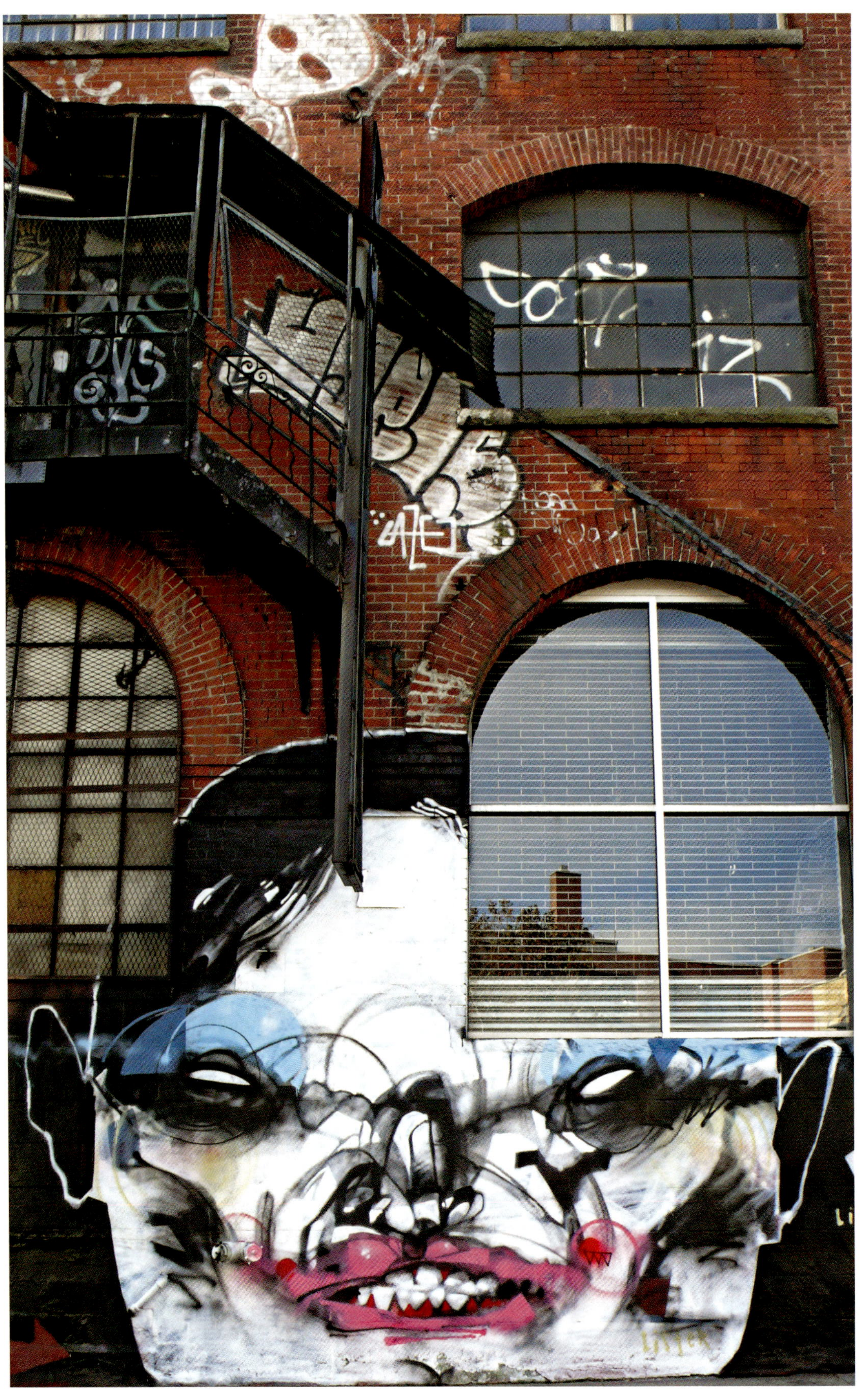

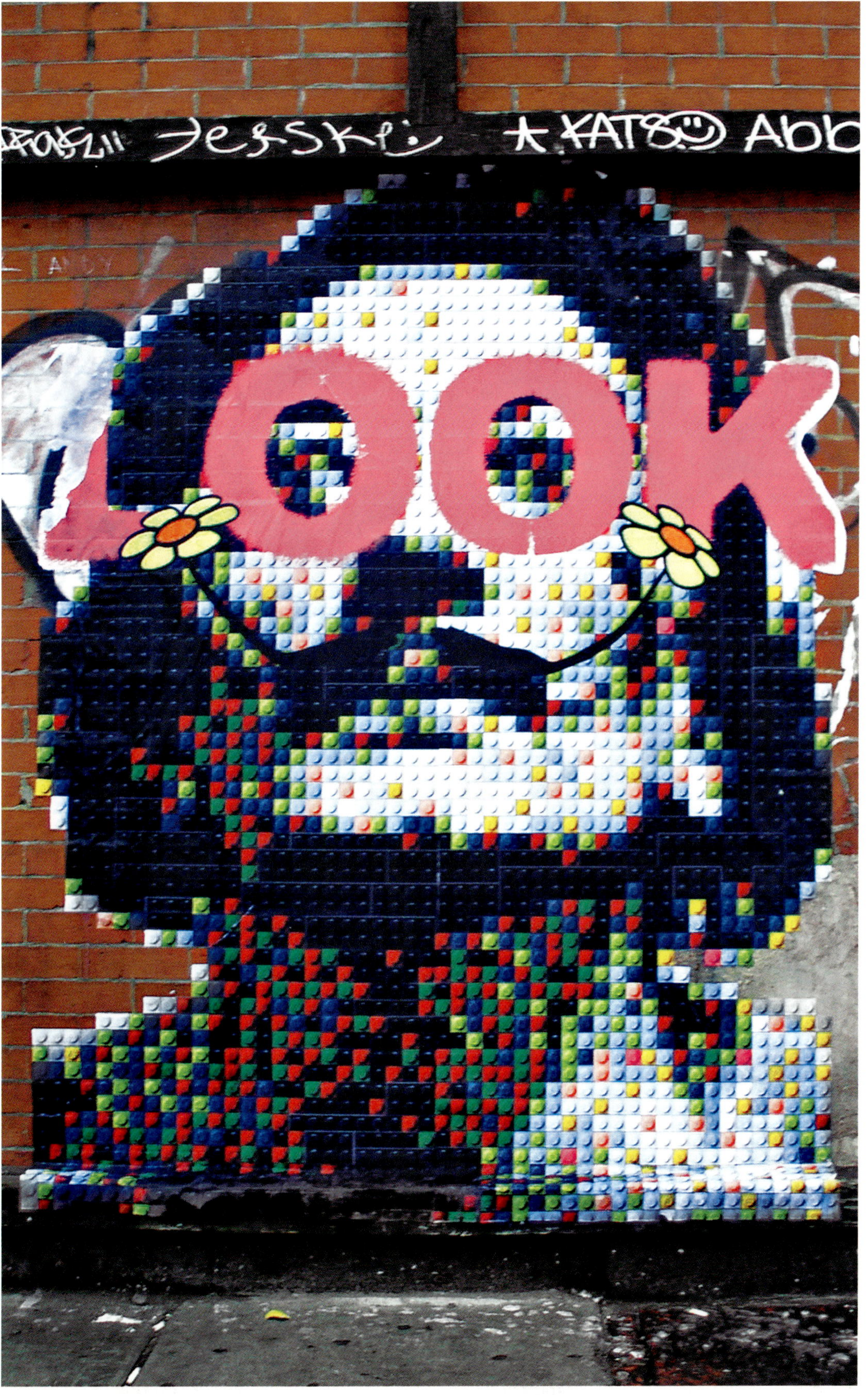
LOOK

KLOWN
05
5036
$ 26.99

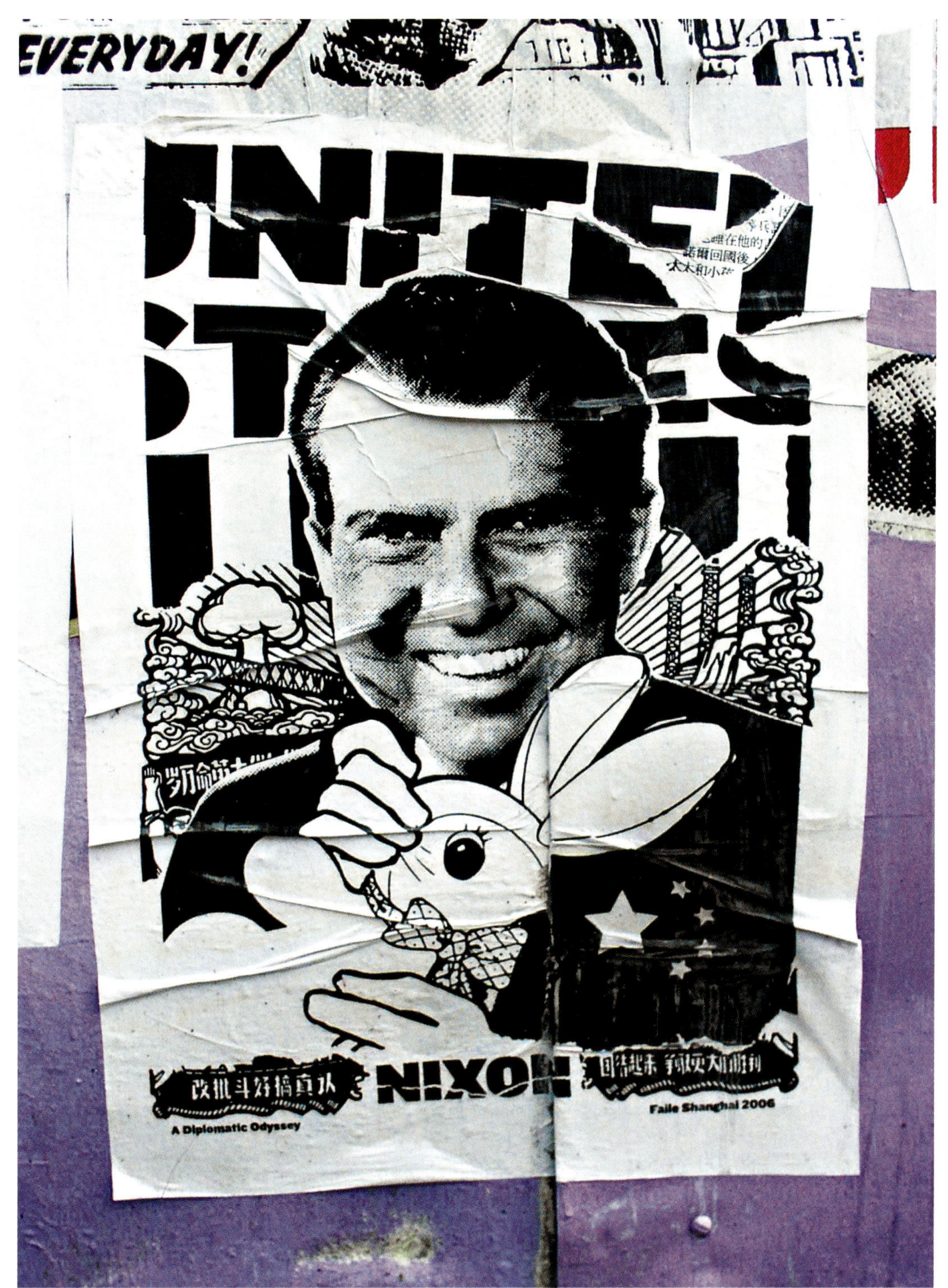
EVERYDAY!
NIXON
A Diplomatic Odyssey
Faile Shanghai 2006

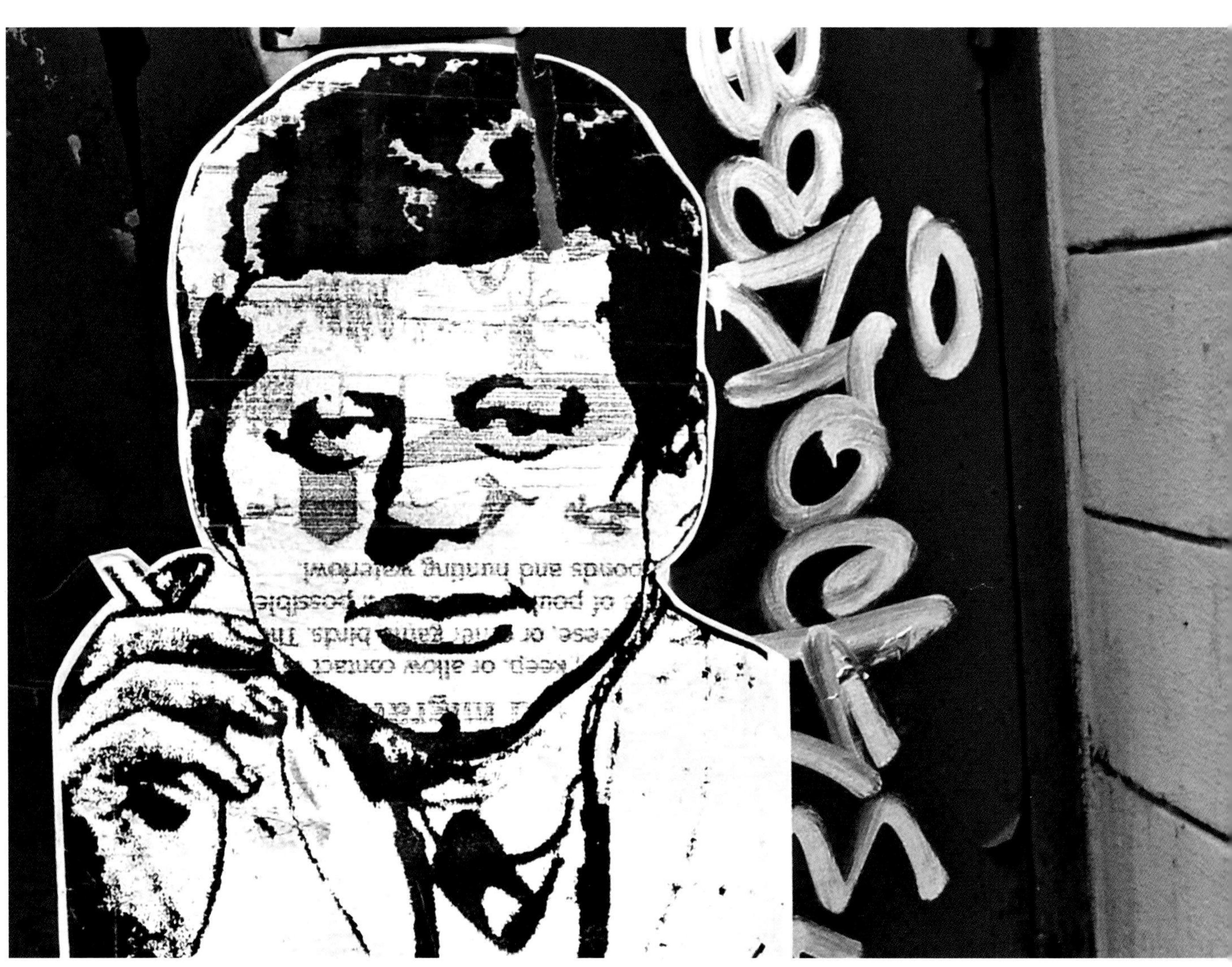

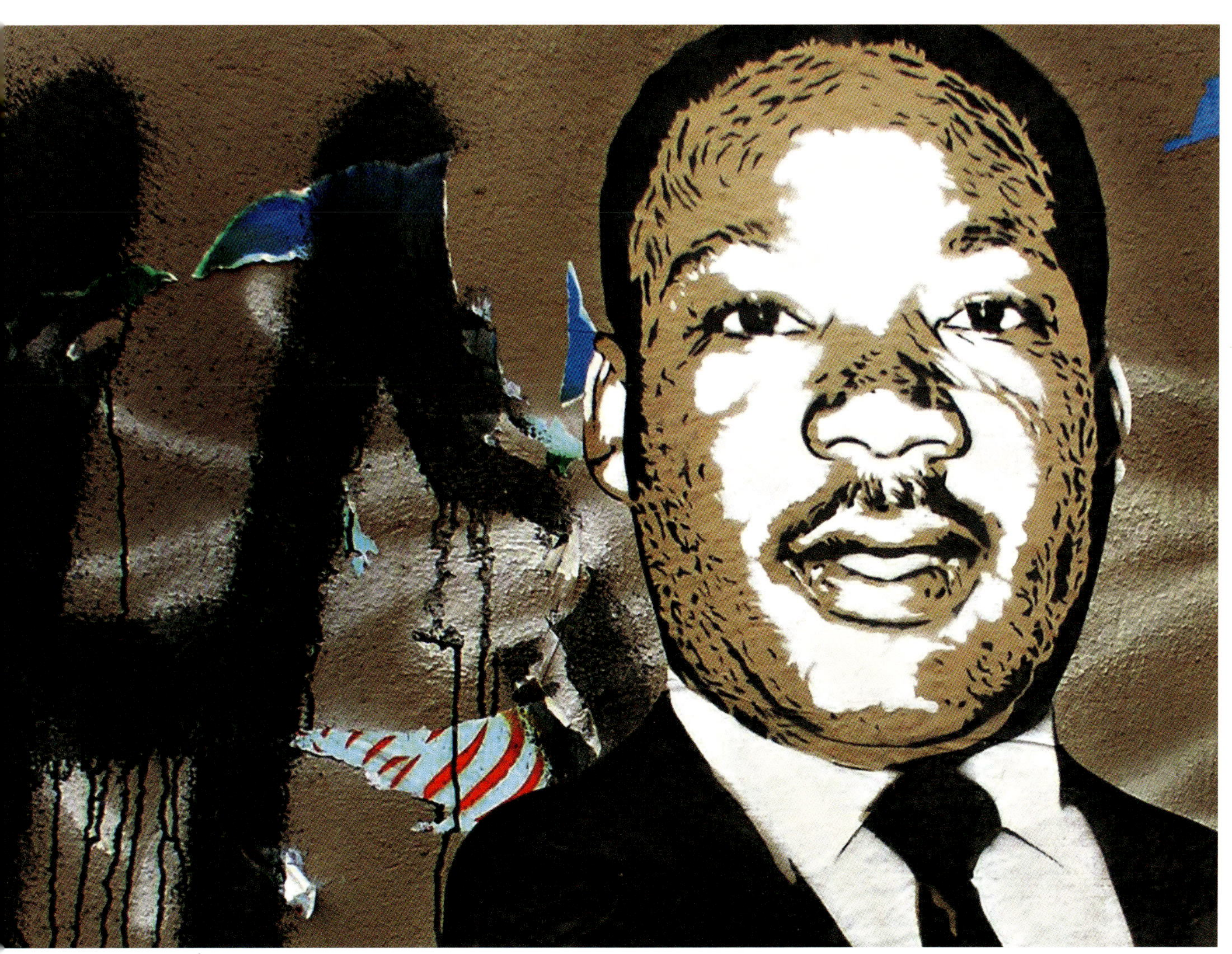

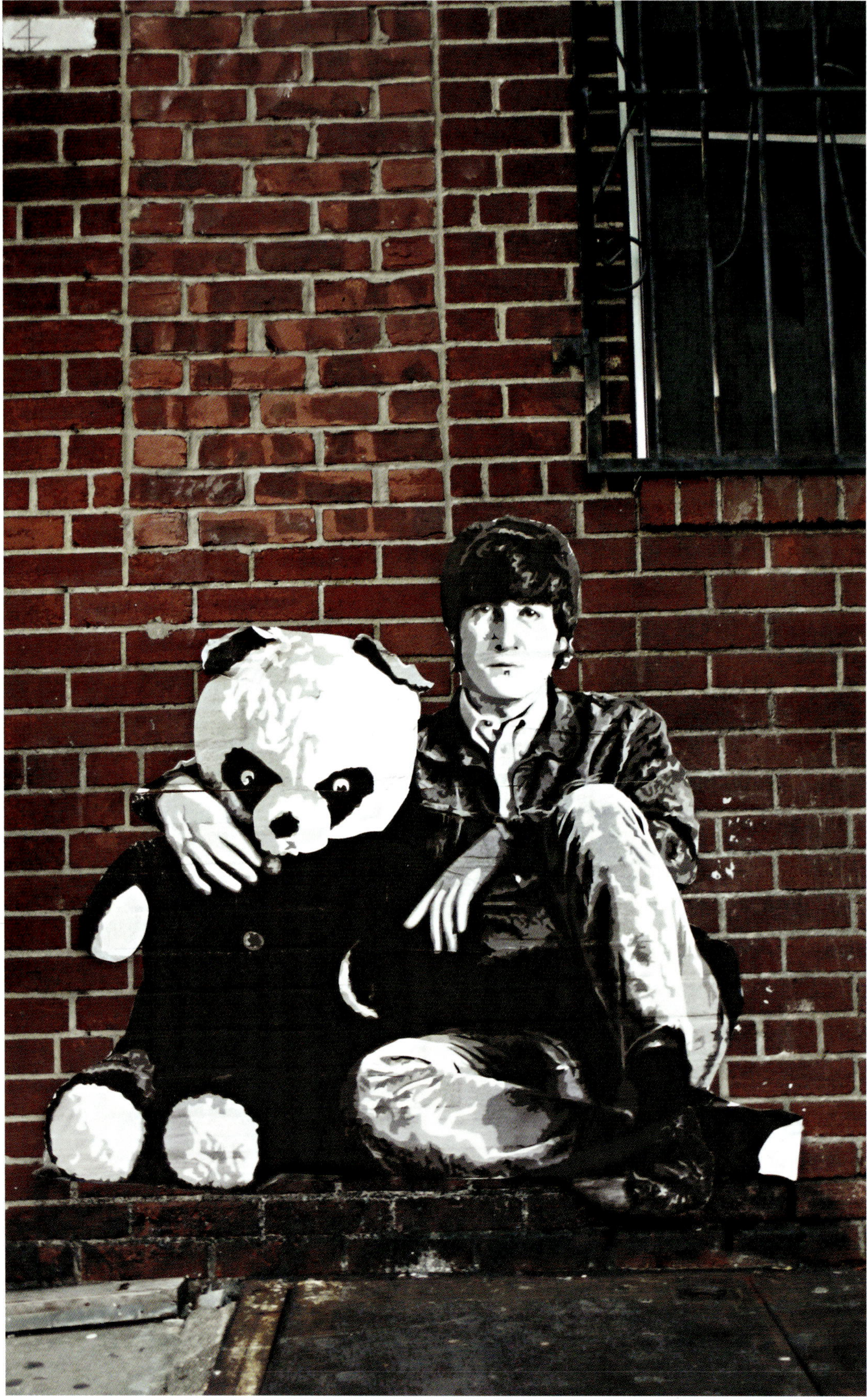

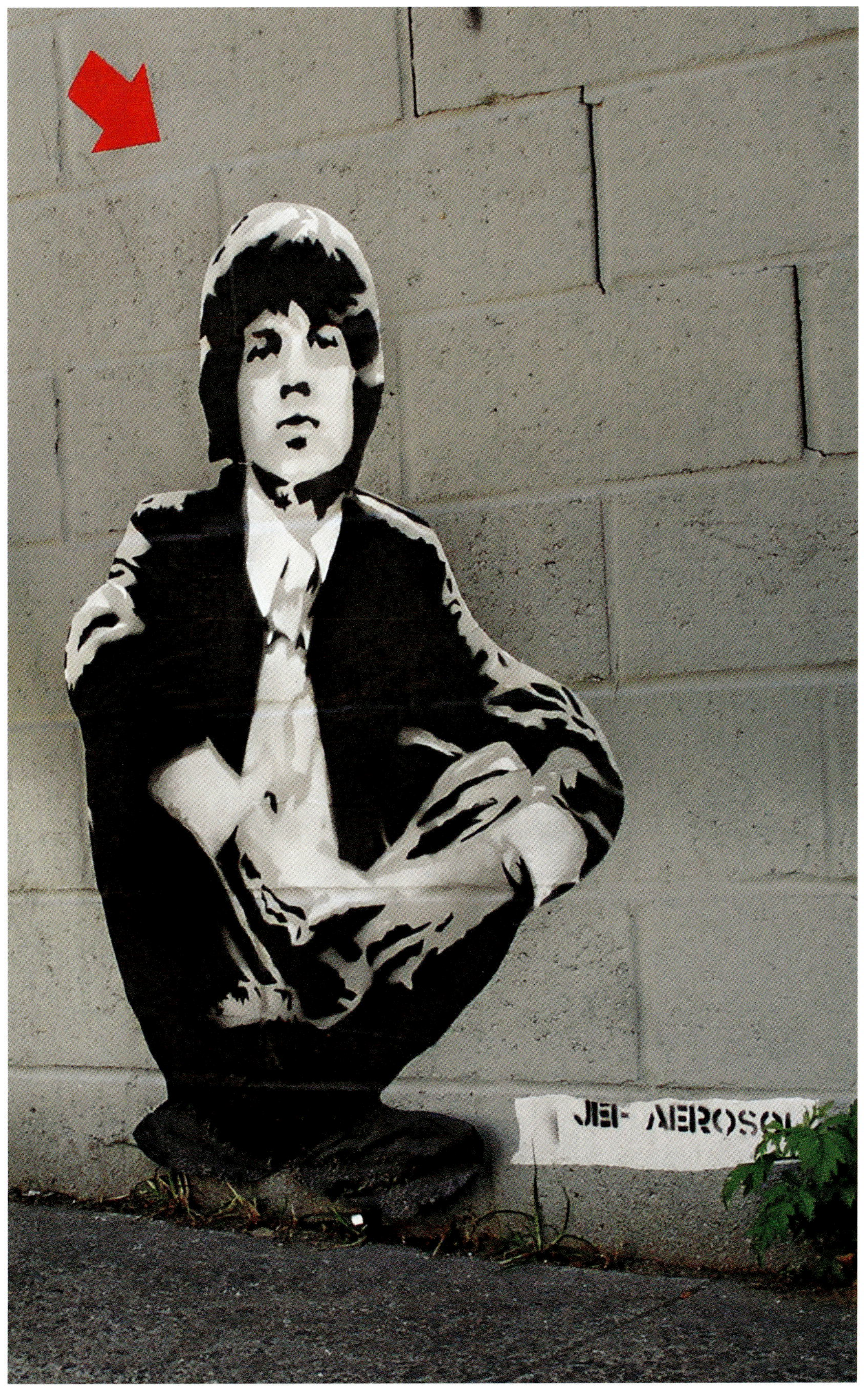

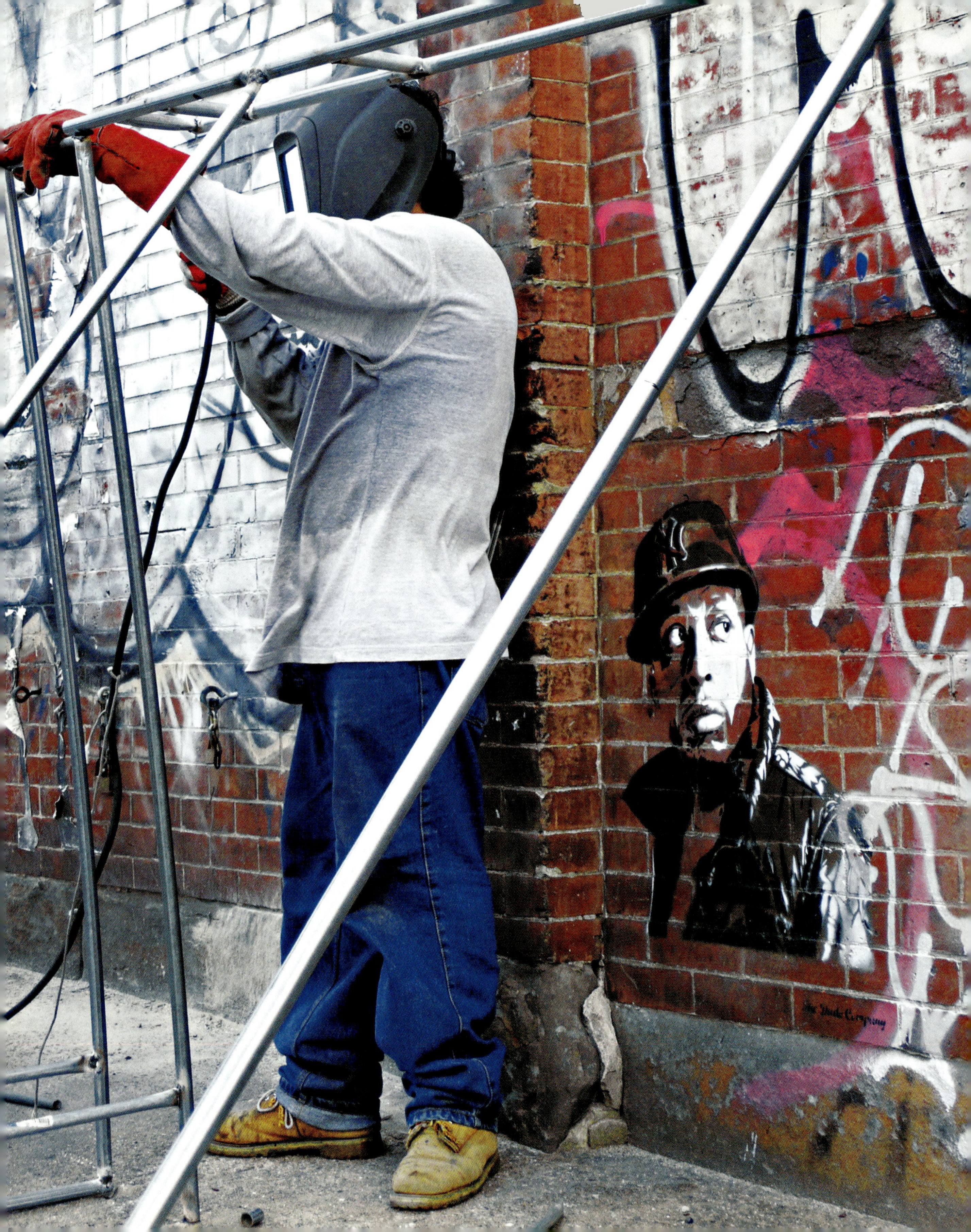

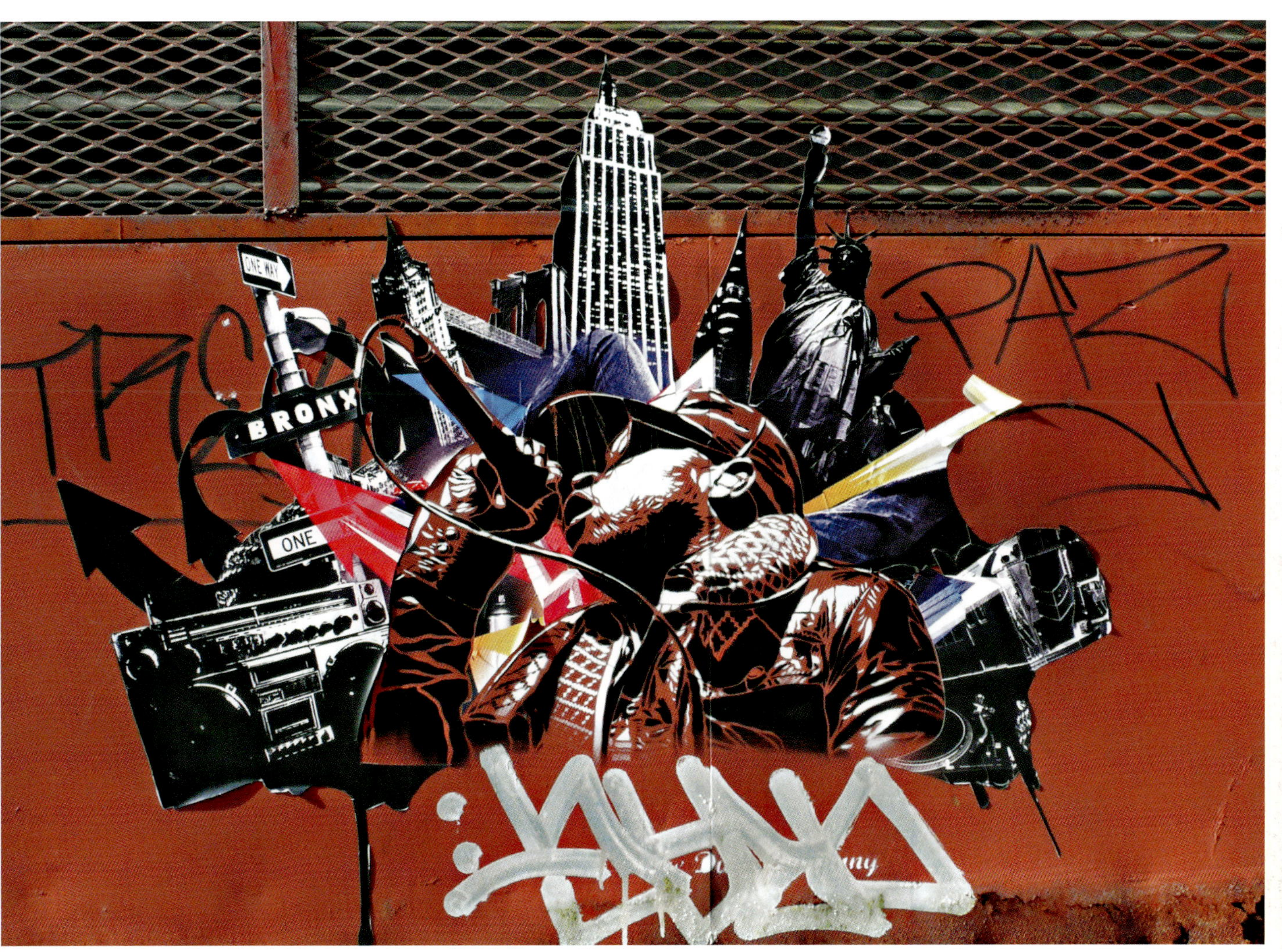
ONE WAY
BRONX
ONE

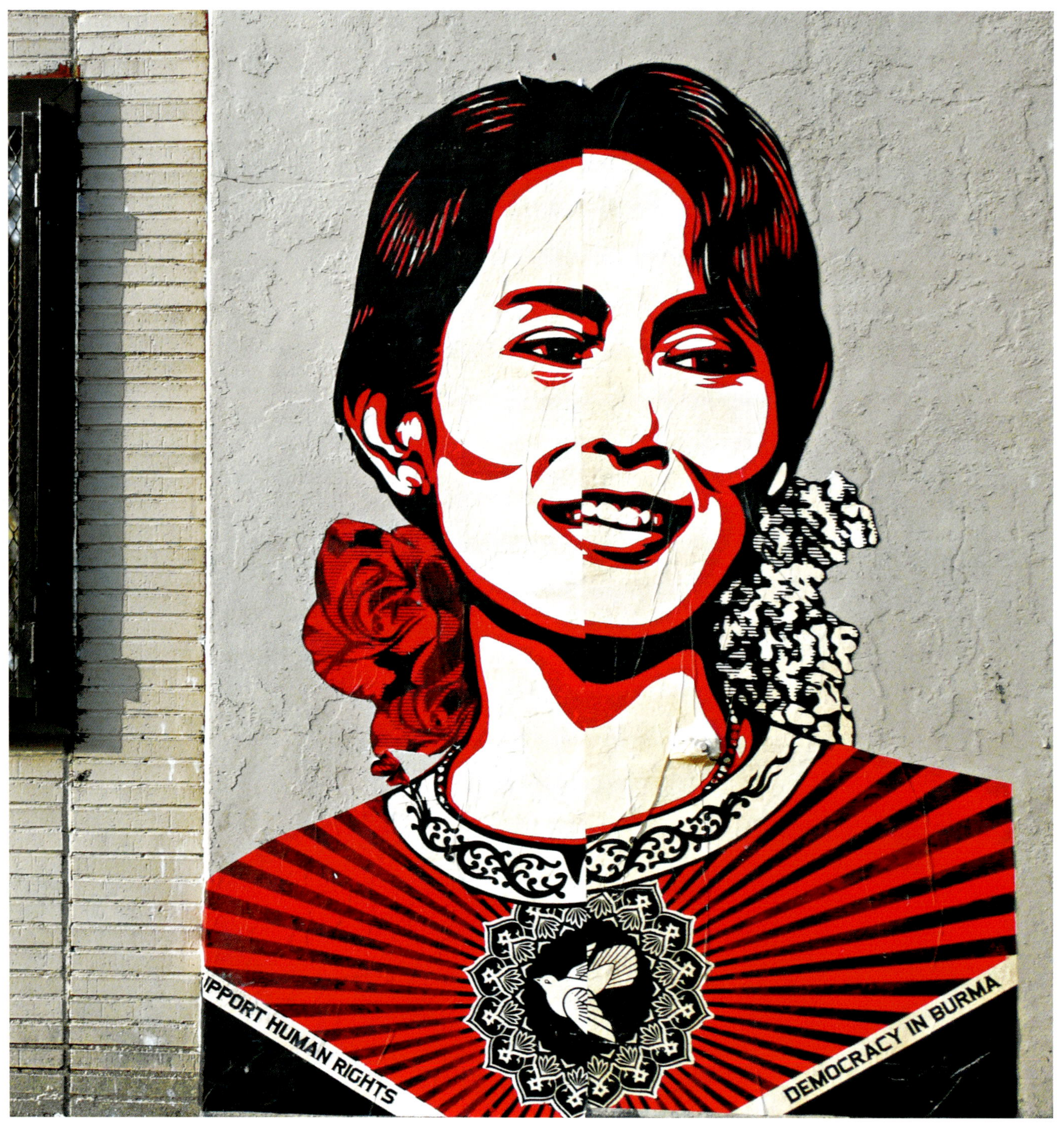
PPORT HUMAN RIGHTS
DEMOCRACY IN BURMA

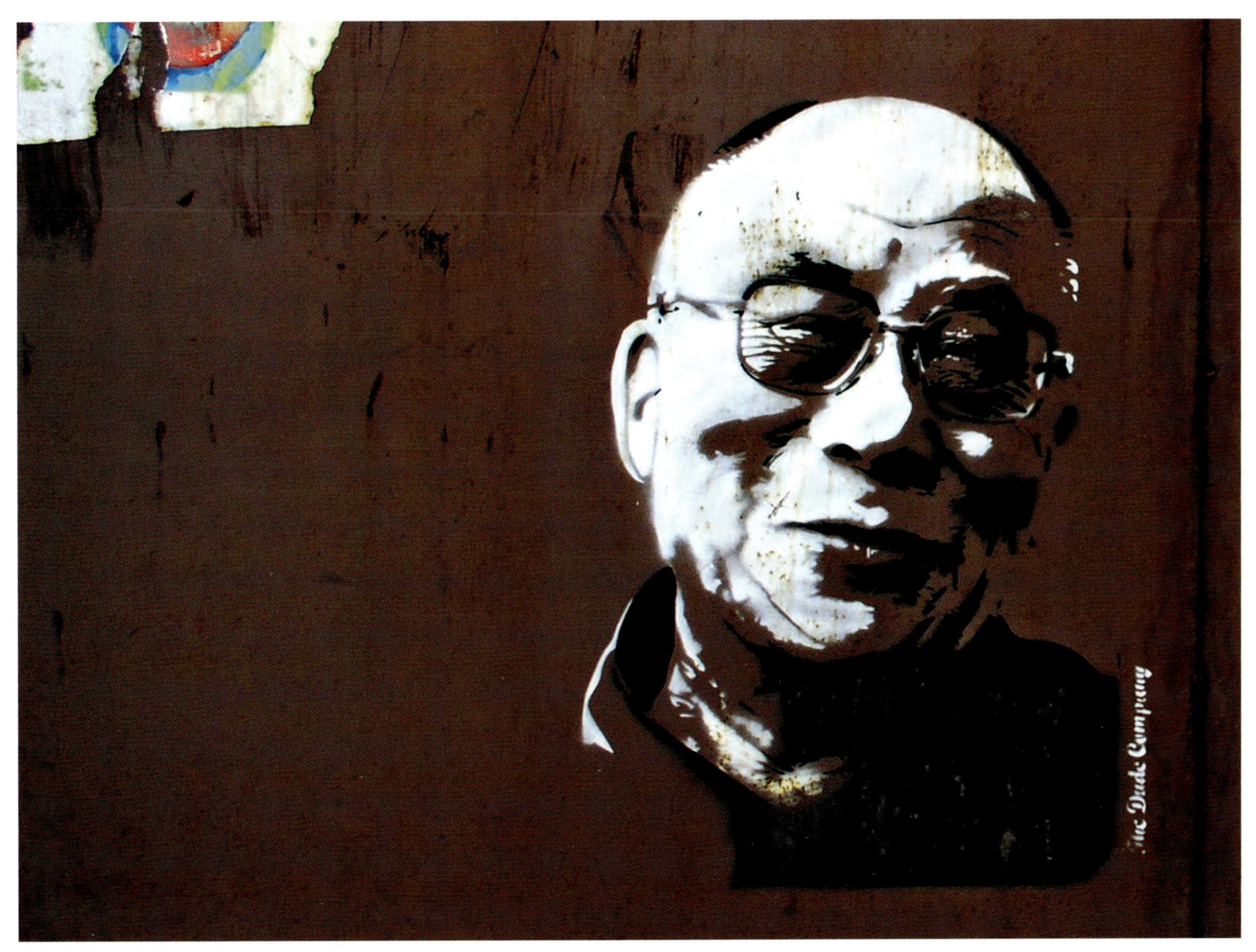
Dude Company

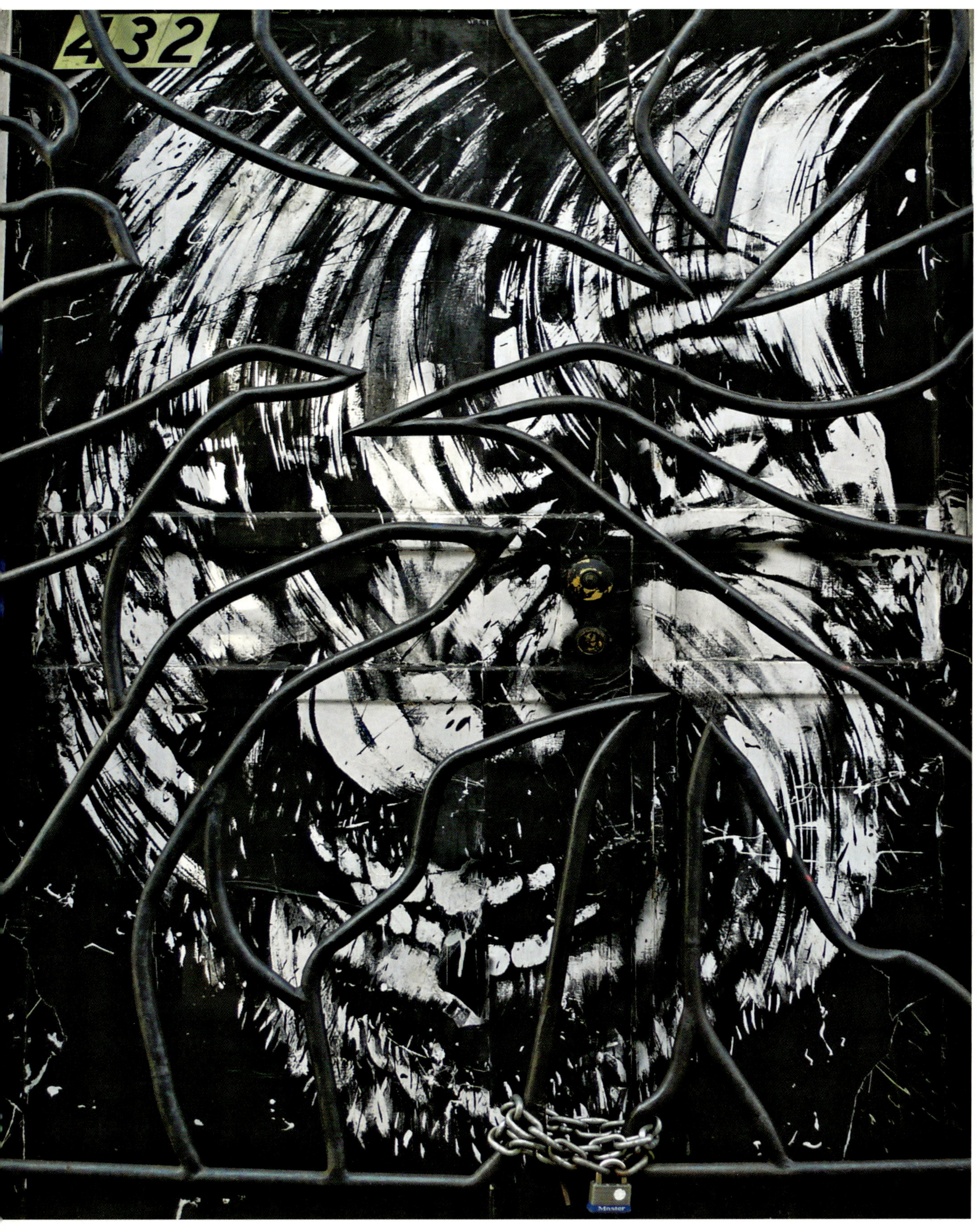
432
Master

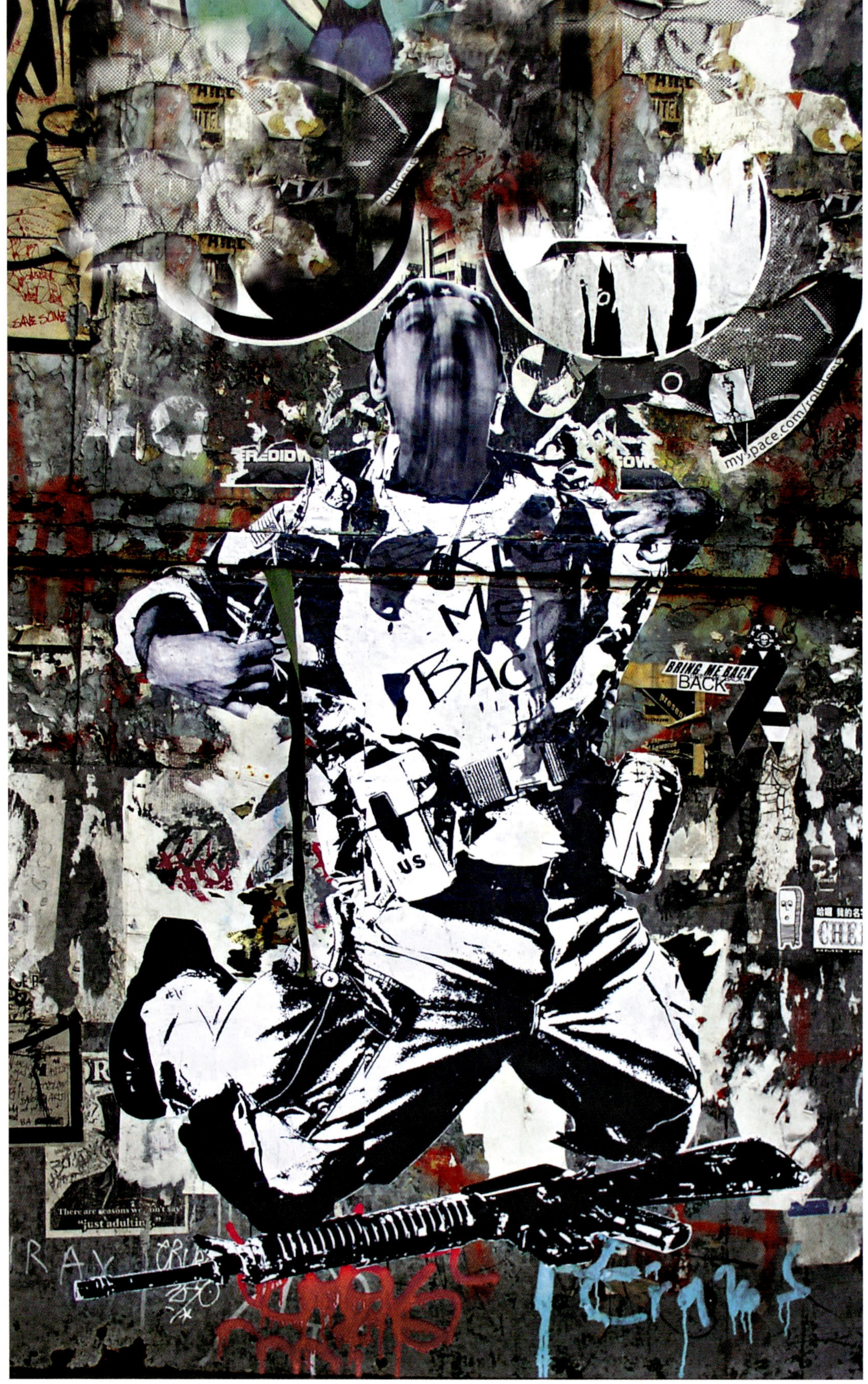
BRING ME BACK
BACK
US

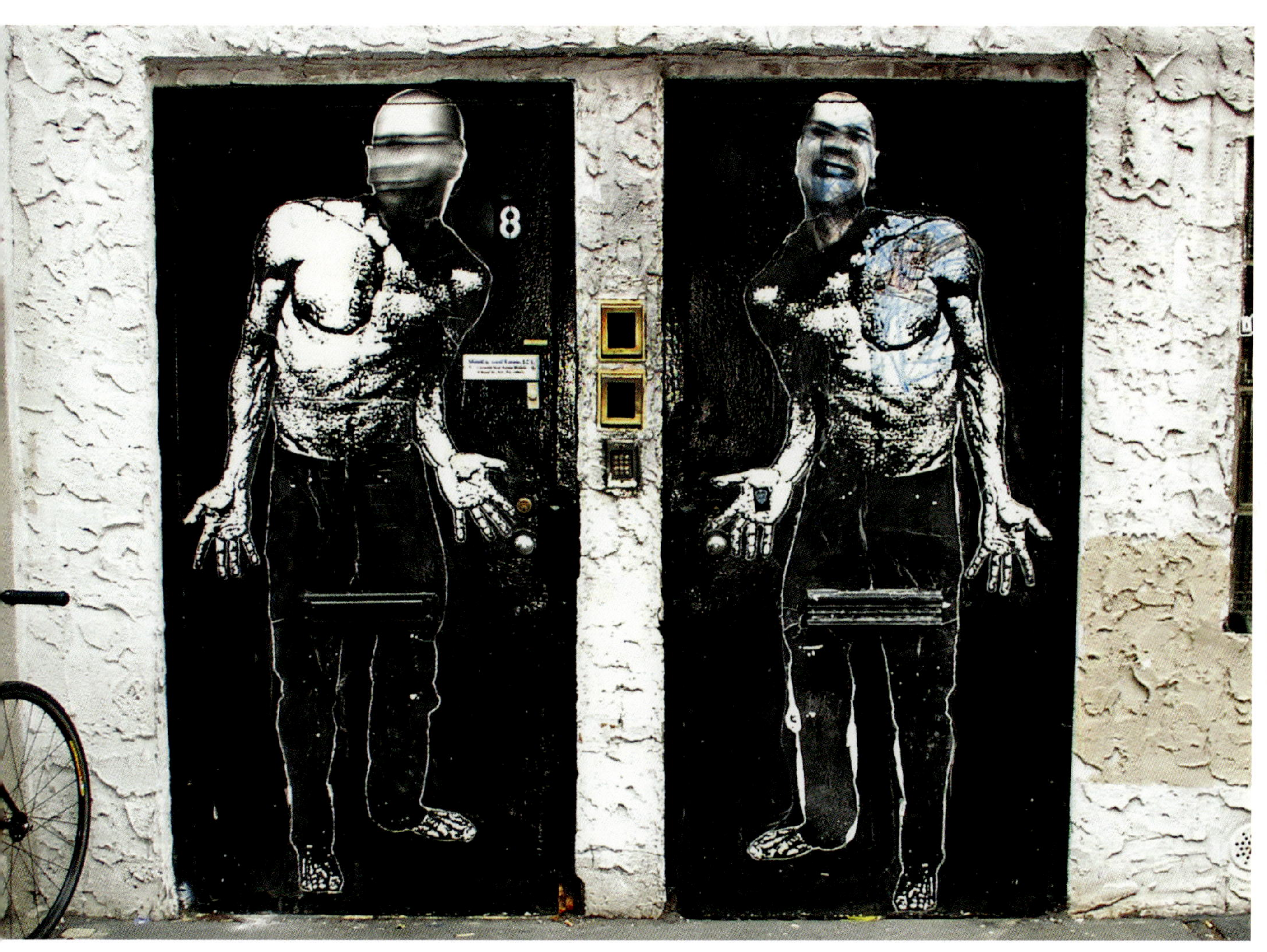
8

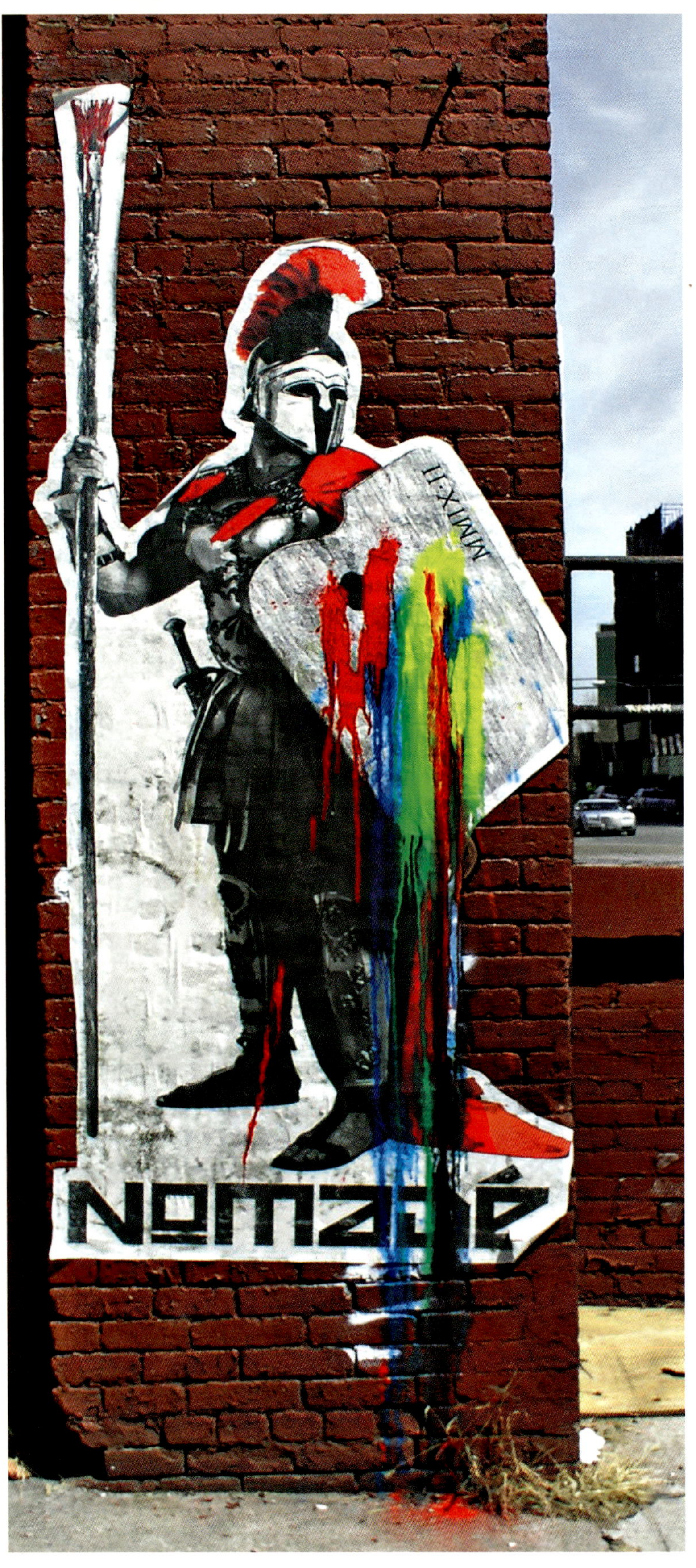
NOMADÉ

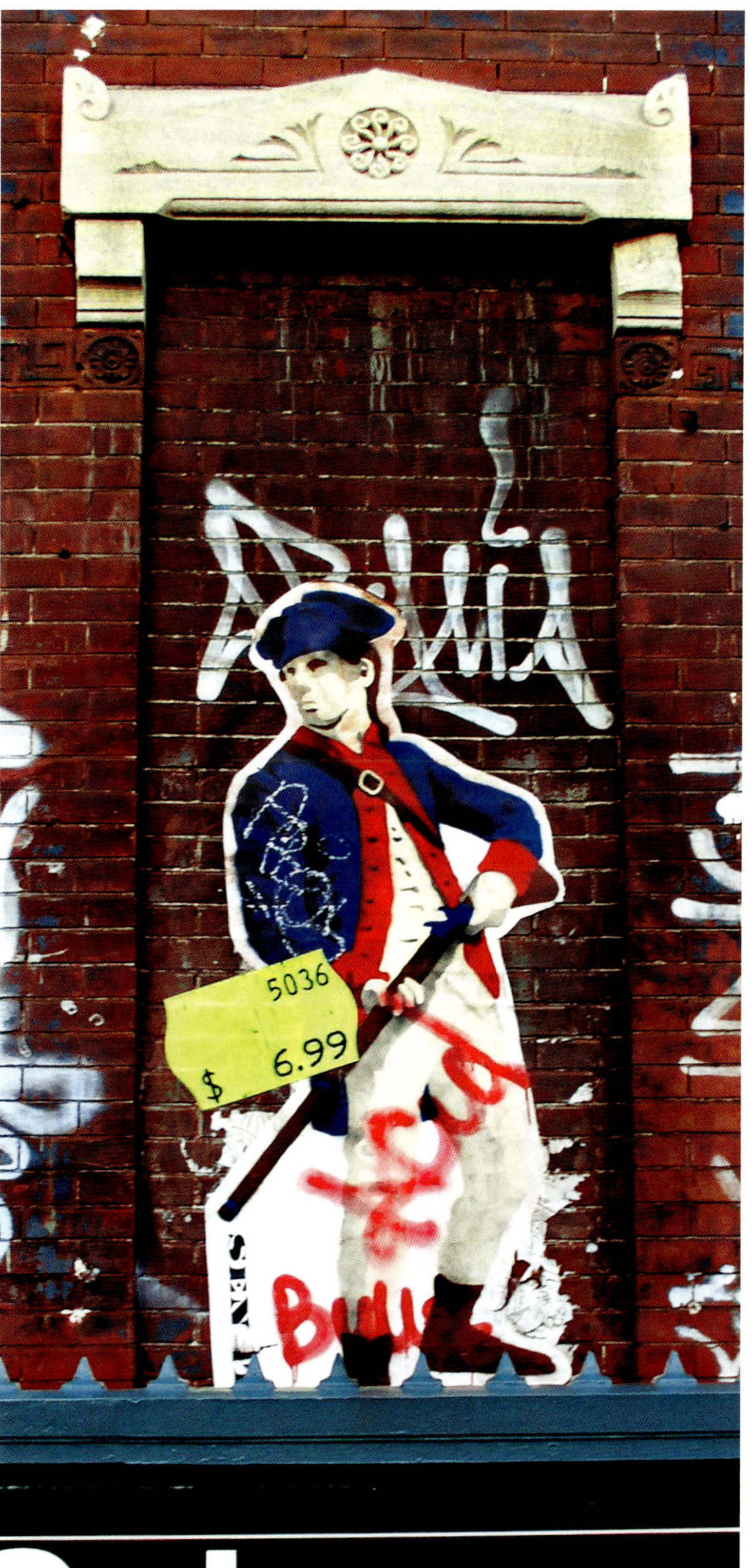

Subway

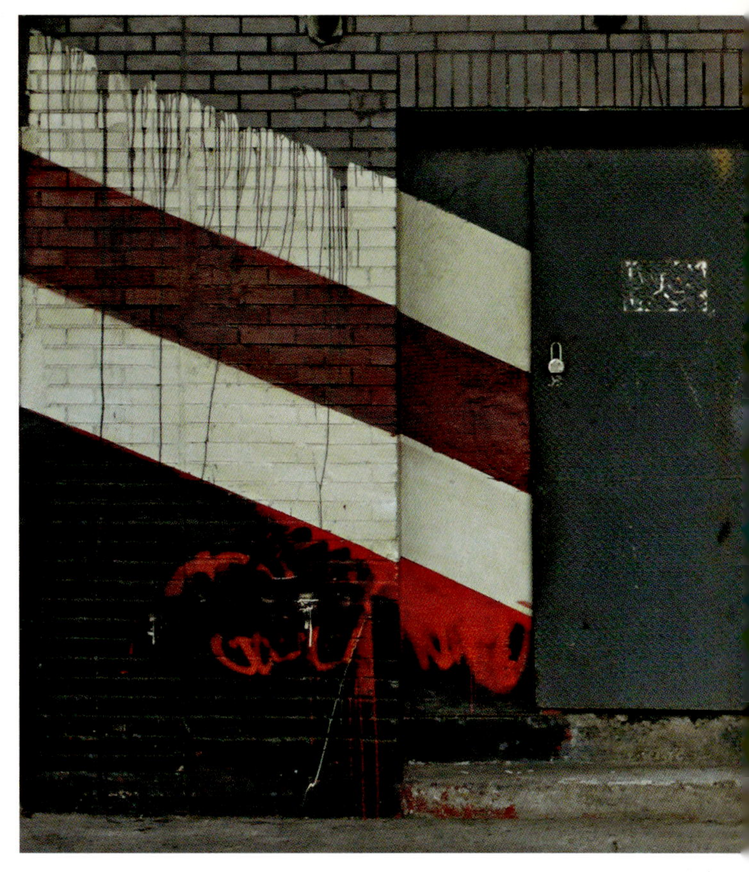

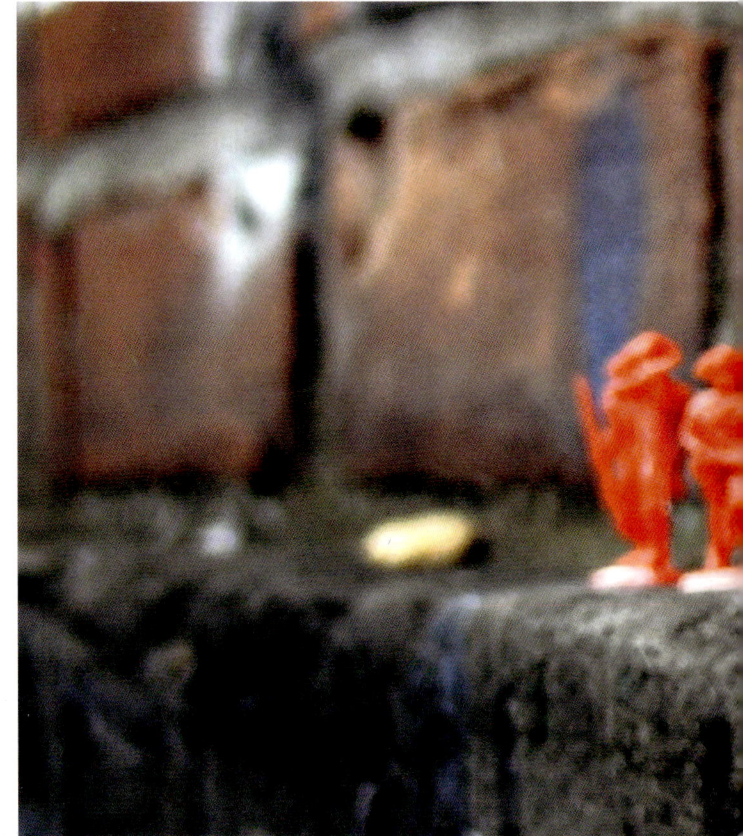

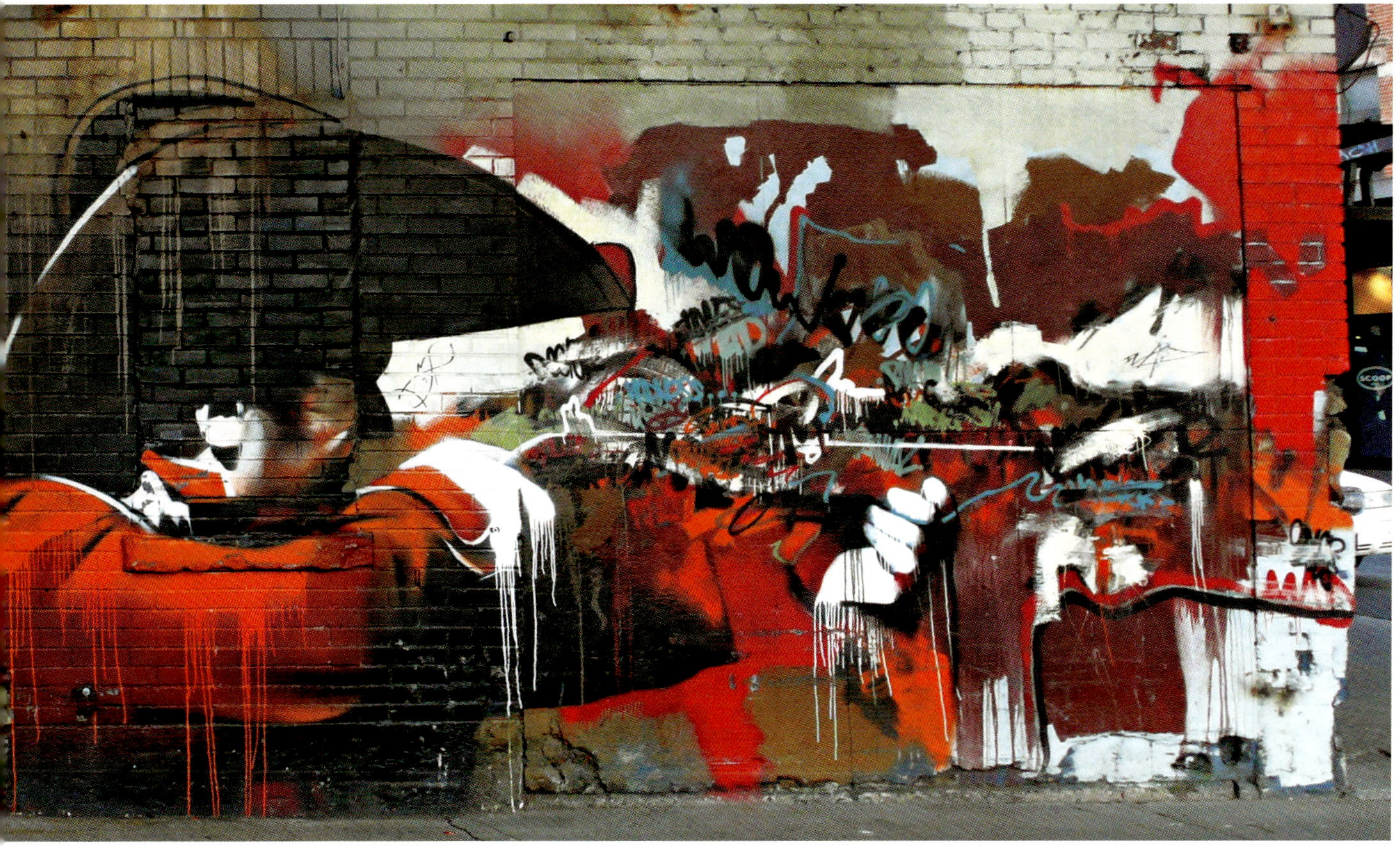

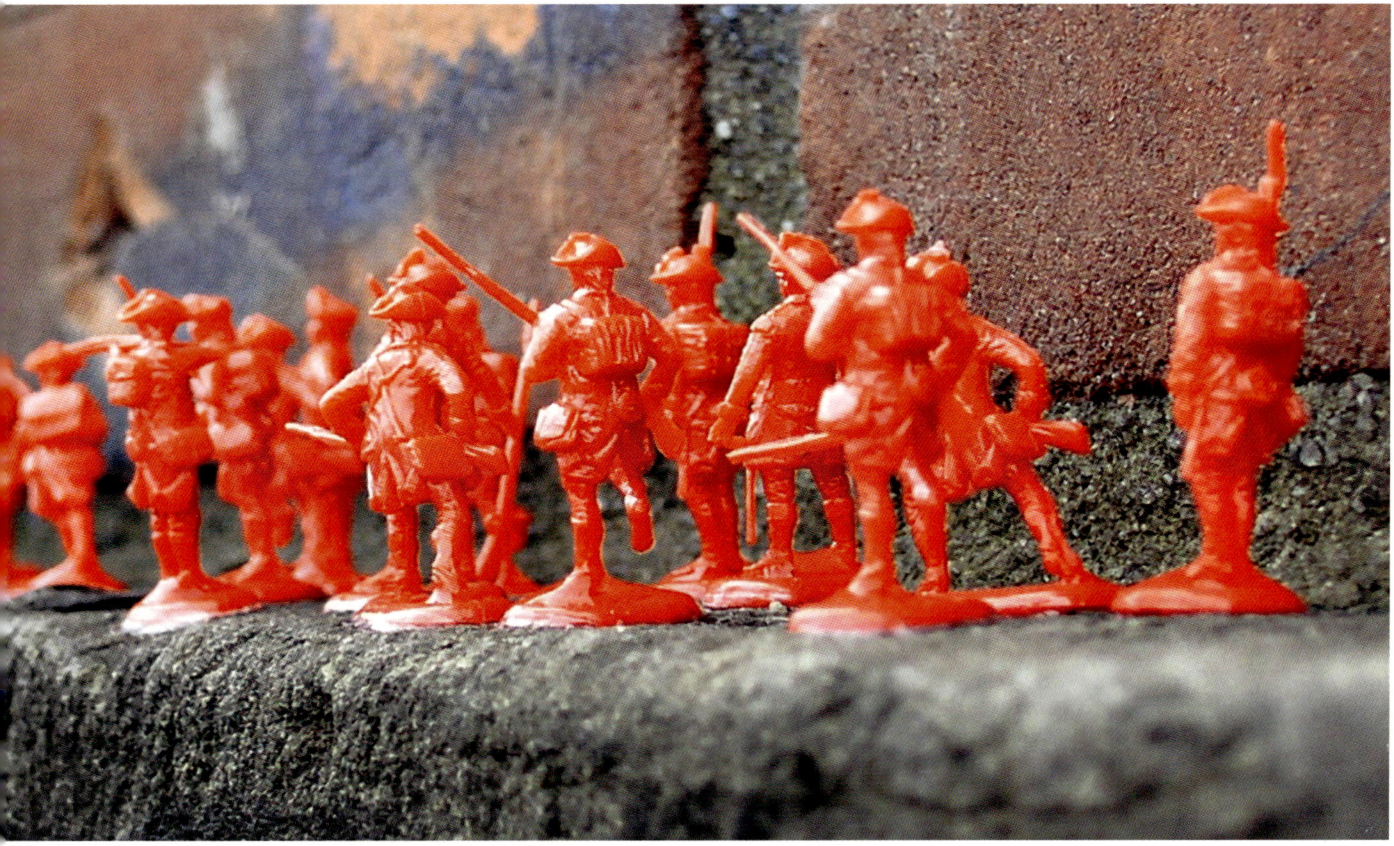

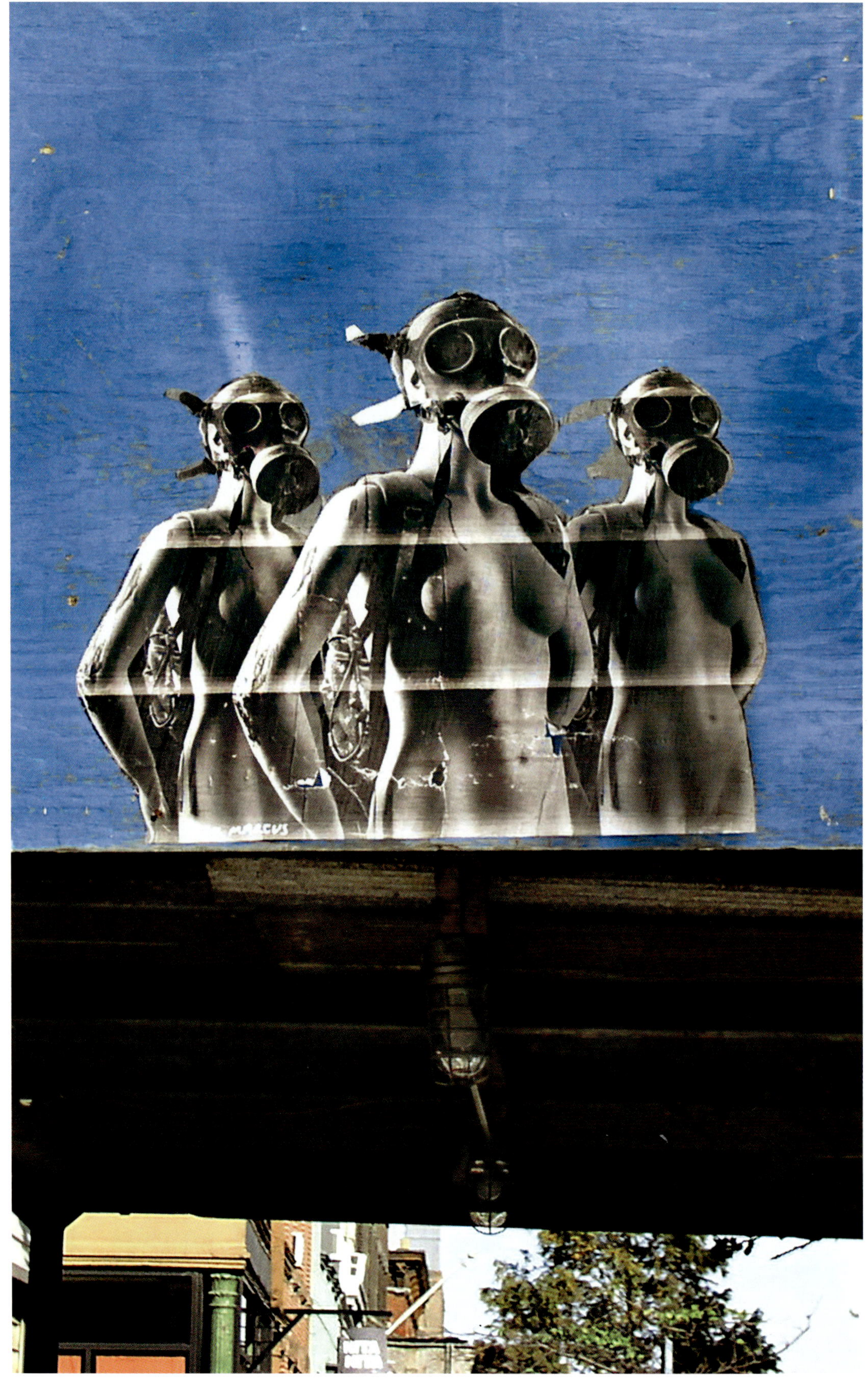
MARCUS

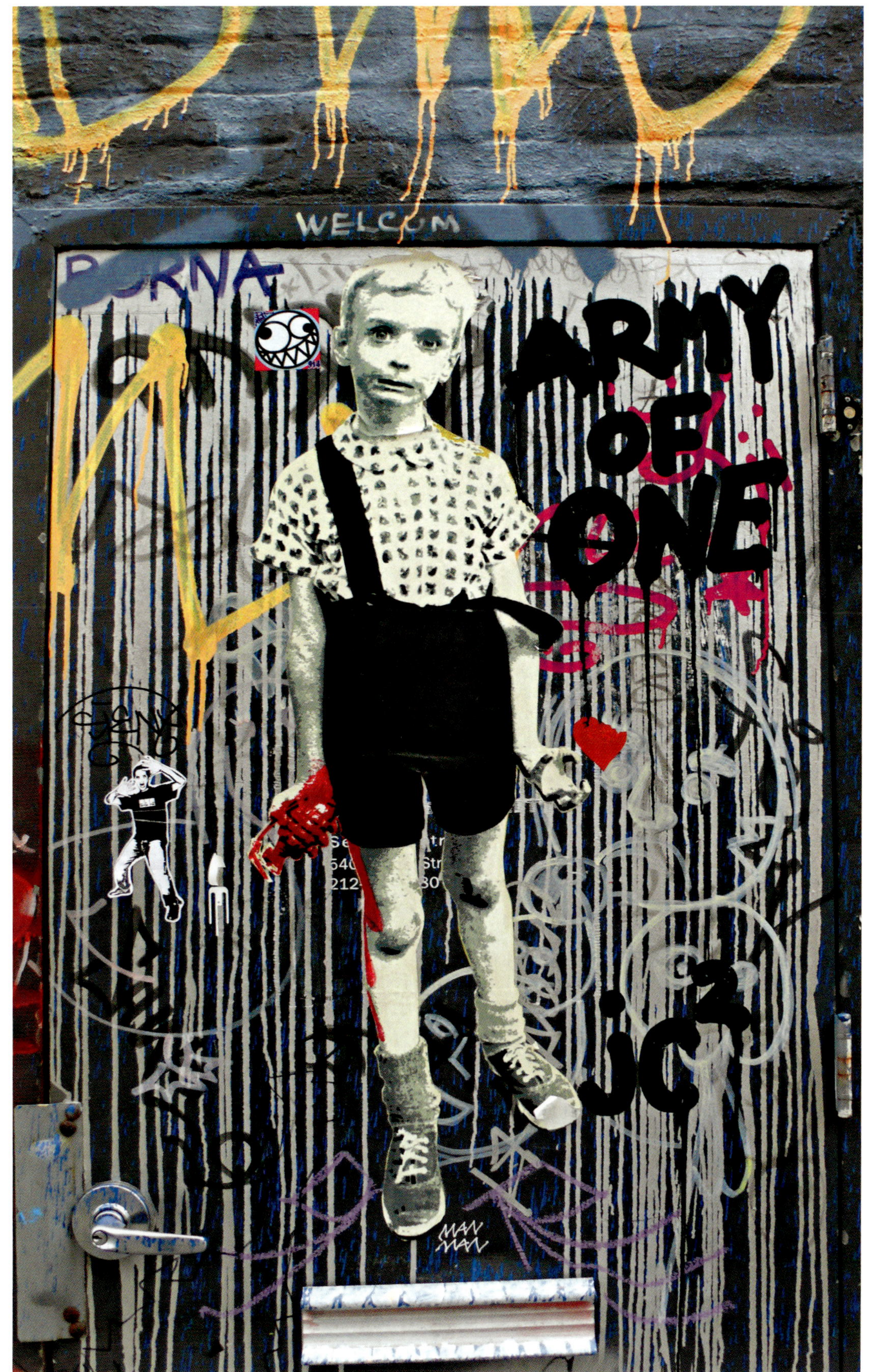
WELCUM
ARMY OF ONE
MAN MAN

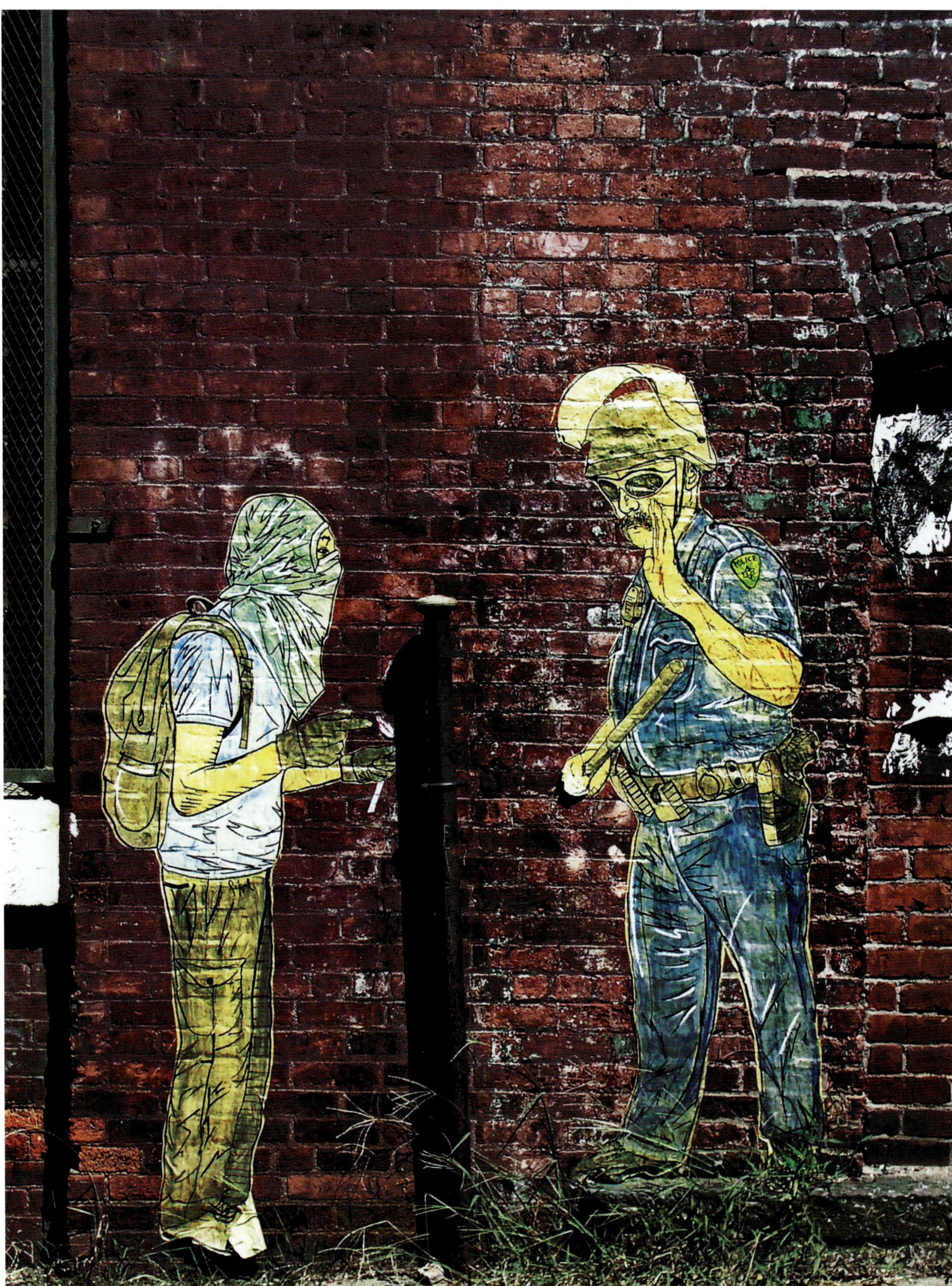
POLICE

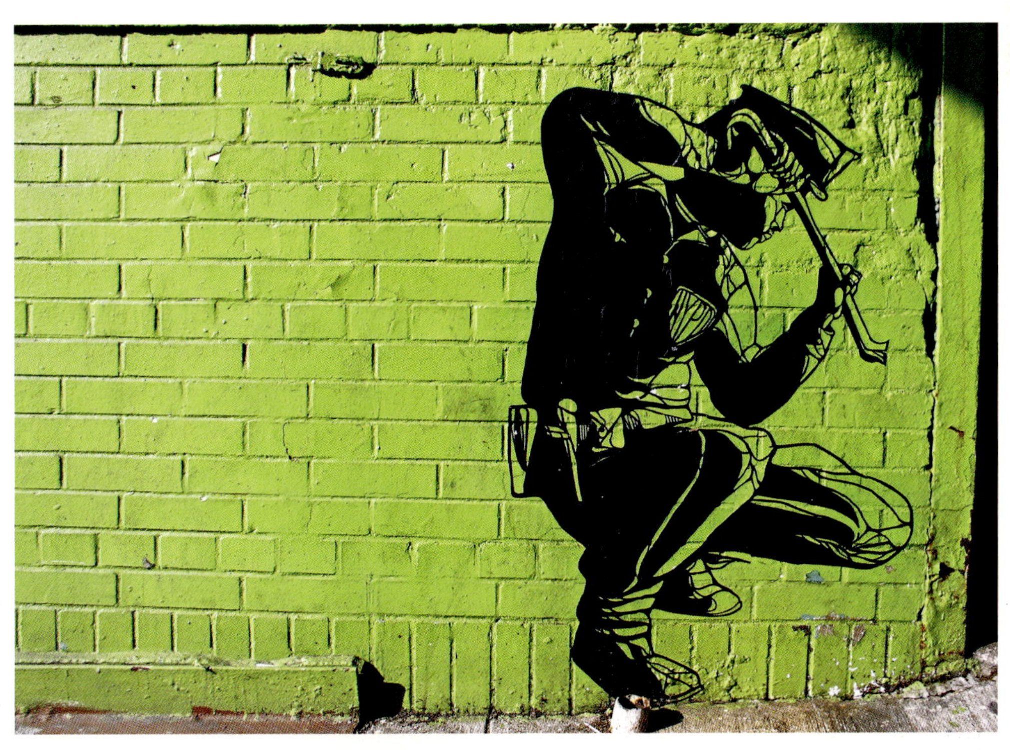

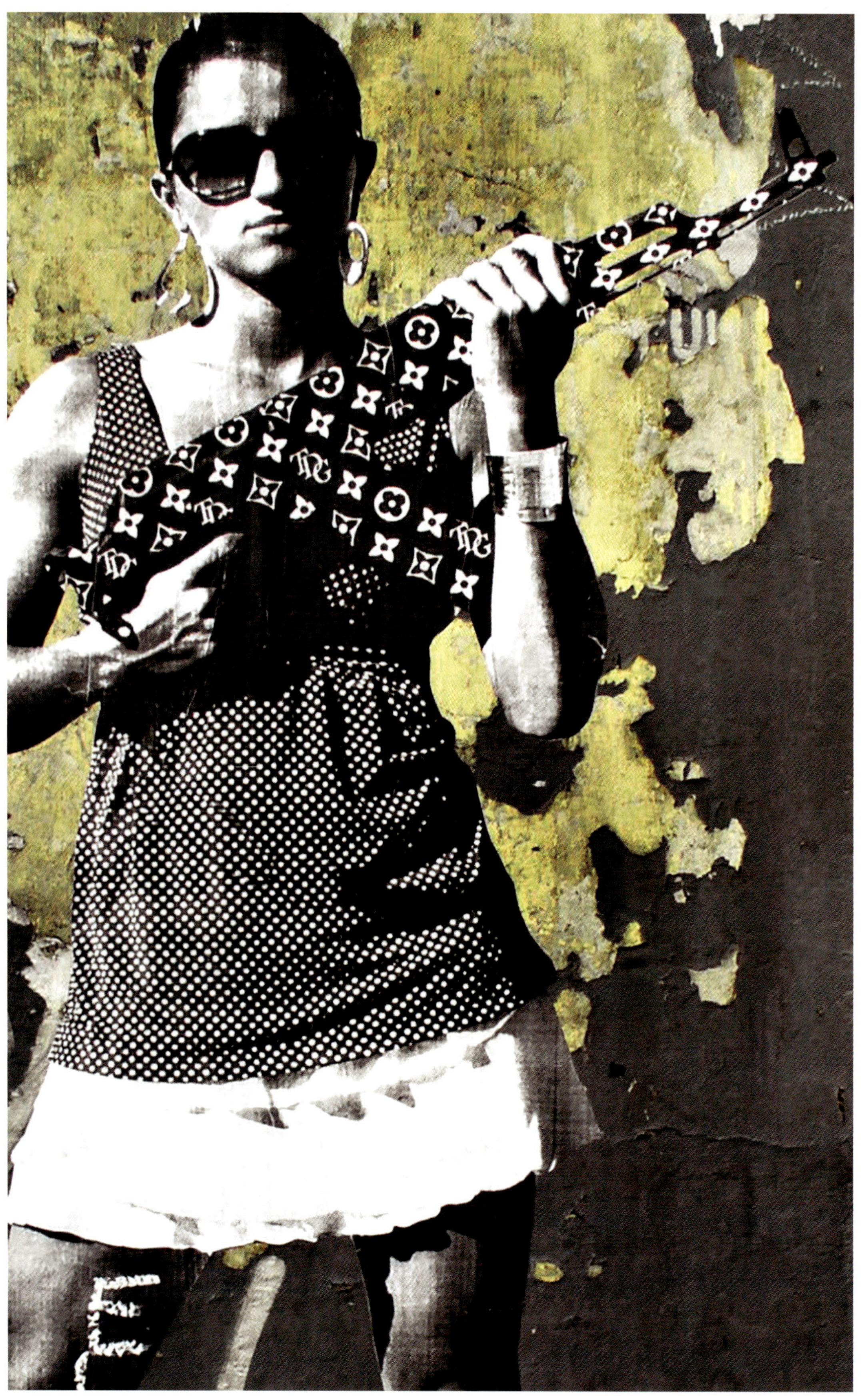

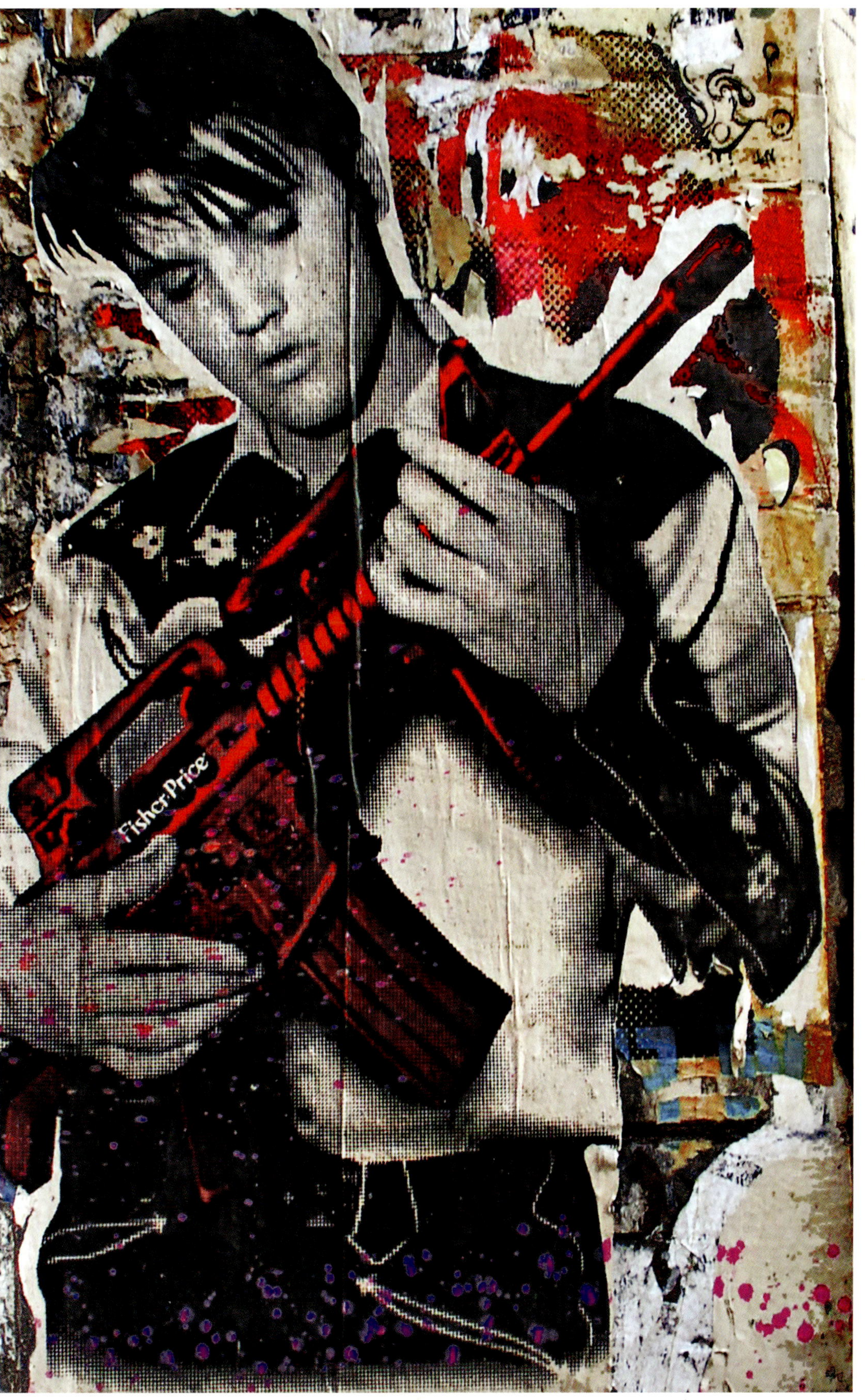
Fisher Price

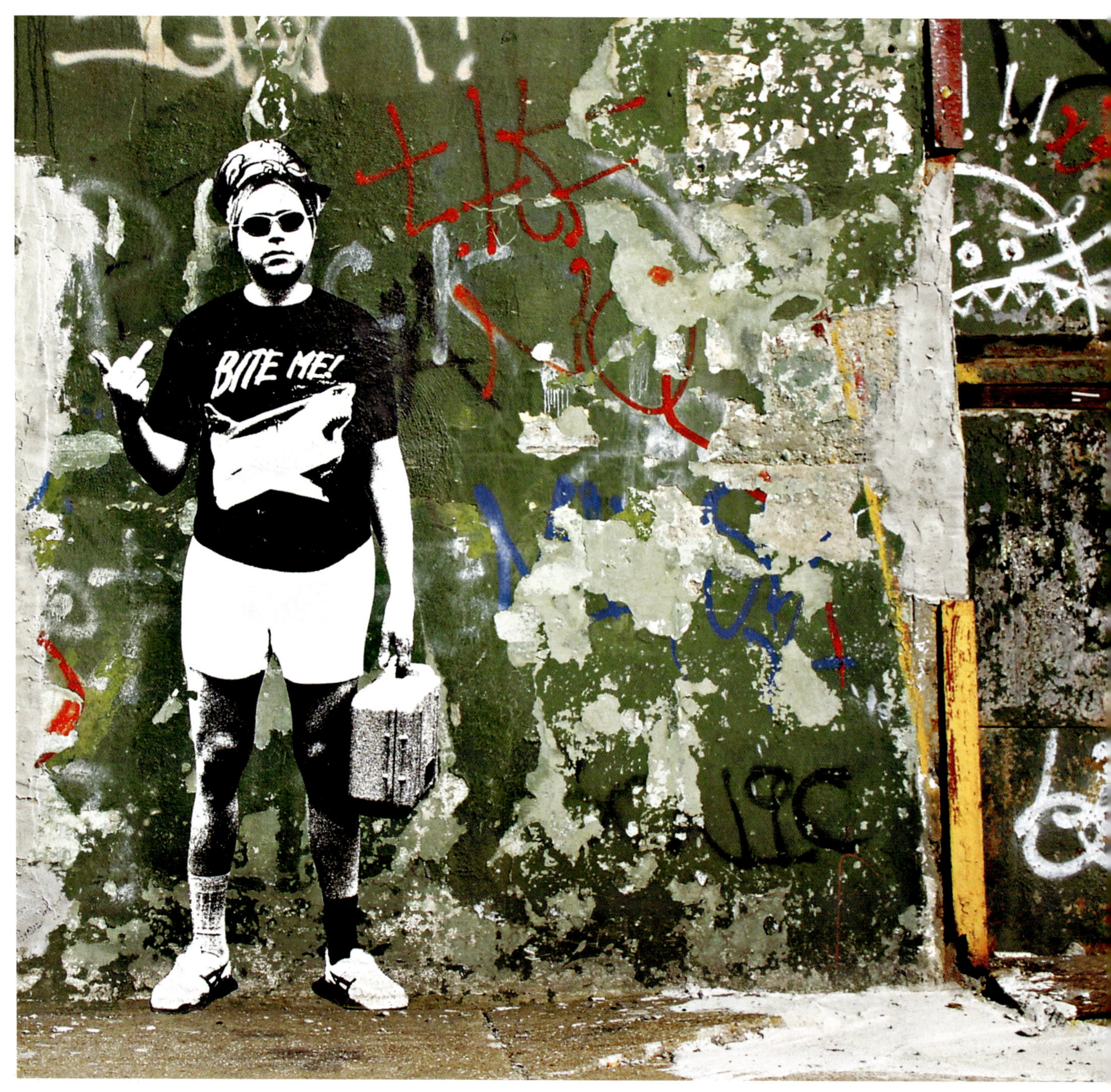
BITE ME!

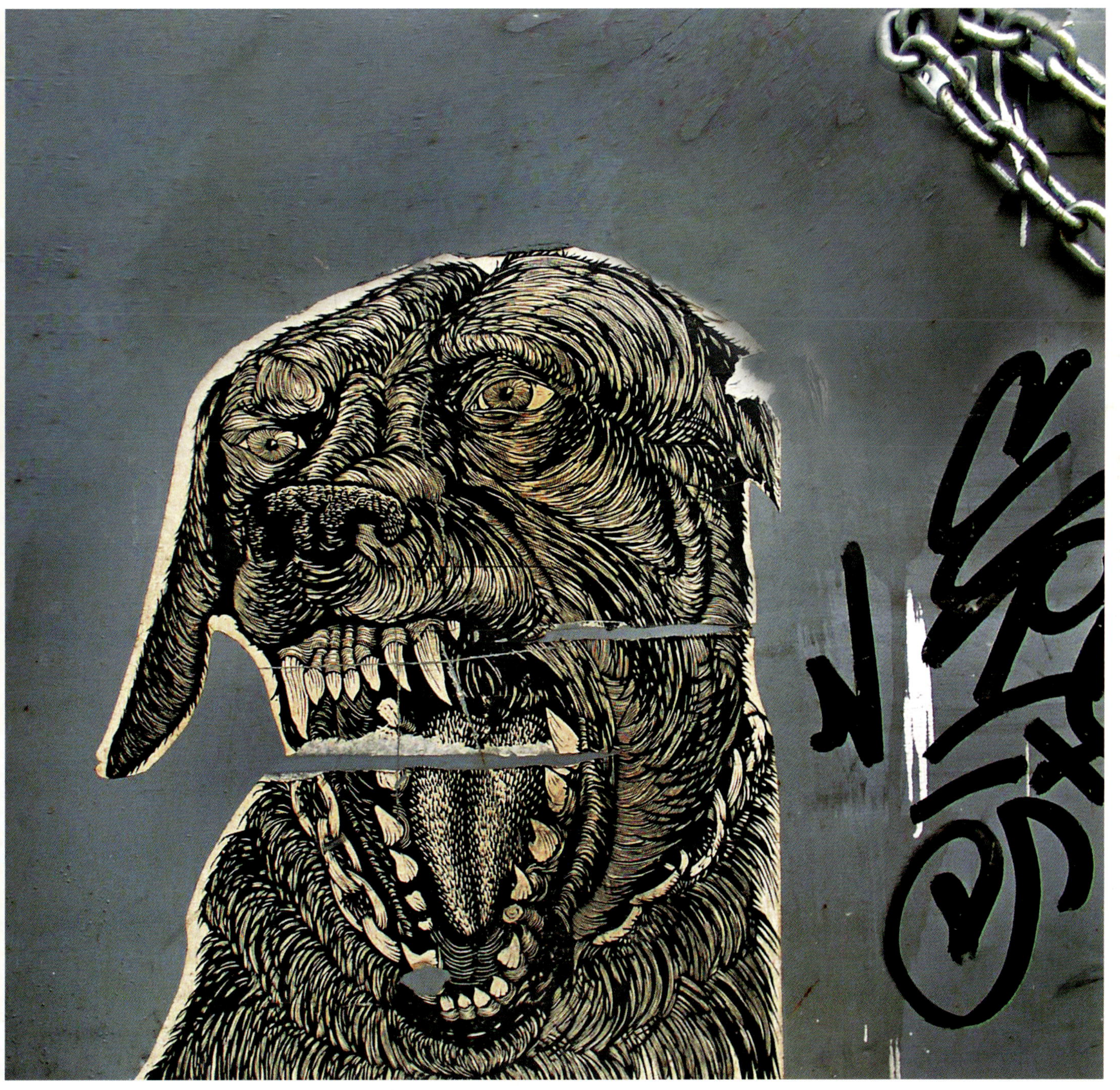

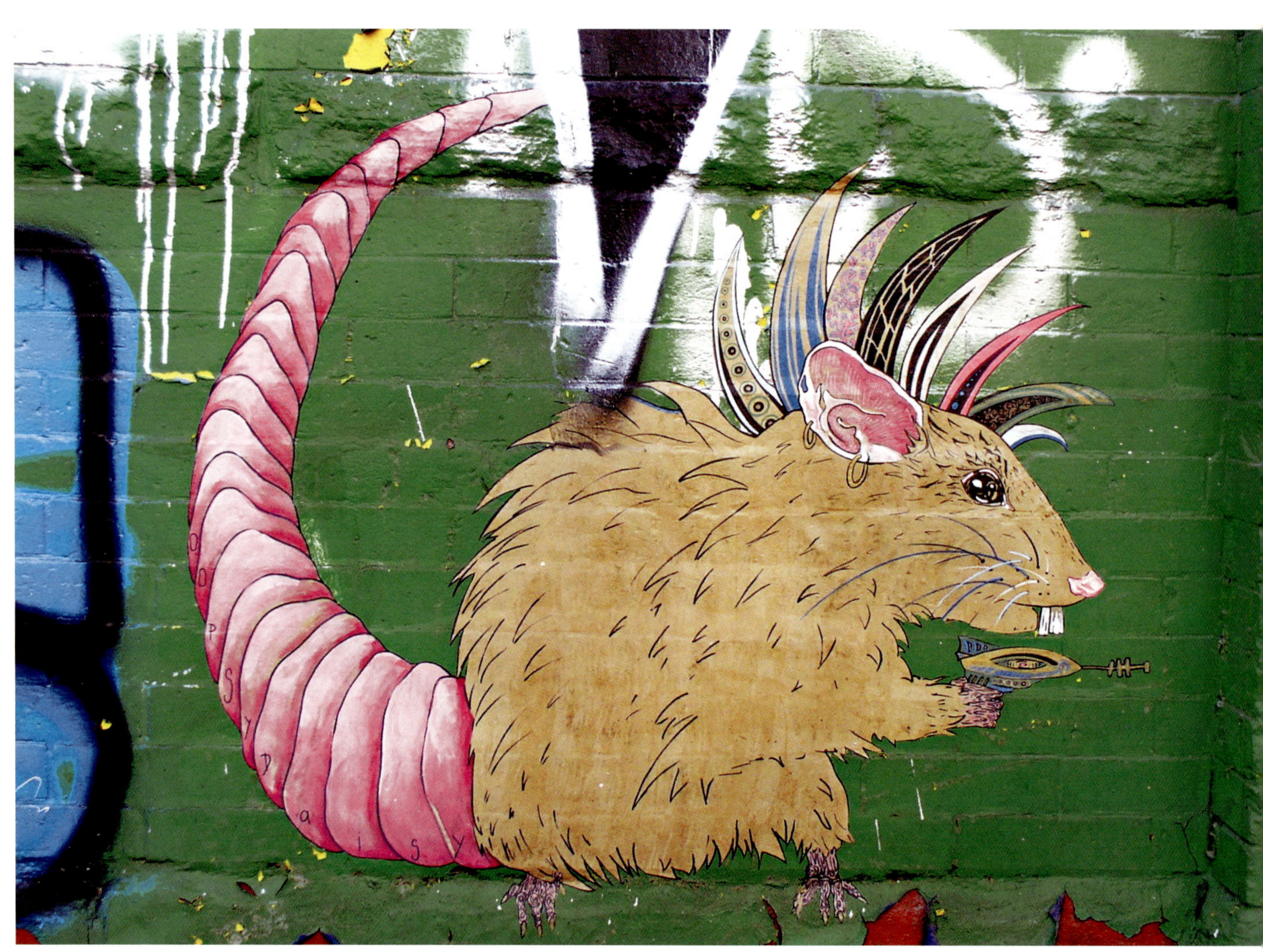
oopsydaisy

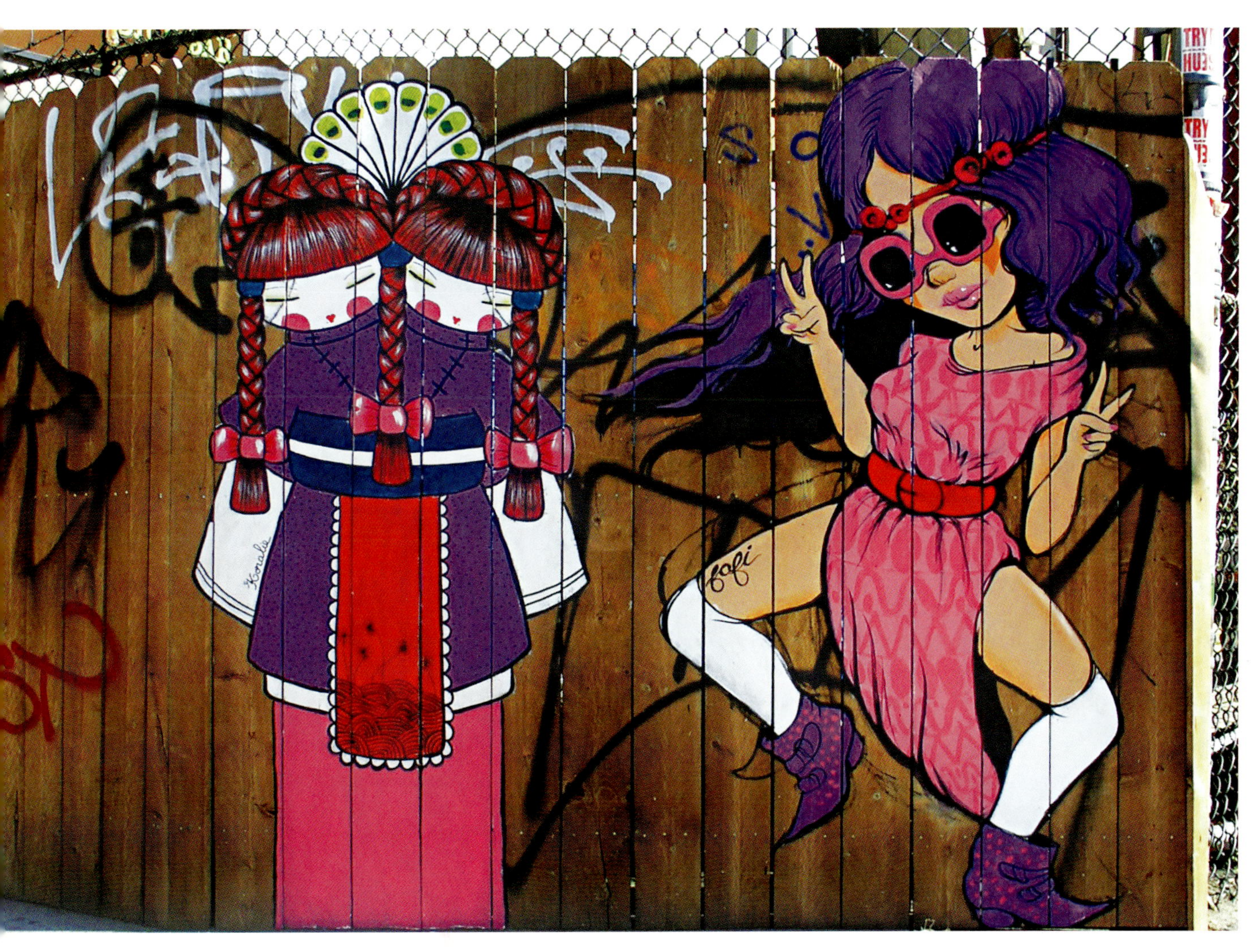
fafi

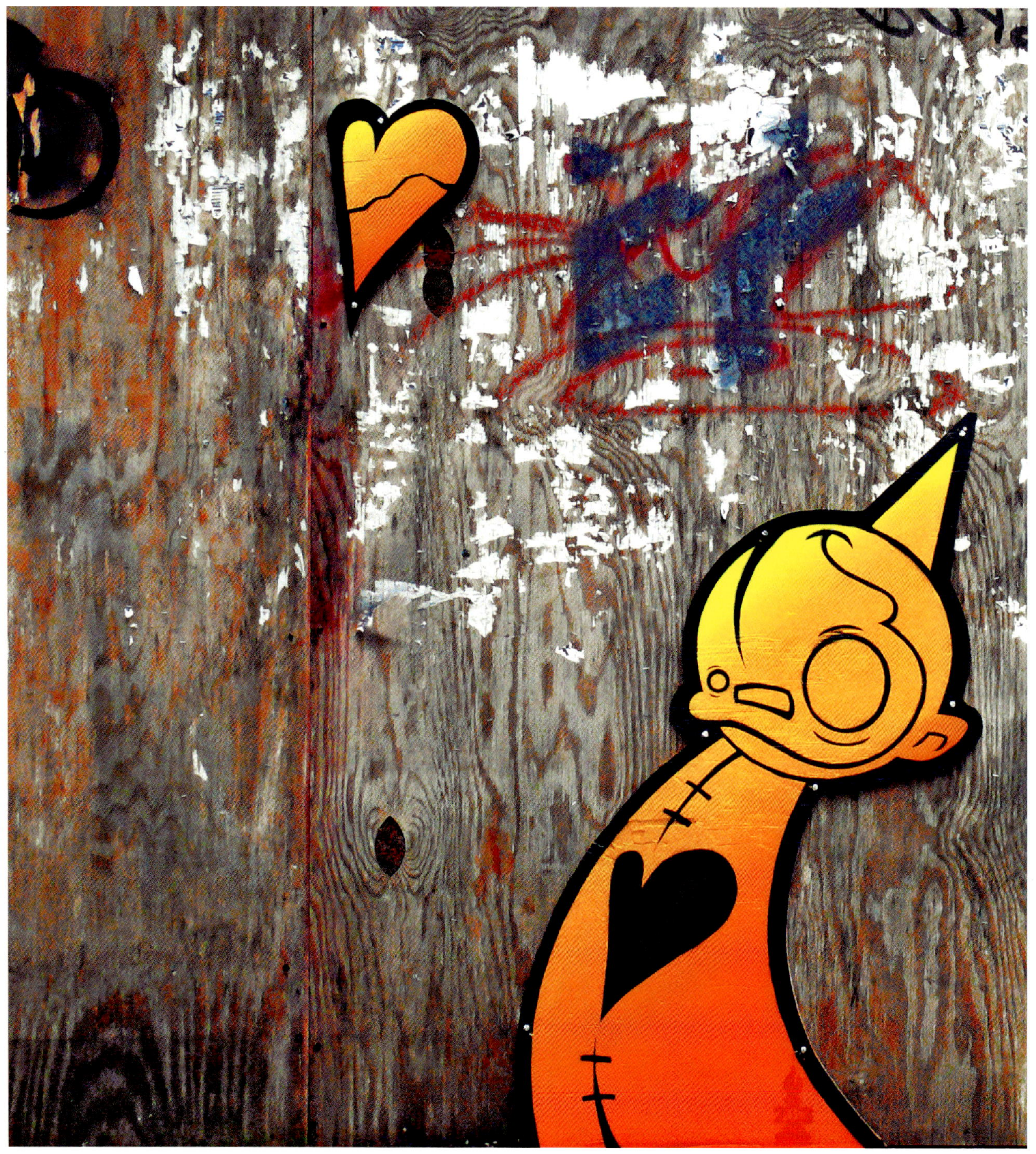

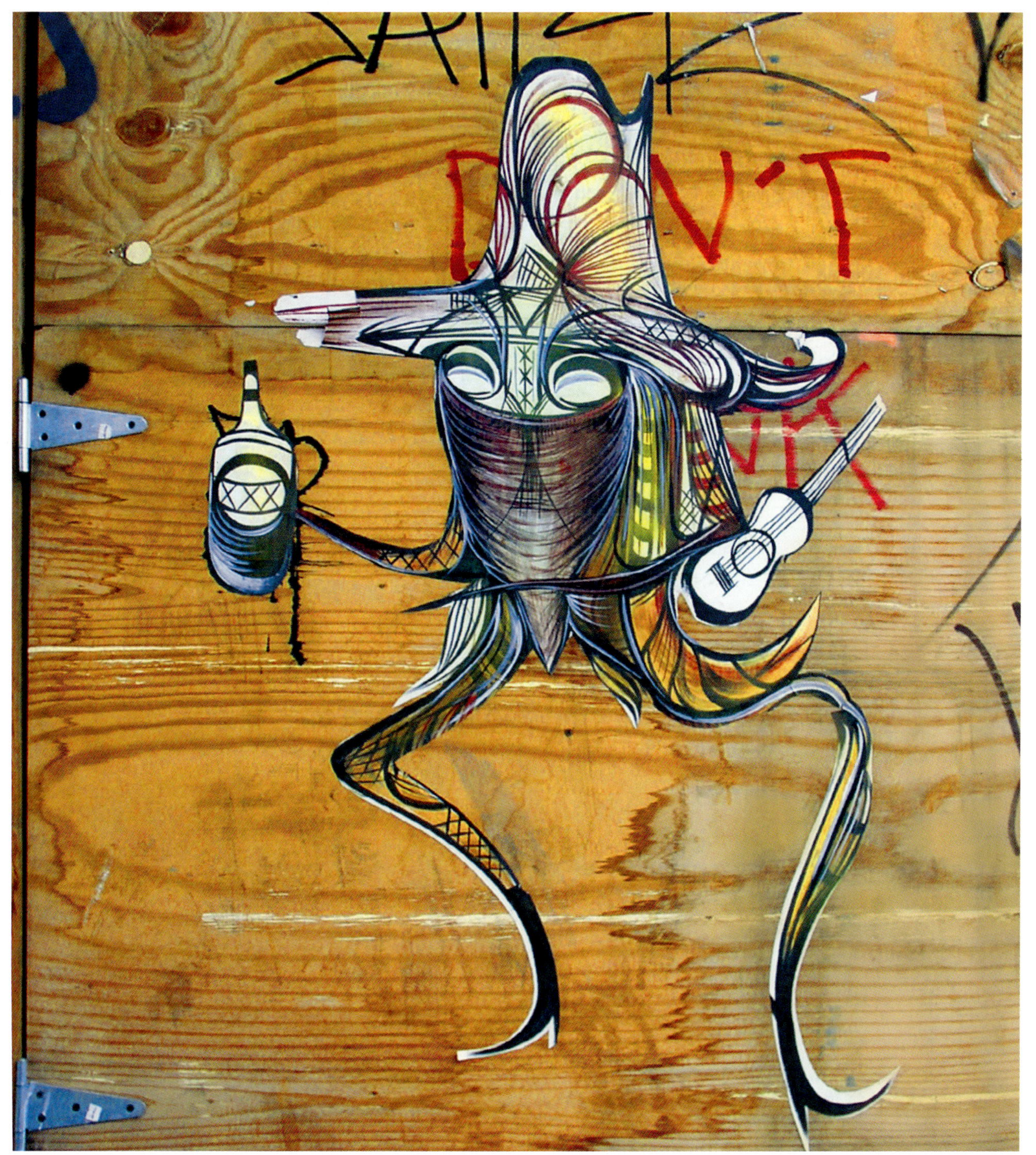

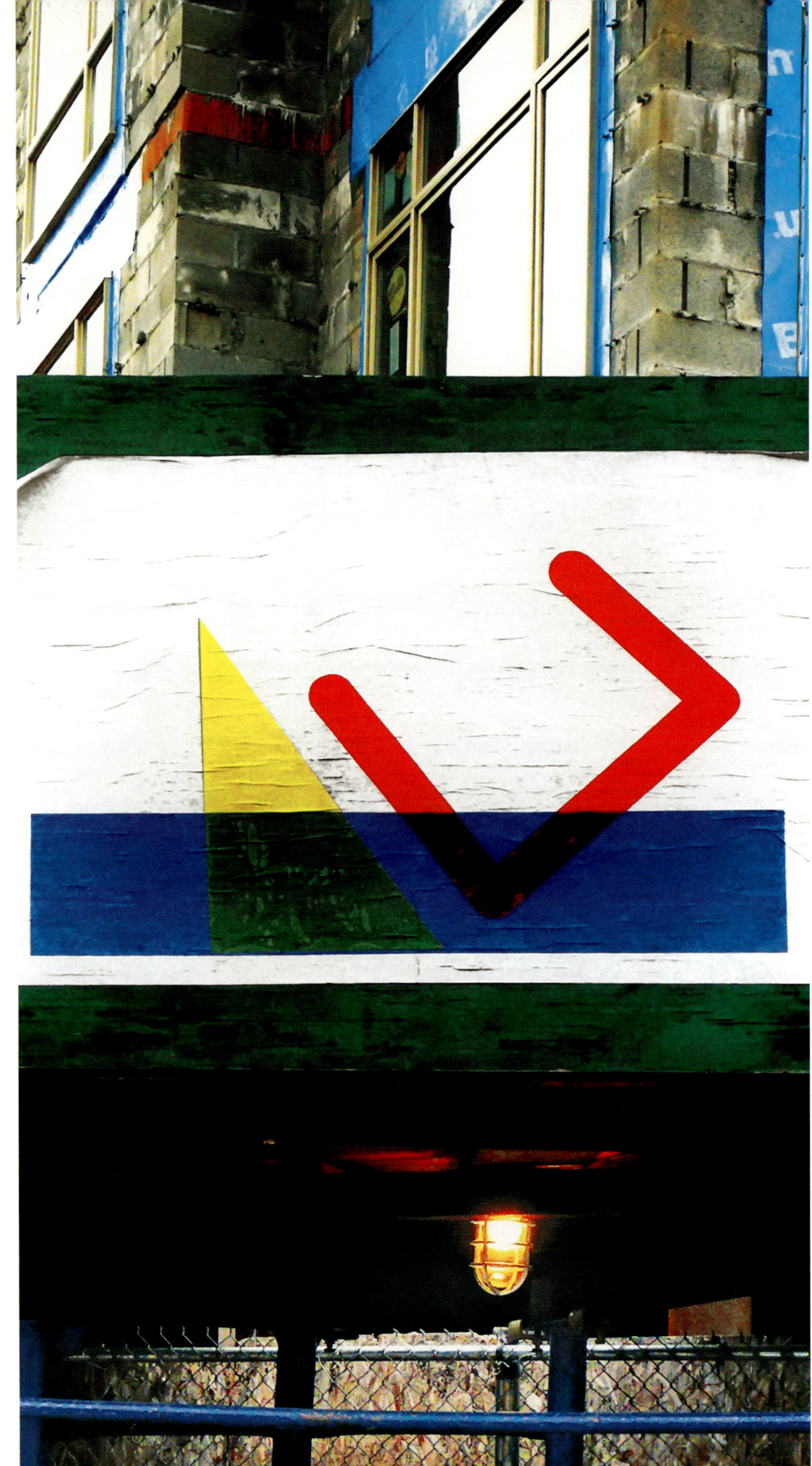

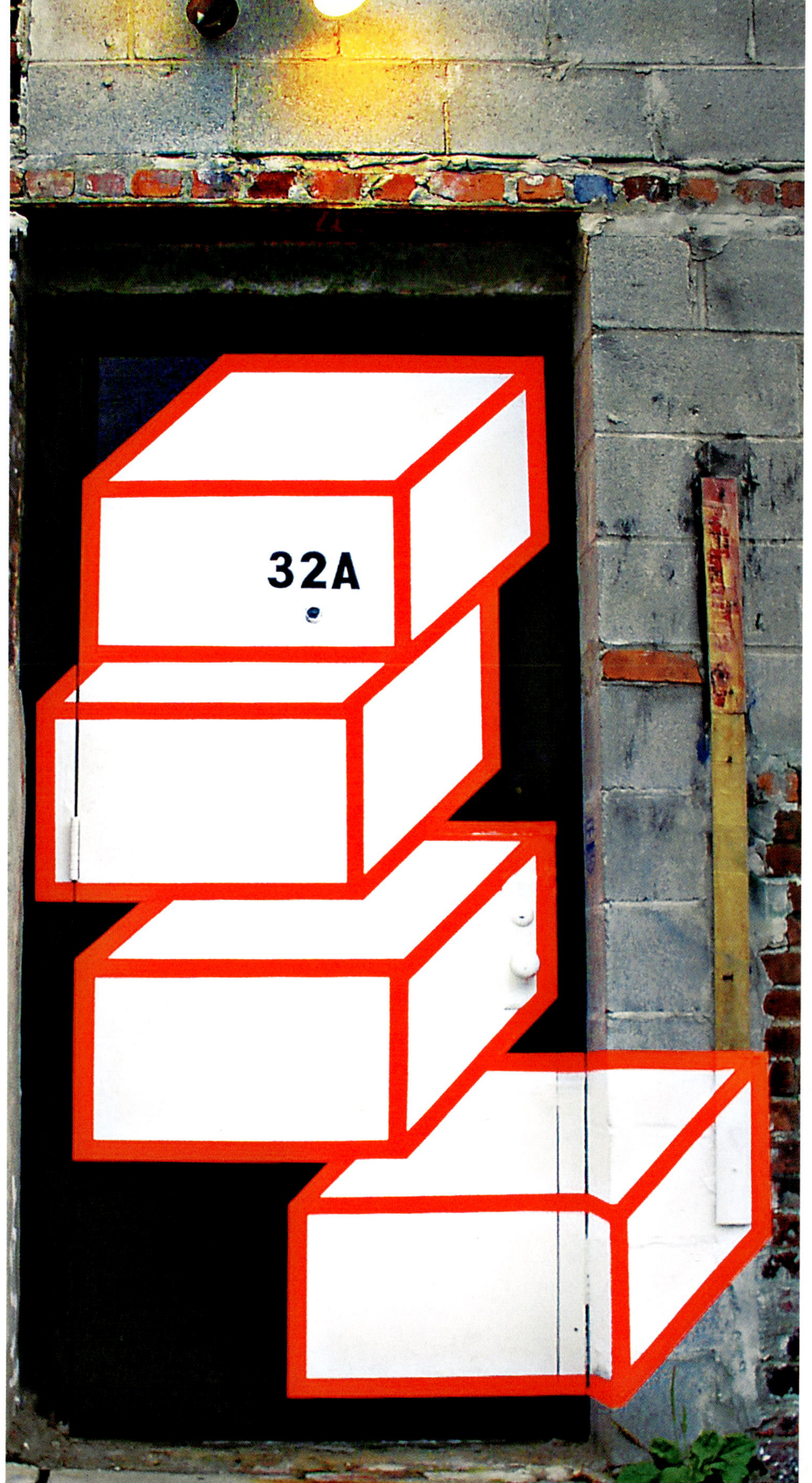
32A

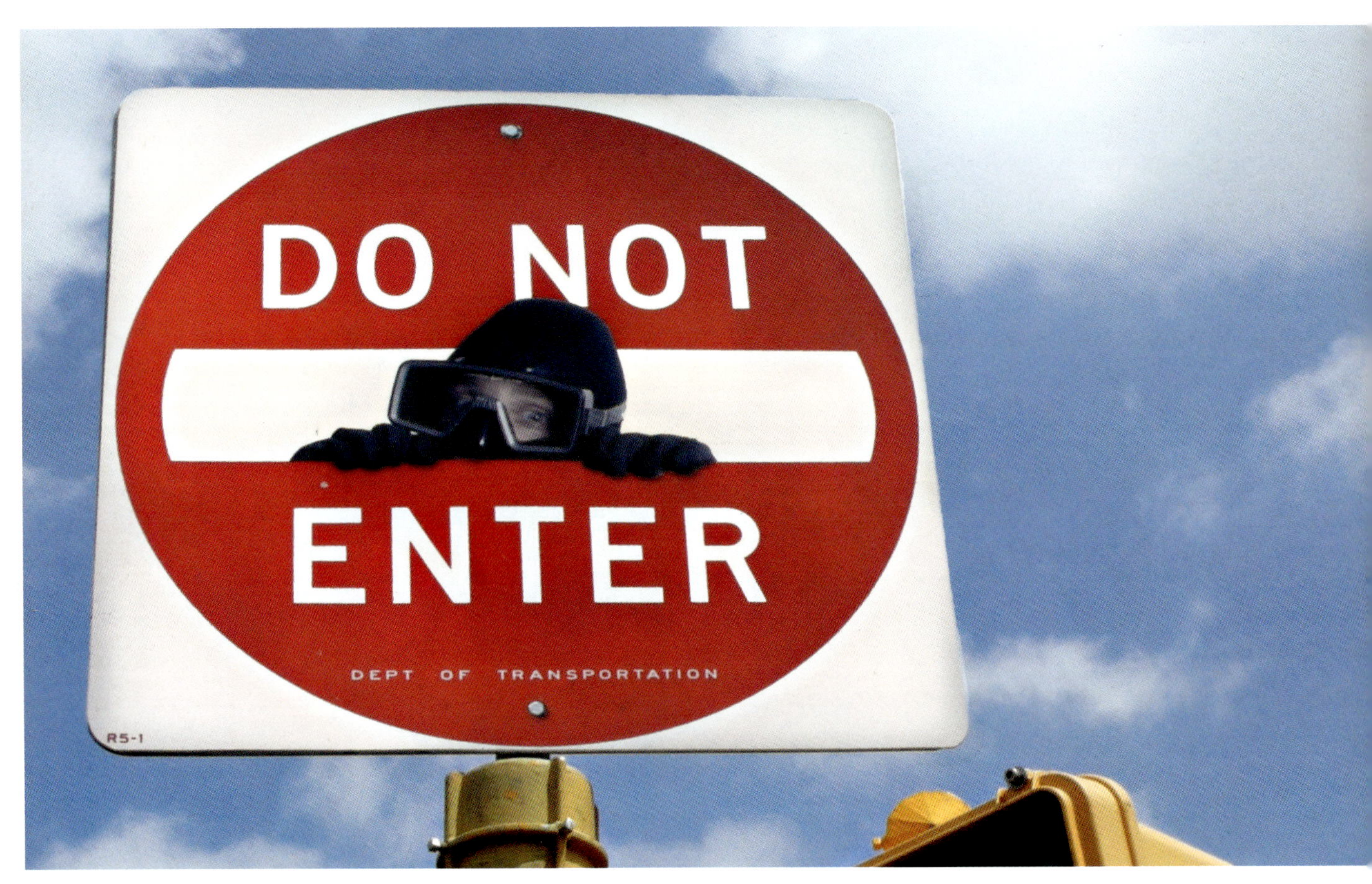
DO NOT
ENTER
DEPT OF TRANSPORTATION
R5-1

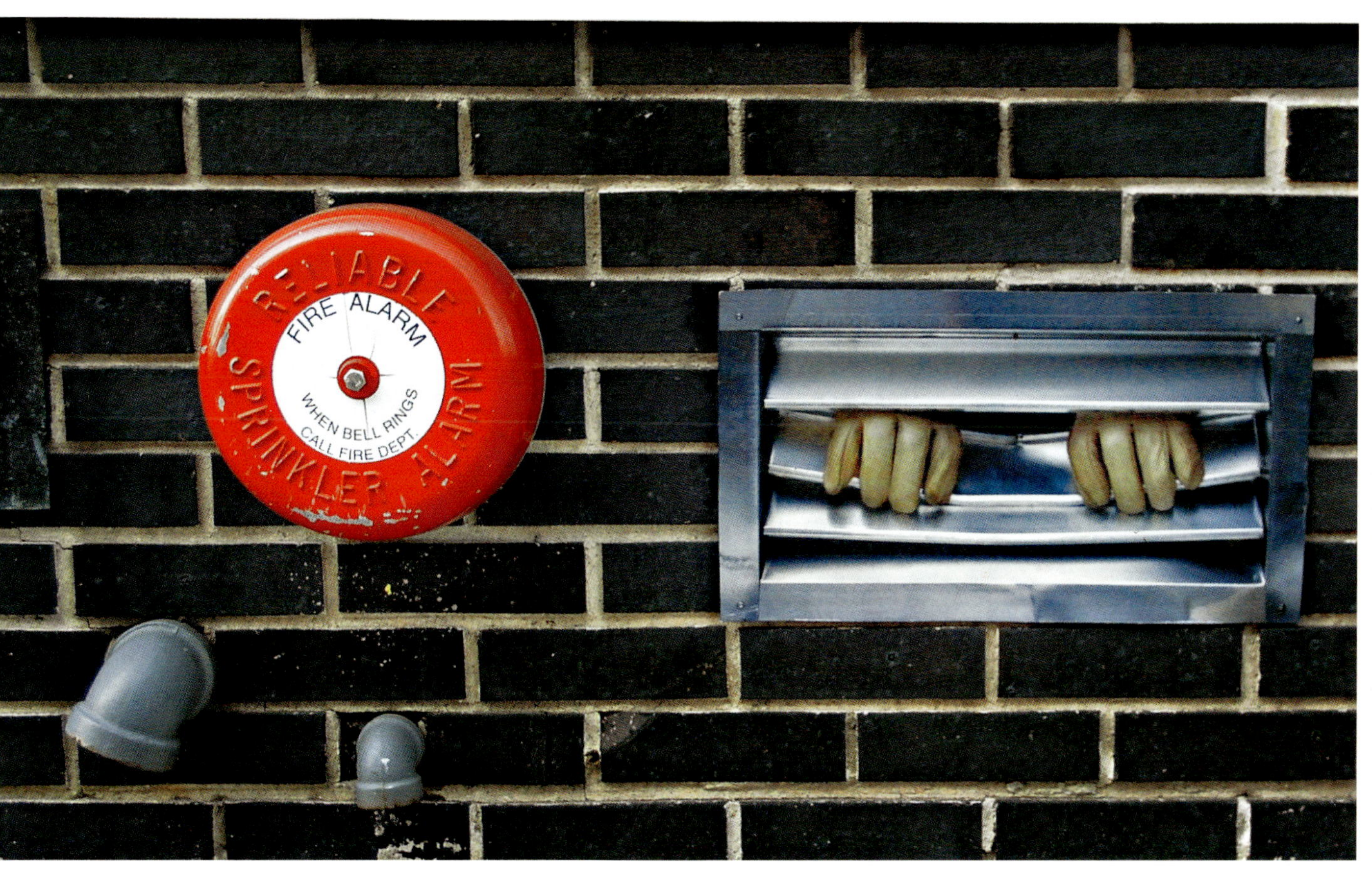
RELIABLE
FIRE ALARM
WHEN BELL RINGS
CALL FIRE DEPT.
SPRINKLER ALARM

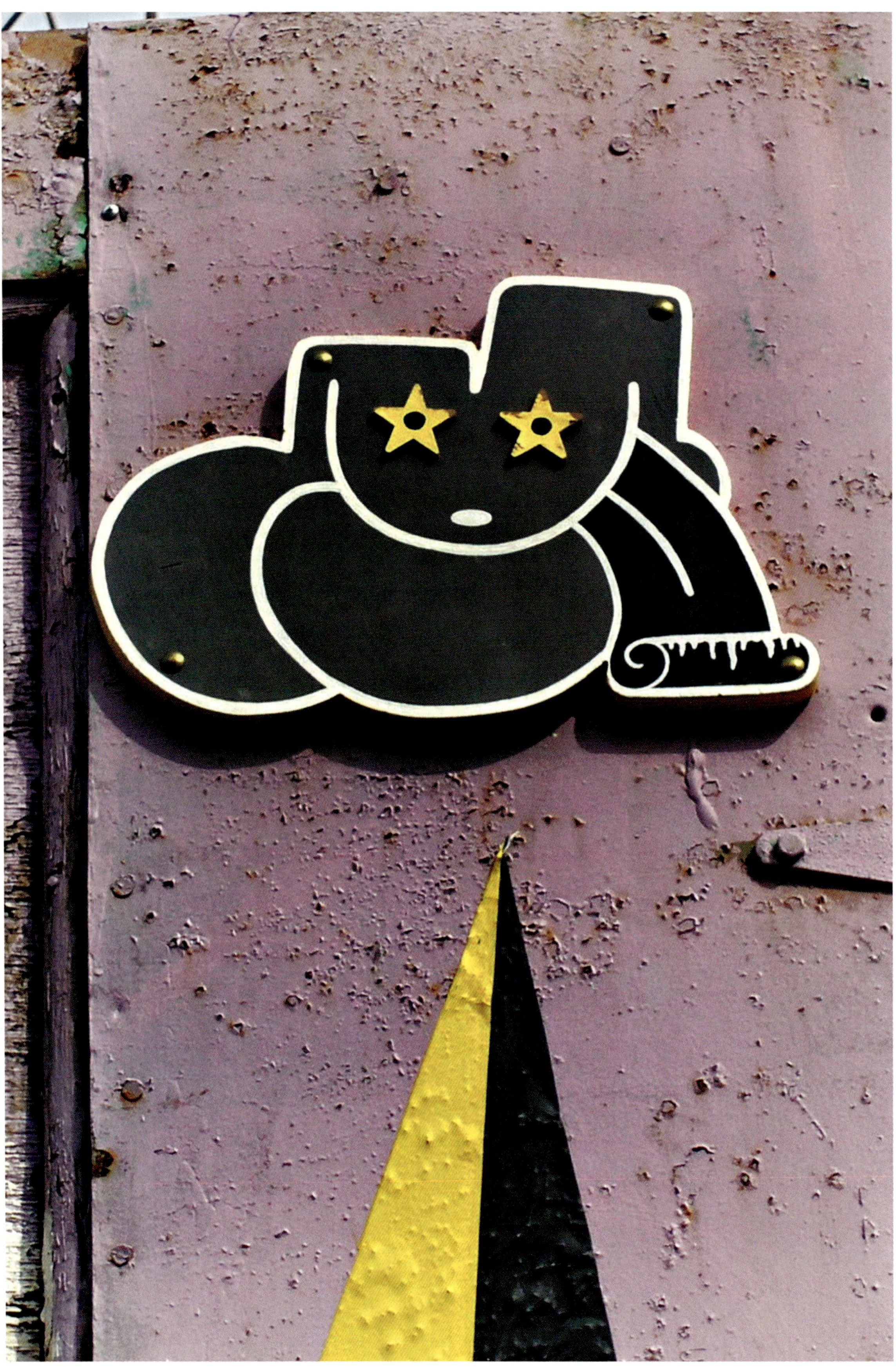

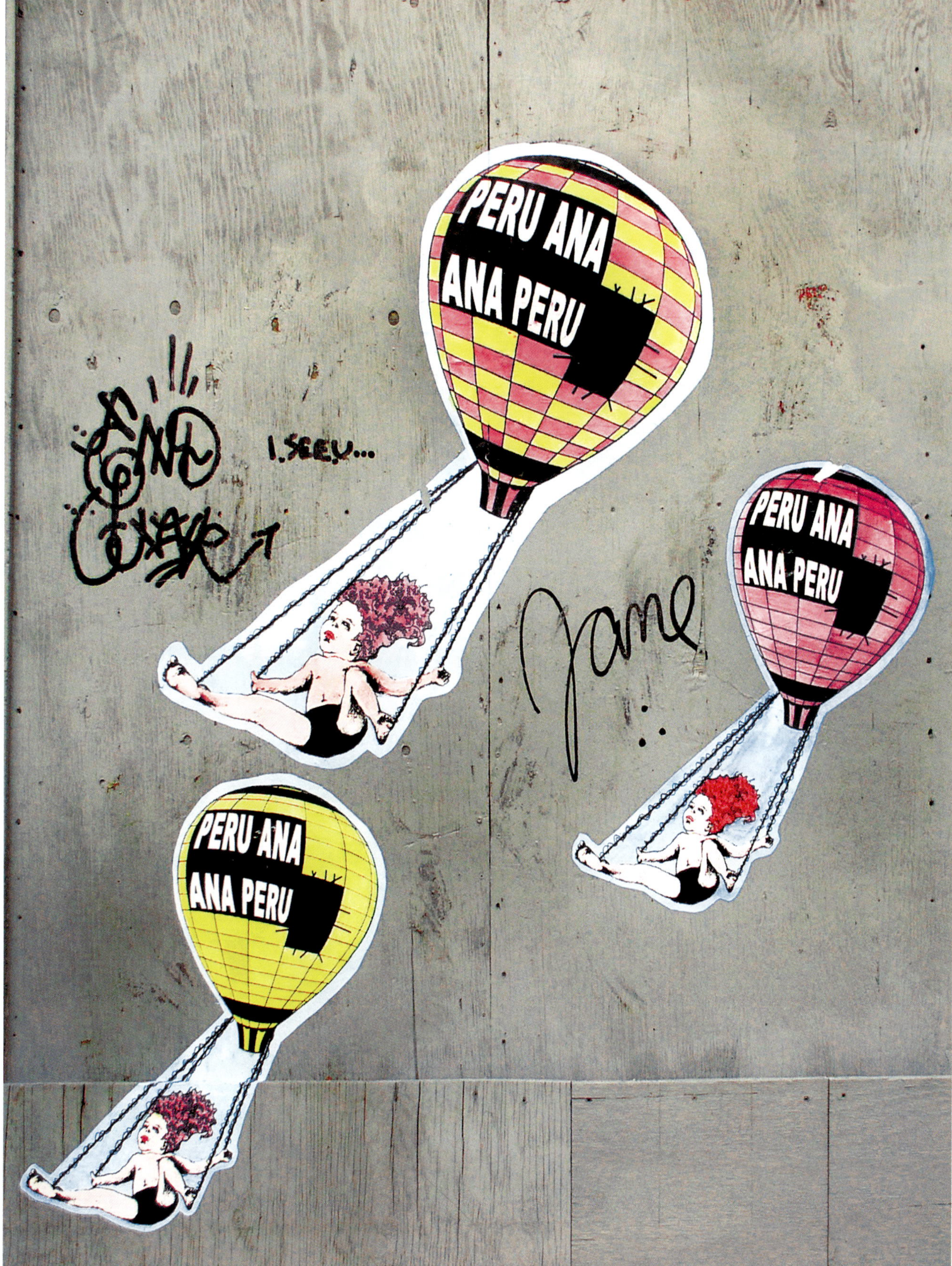

PERU ANA
ANA PERU
I.SEE.U...
PERU ANA
ANA PERU
Jane
PERU ANA
ANA PERU

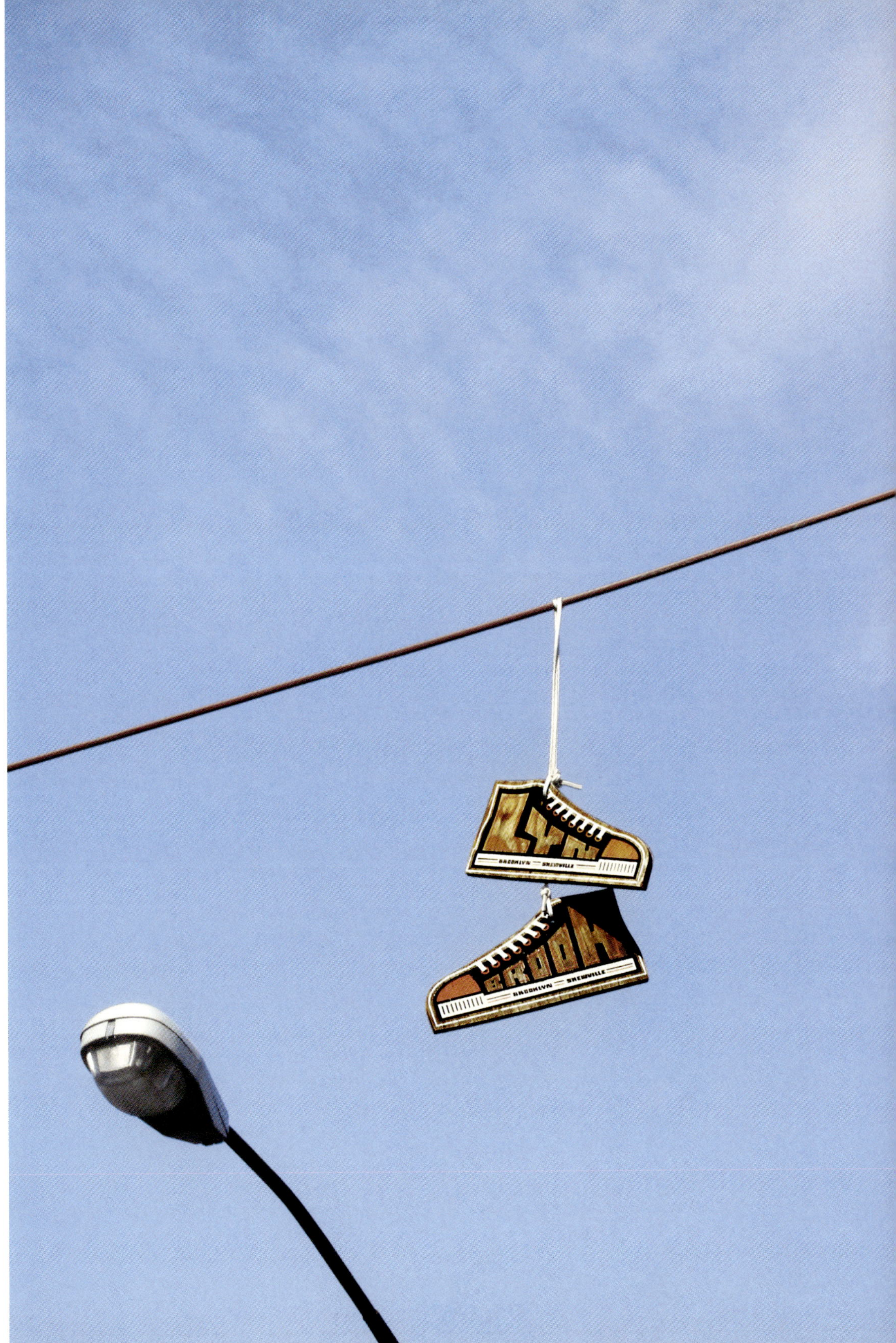

LYN
BROOK
BROOKLYN

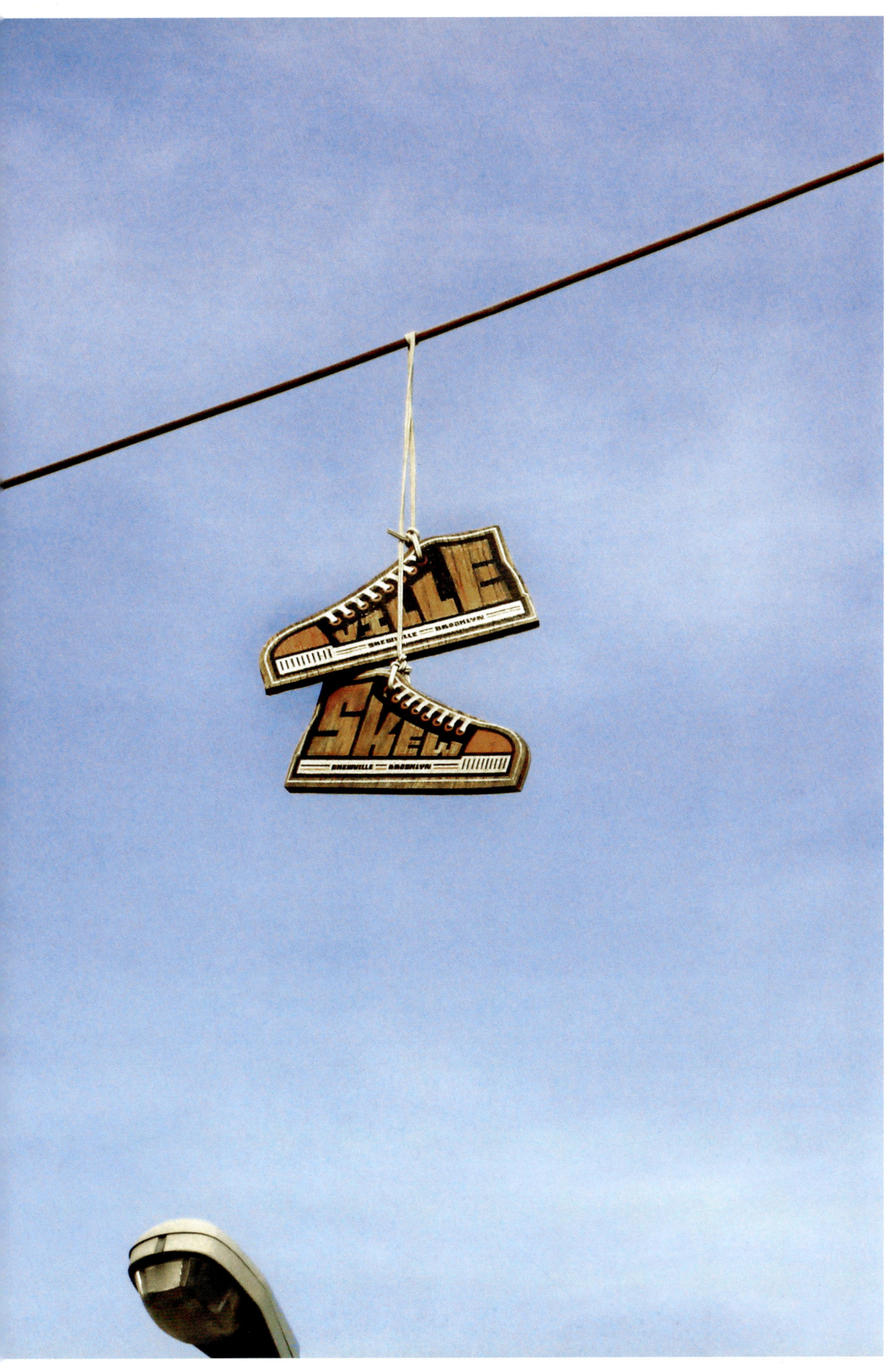
VILLE
SKEW

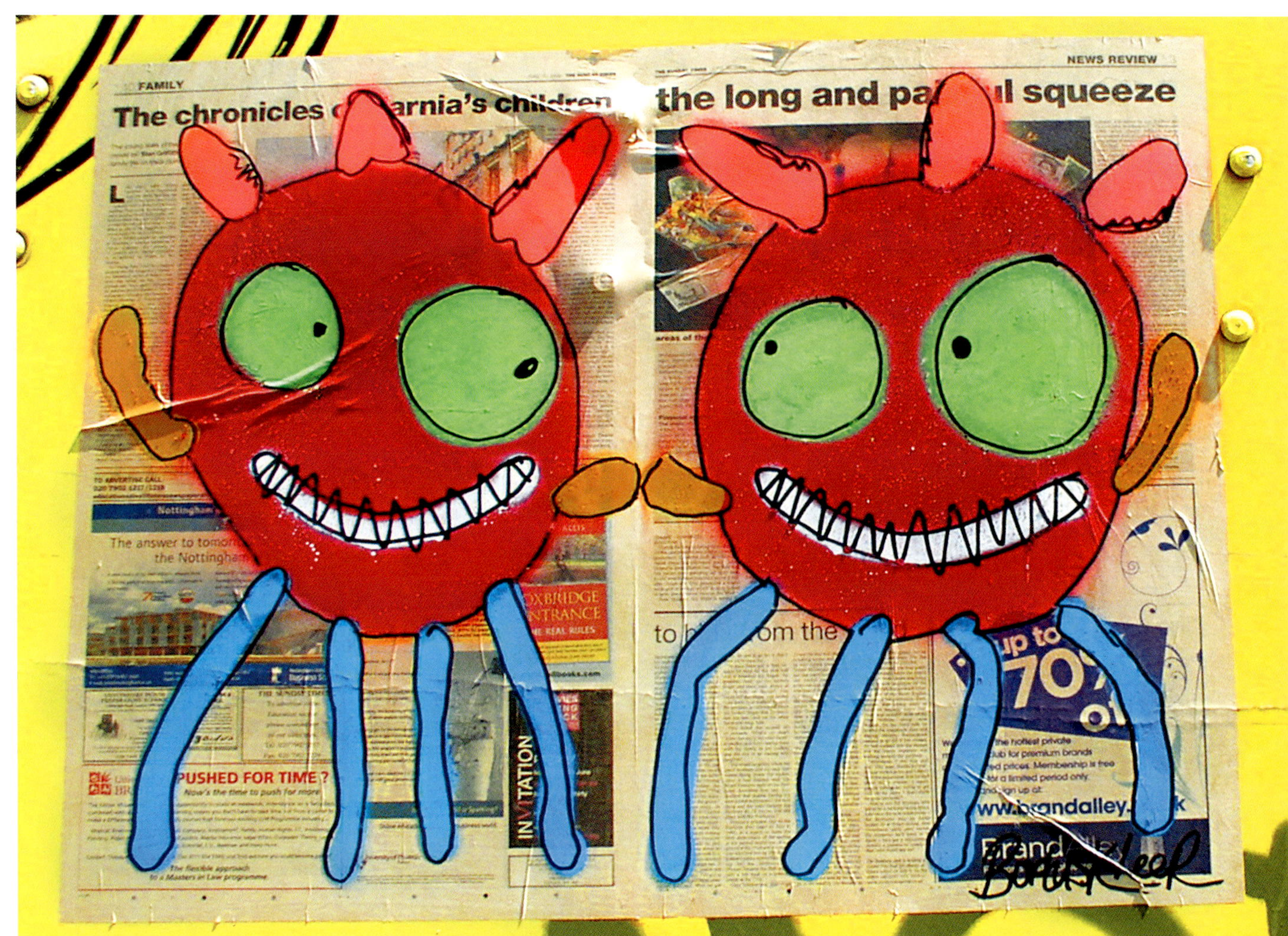
FAMILY
NEWS REVIEW
the long and pa ul squeeze
PUSHED FOR TIME ?
INVITATION
OXBRIDGE
NTRANCE
www.brandalley

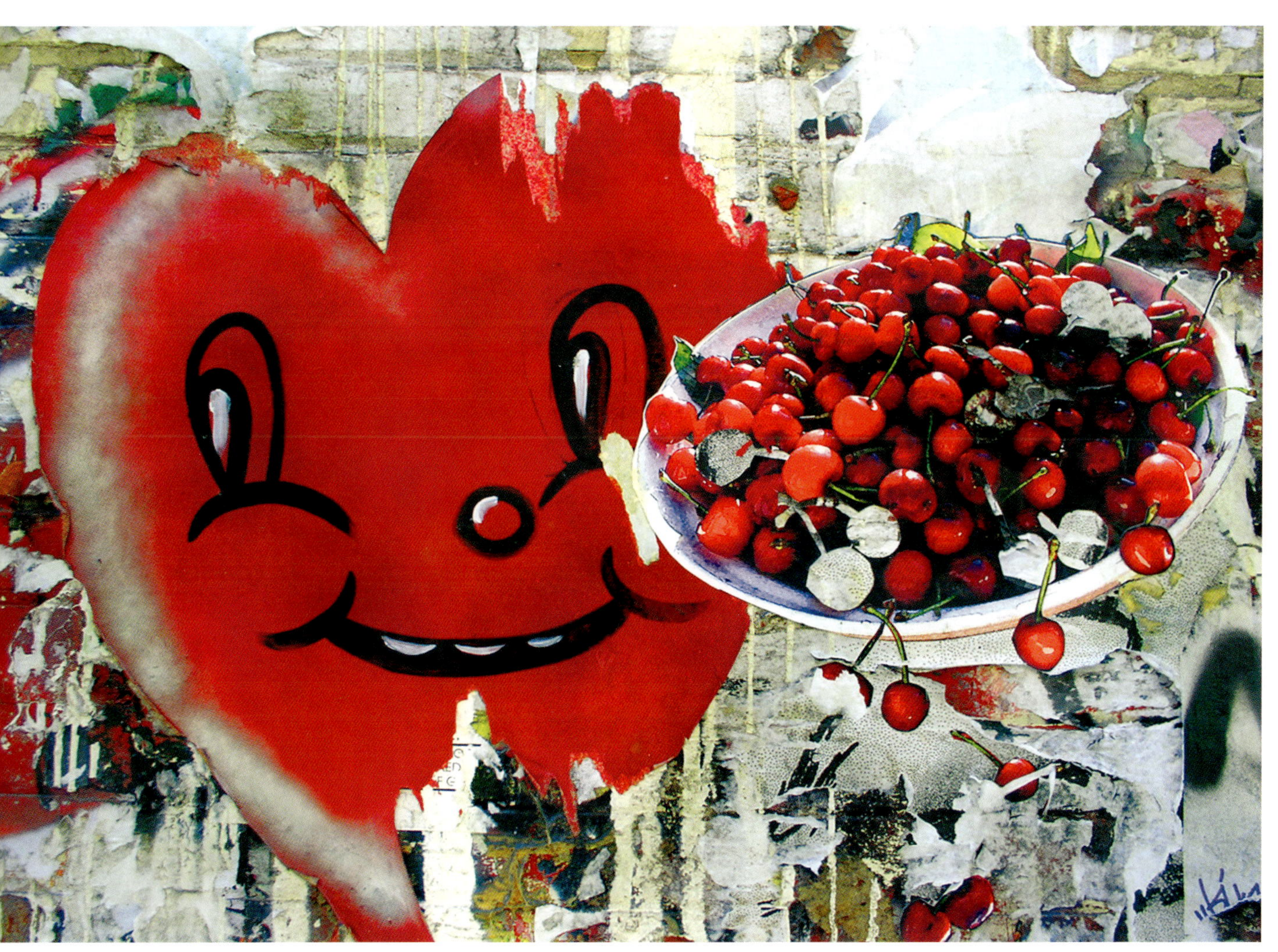

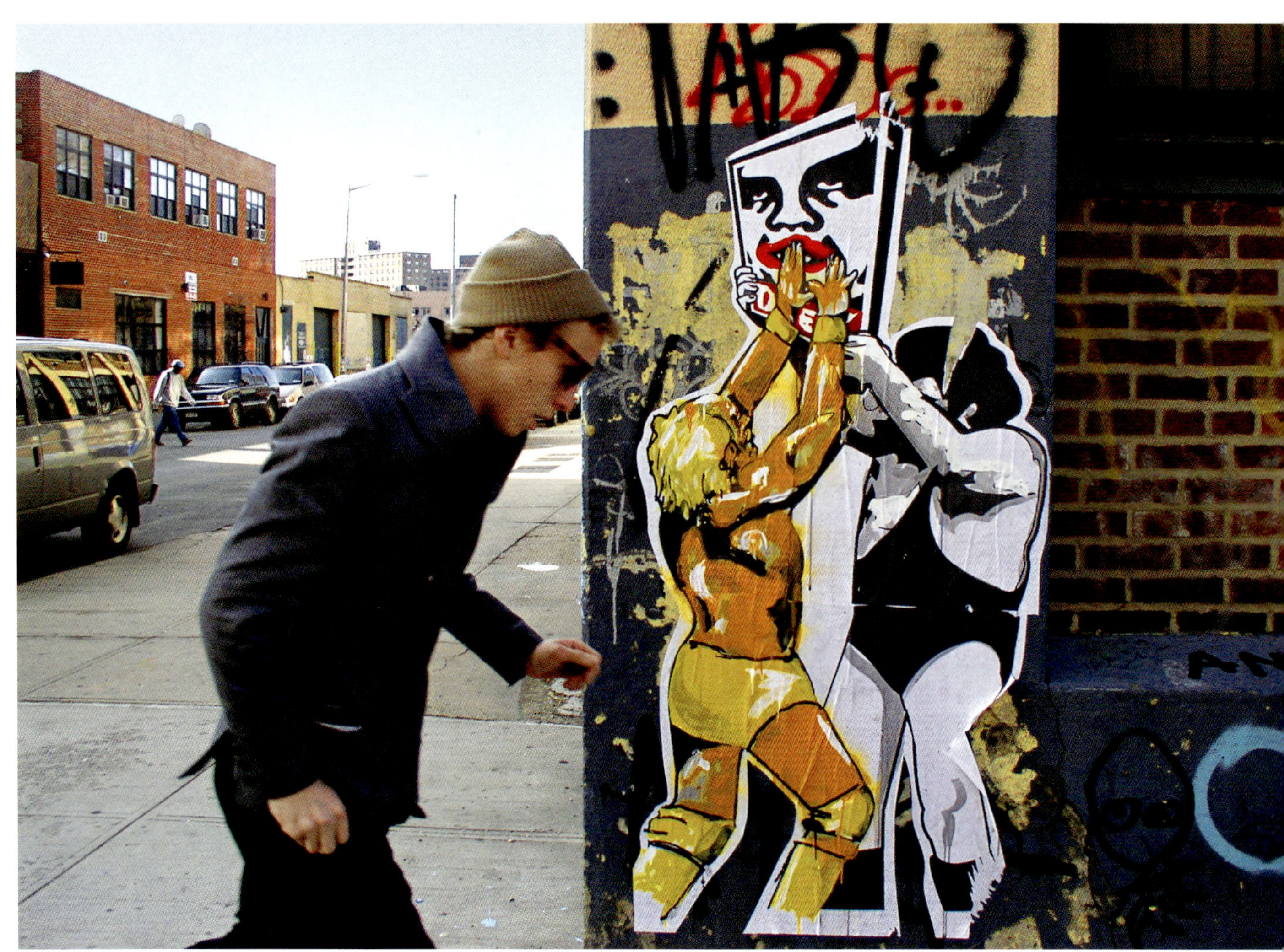

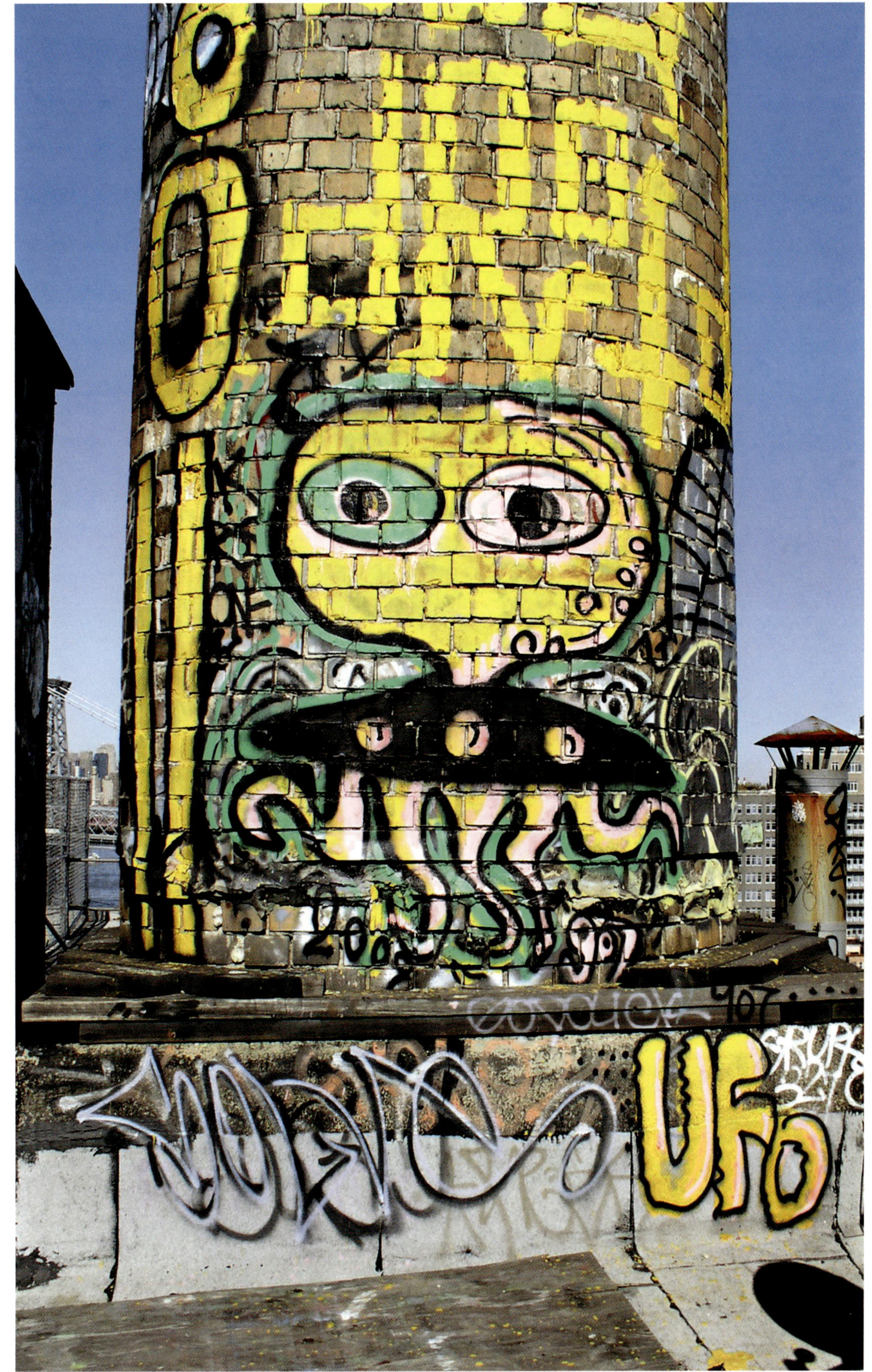
UFO

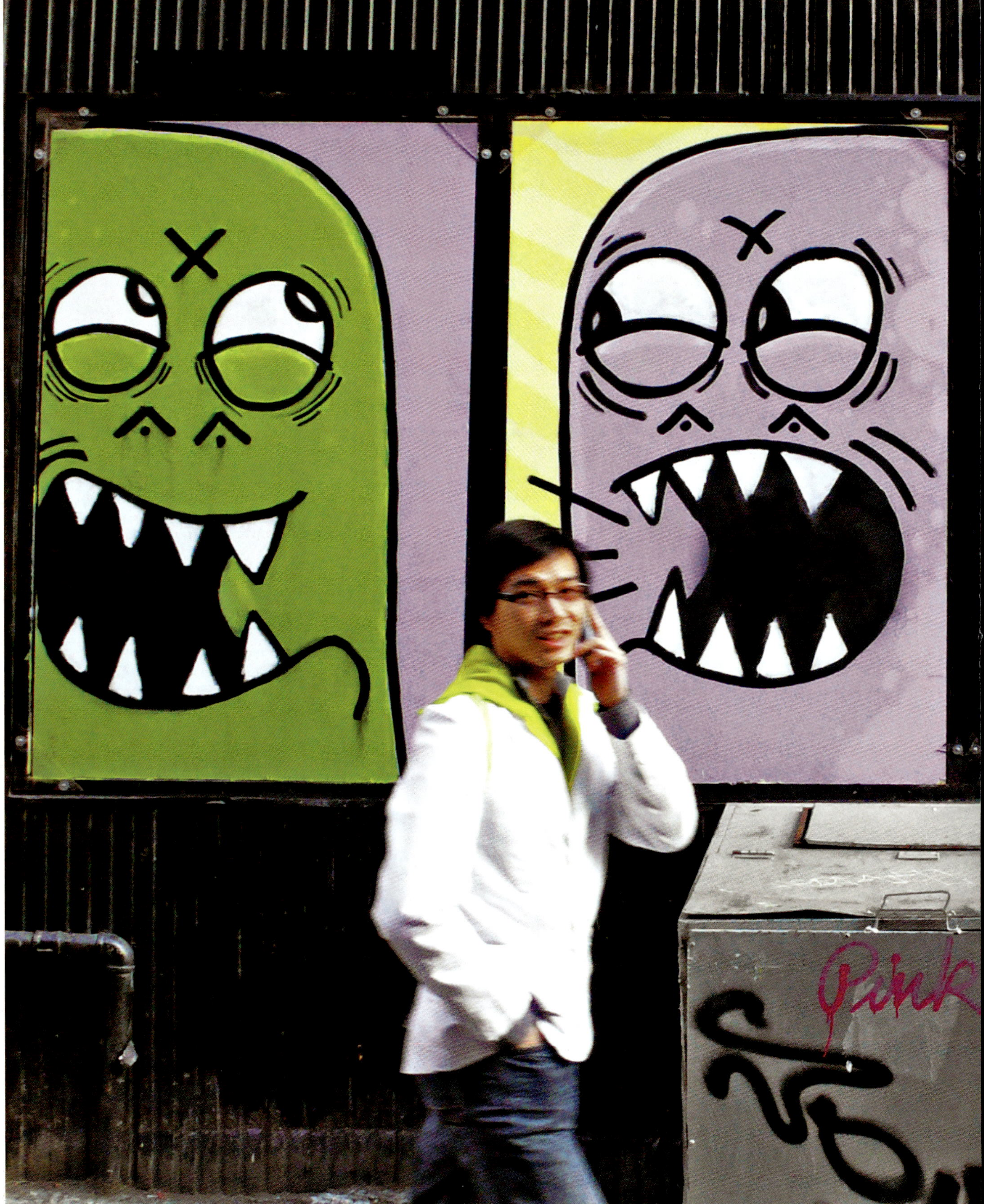
Pink

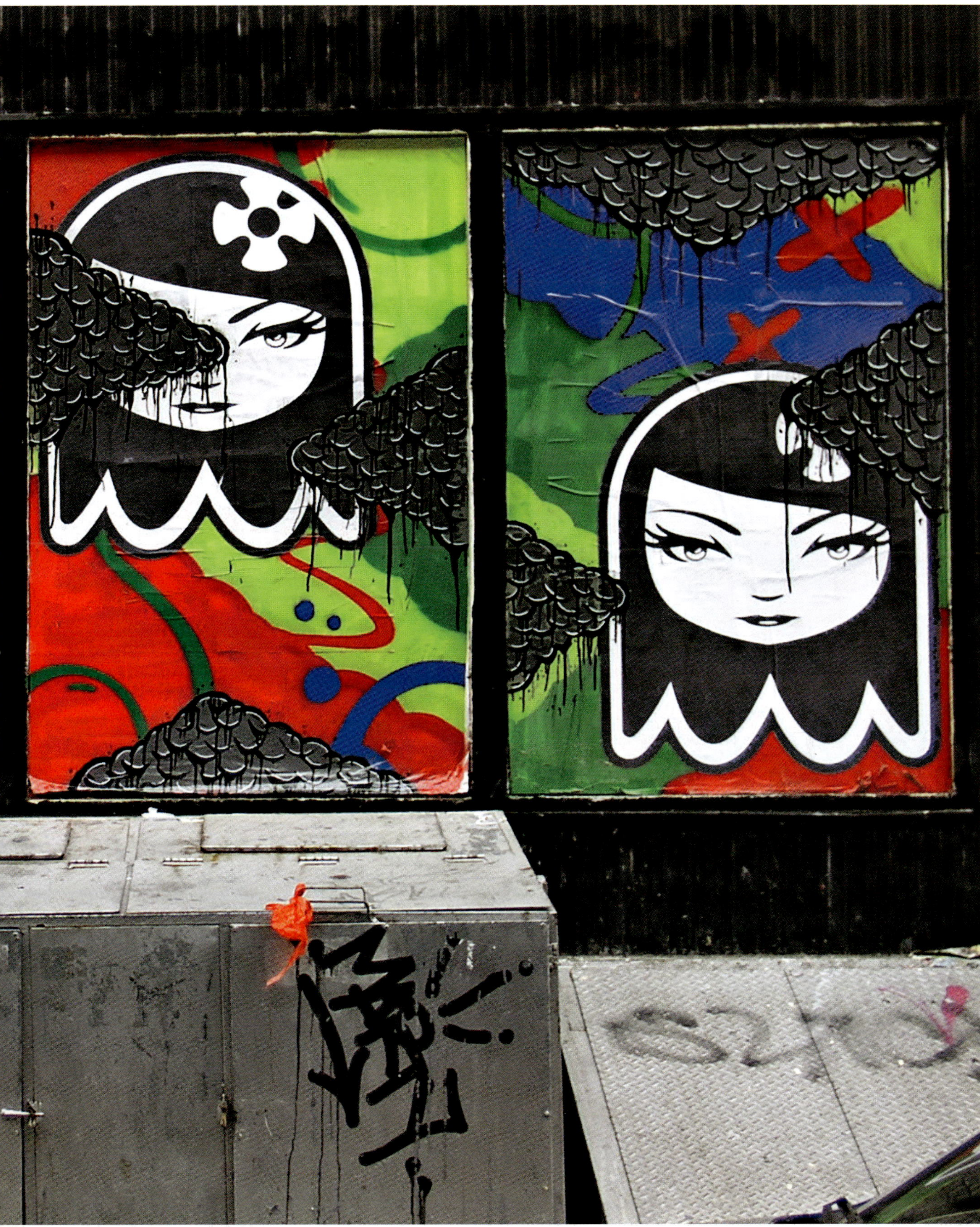

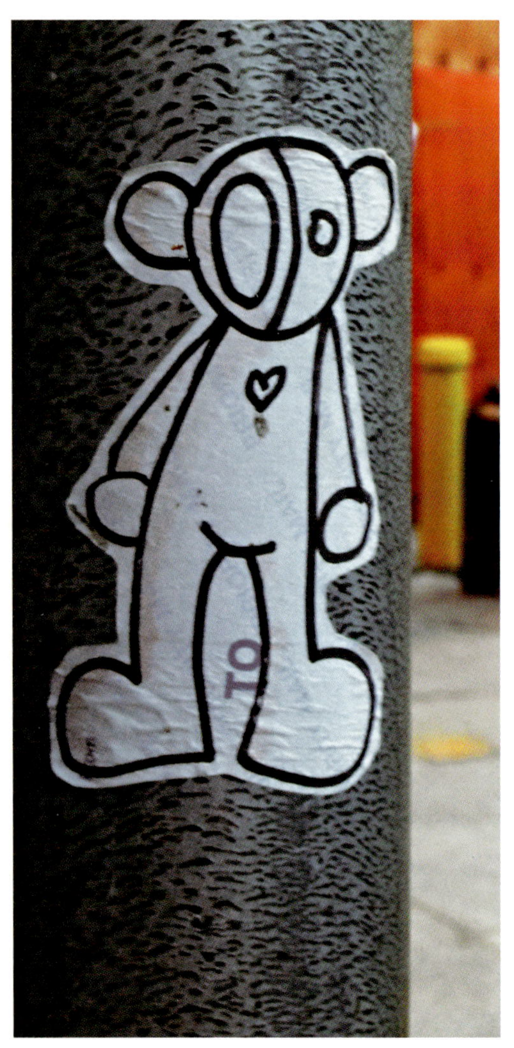
TO

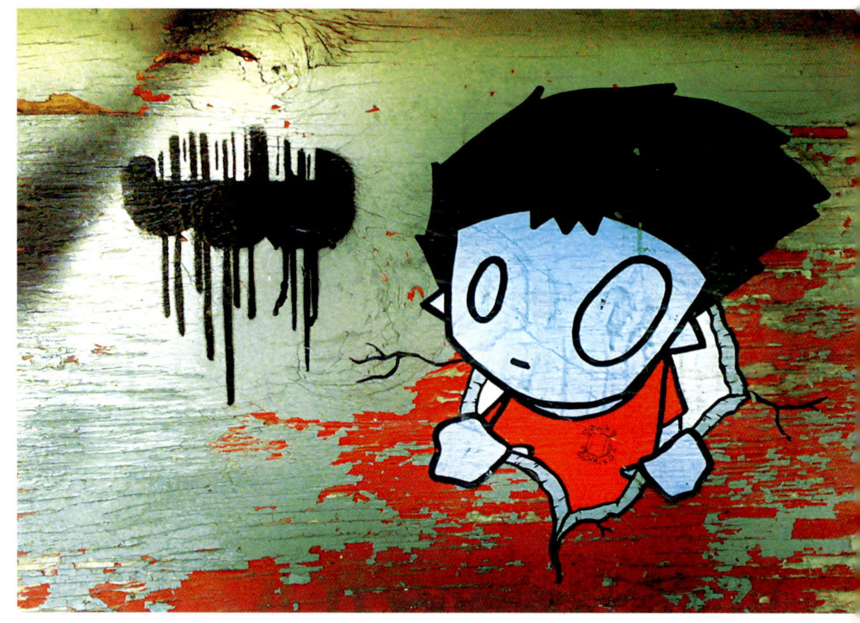

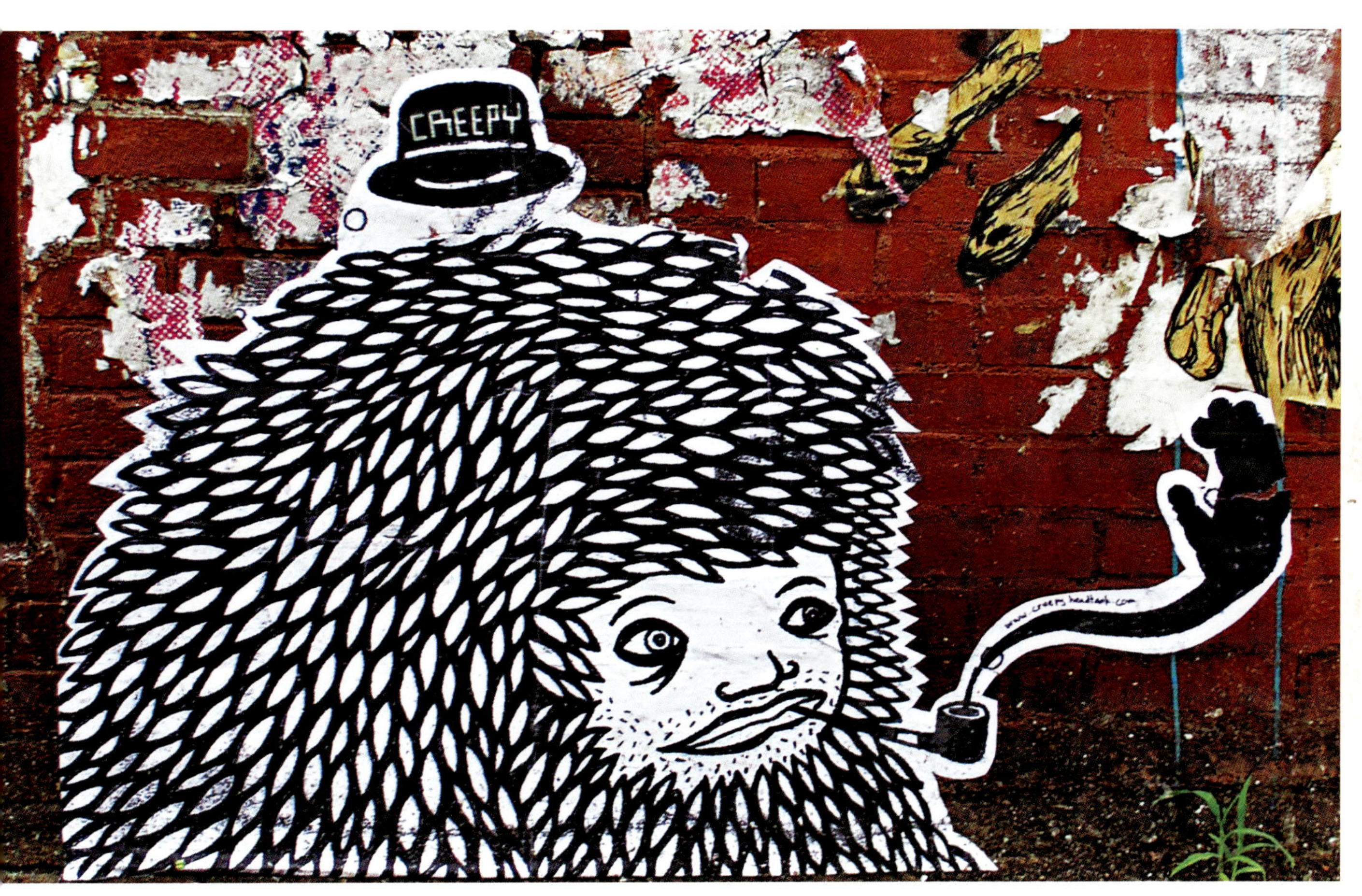
CREEPY

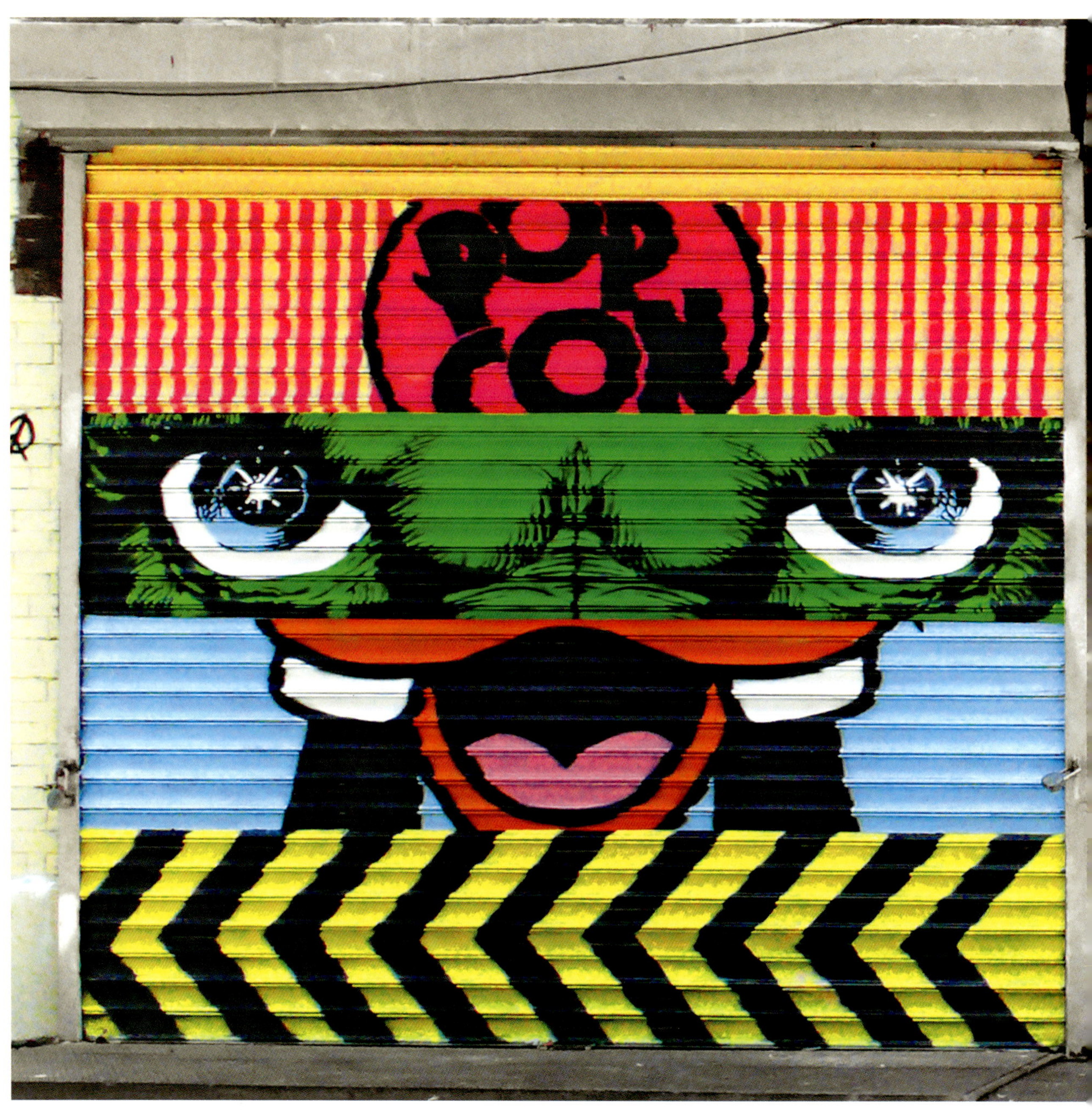

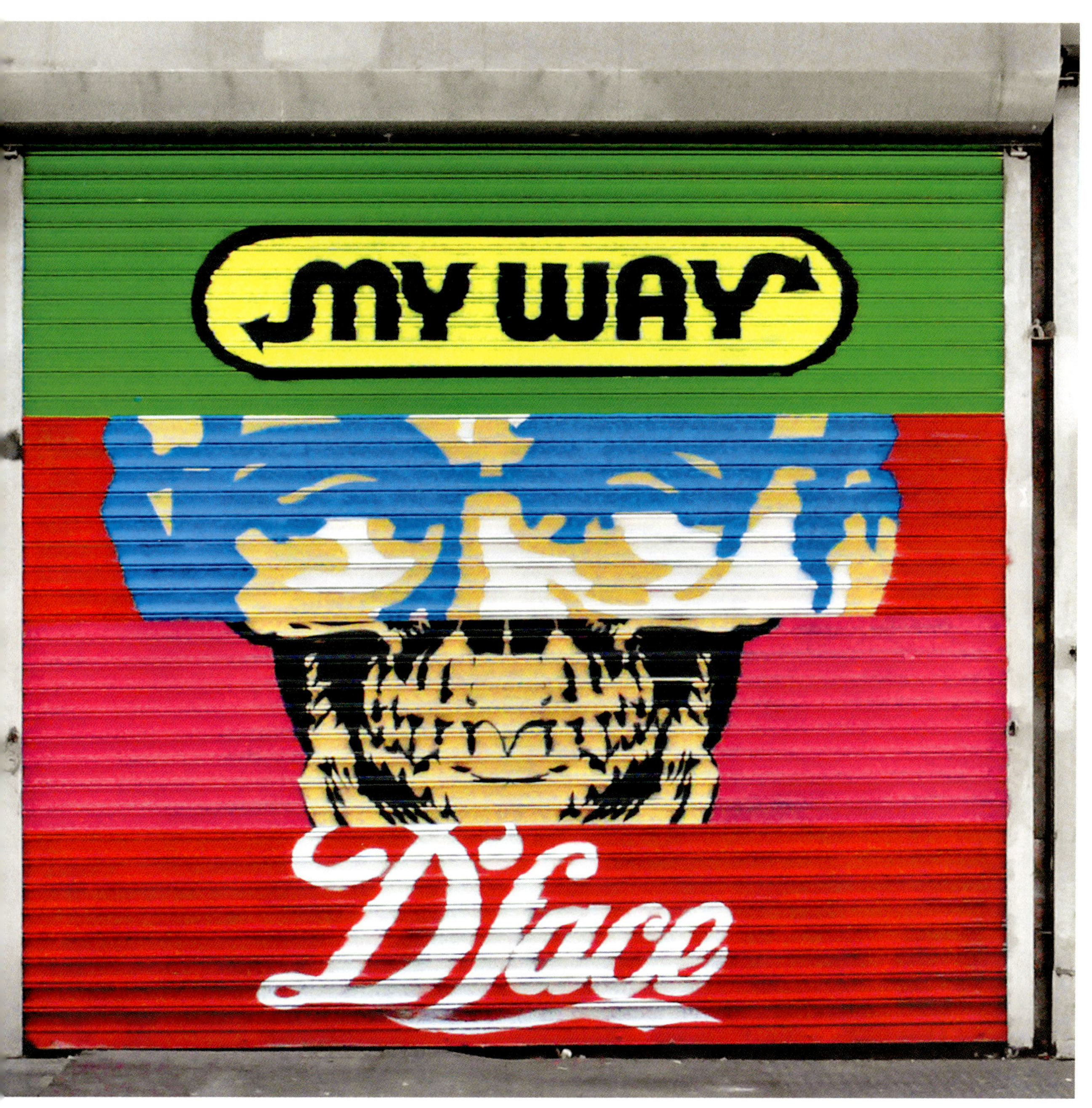
MY WAY
D*face

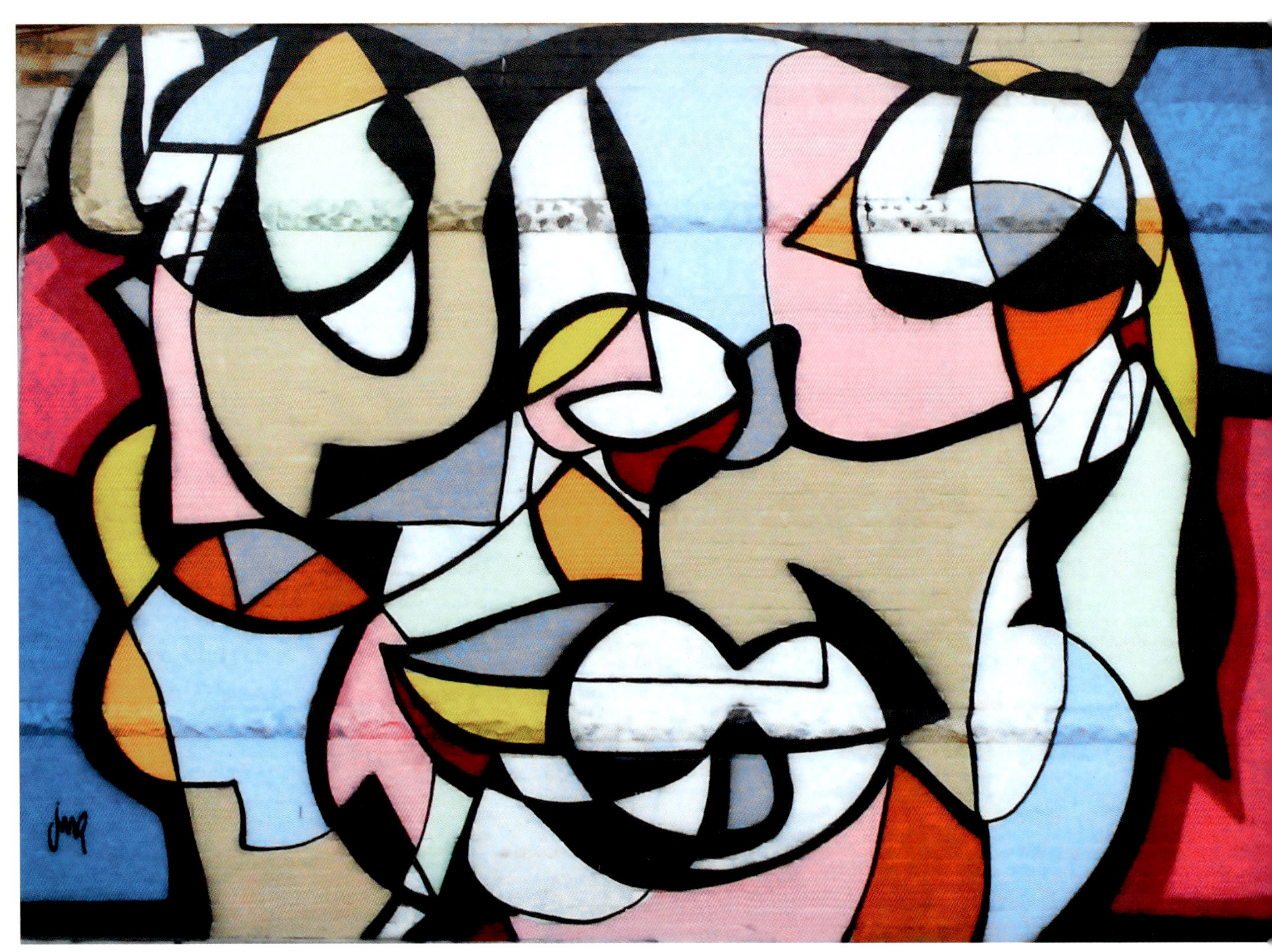

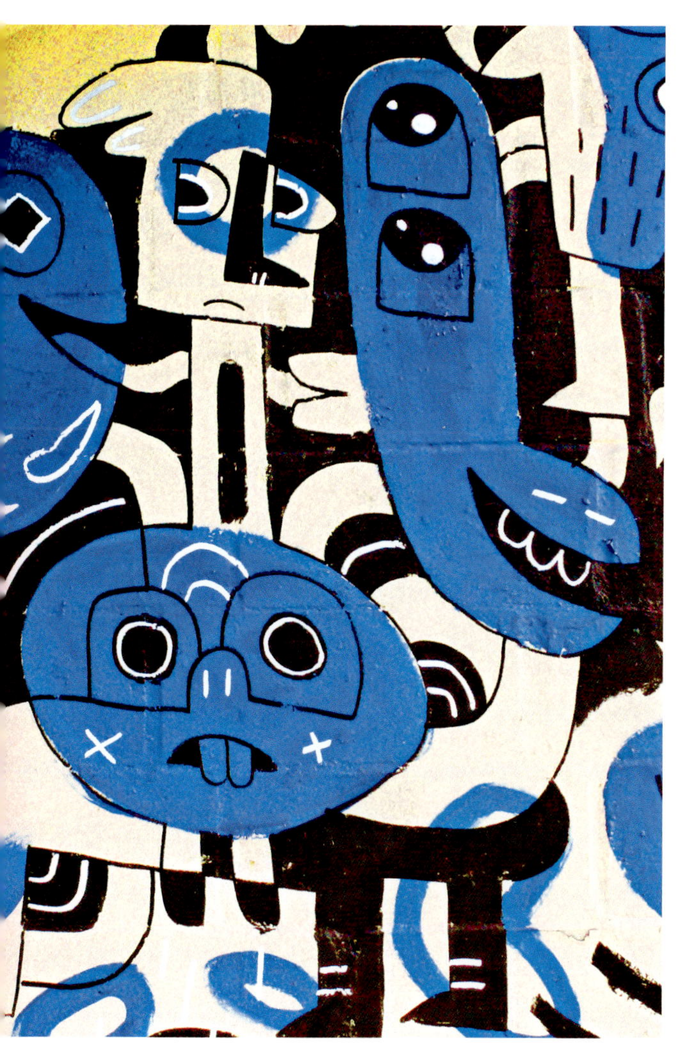

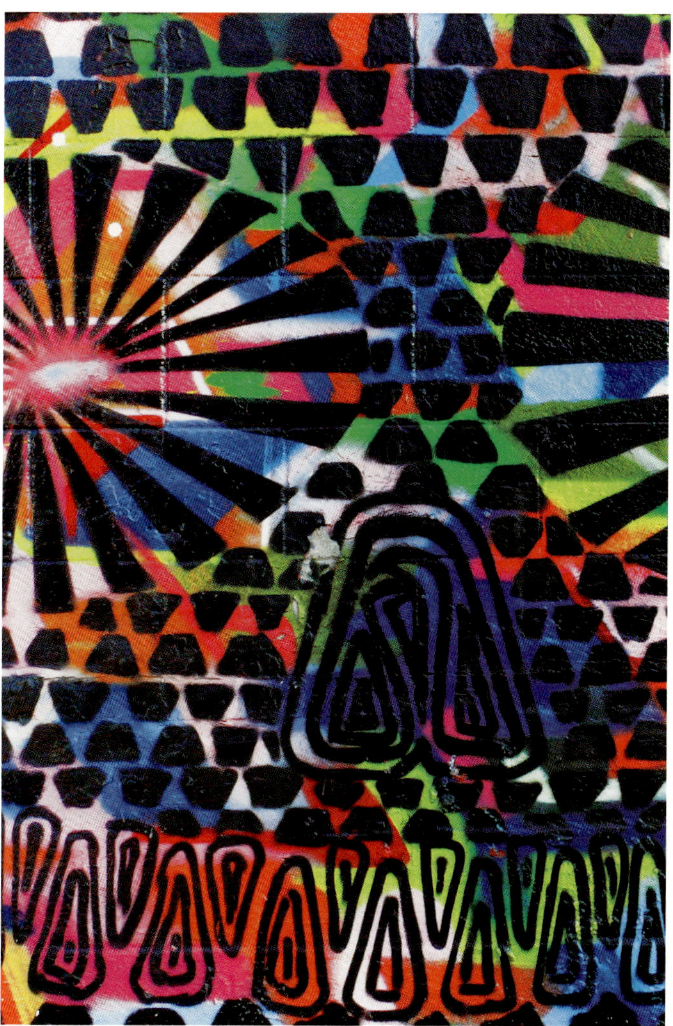

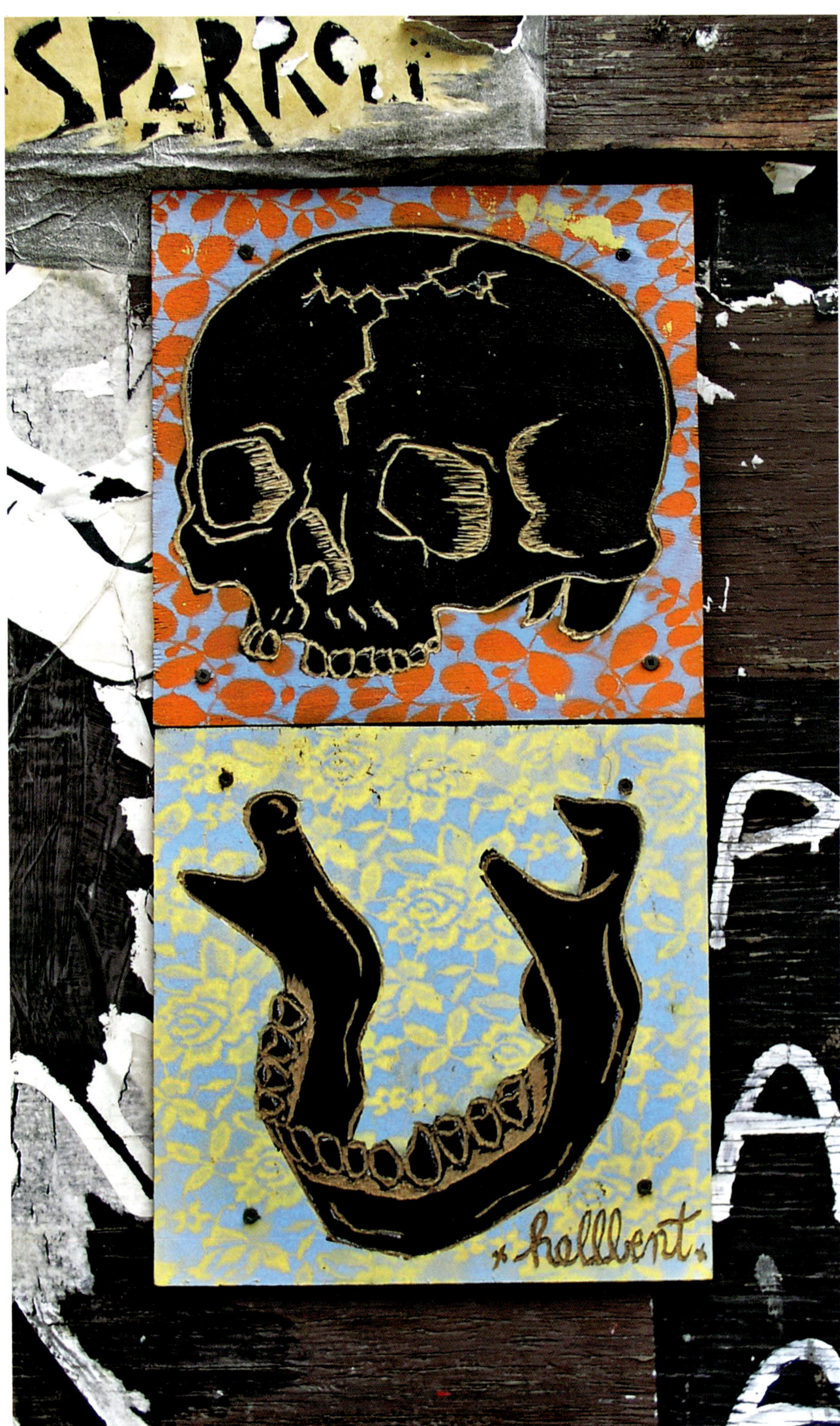
hellbent

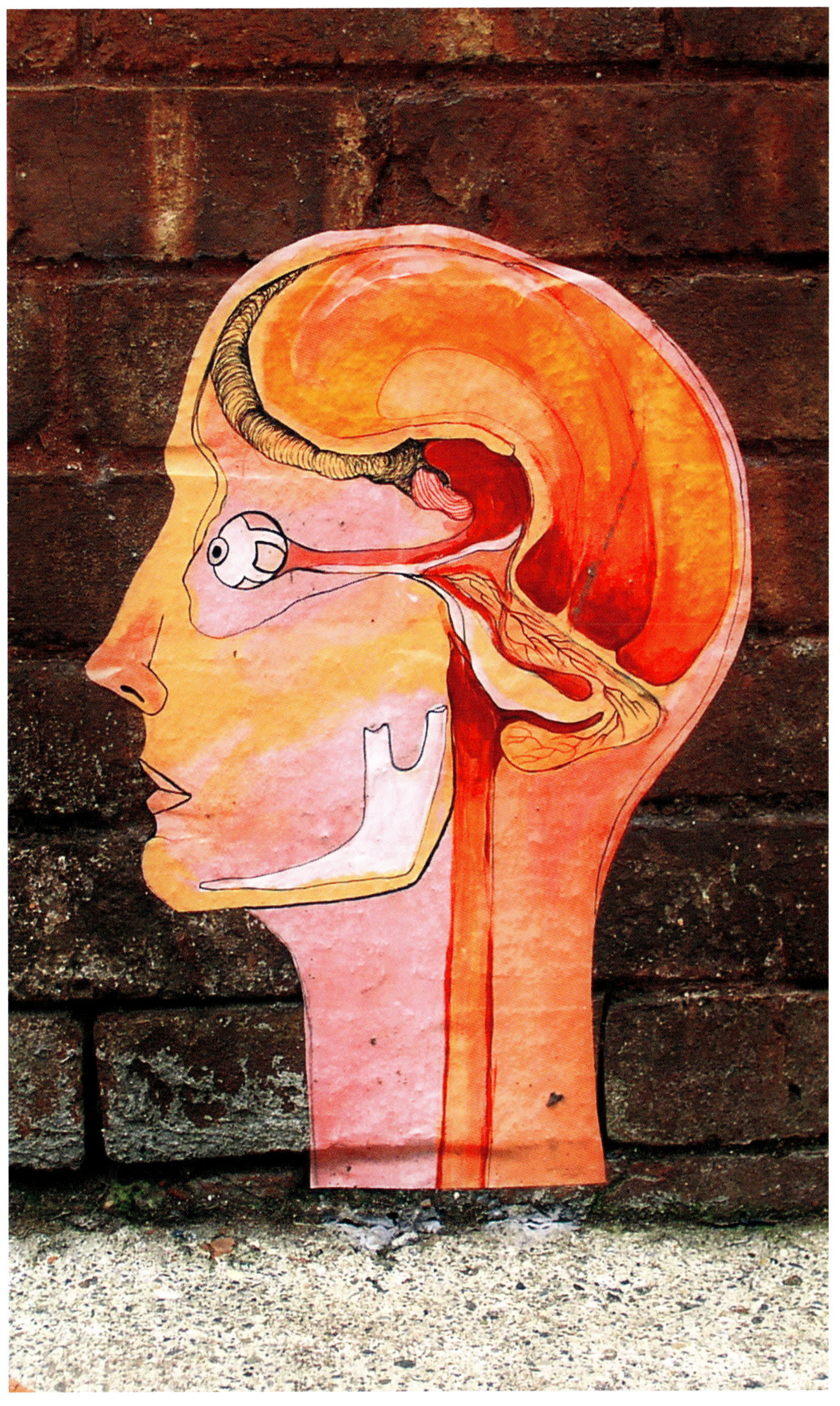

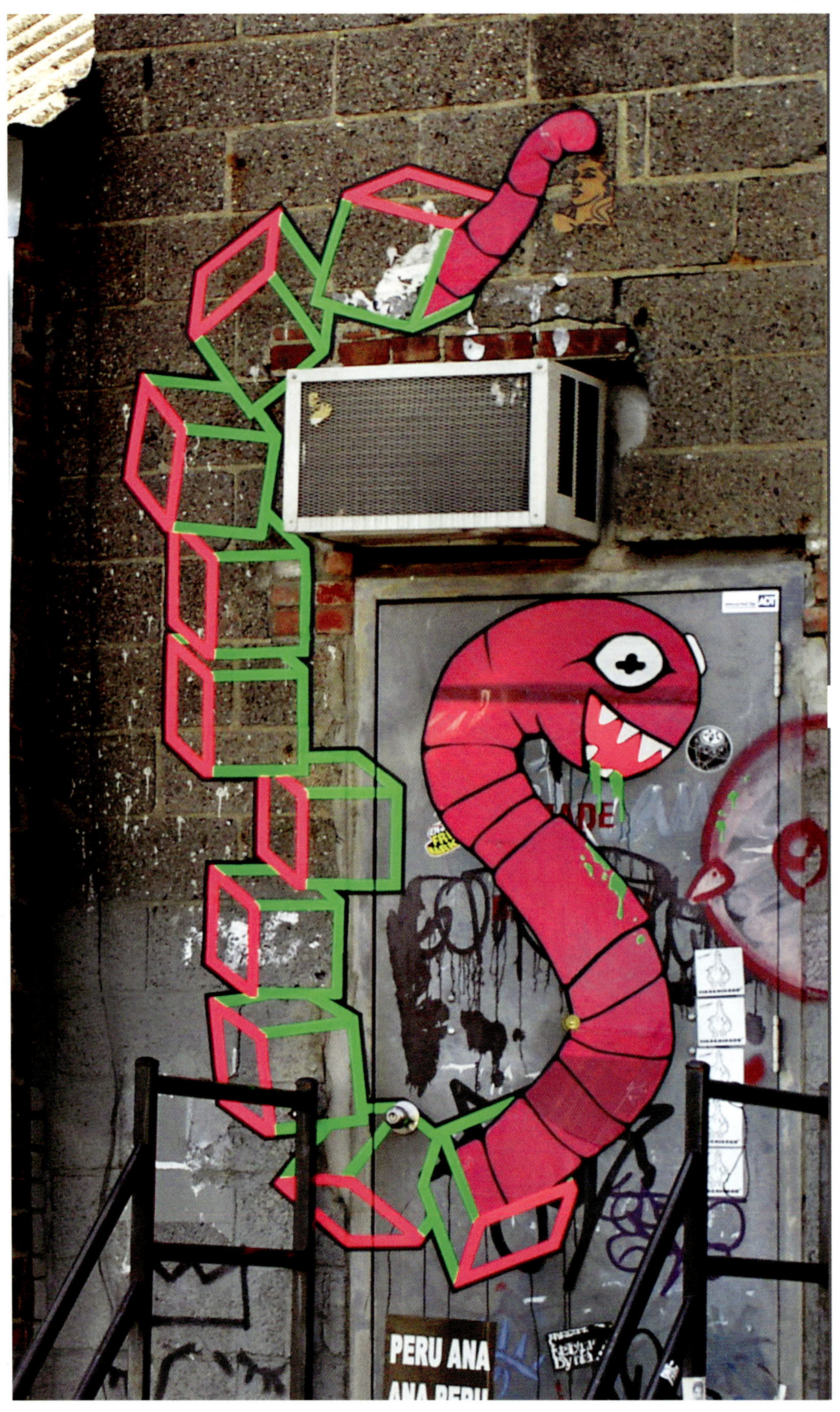
PERU ANA

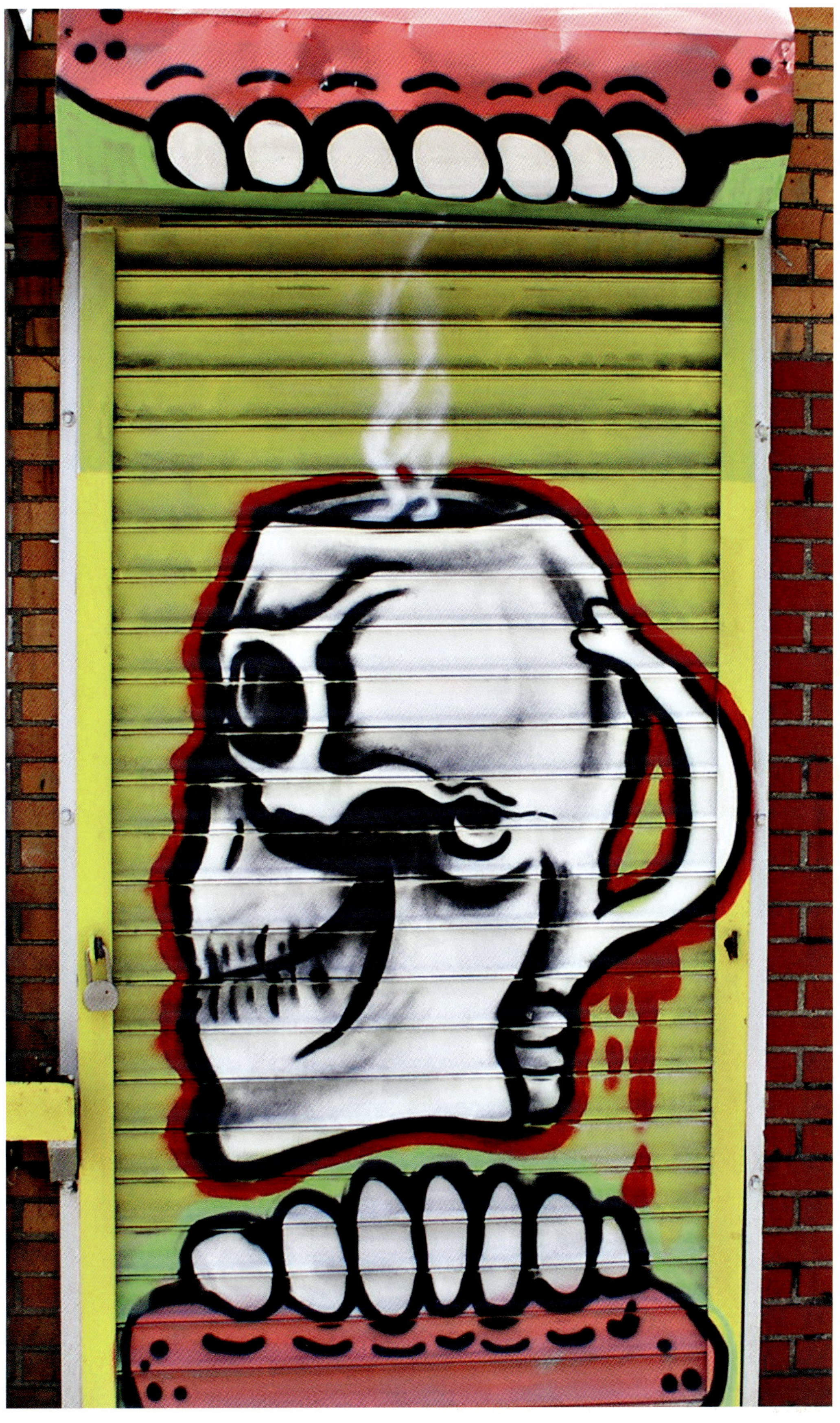

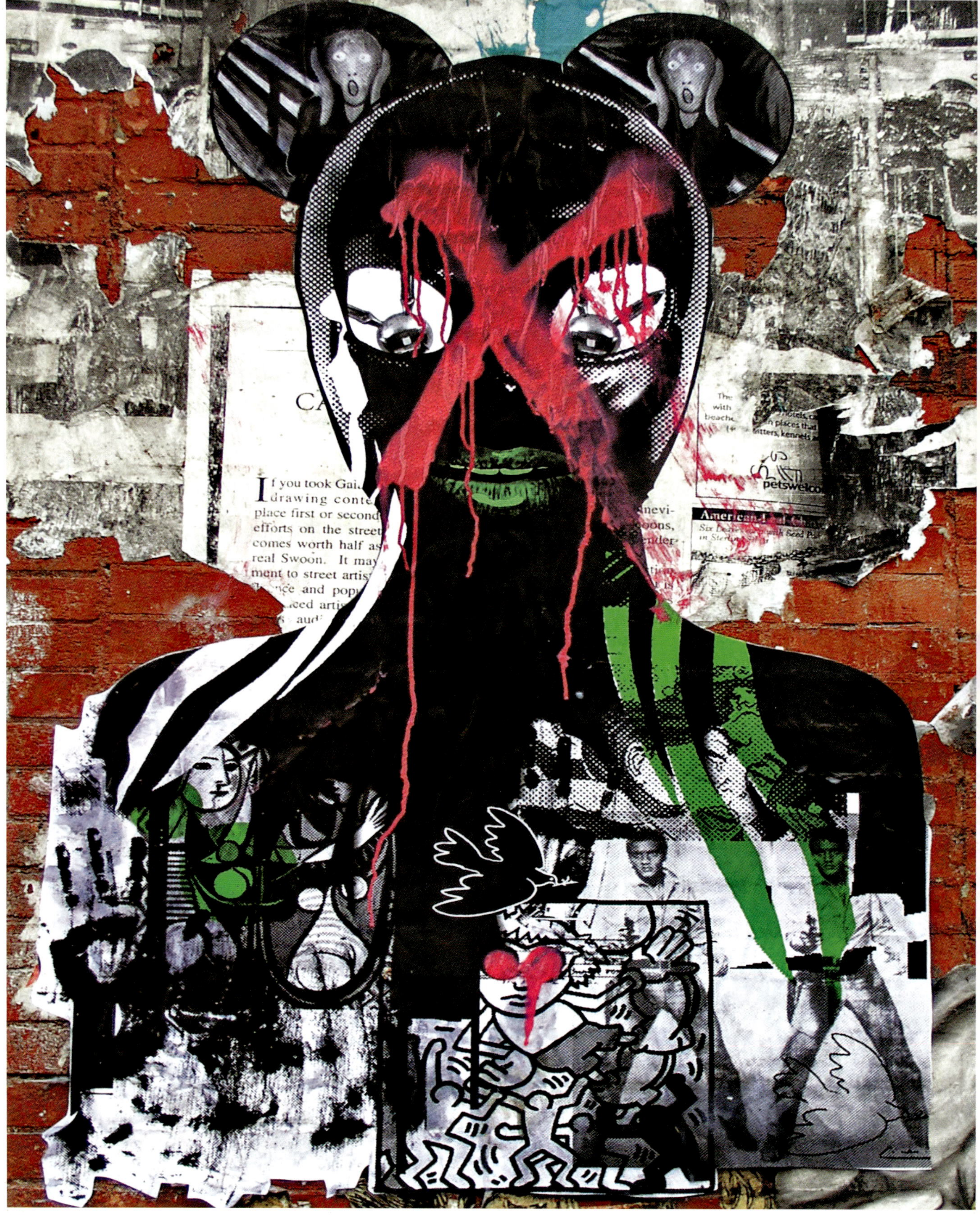
If you took
drawing
place first or
efforts on the
comes worth half
real Swoon. It
ment to street
and
petswelco

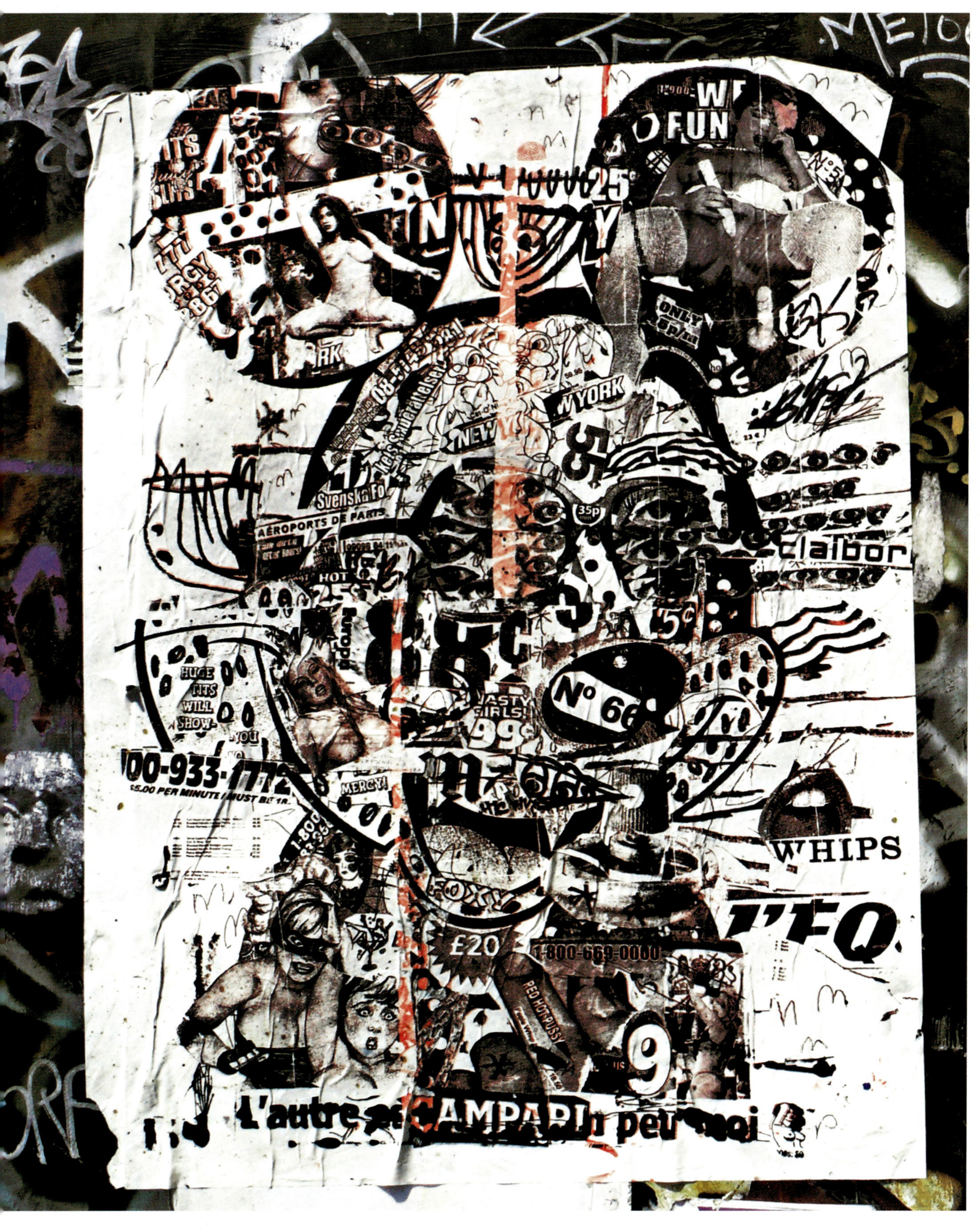

WE
FUN
N°5
ORGY
NEW YORK
Svenska Fo
AÉROPORTS DE PARIS
HOT
claibor
35p
5¢
N° 66
NASTY
GIRLS!
99¢
HUGE
TITS
WILL
SHOW
YOU
00-933-1772
$5.00 PER MINUTE / MUST BE 18.
MERCY!
WHIPS
FOXY
£20
1-800-669-0000
RED HOT PUSSY
9
CAMPARI

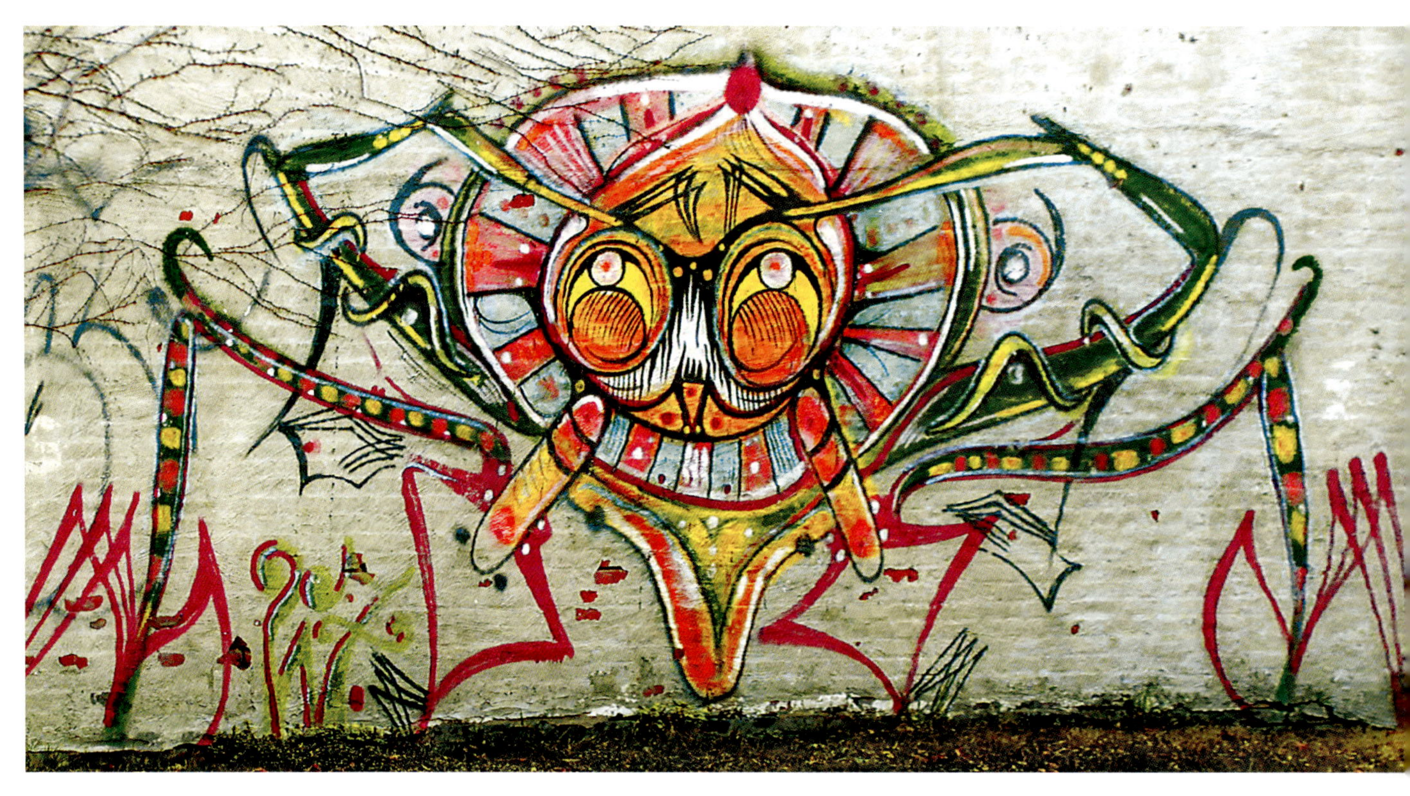

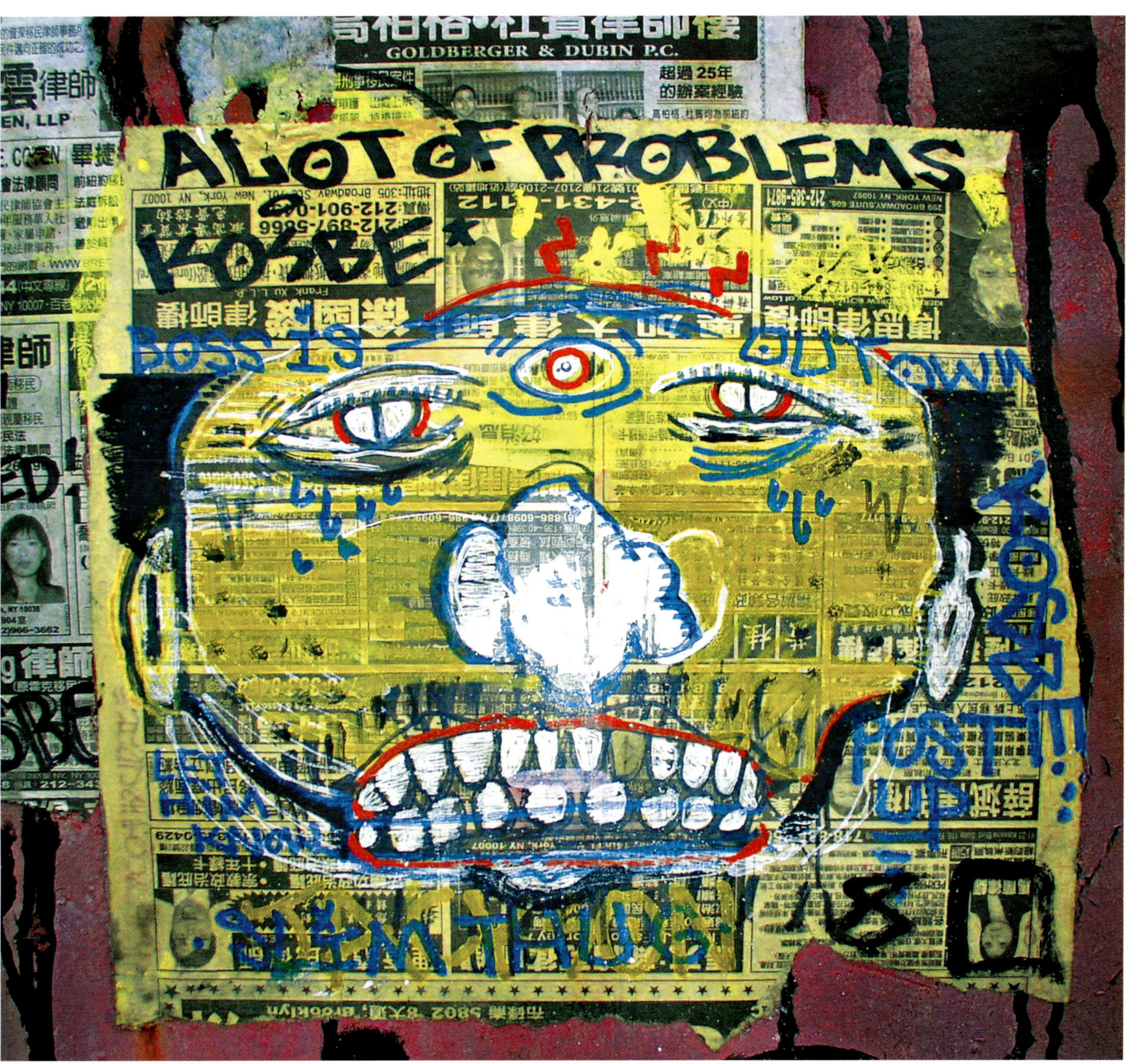
ALOT OF PROBLEMS
KOSBE
BOSS IS
OUTOWN
KOSBE
POST UP
LET HIM KNOW
GOLDBERGER & DUBIN P.C.
超過 25年
的辦案經驗

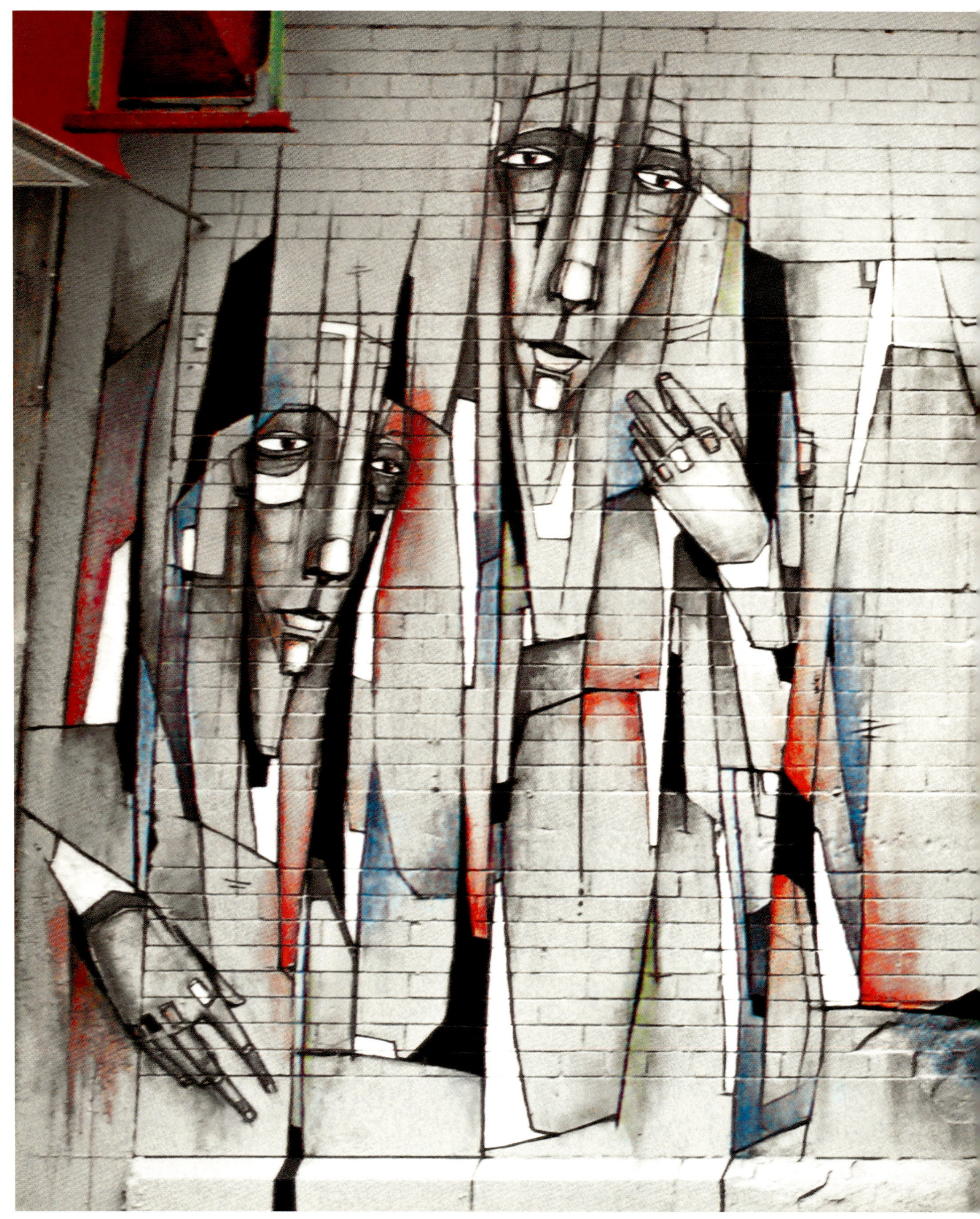

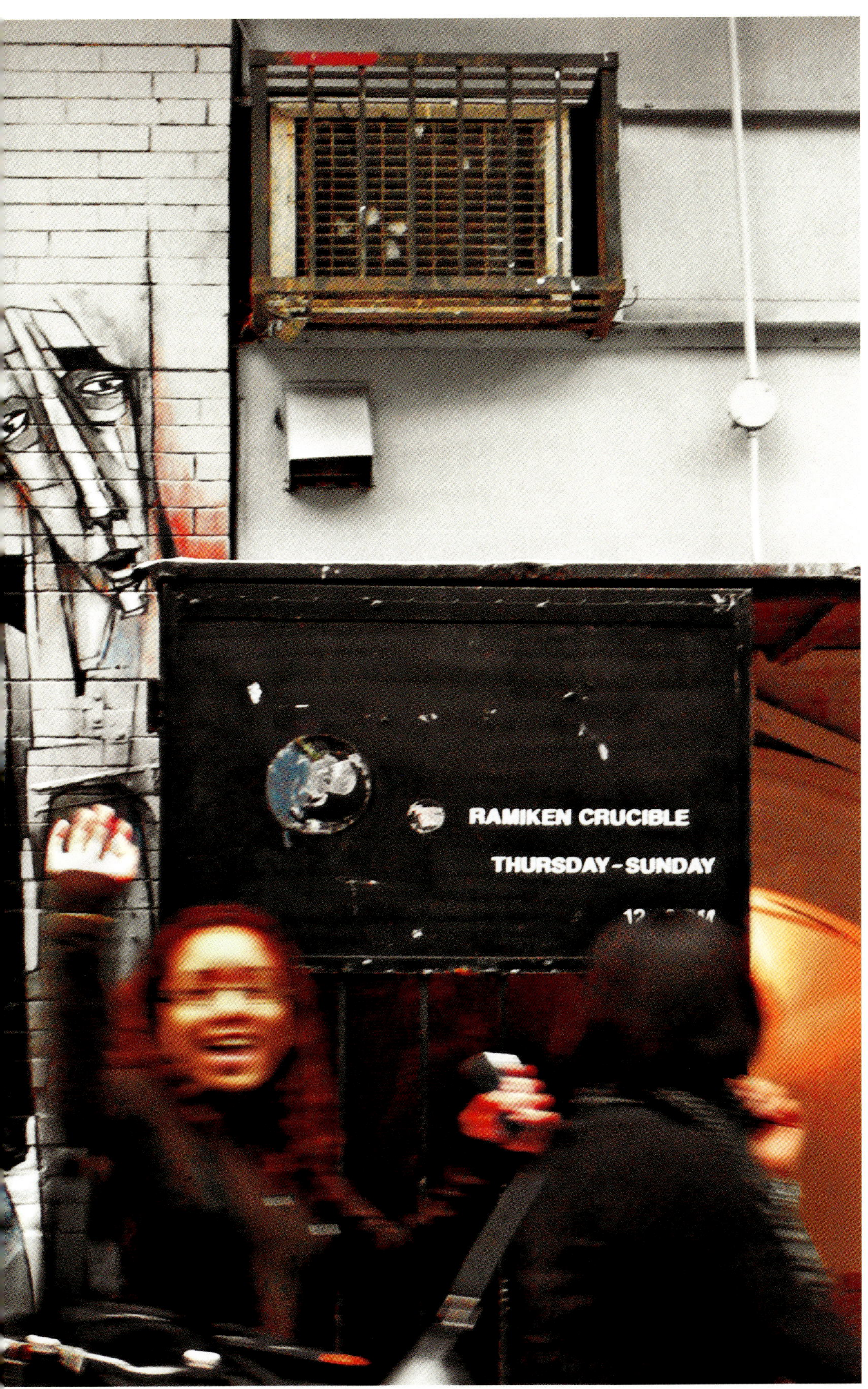
RAMIKEN CRUCIBLE
THURSDAY - SUNDAY

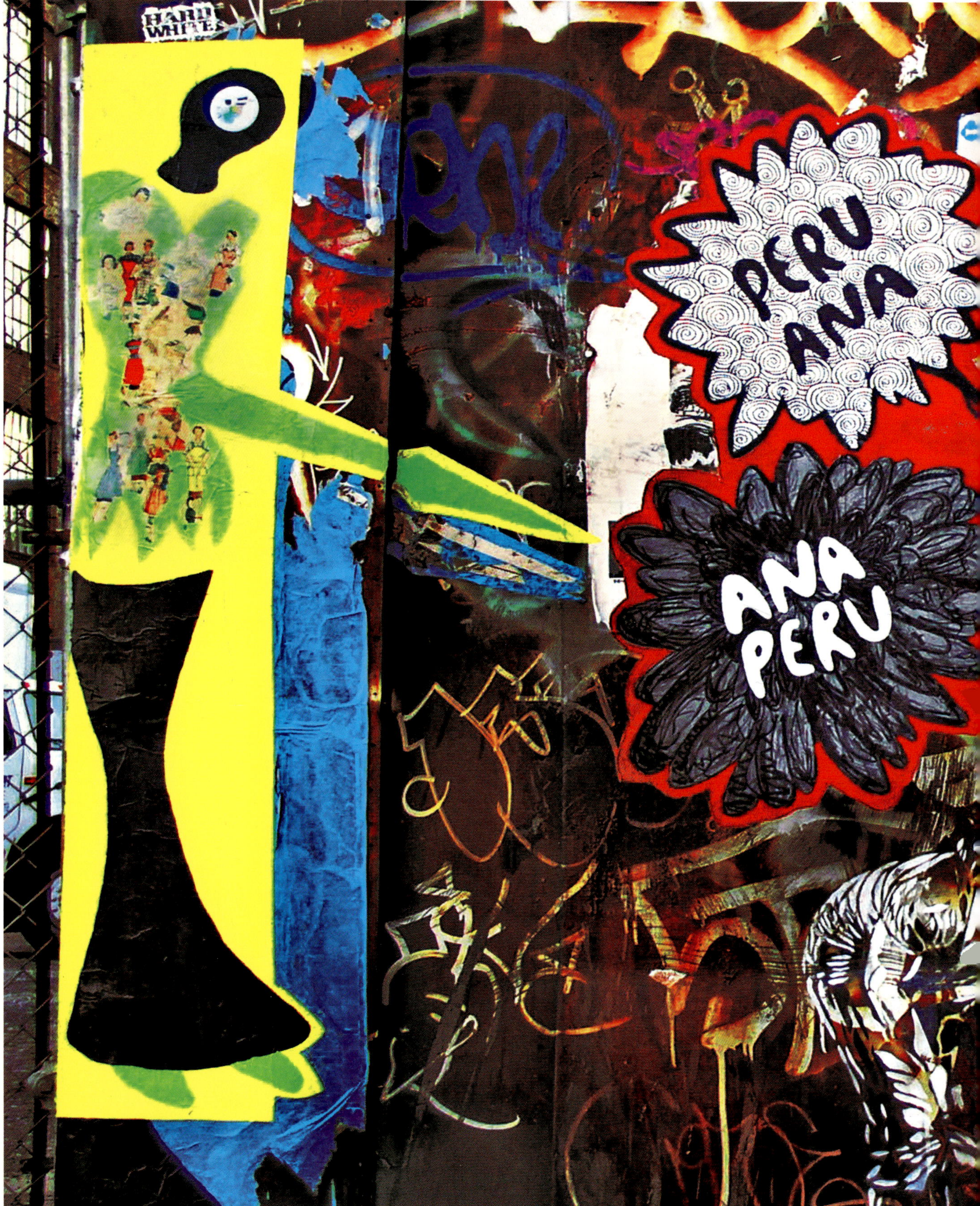
HARD WHITE
PERU ANA
ANA PERU

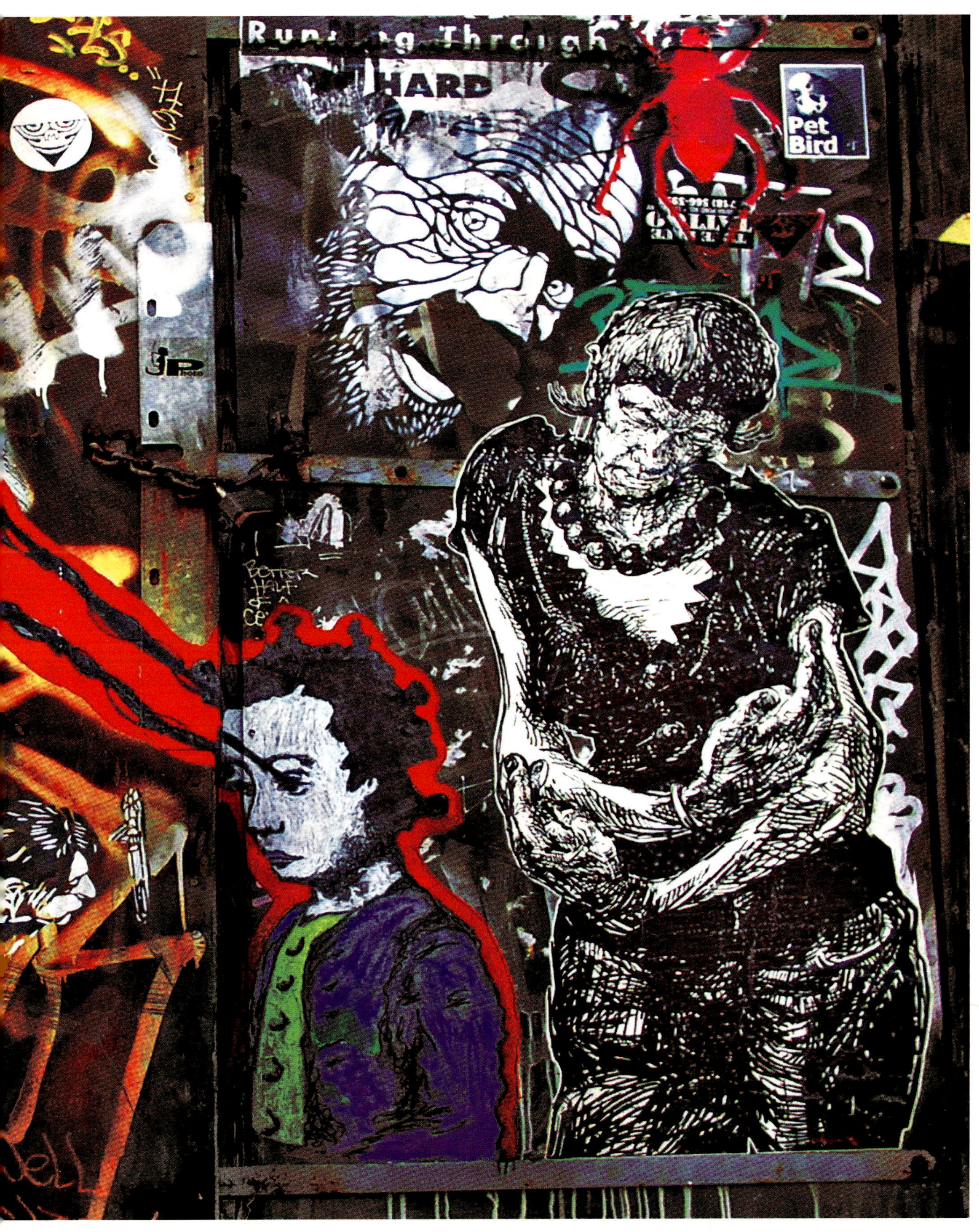
HARD
Pet Bird

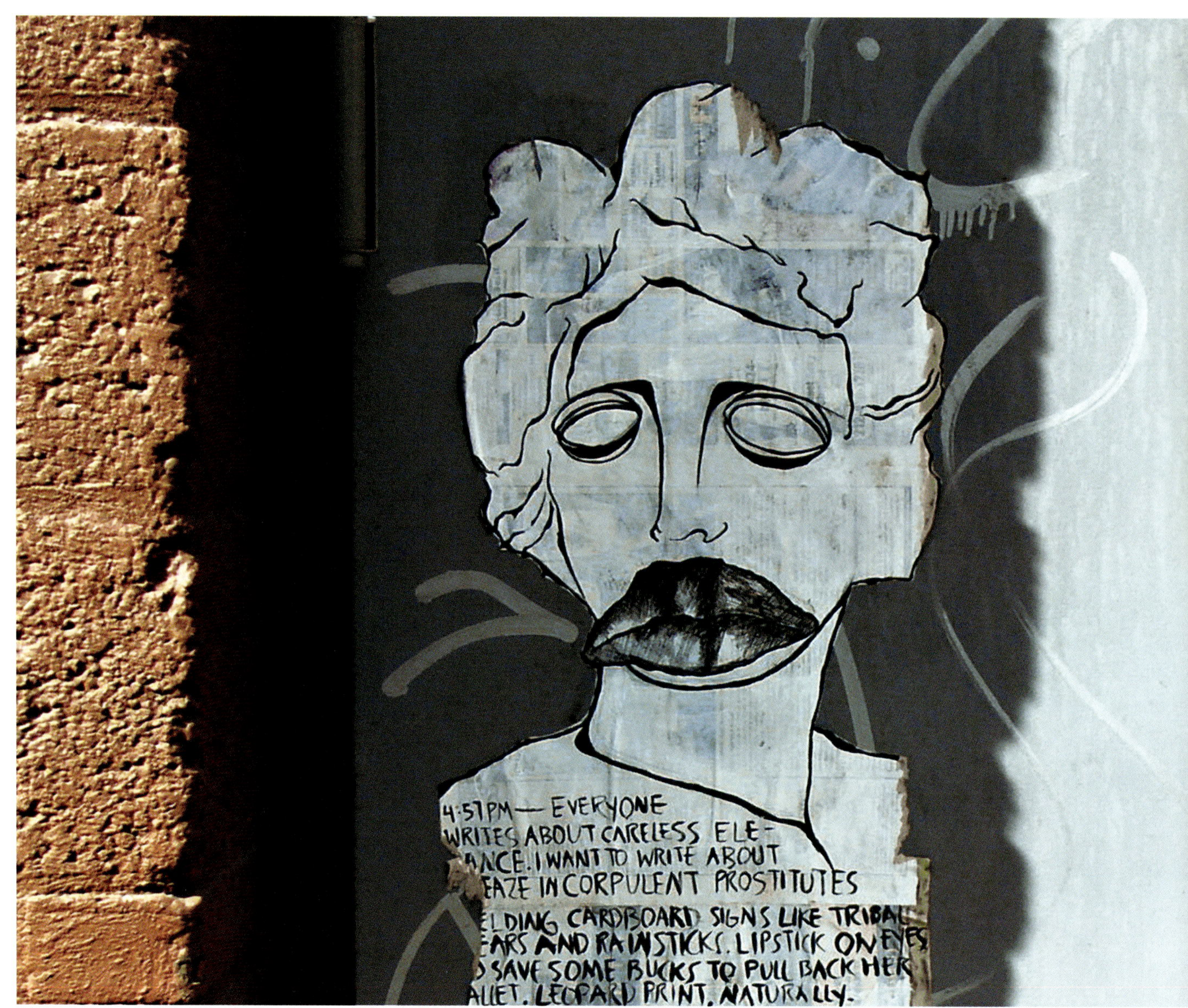
4:57PM — EVERYONE
WRITES ABOUT CARELESS ELE-
ANCE. I WANT TO WRITE ABOUT
EAZE IN CORPULENT PROSTITUTES
ELDING CARDBOARD SIGNS LIKE TRIBA
EARS AND RAINSTICKS. LIPSTICK ON EYES
SAVE SOME BUCKS TO PULL BACK HER
ALLET. LEOPARD PRINT. NATURALLY.

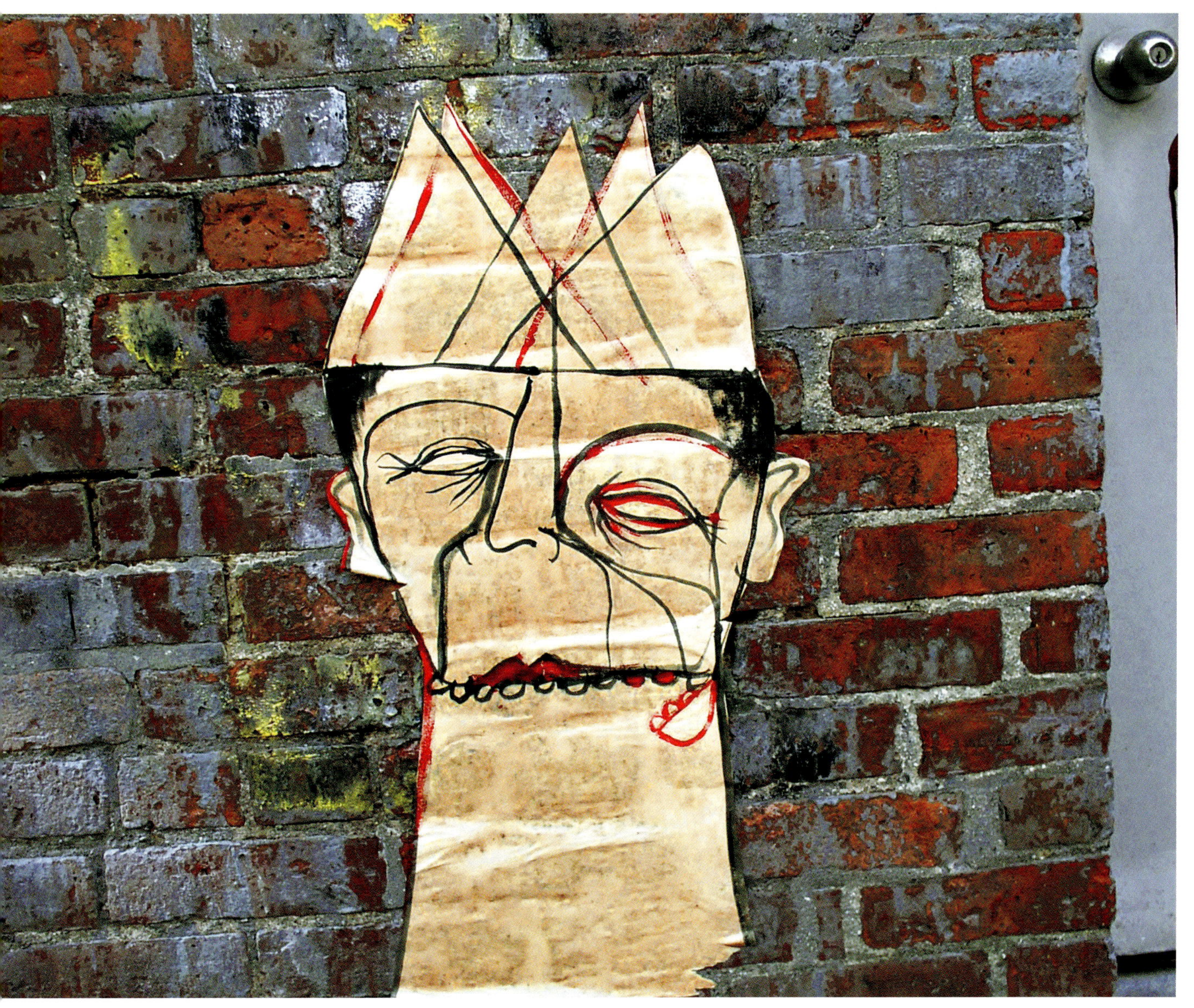

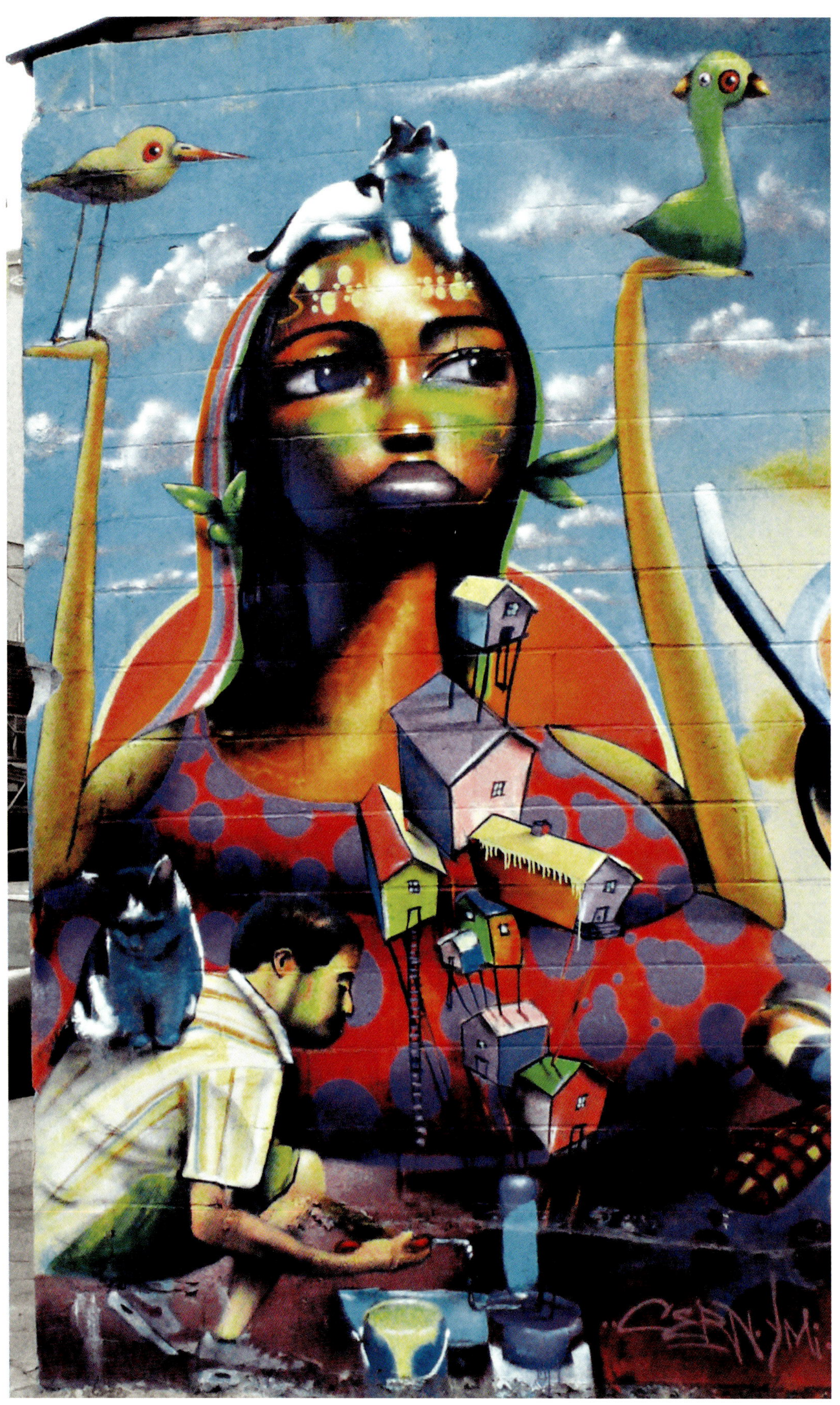

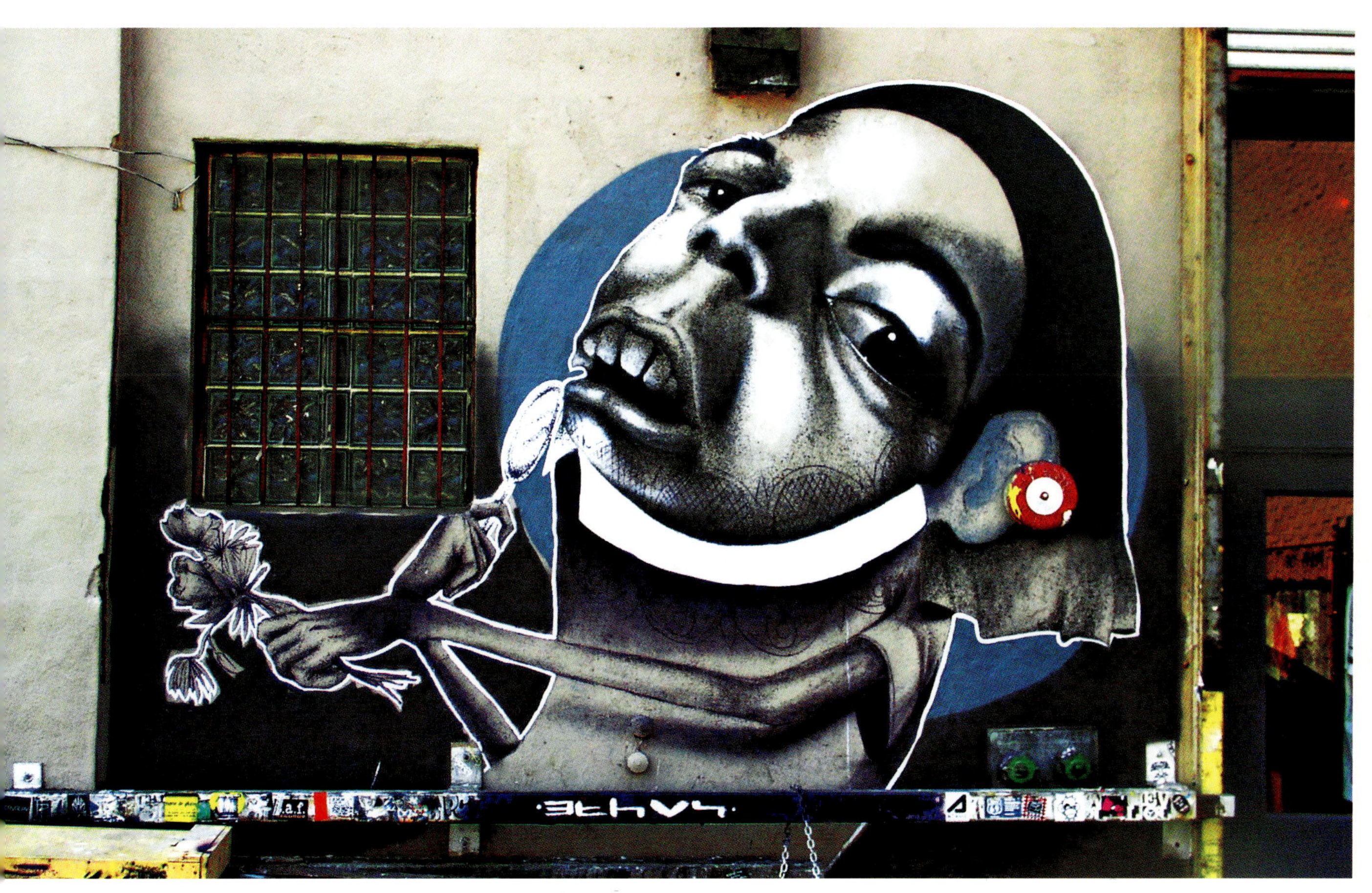

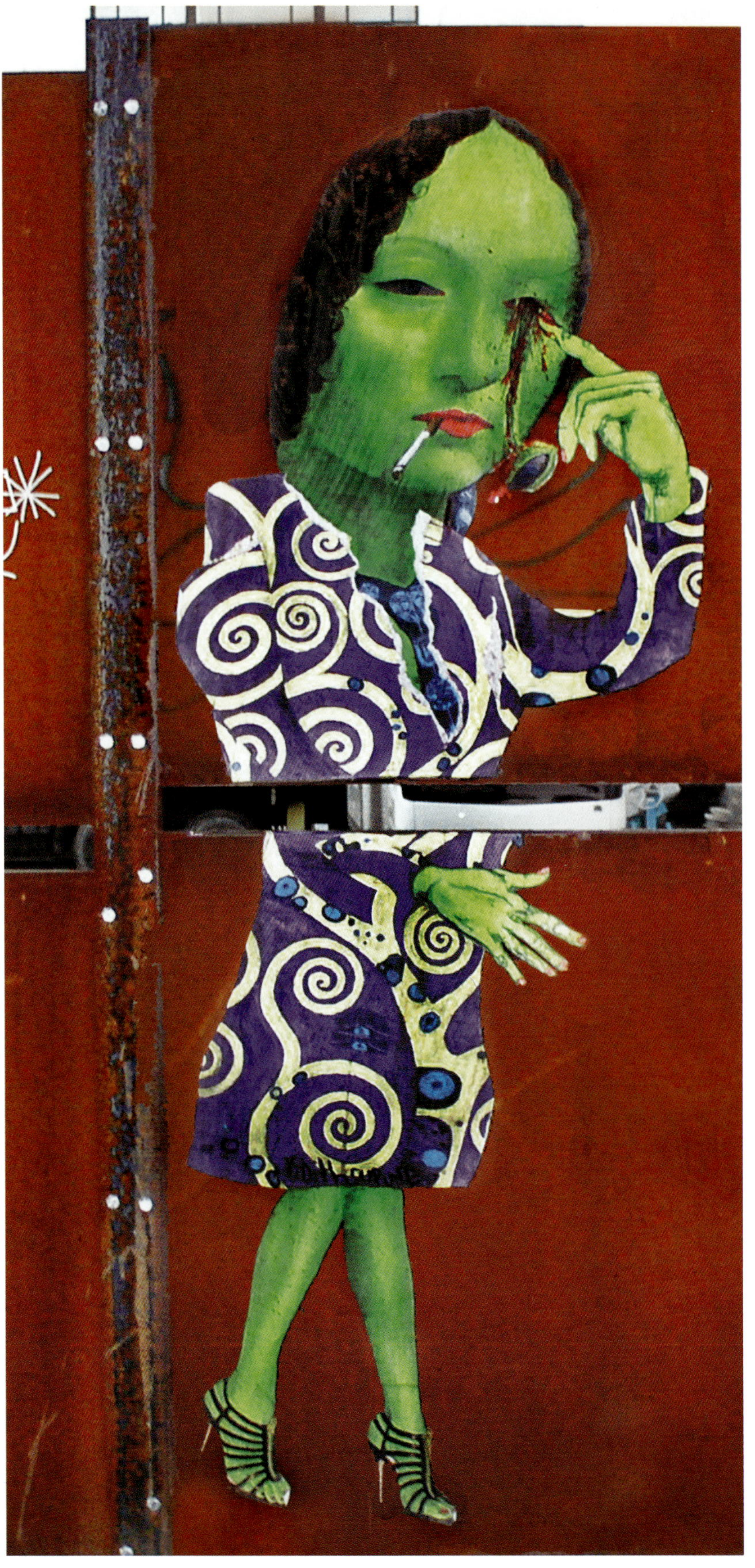

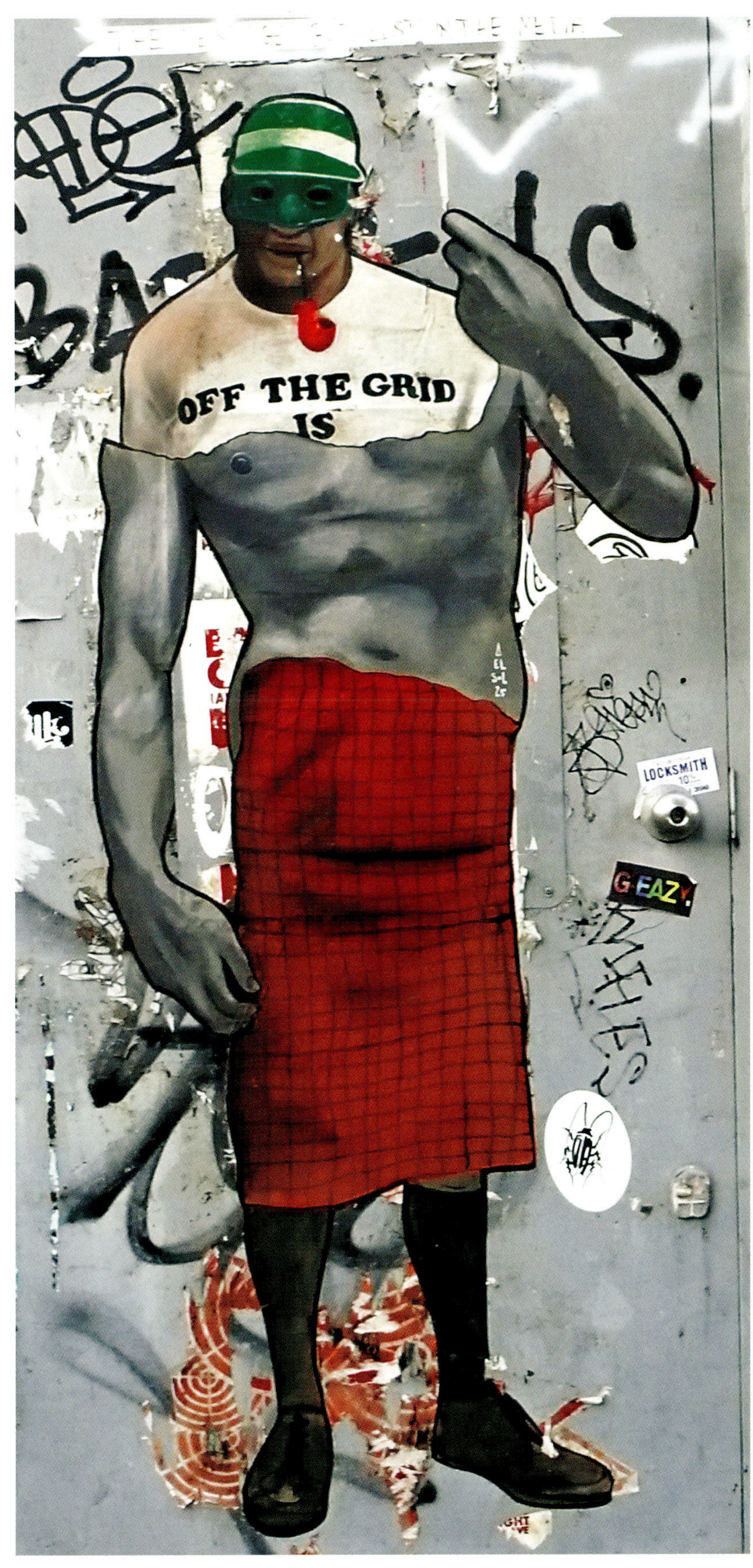
OFF THE GRID
IS
LOCKSMITH
G-EAZY

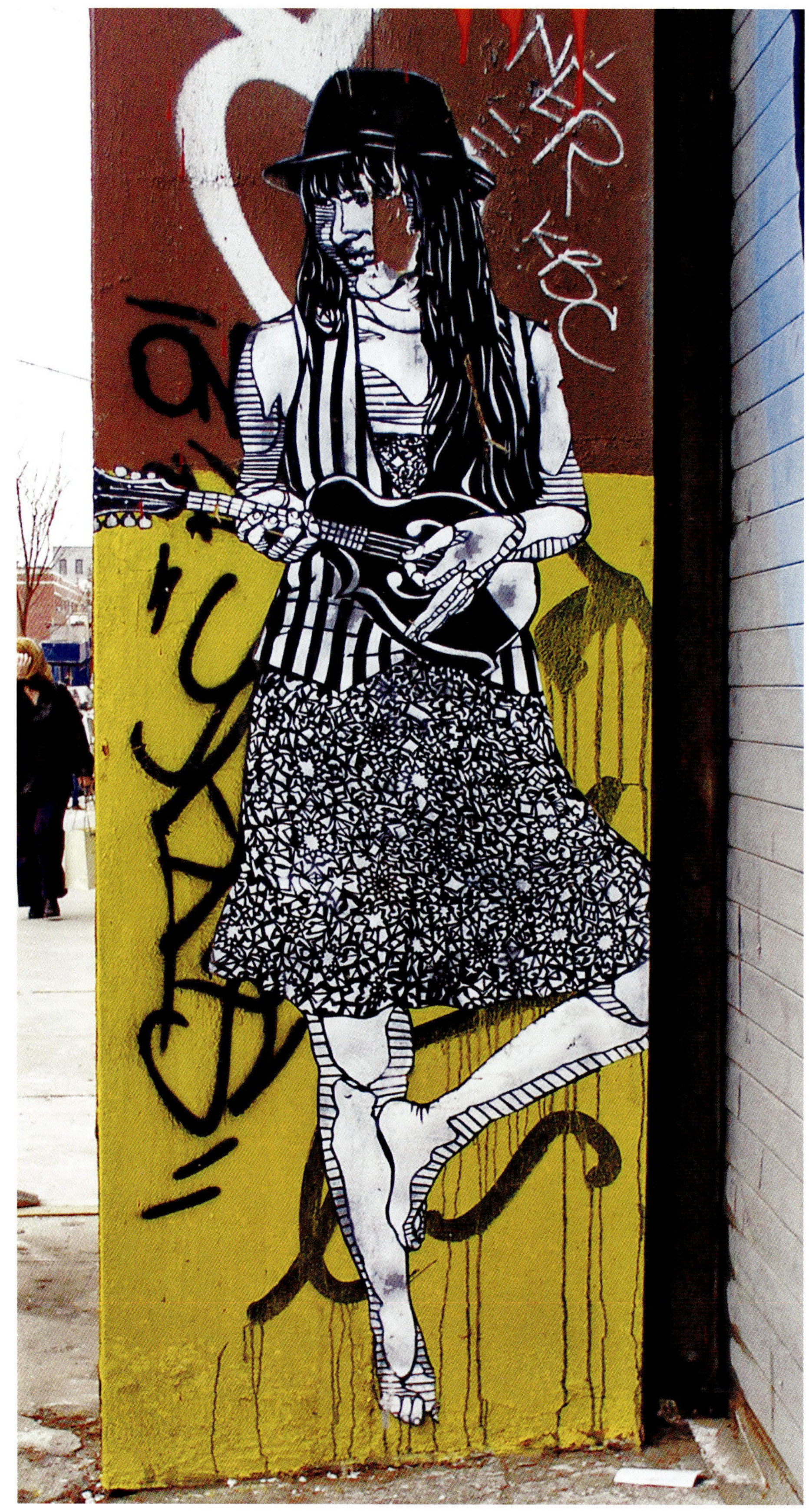

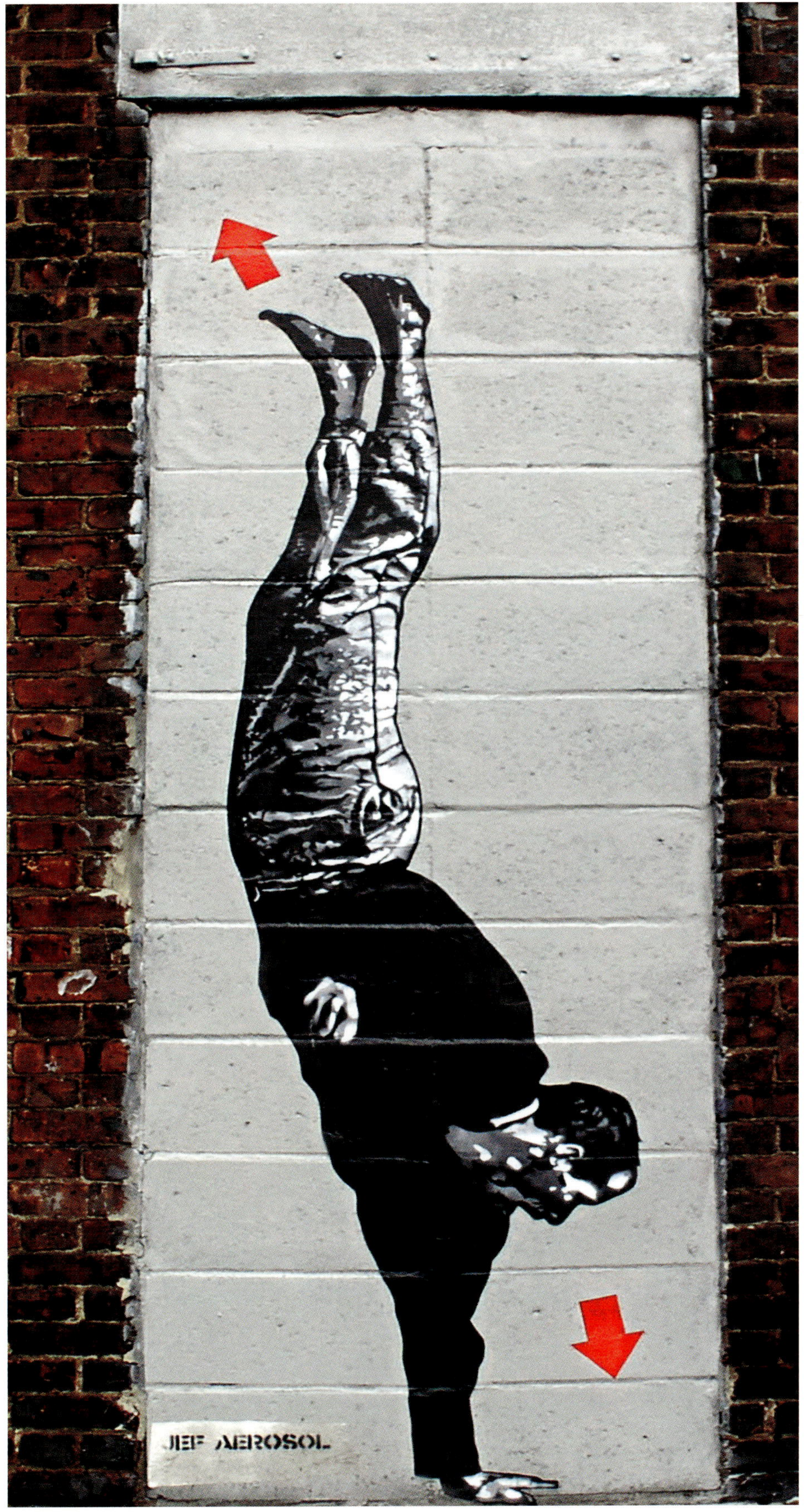
JEF AEROSOL

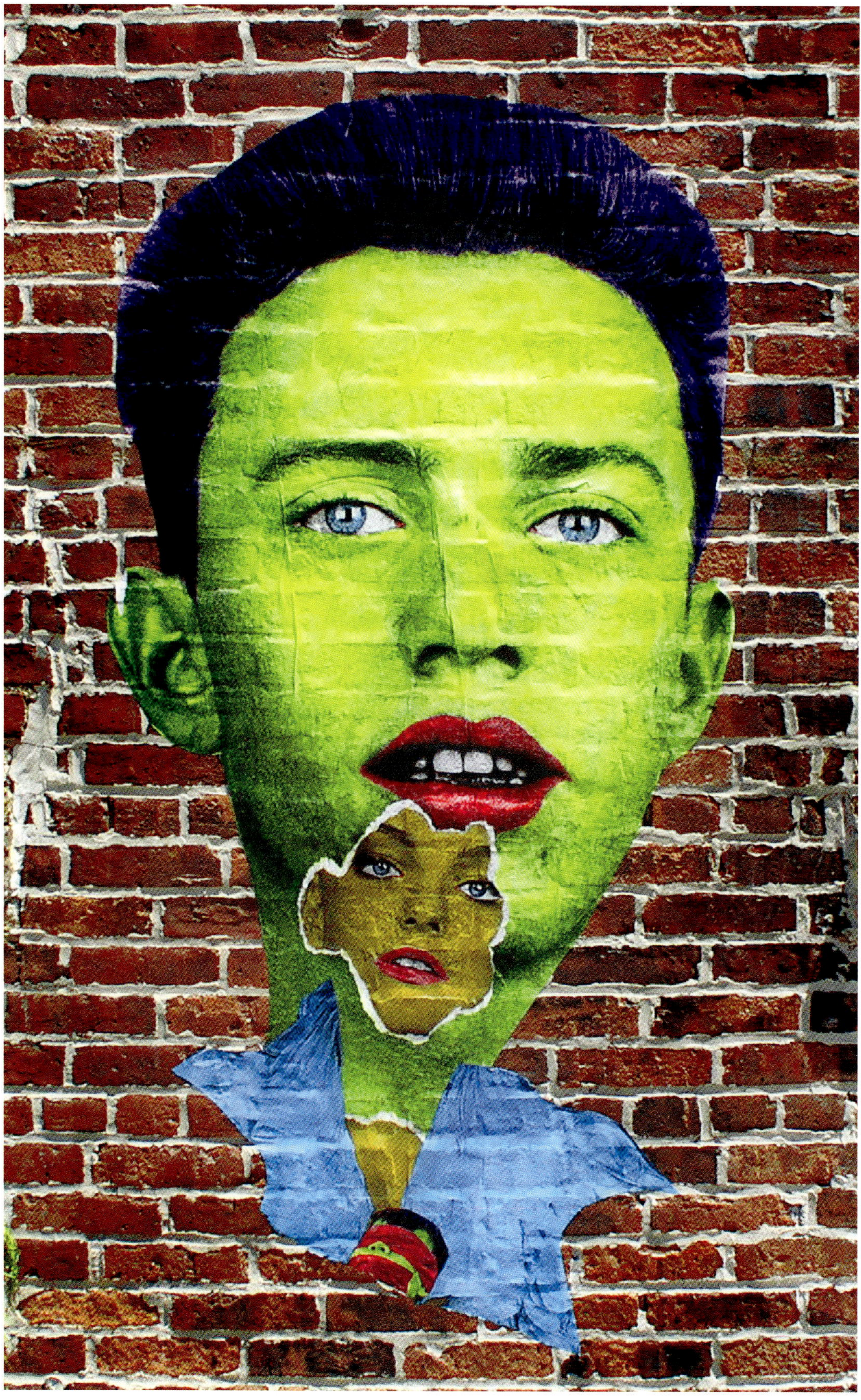

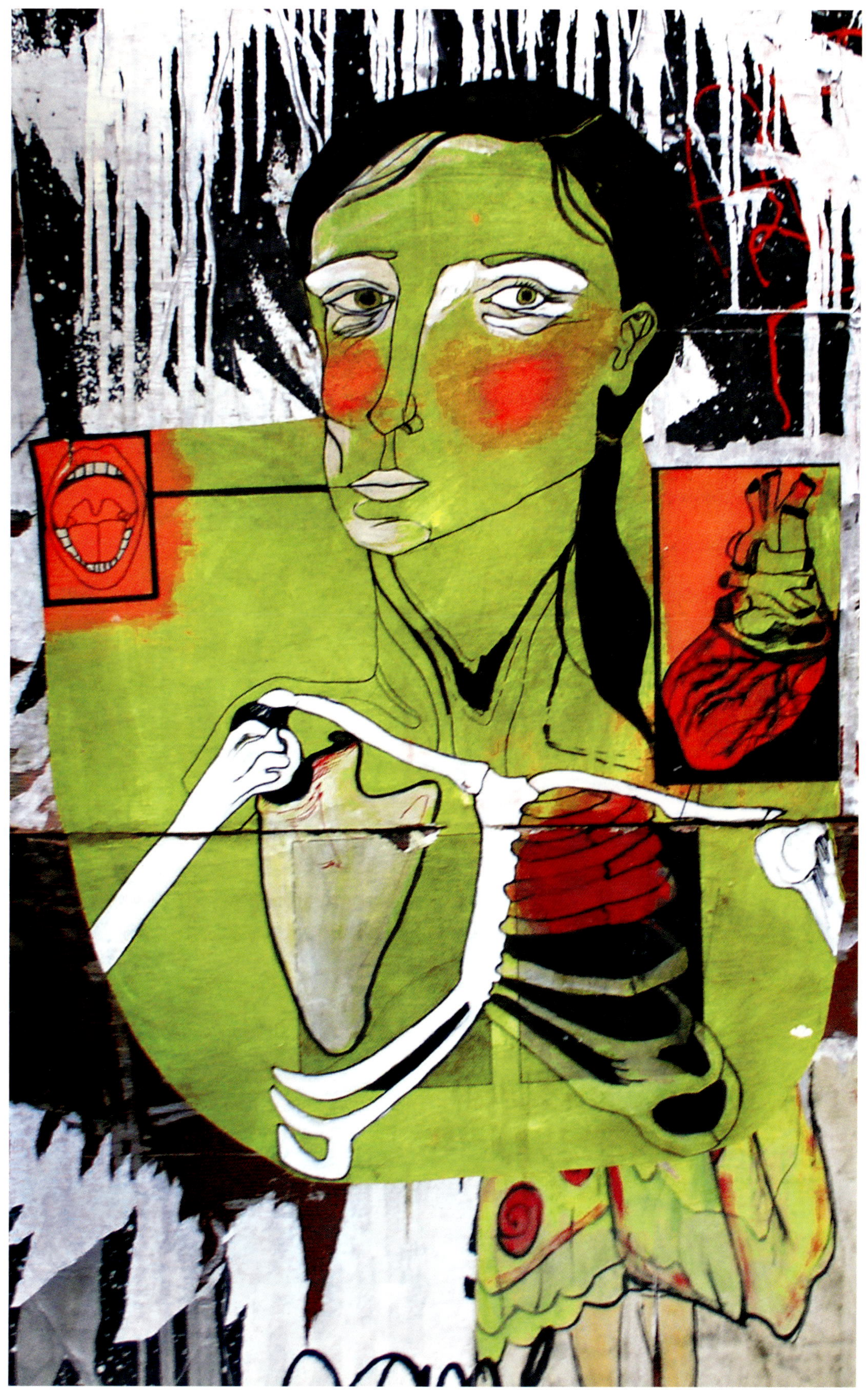

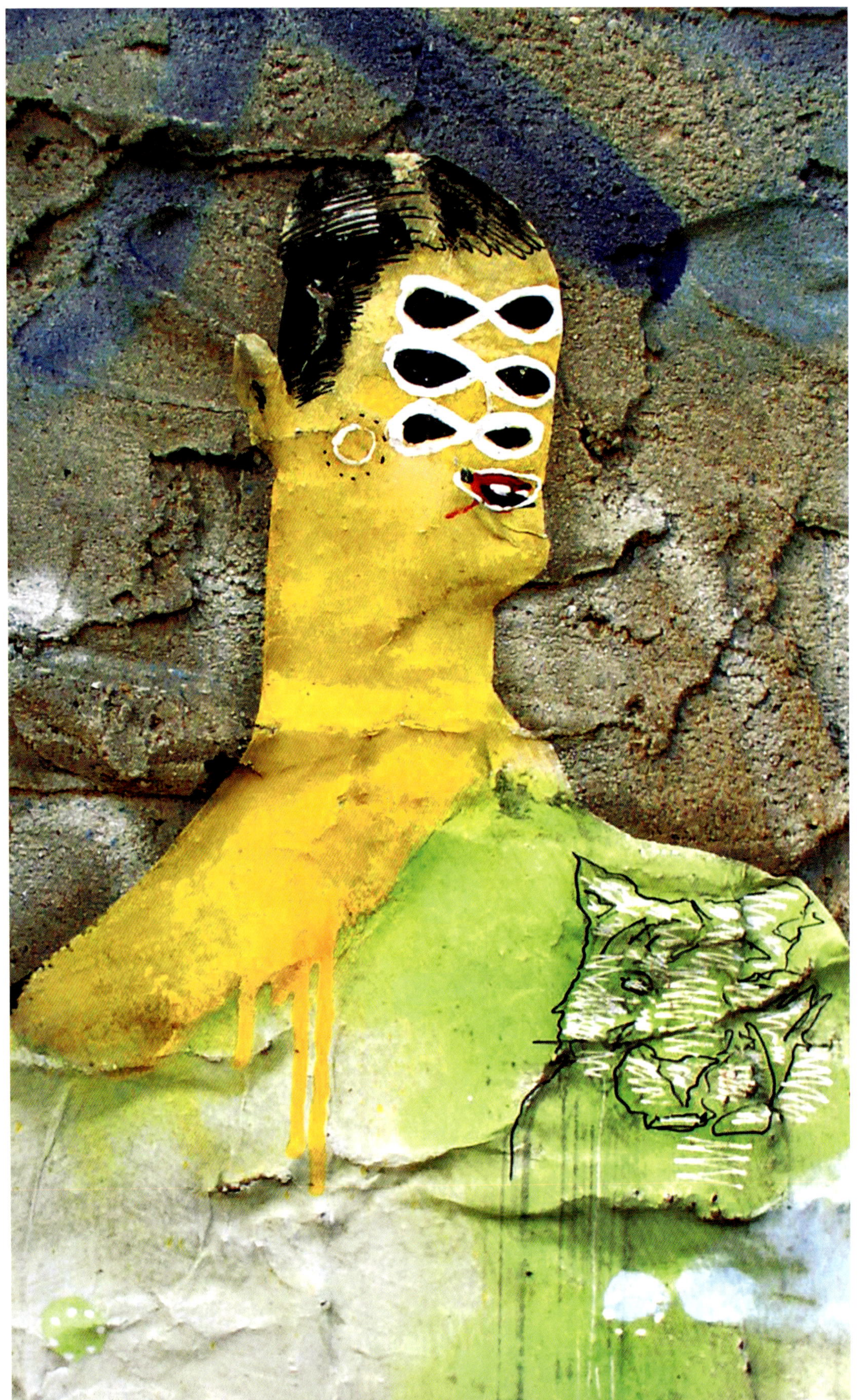

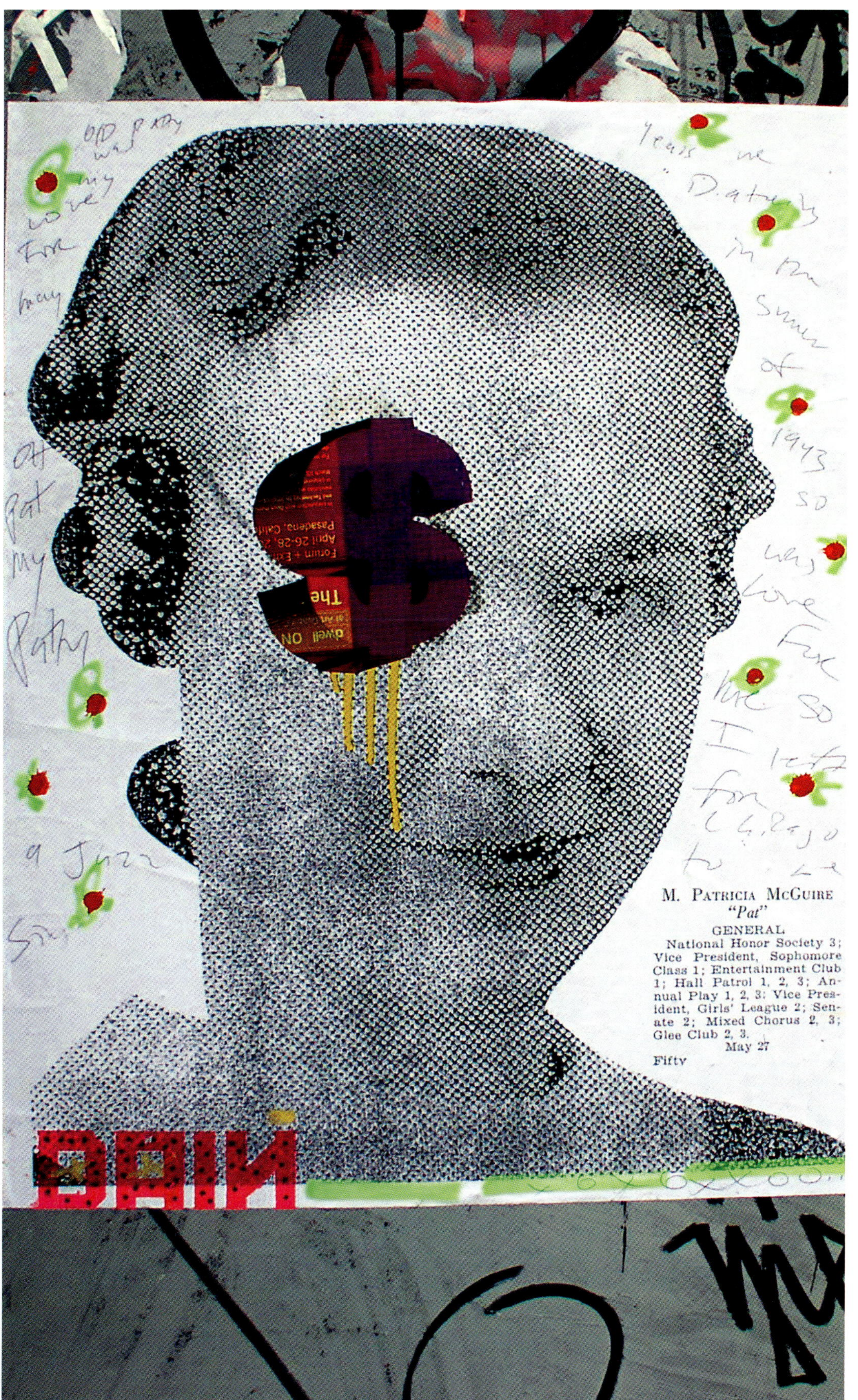
M. PATRICIA McGUIRE
"Pat"
GENERAL
National Honor Society 3; Vice President, Sophomore Class 1; Entertainment Club 1; Hall Patrol 1, 2, 3; Annual Play 1, 2, 3; Vice President, Girls' League 2; Senate 2; Mixed Chorus 2, 3; Glee Club 2, 3.
May 27
Fifty

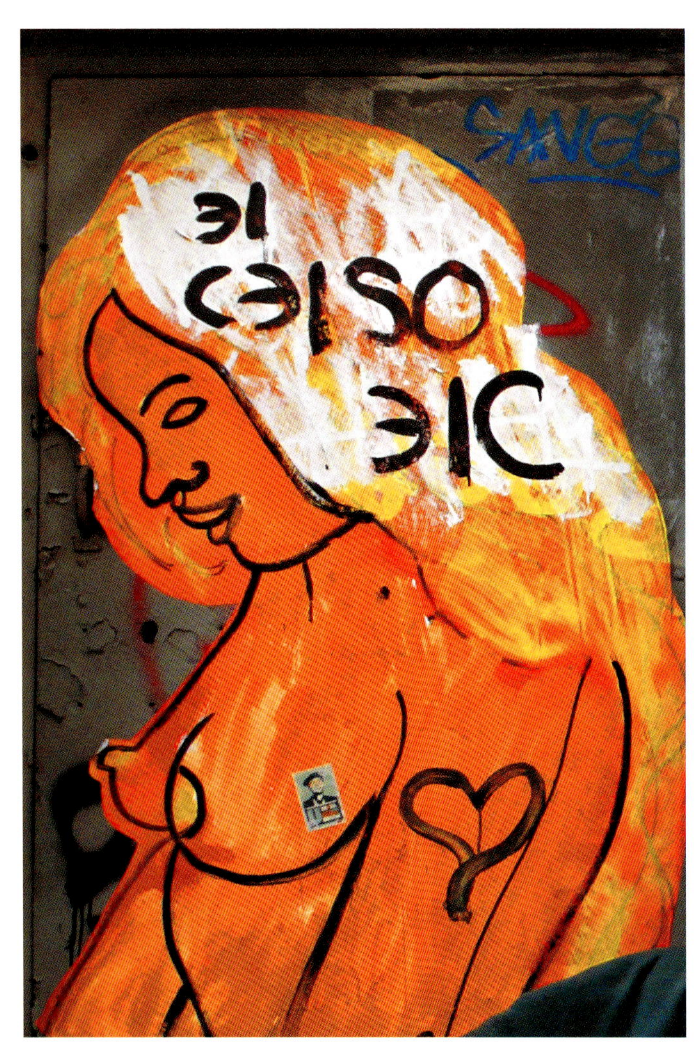

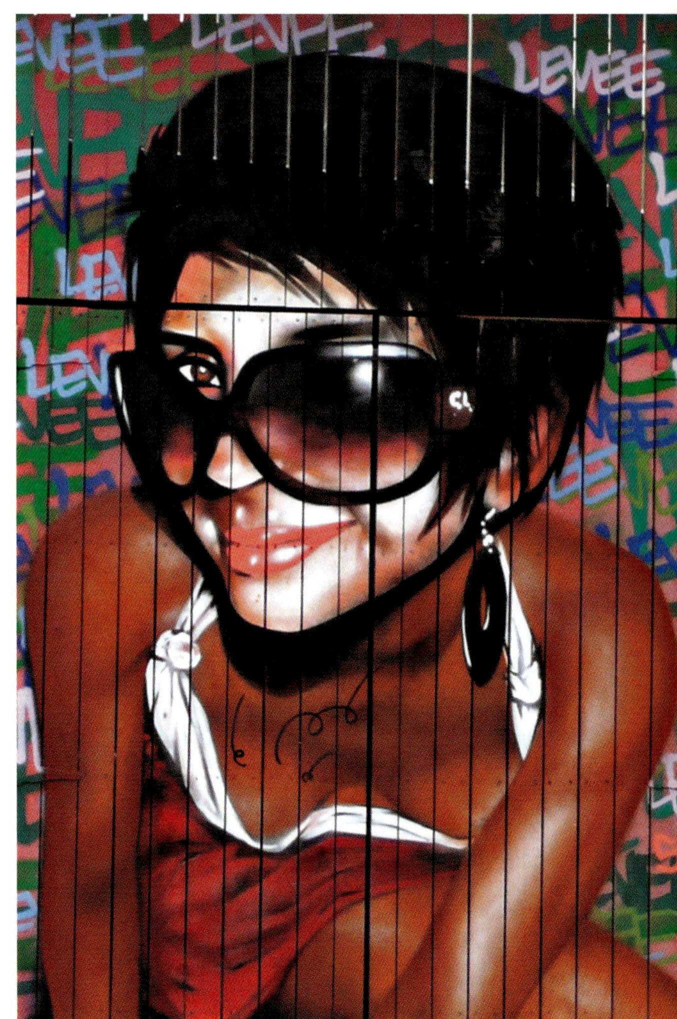
LEVEE

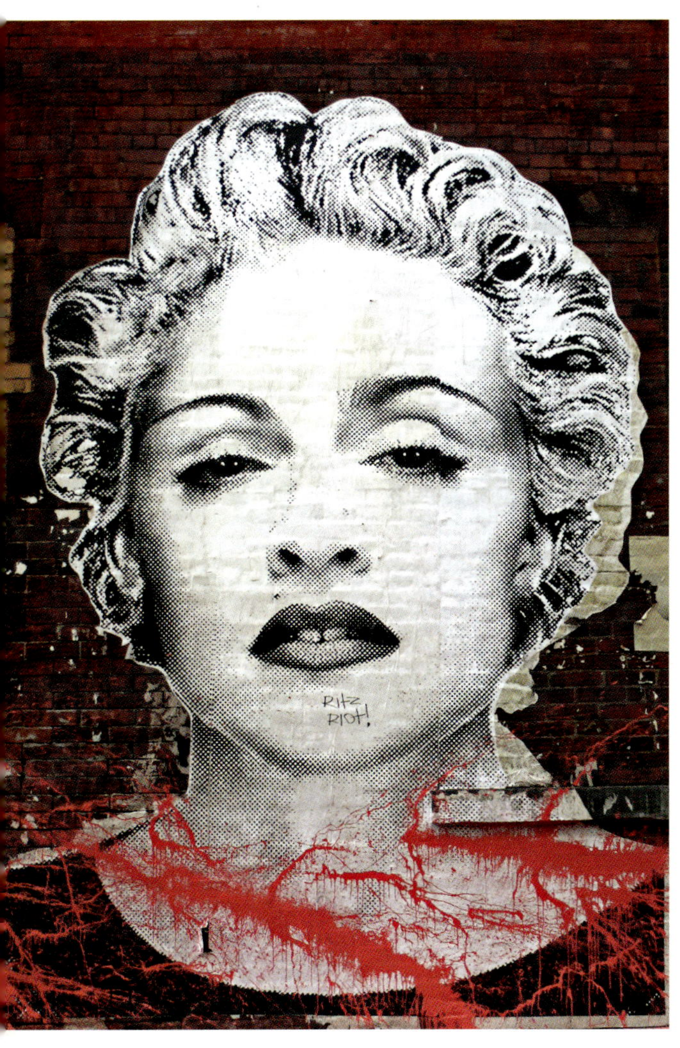
Ritz
Riot!

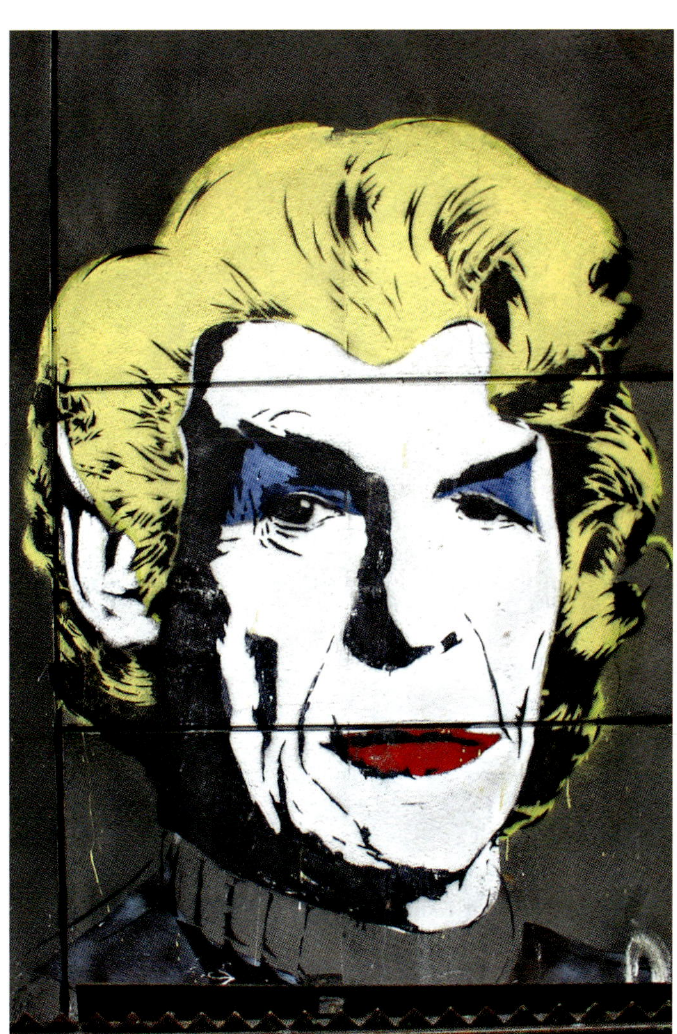

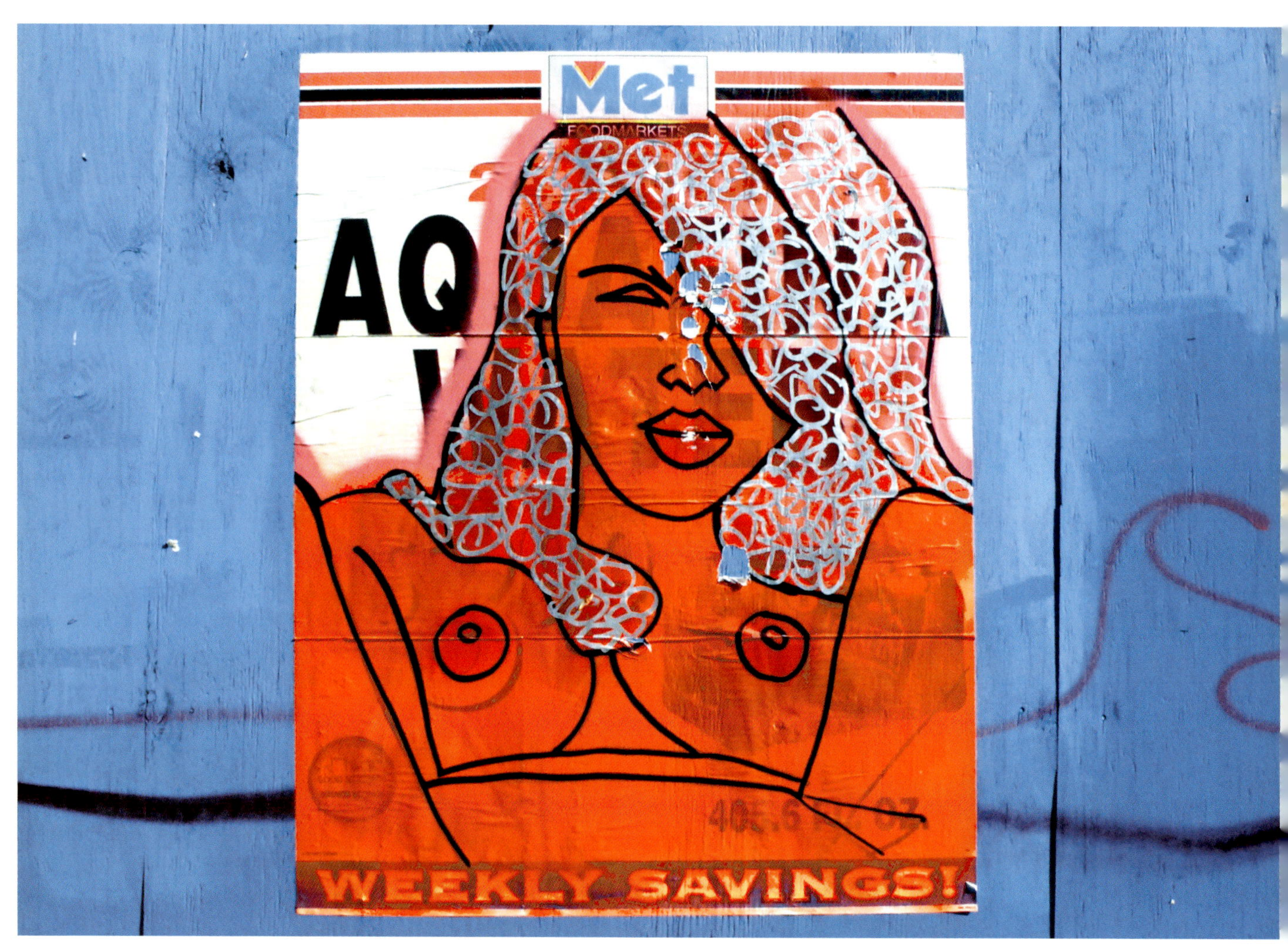
Met
FOODMARKETS
AQ
WEEKLY SAVINGS!

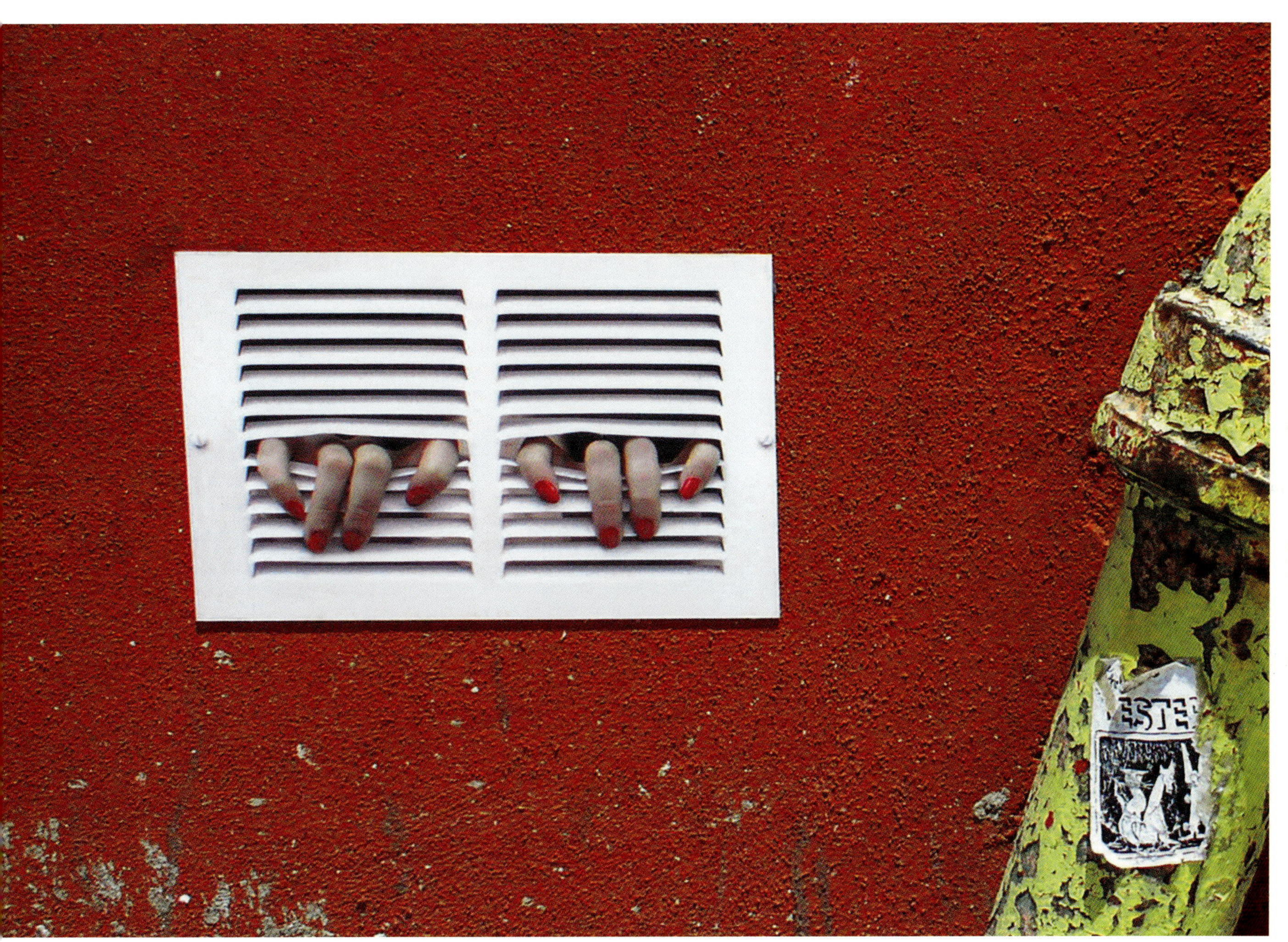

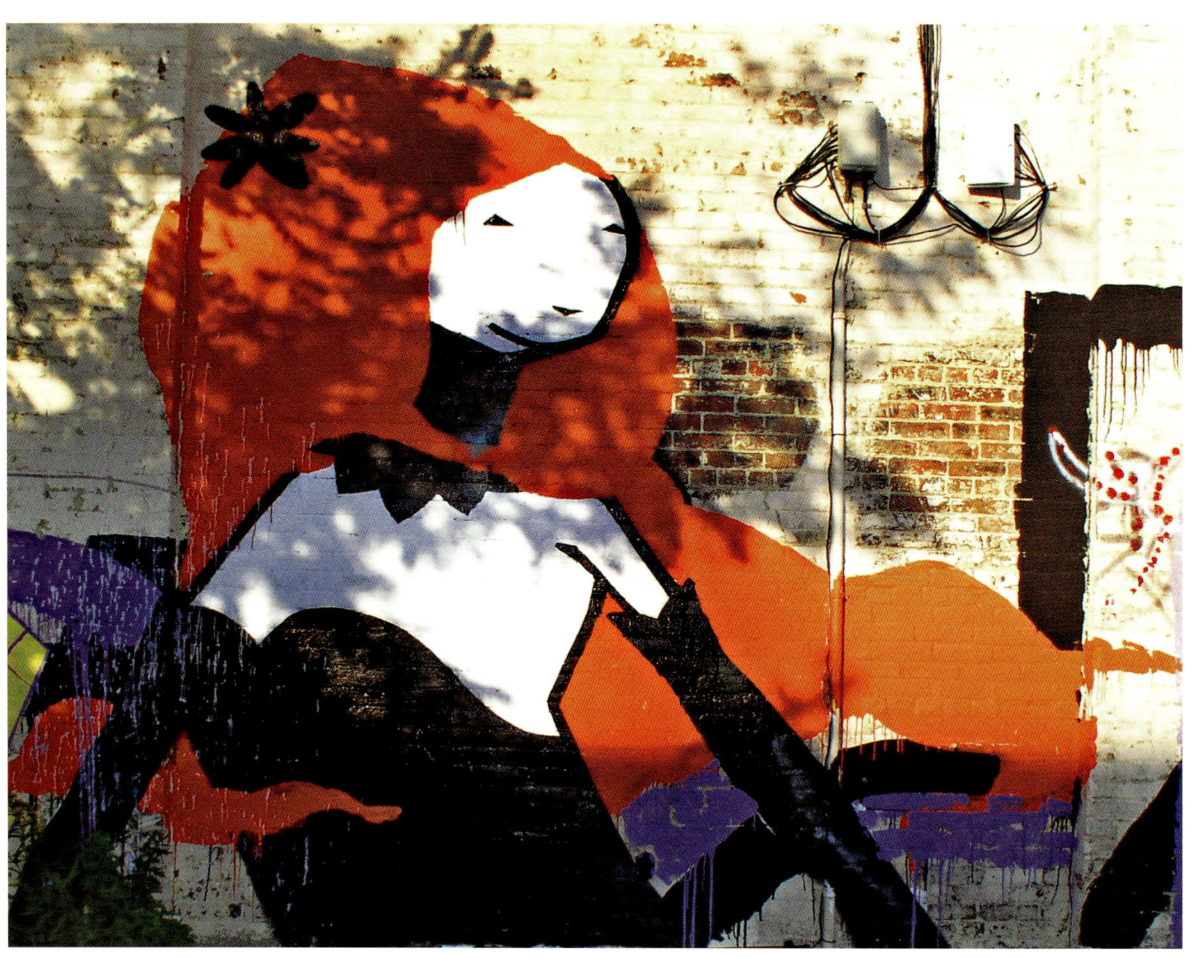

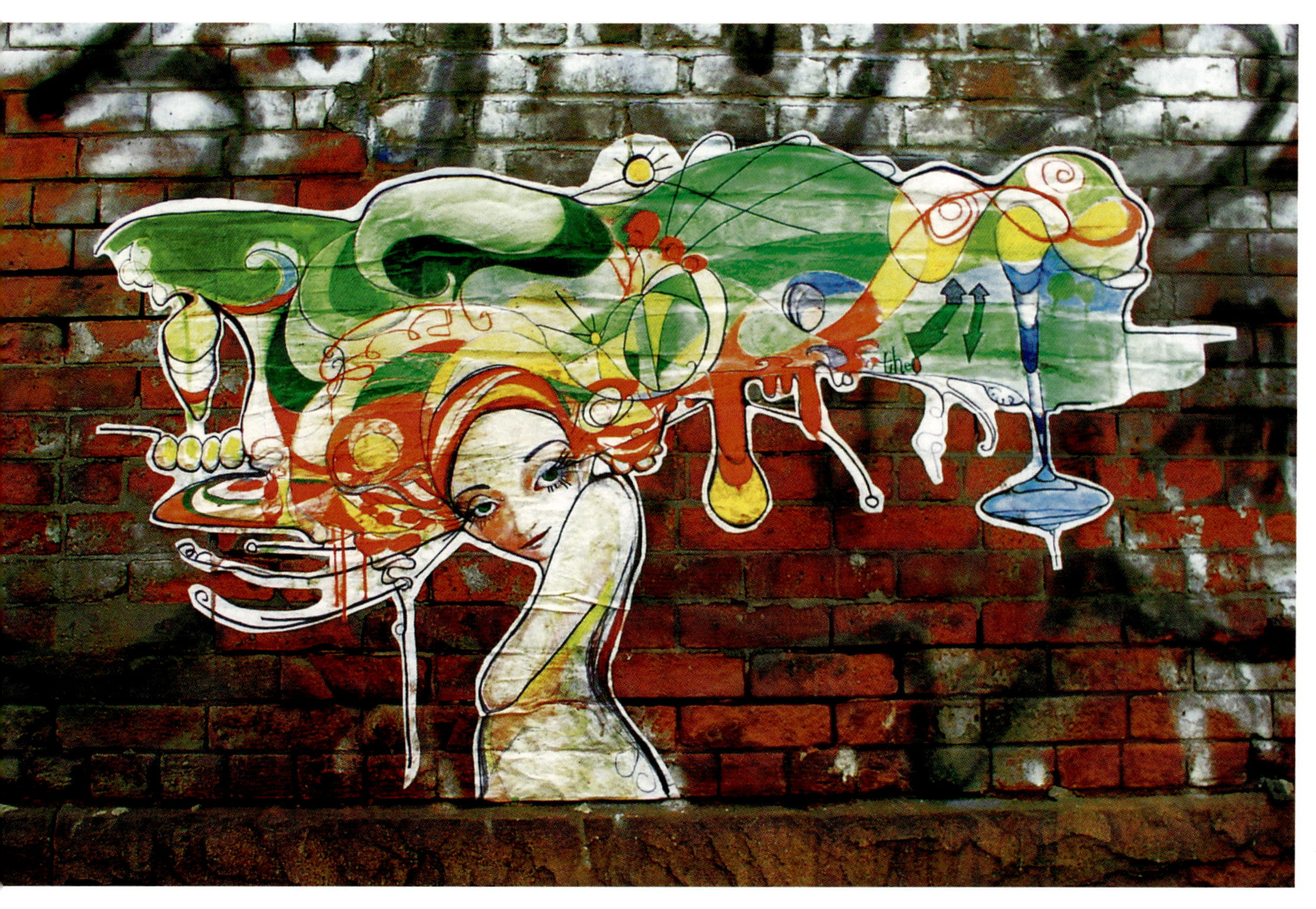
the

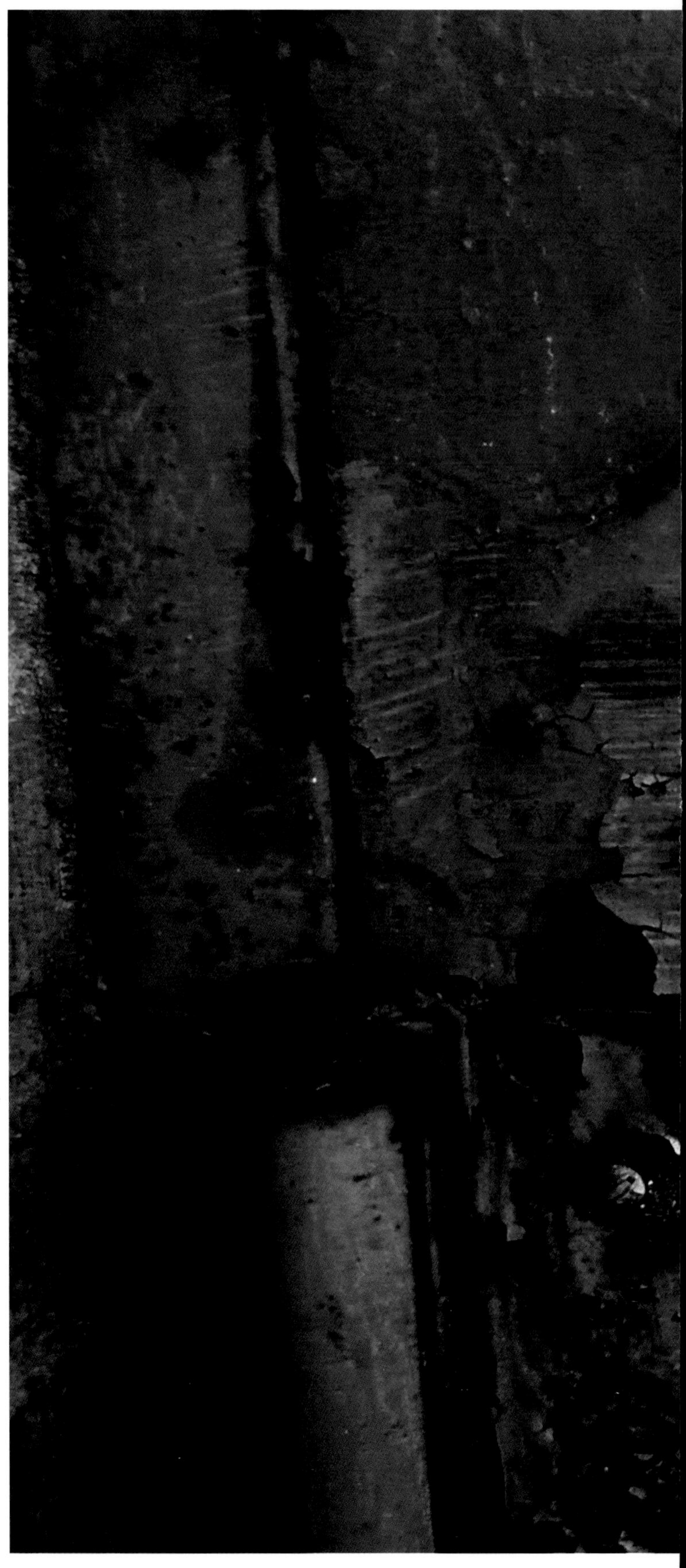

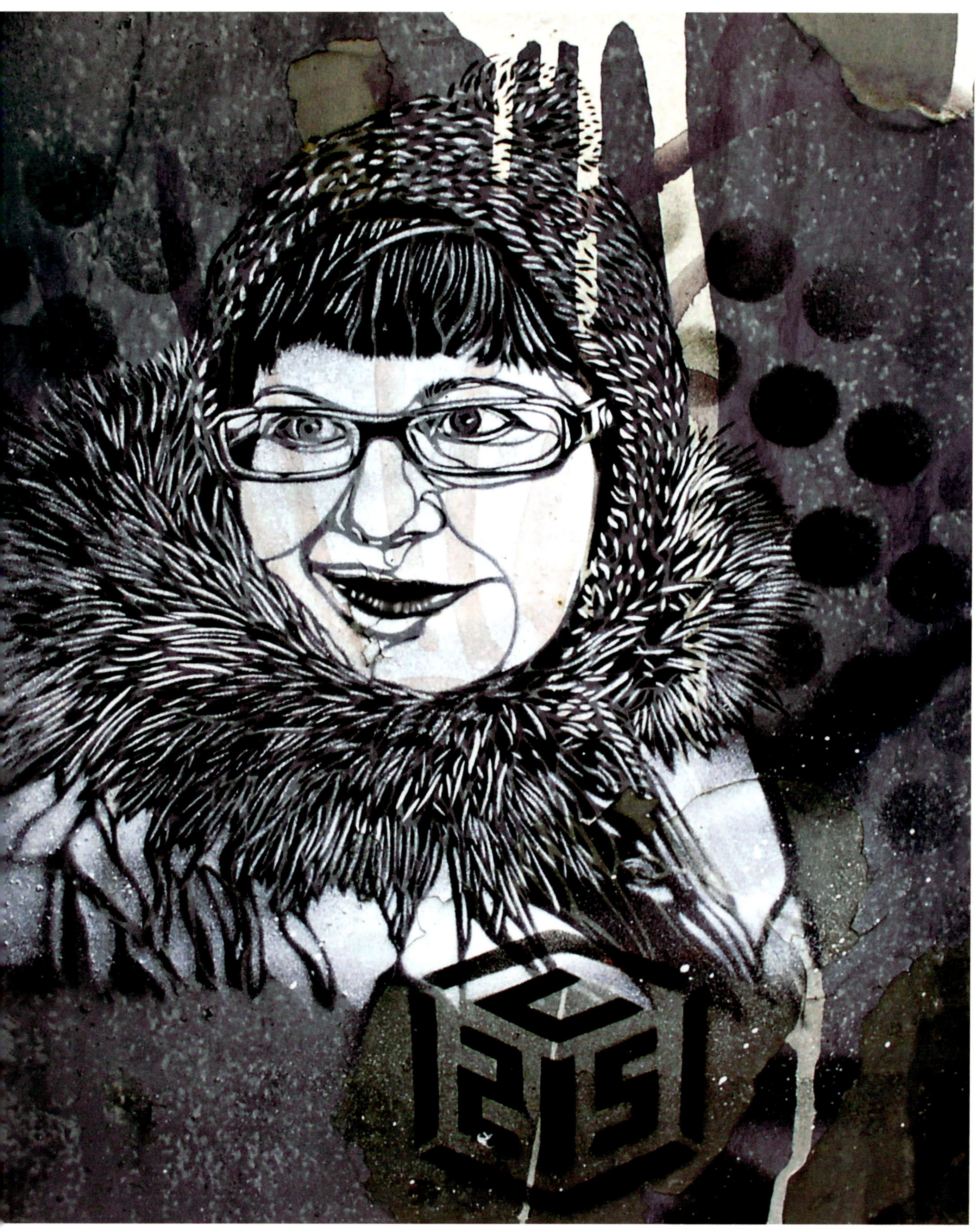
C215

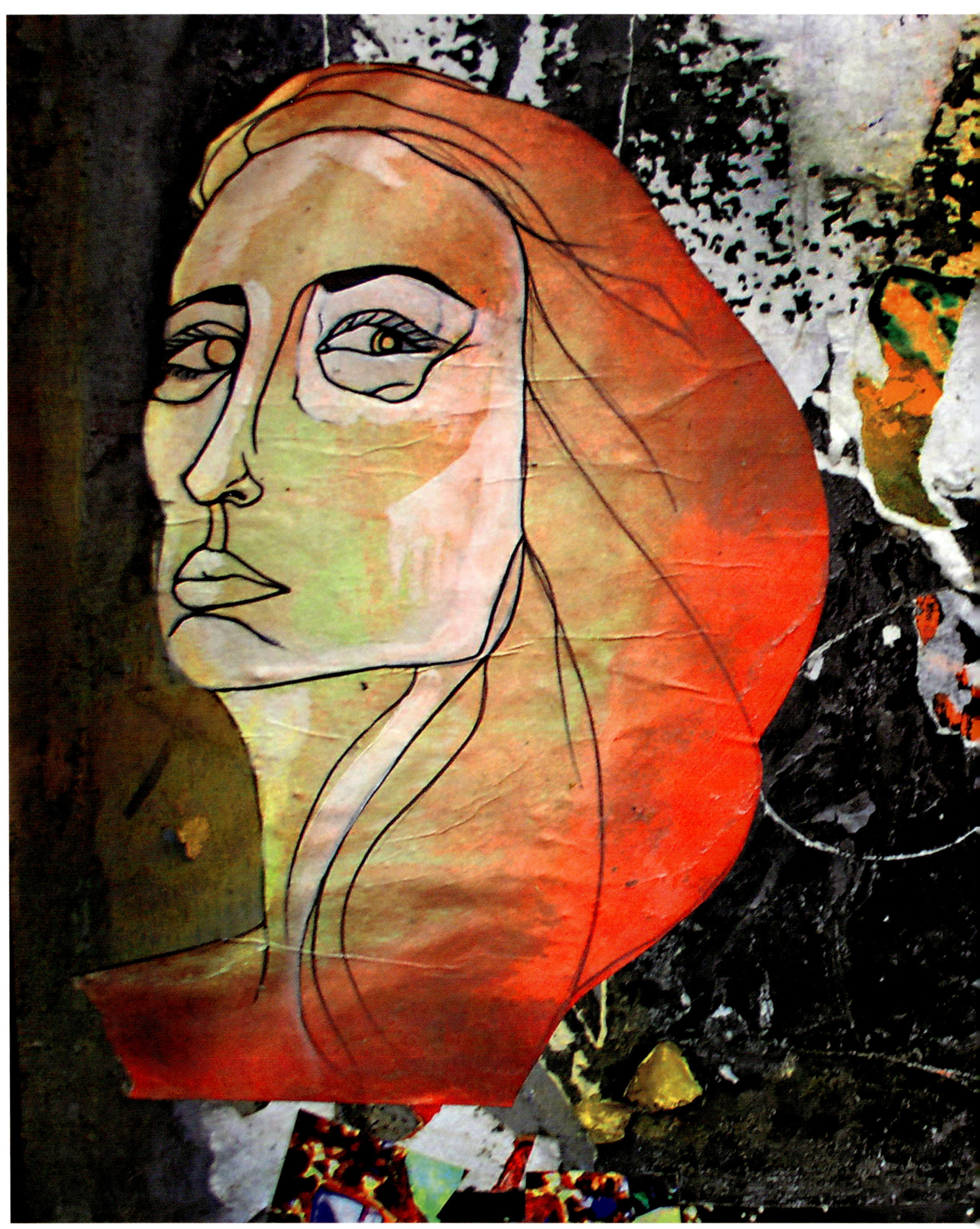

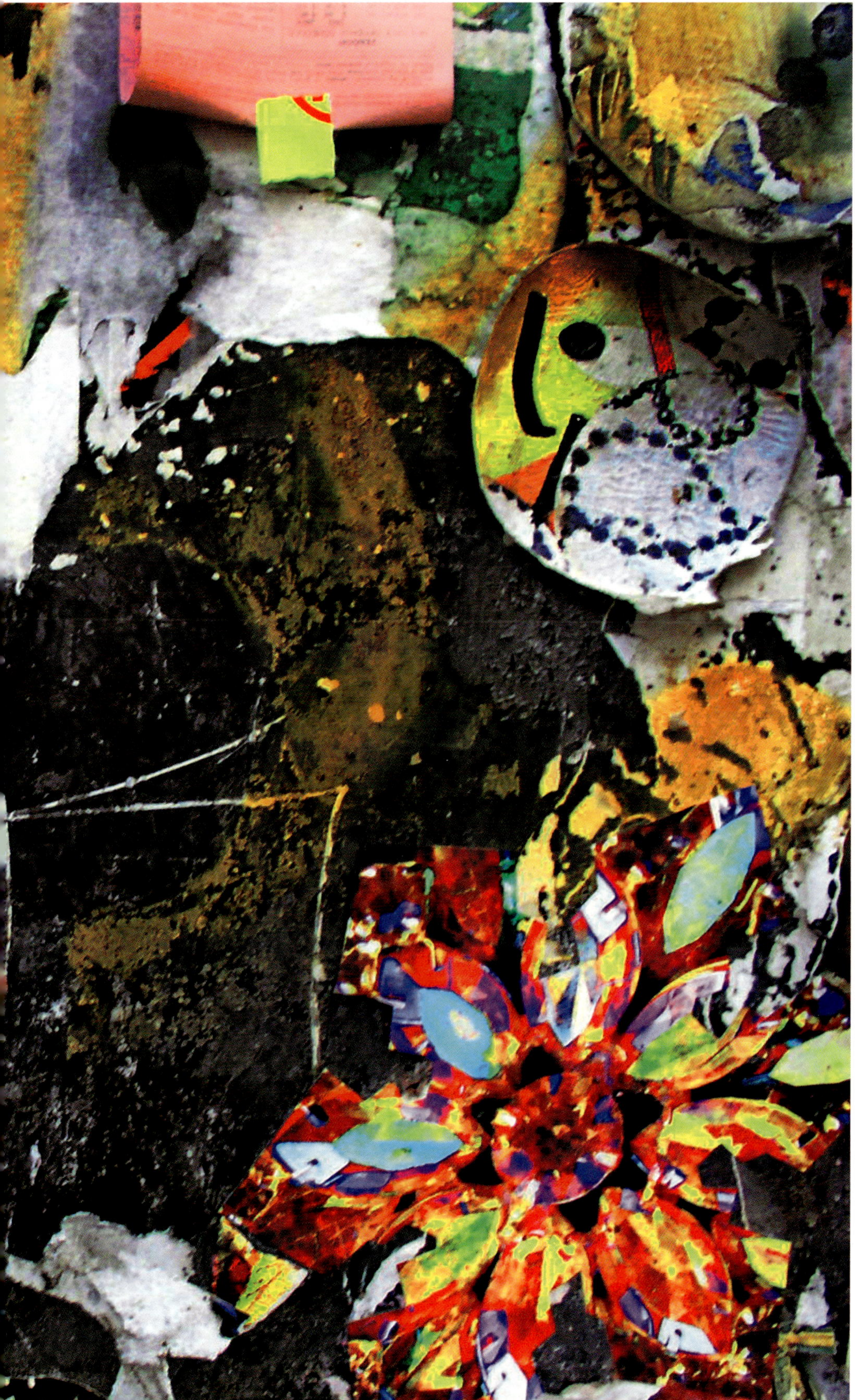

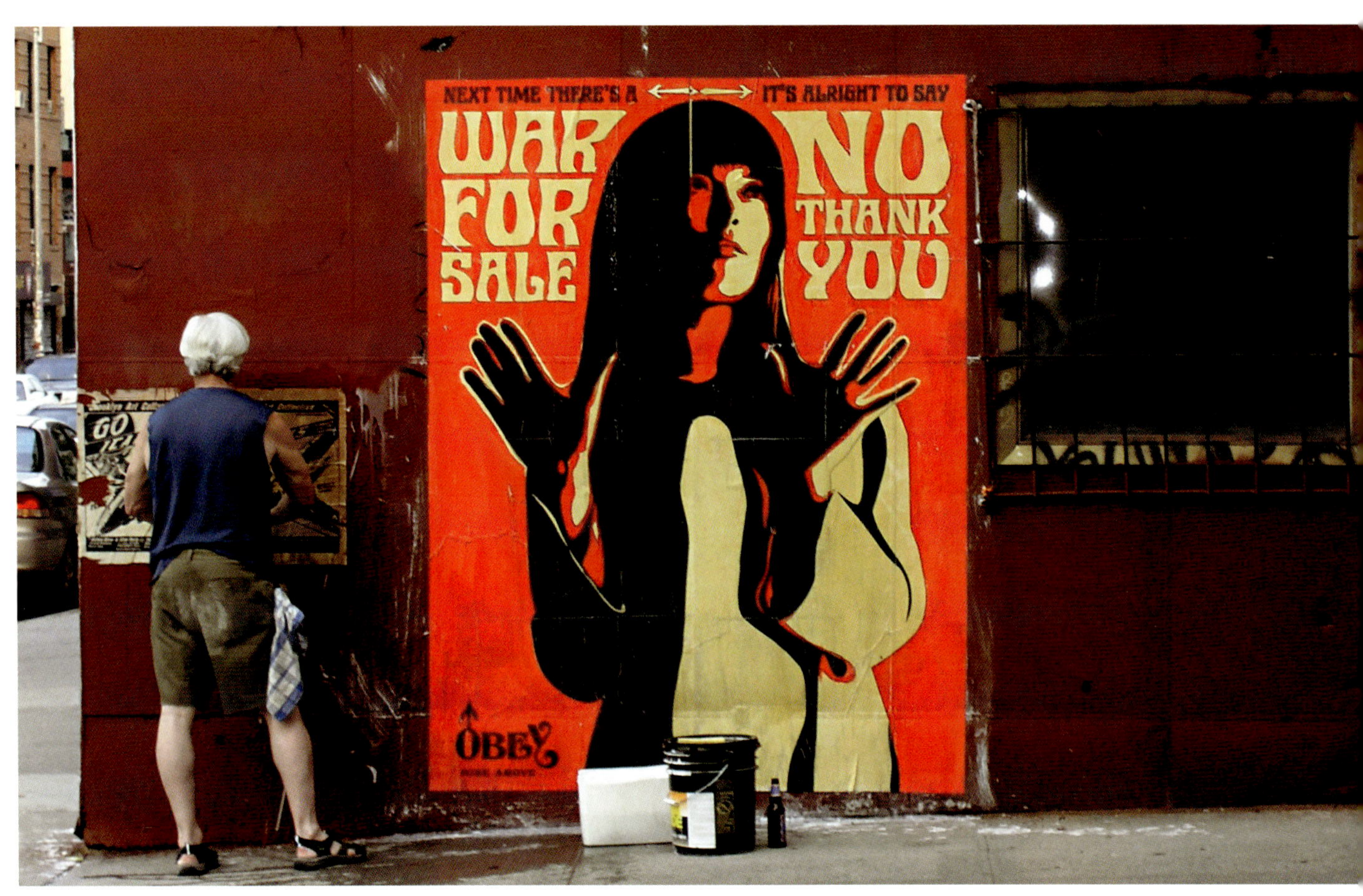
NEXT TIME THERE'S A
IT'S ALRIGHT TO SAY
WAR FOR SALE
NO THANK YOU
OBEY

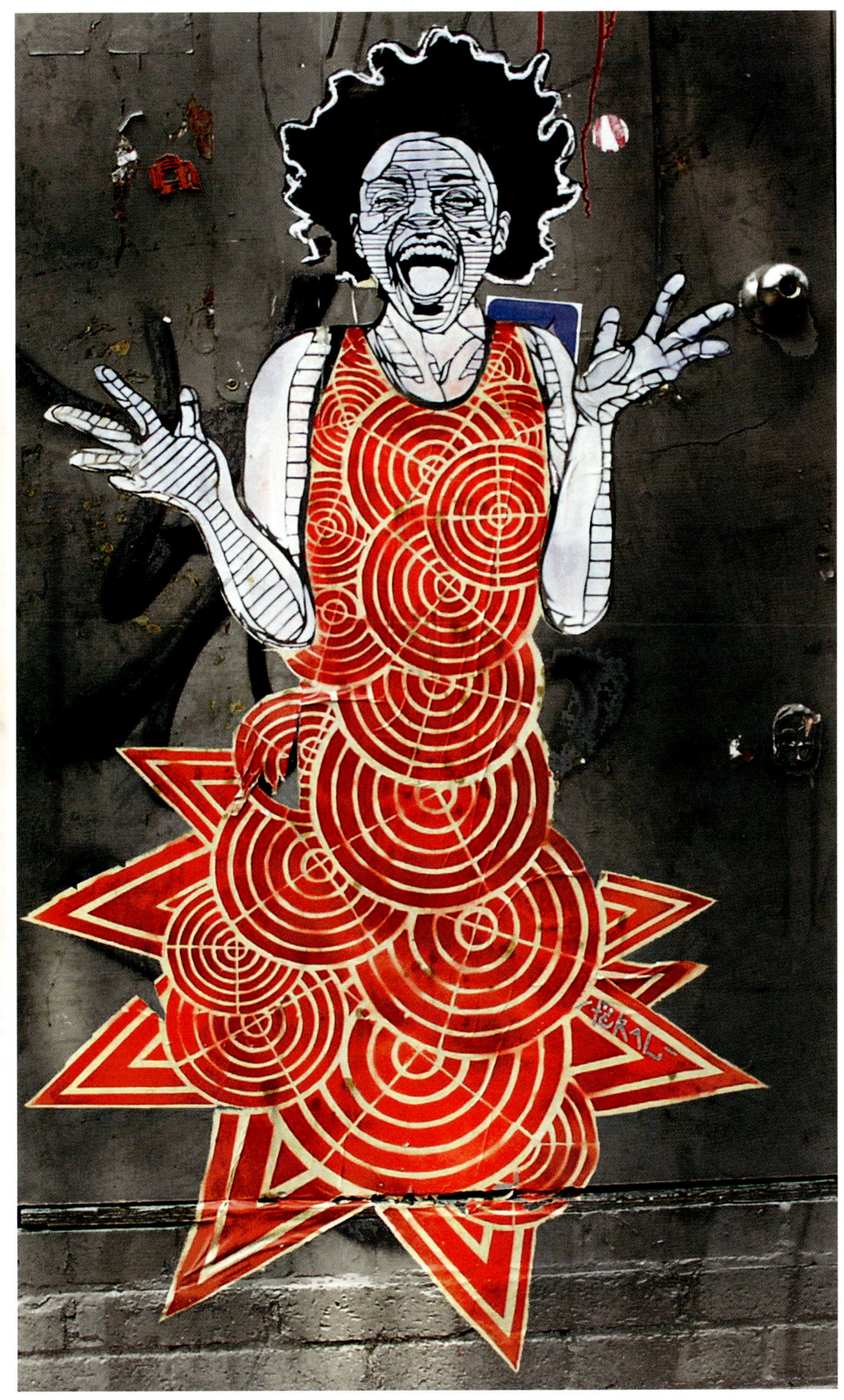

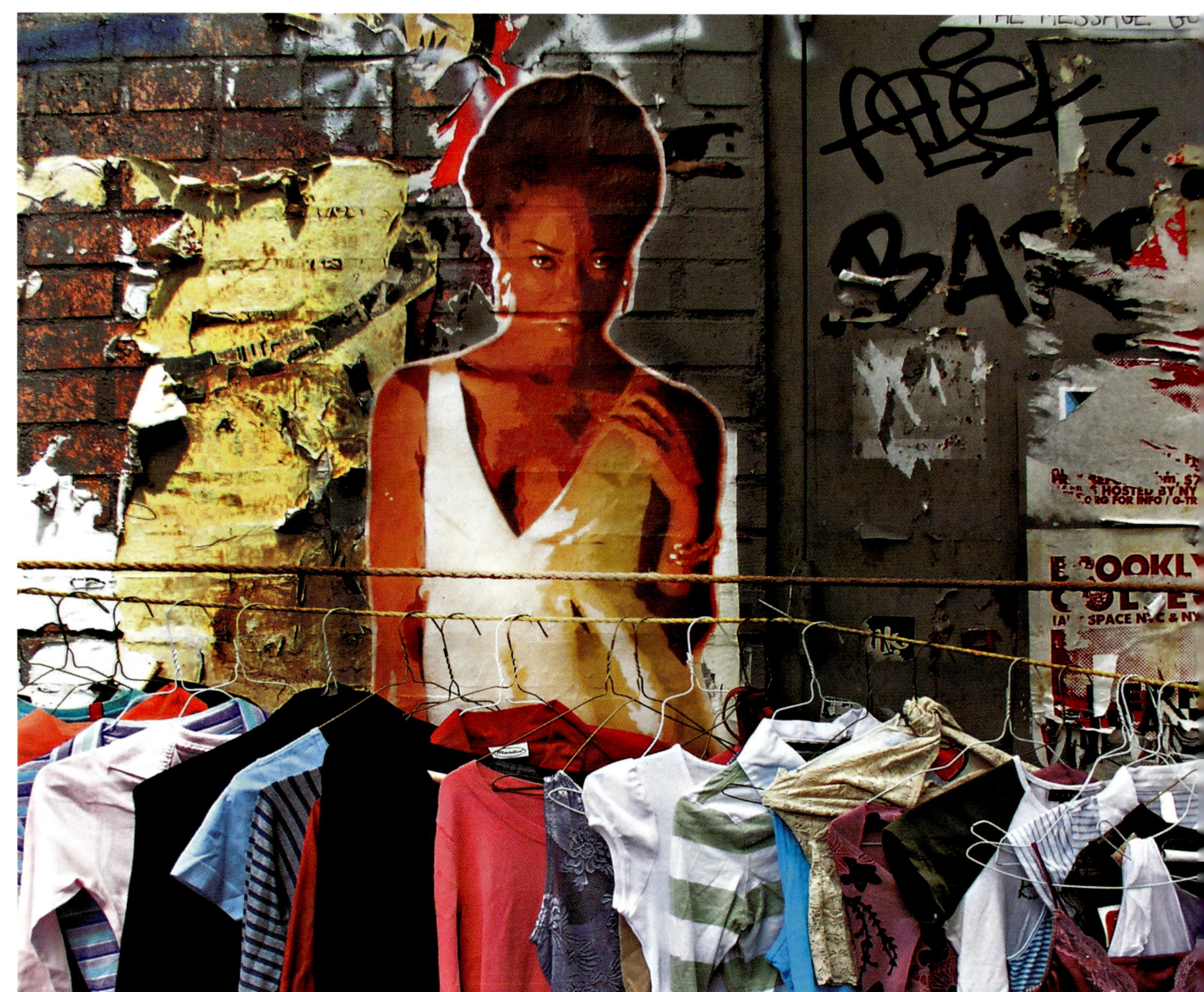

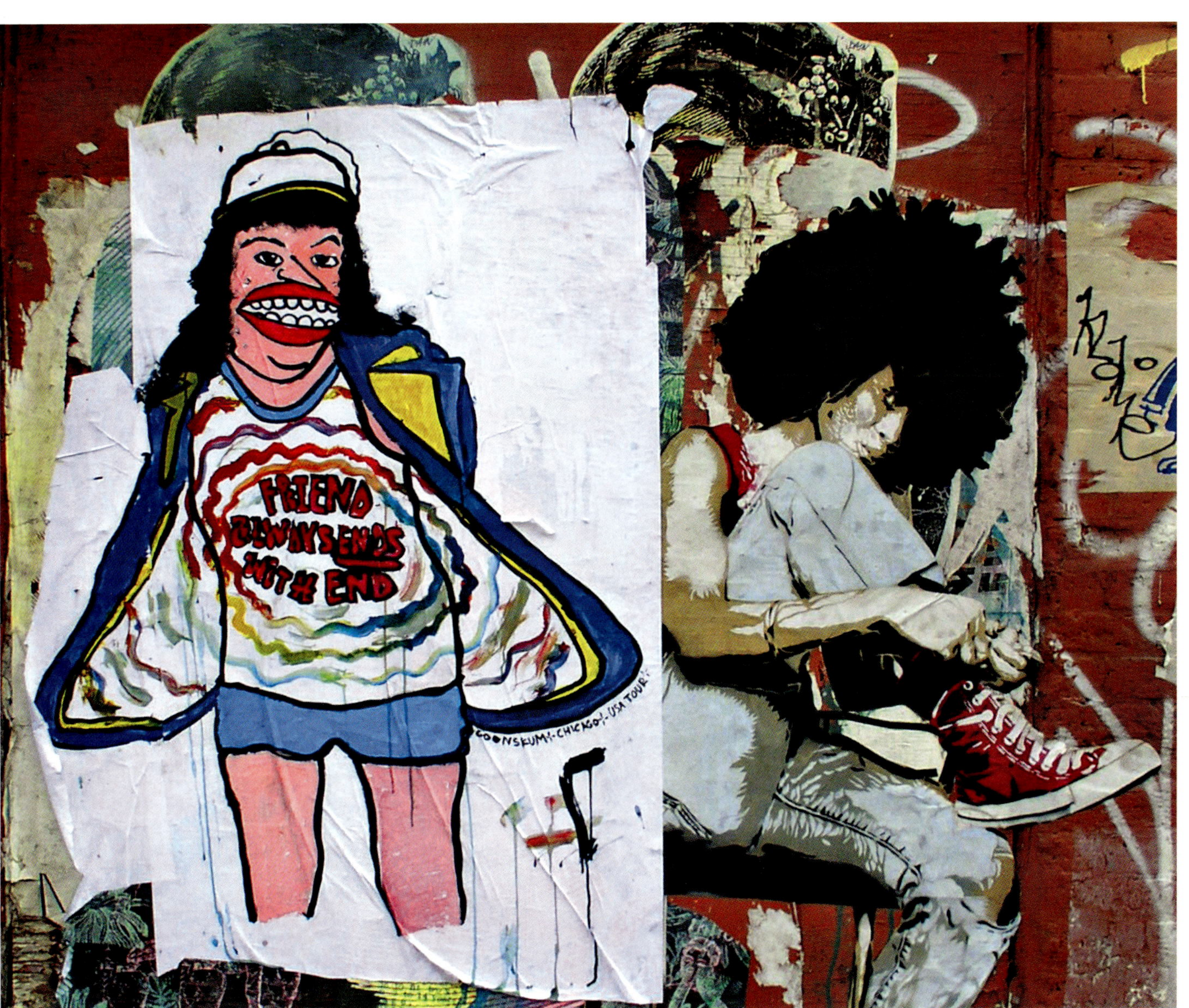
FRIEND
ALWAYS ENDS
WITH END
GOONSKUM-CHICAGO-USA TOUR

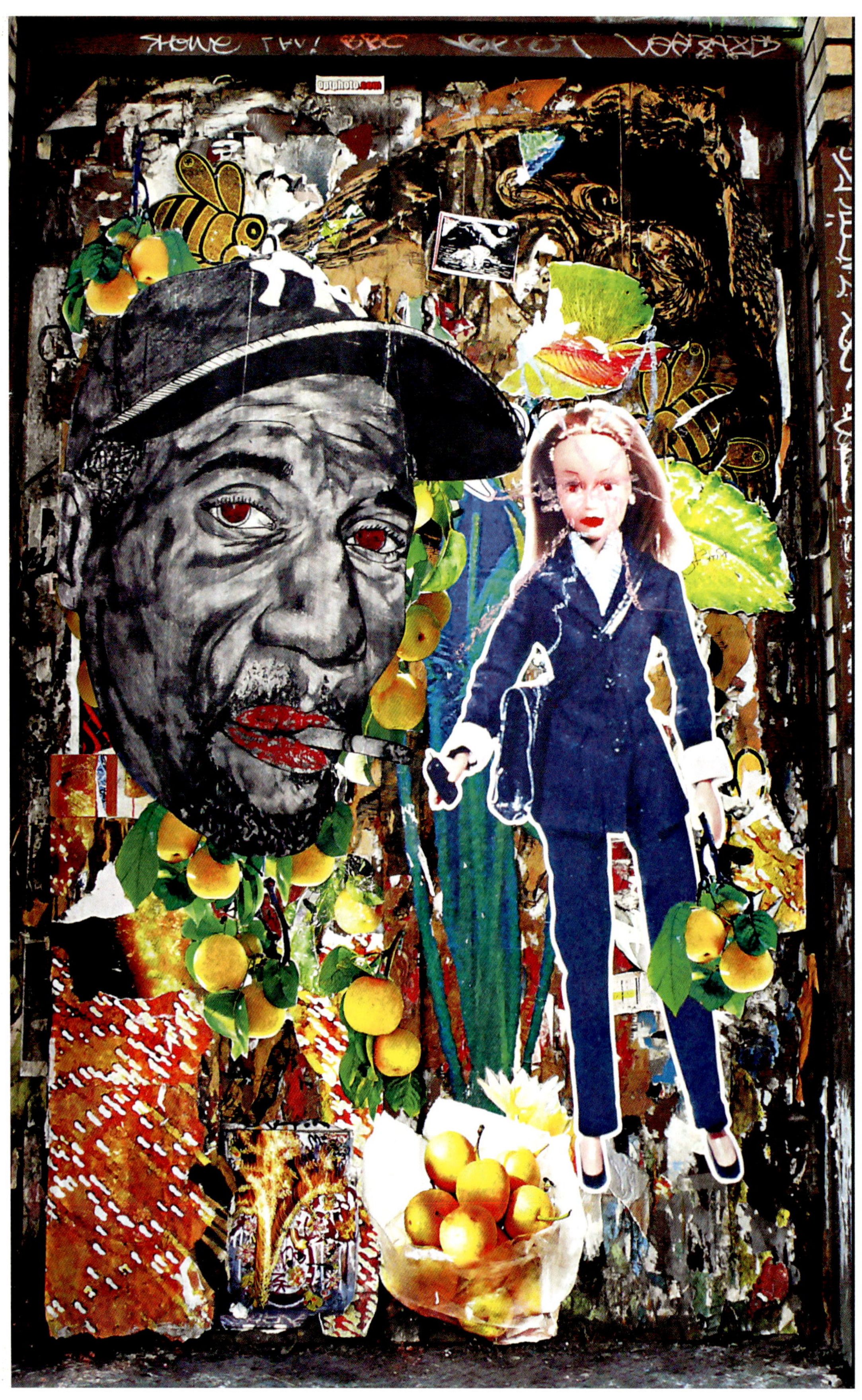

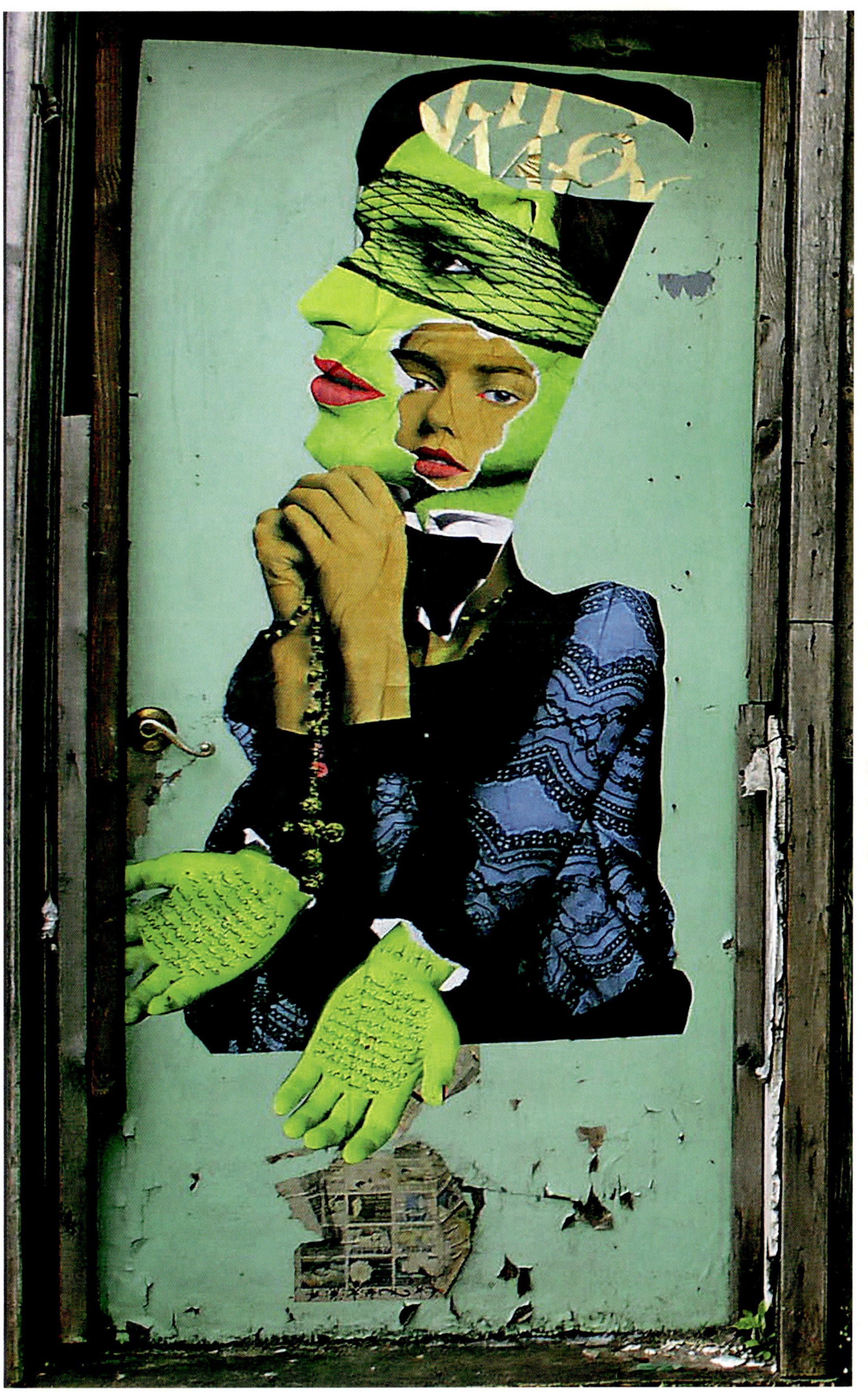

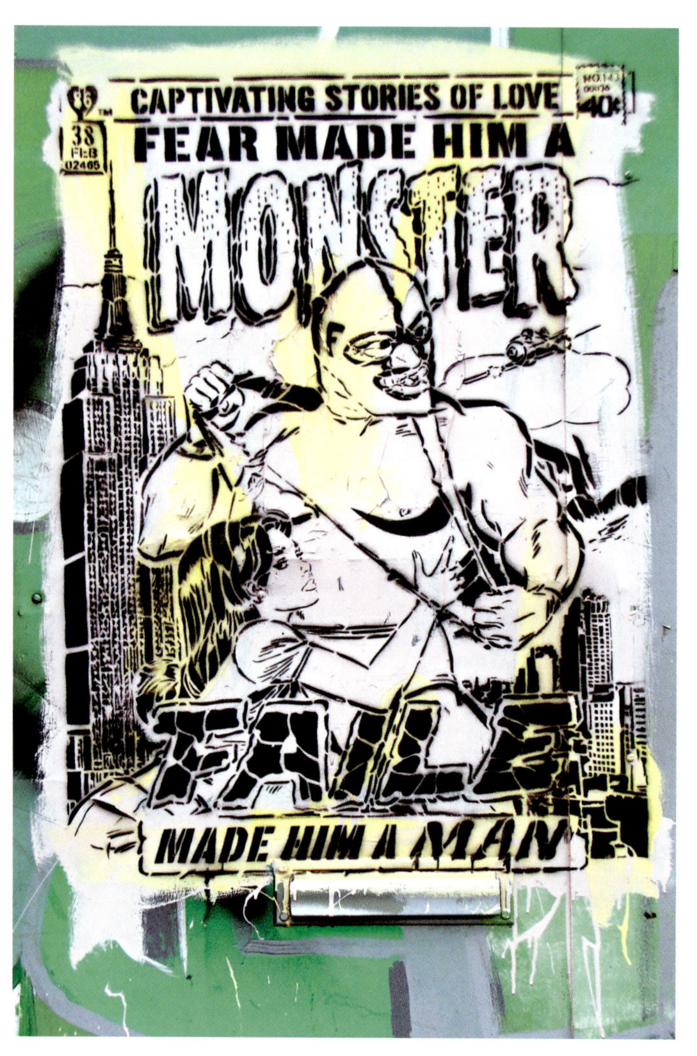
CAPTIVATING STORIES OF LOVE
38 FEB 02465
40¢
FEAR MADE HIM A
MONSTER
FAILE
MADE HIM A MAN

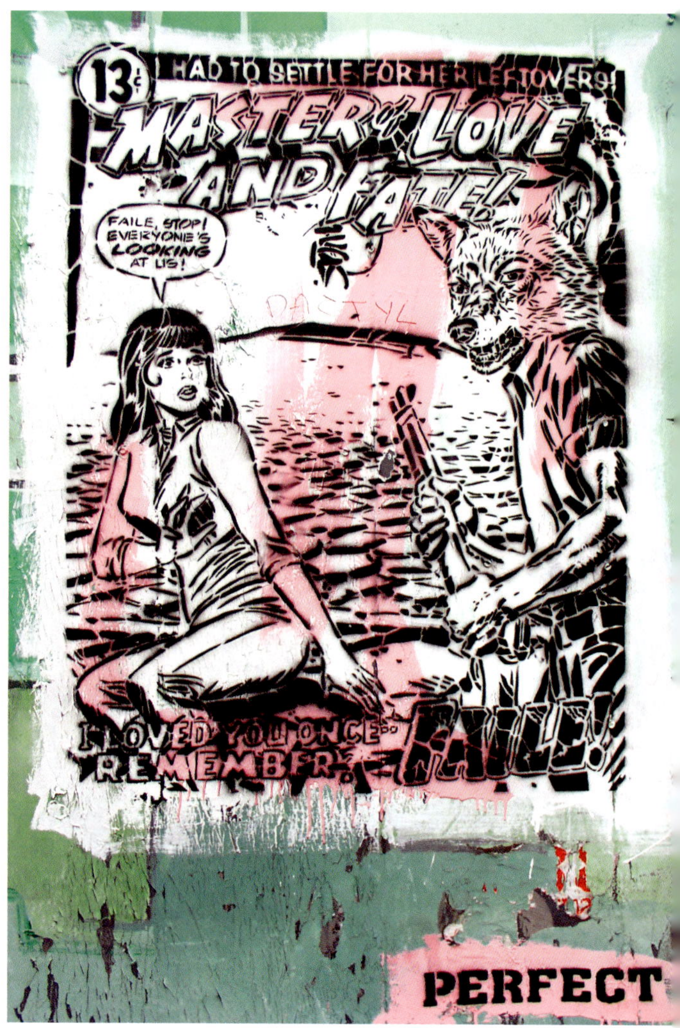
13¢
HAD TO SETTLE FOR HER LEFTOVERS
MASTER of LOVE AND FATE
FAILE, STOP! EVERYONE'S LOOKING AT US!
I LOVED YOU ONCE...
REMEMBER...
FAILE!
PERFECT

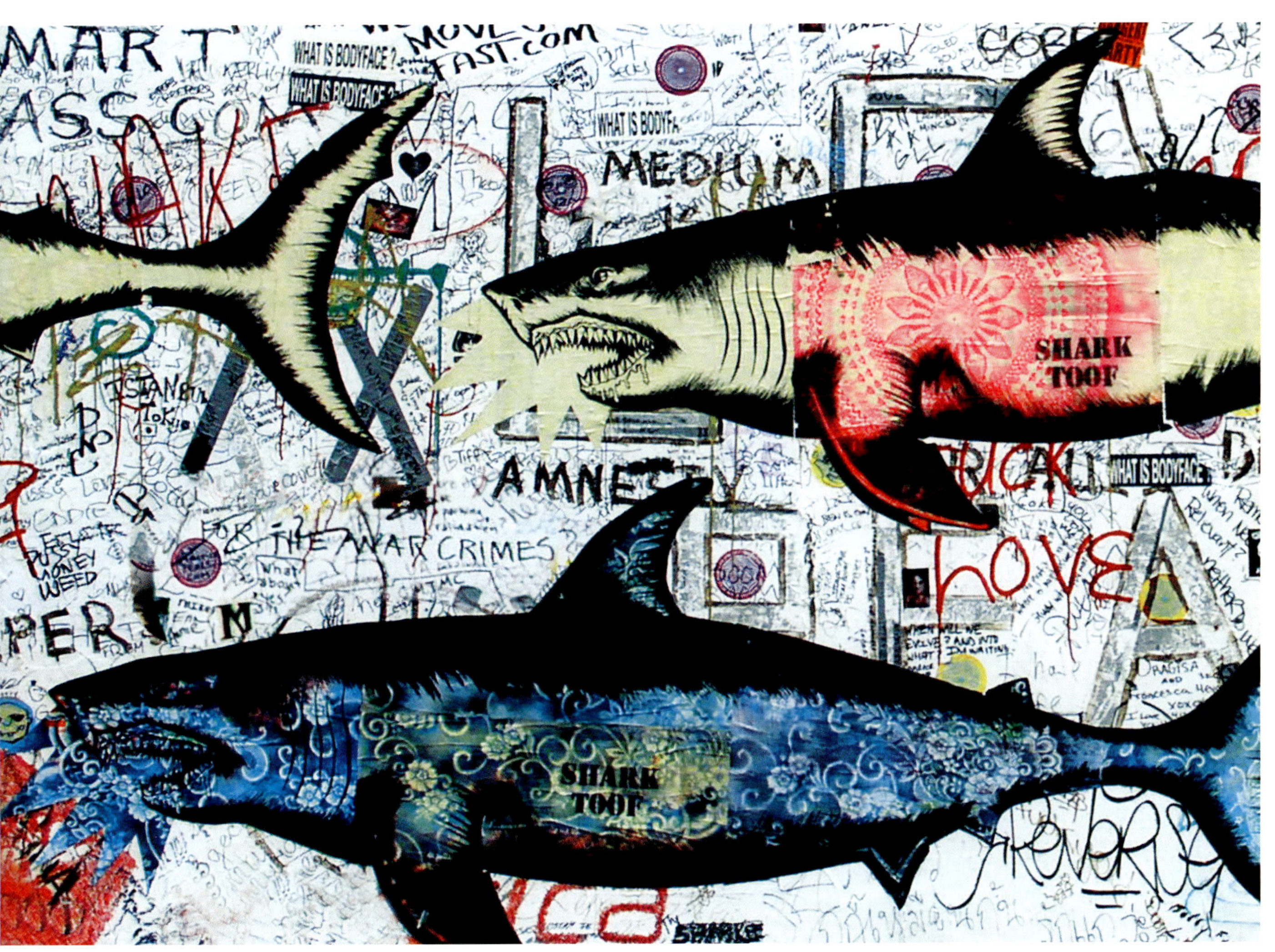
WHAT IS BODYFACE ?
FAST.COM
MEDIUM
SHARK TOOF
FOR THE WAR CRIMES
Love
WHAT IS BODYFACE
SHARK TOOF

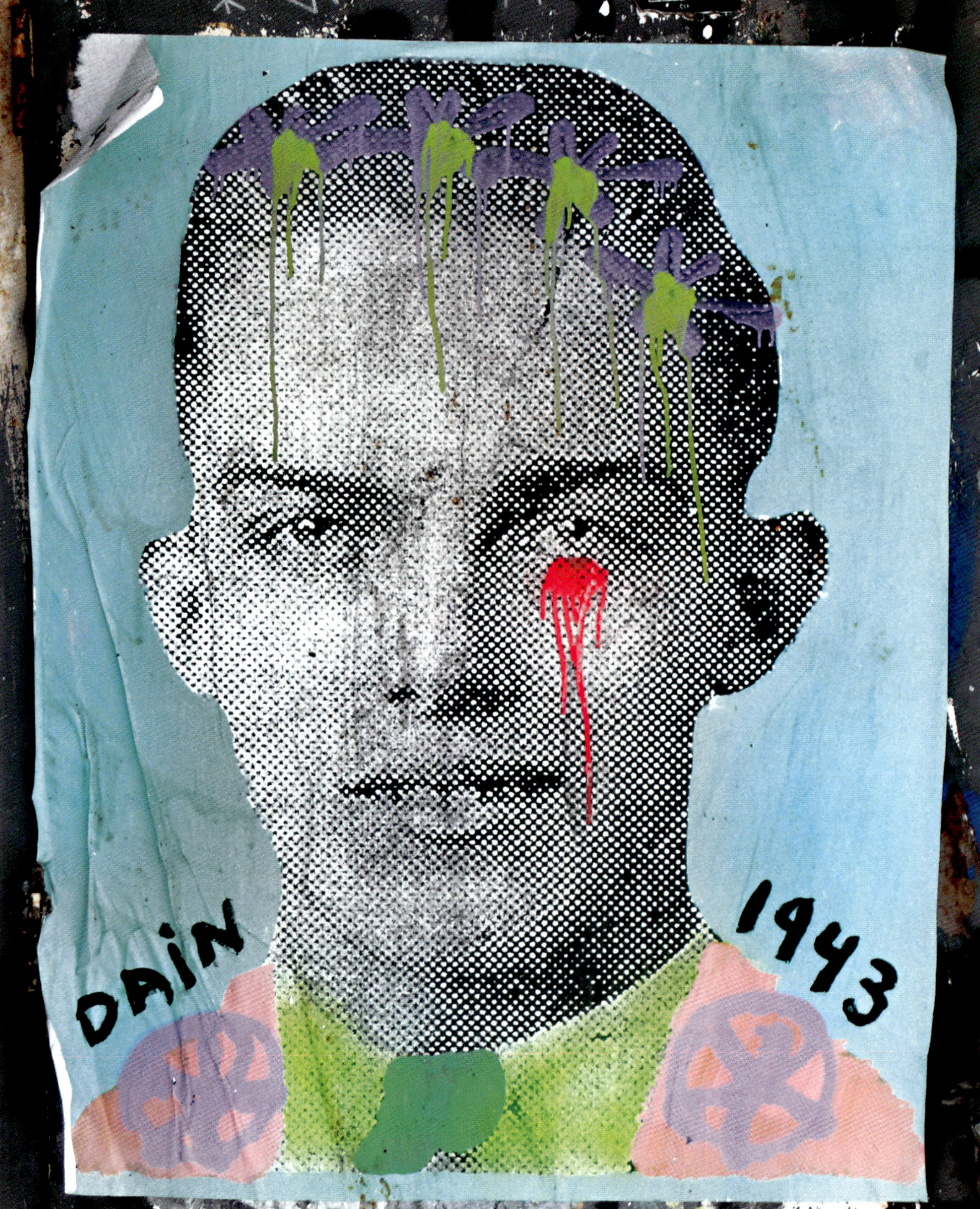
DAIN
1943

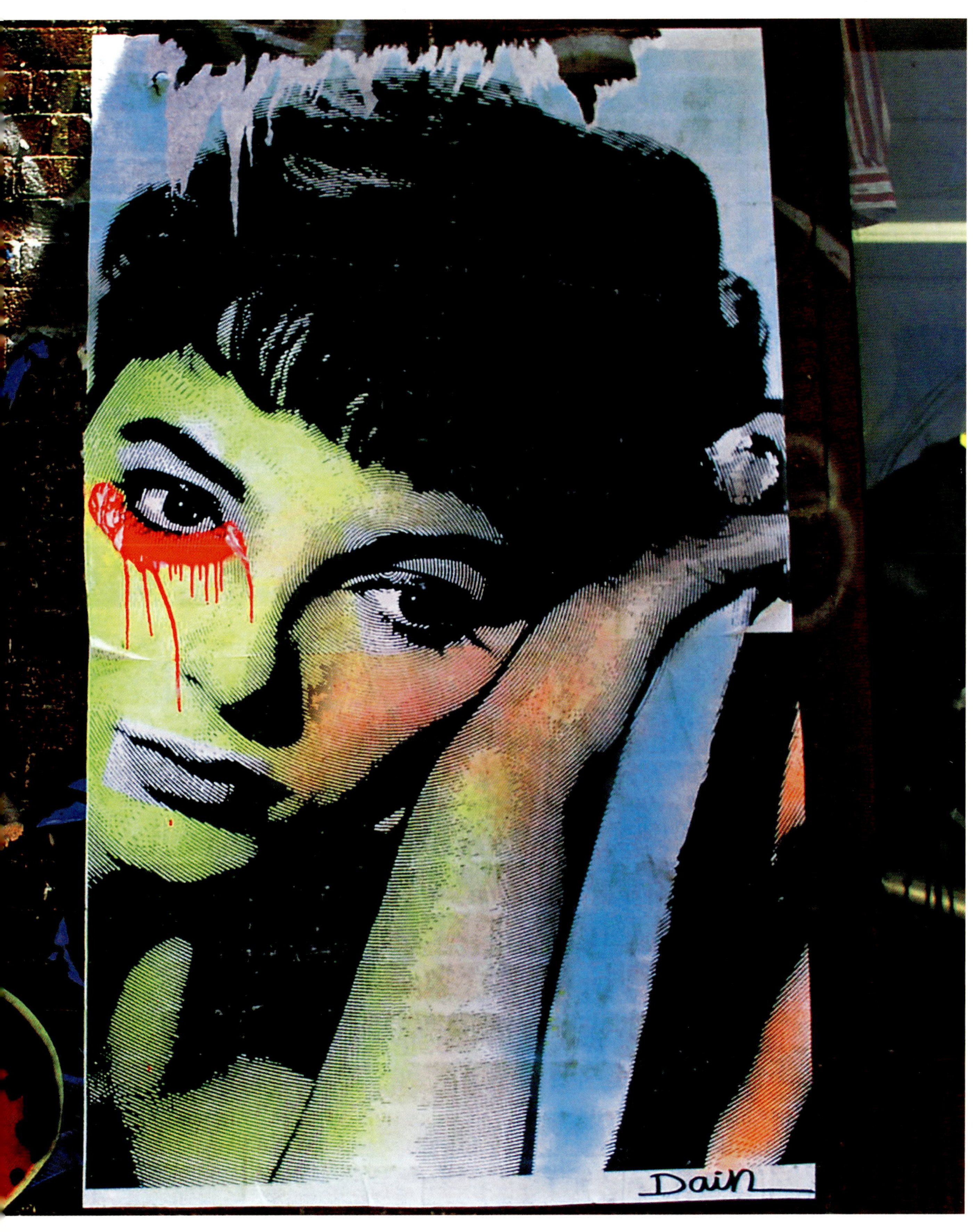
Dain

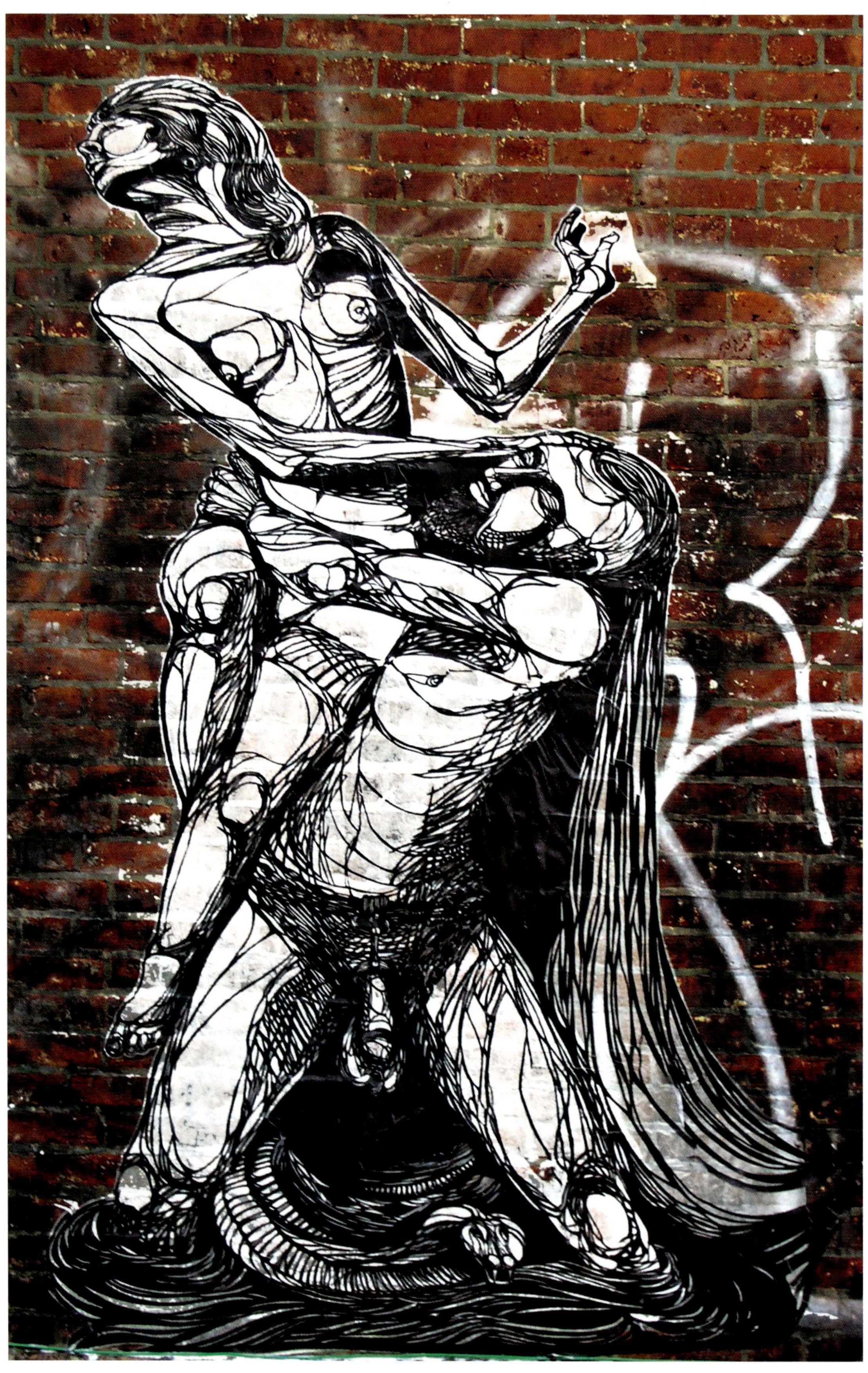

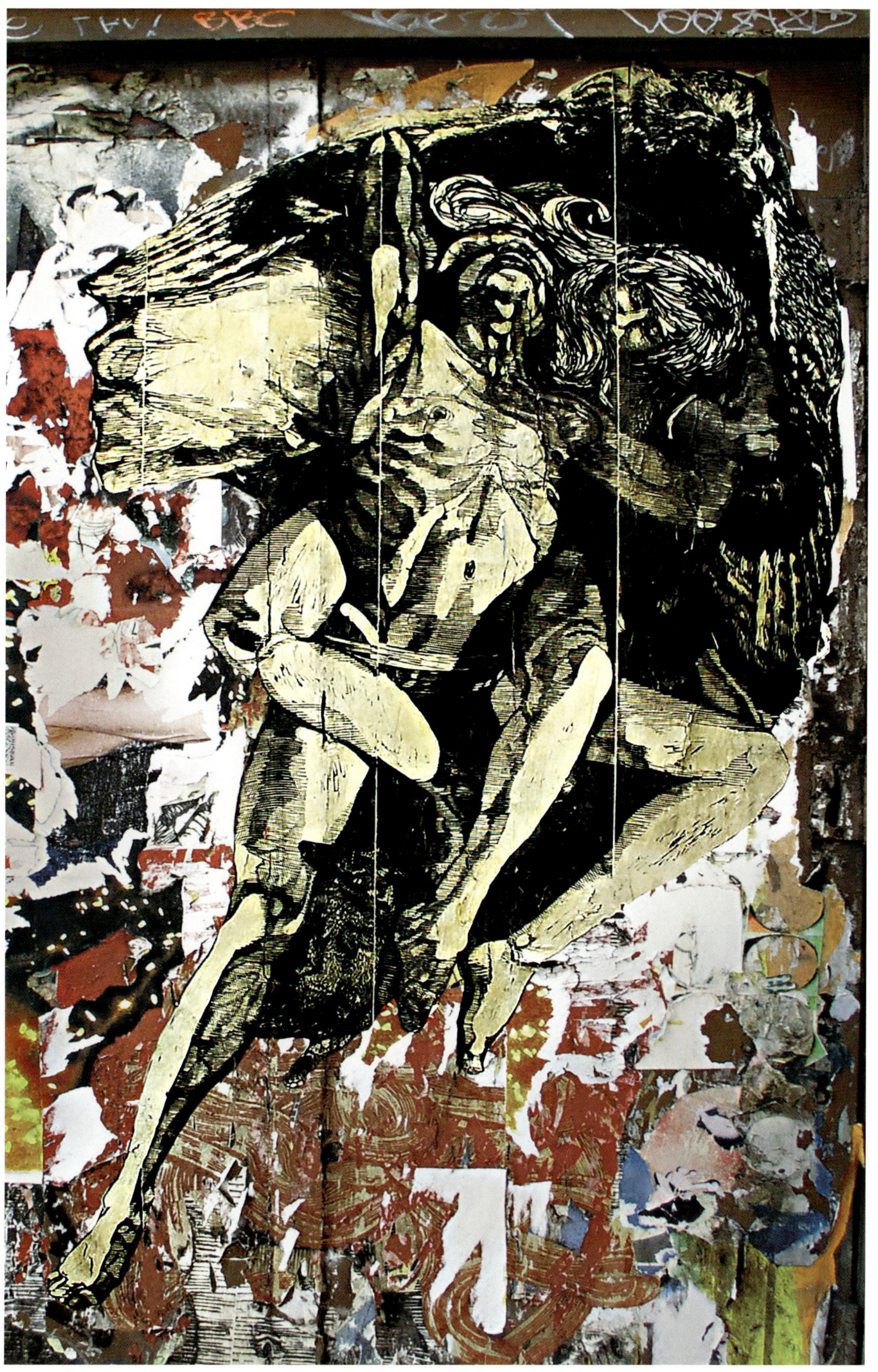

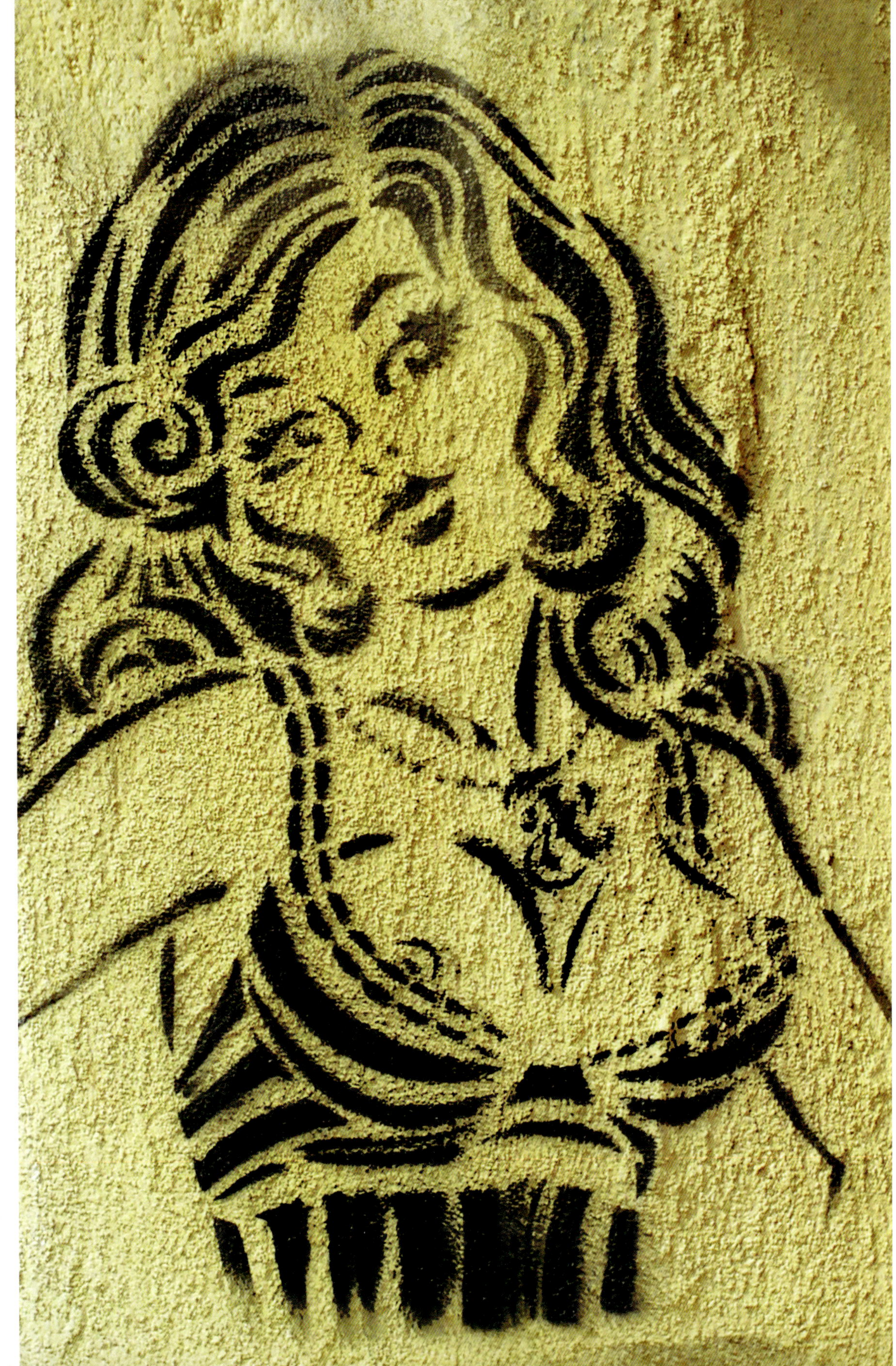

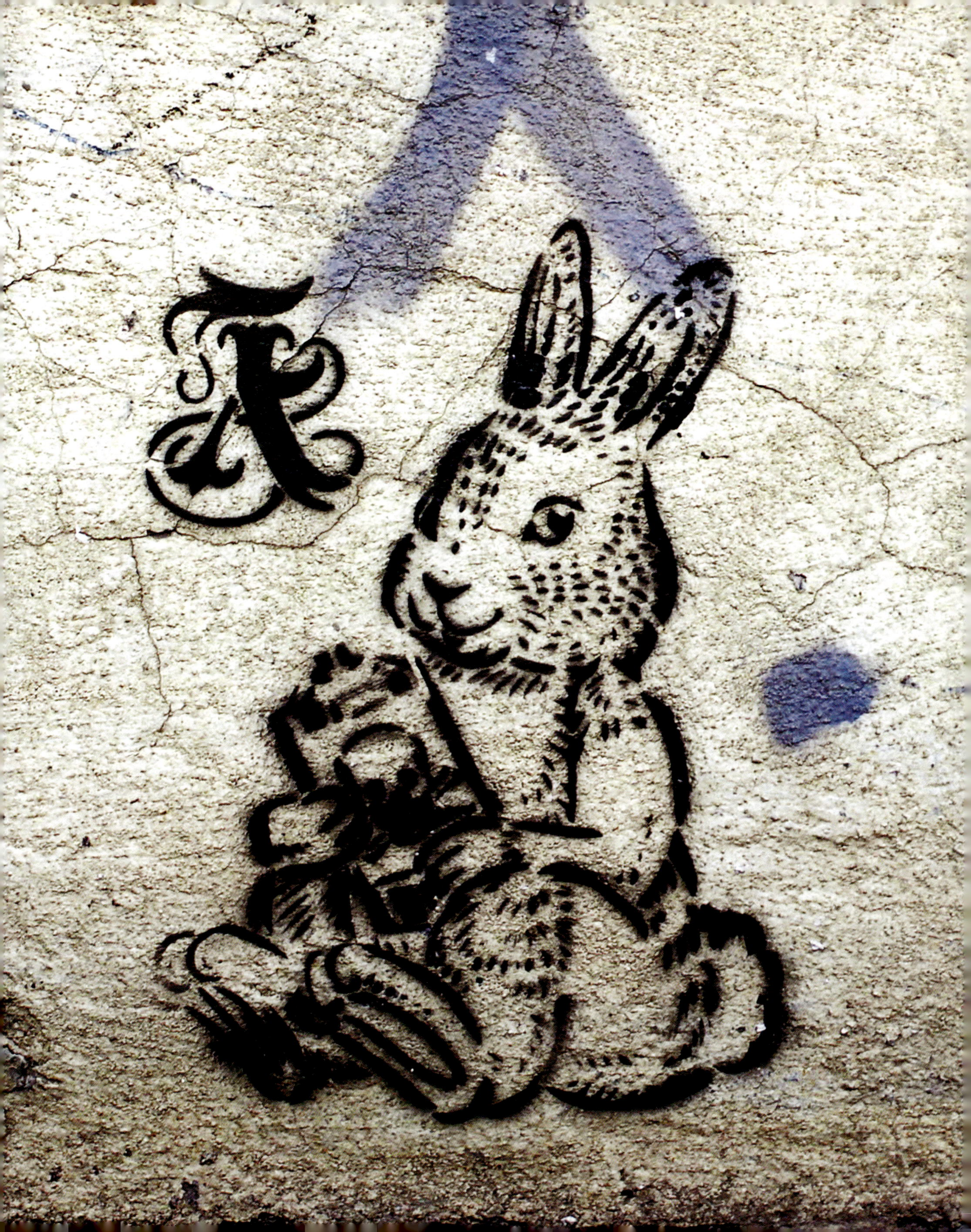

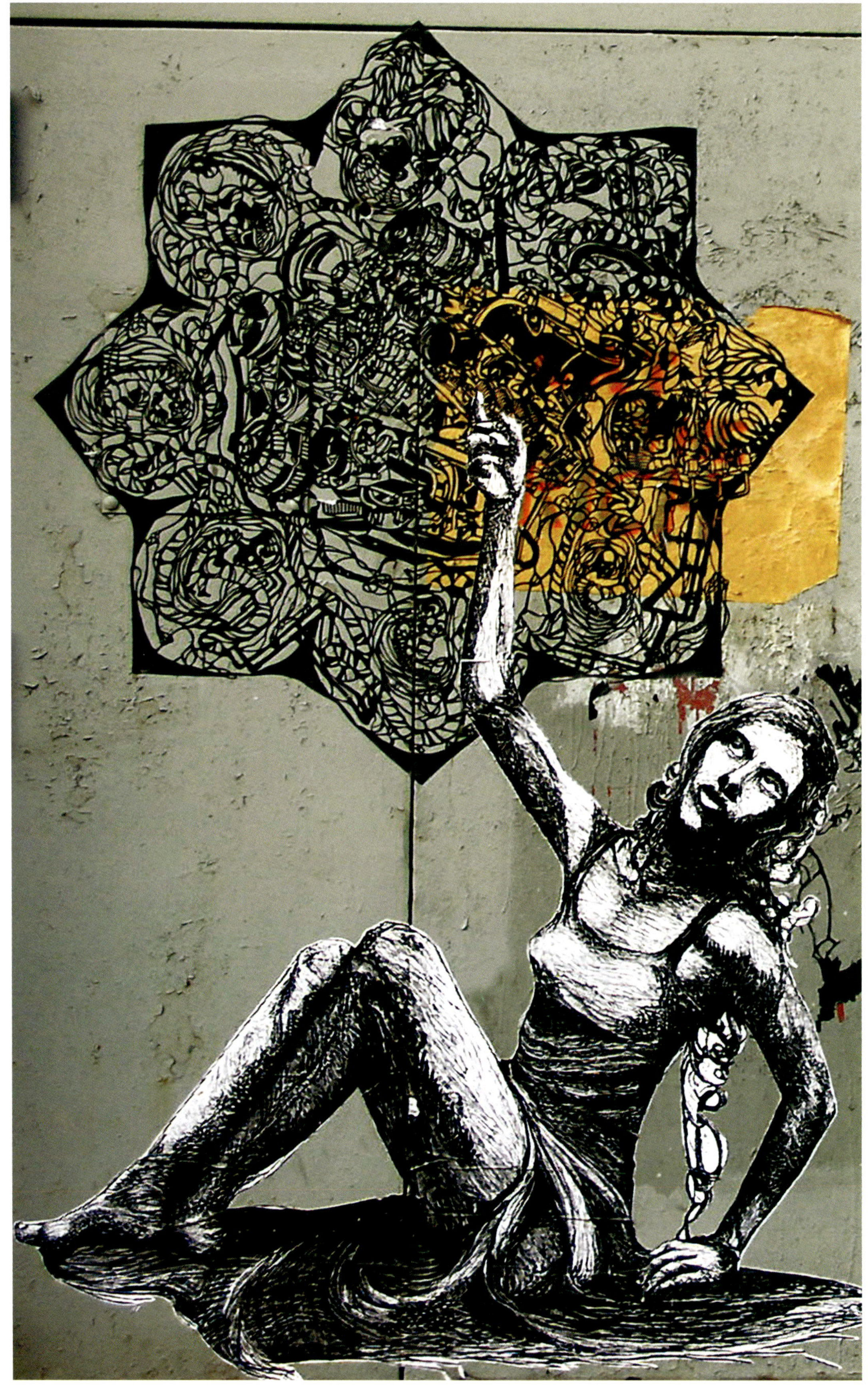

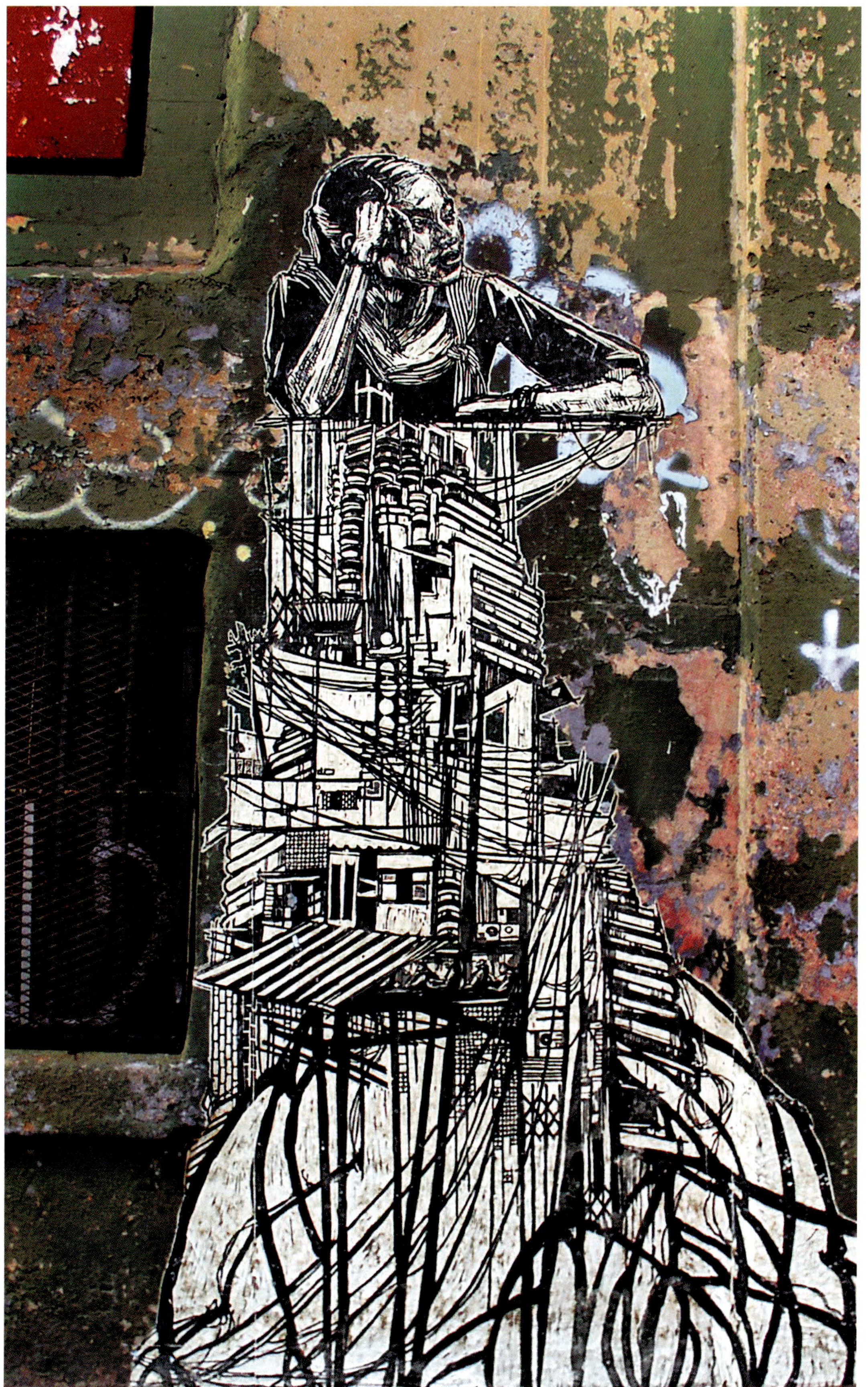

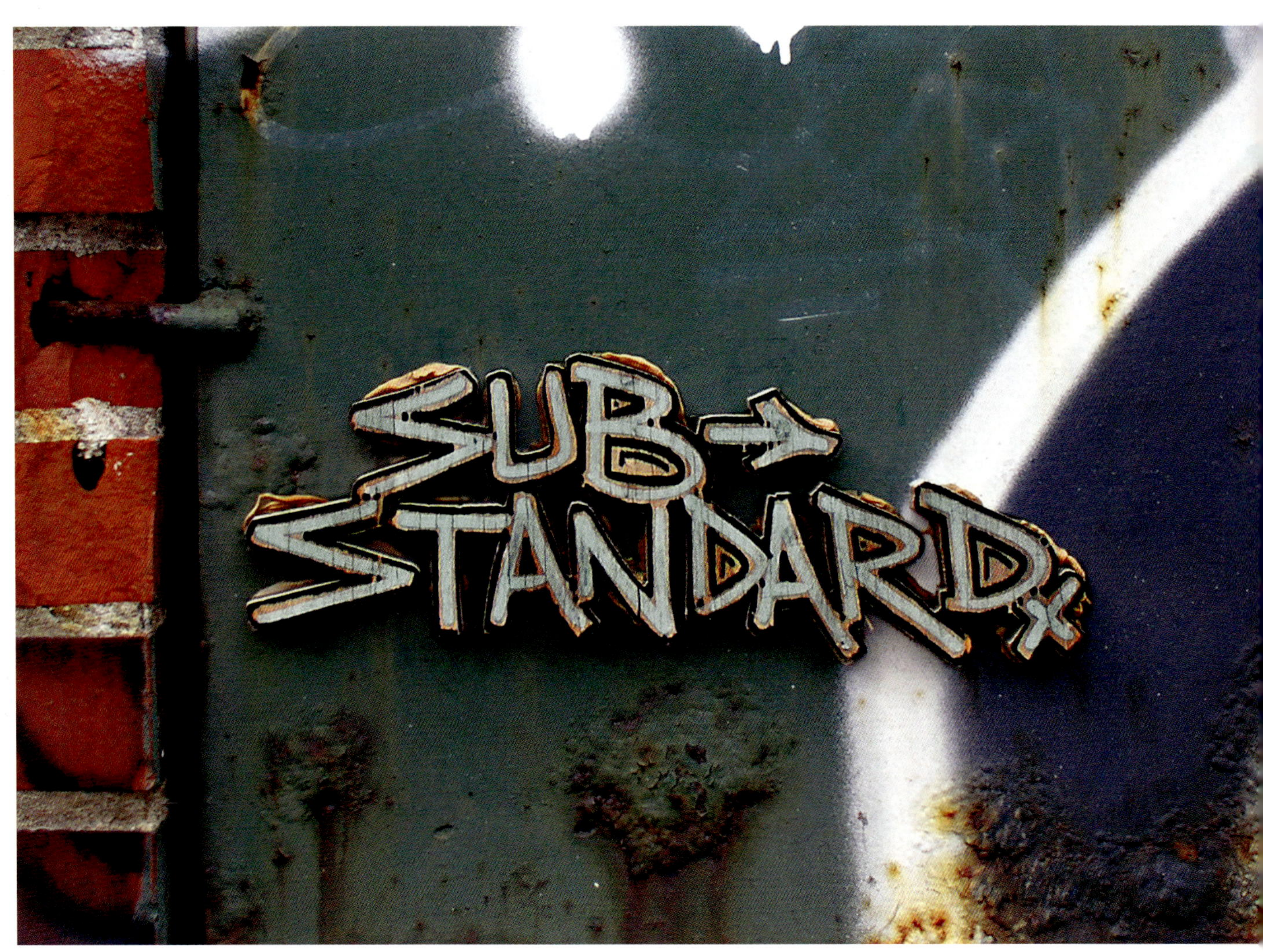
SUB-
STANDARD

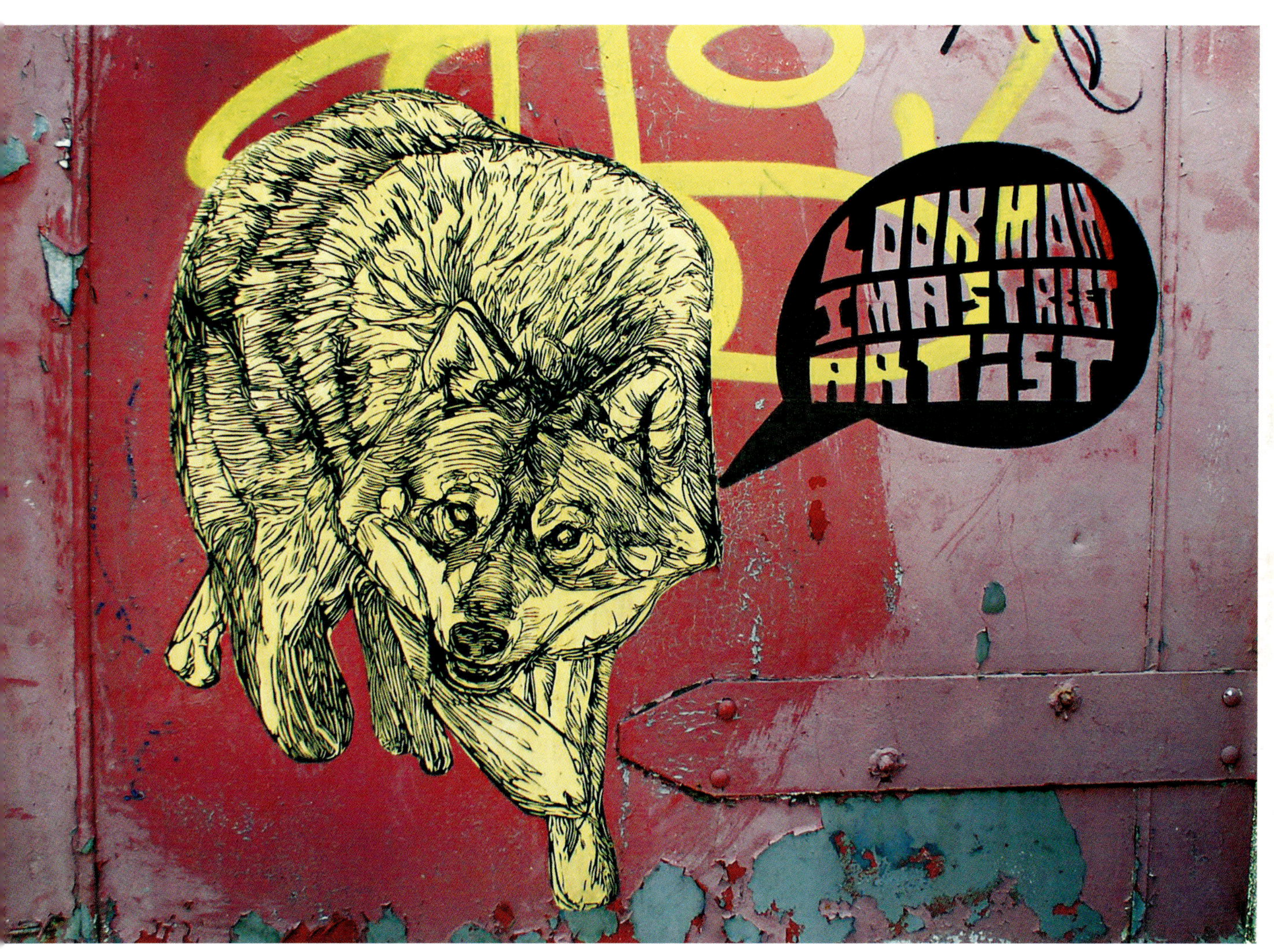
LOOK MOM
IMASTREET
ARTIST

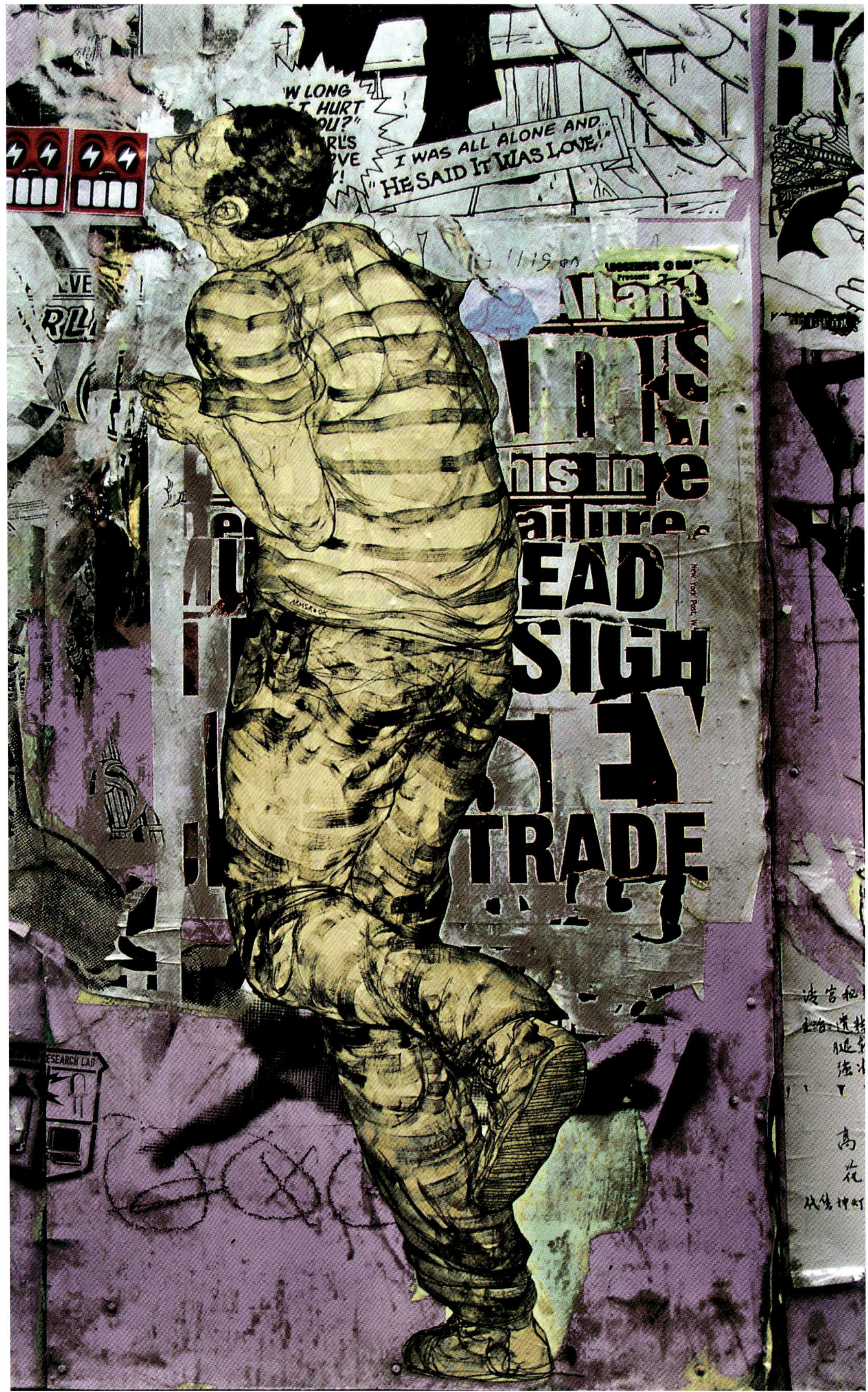
I WAS ALL ALONE AND..
"HE SAID IT WAS LOVE!"
EAD
SIGH
TRADE

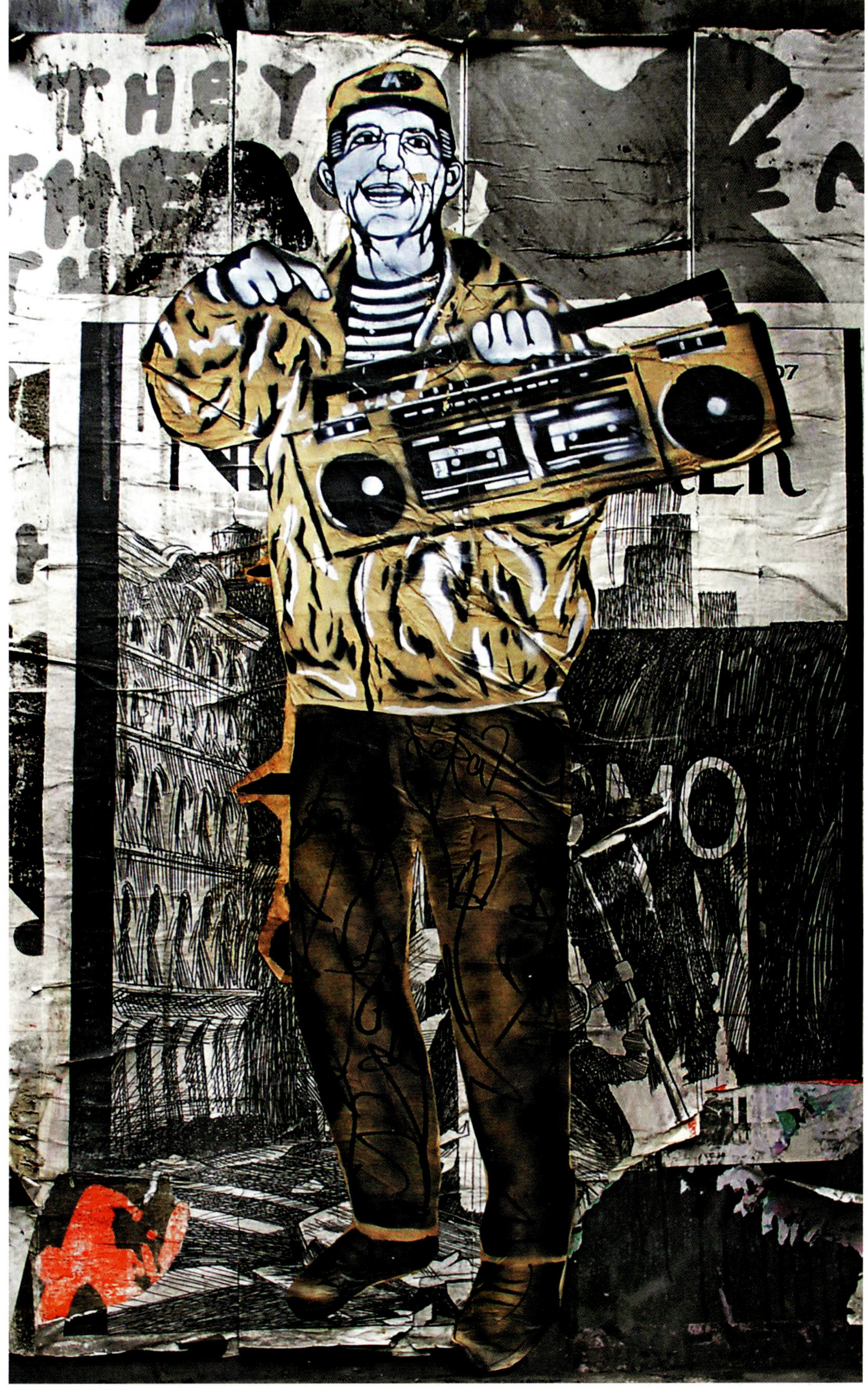
THEY

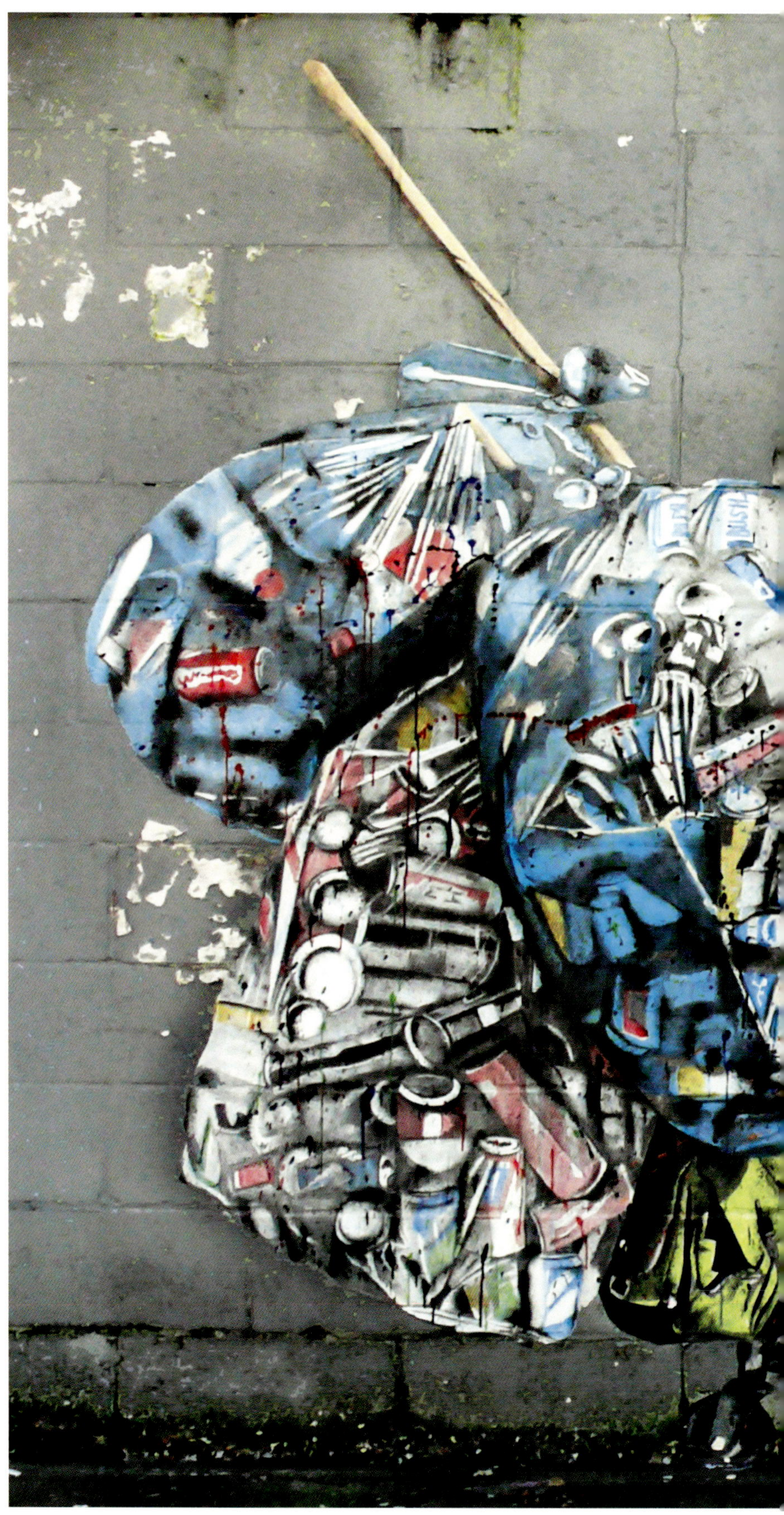

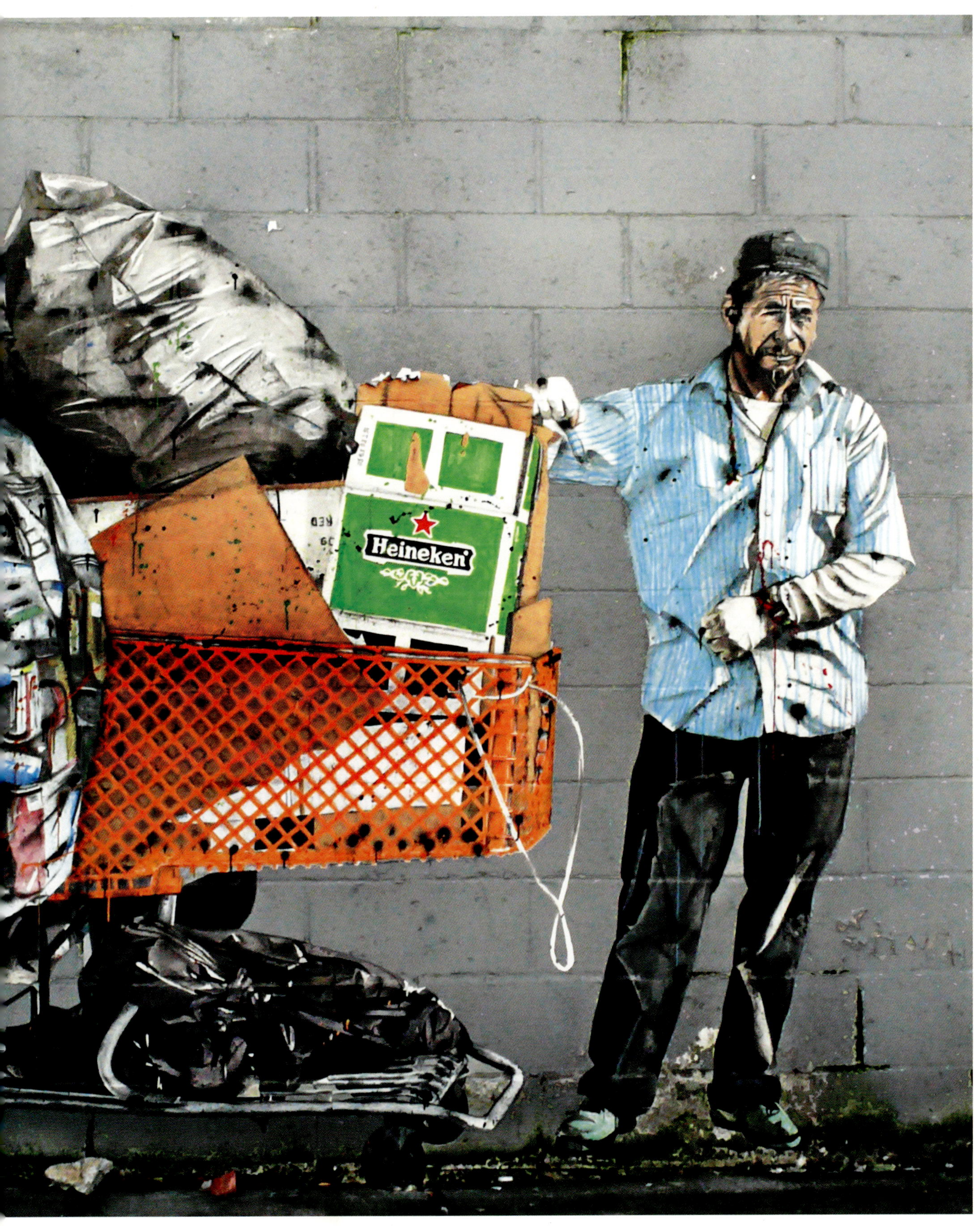
Heineken

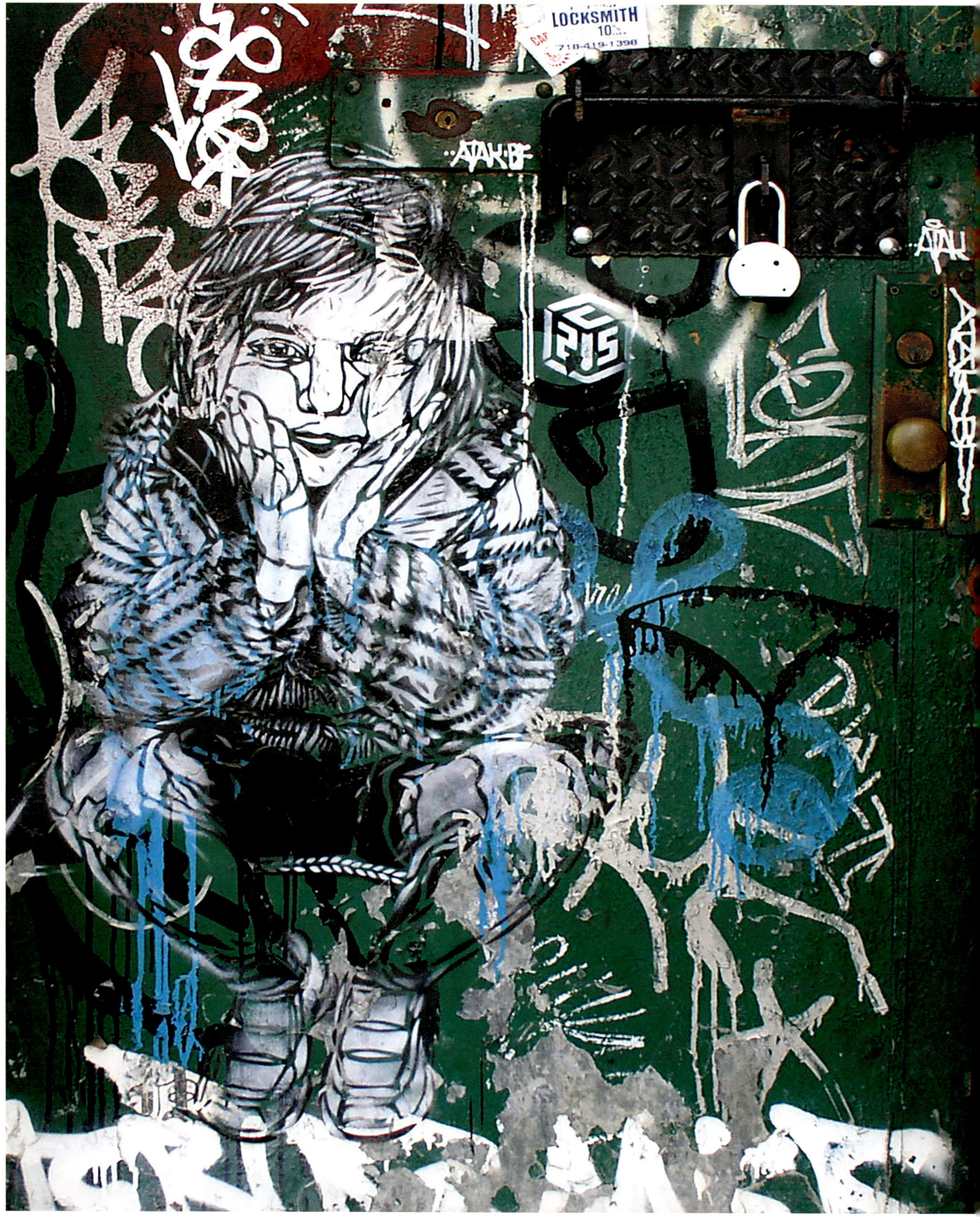
LOCKSMITH

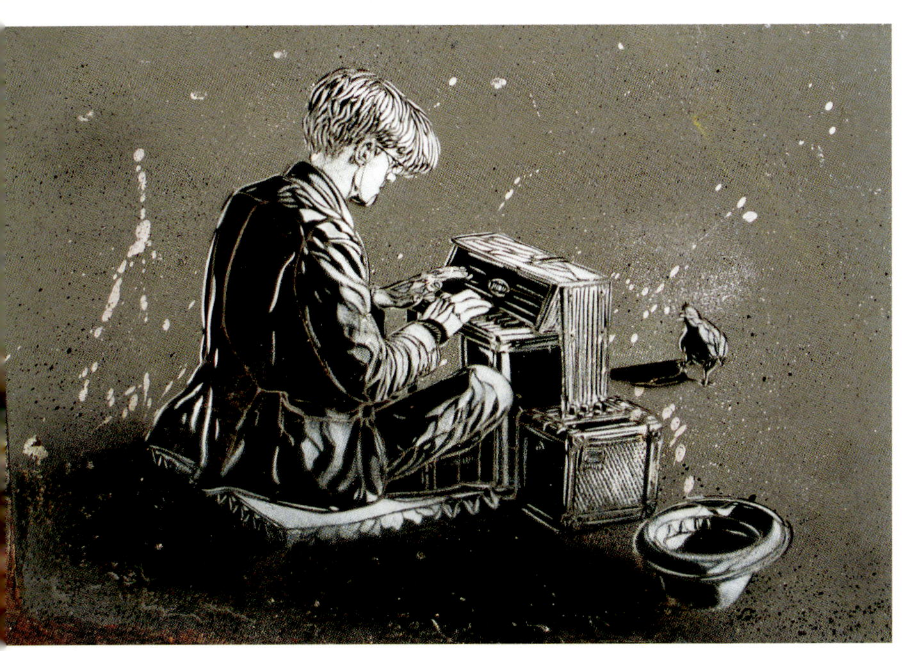

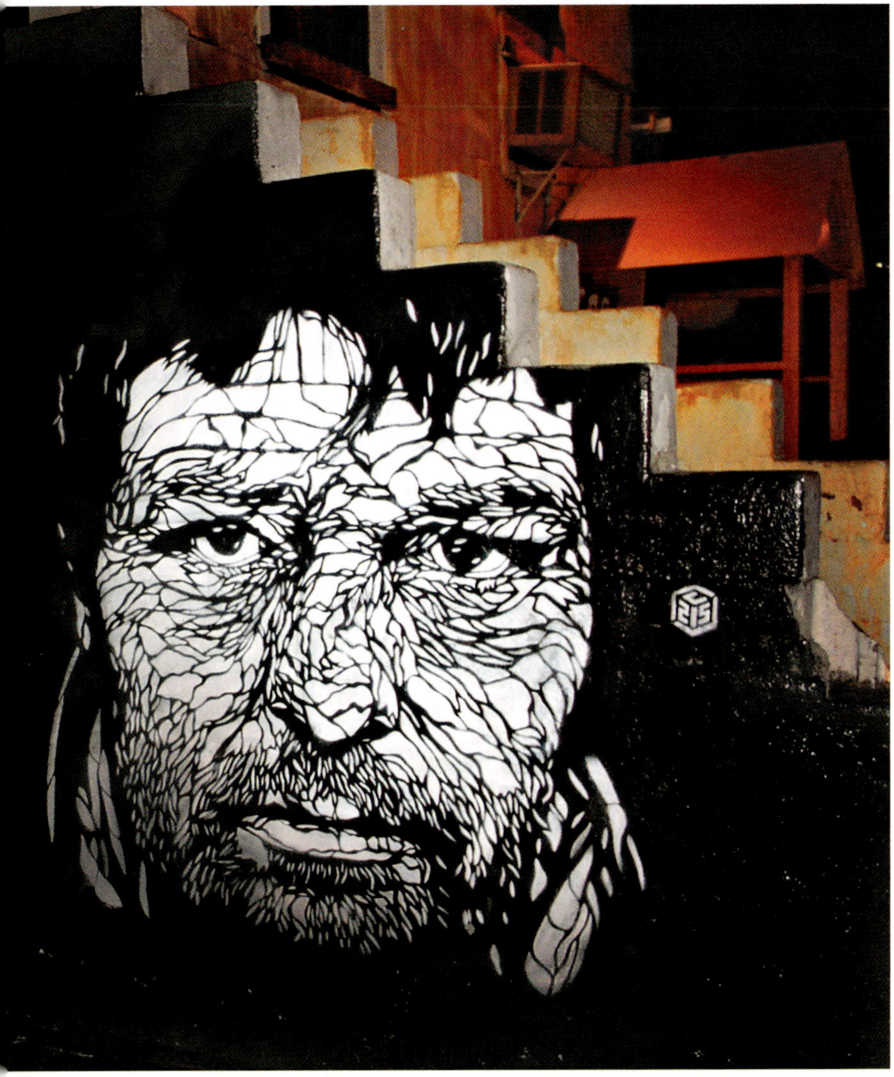

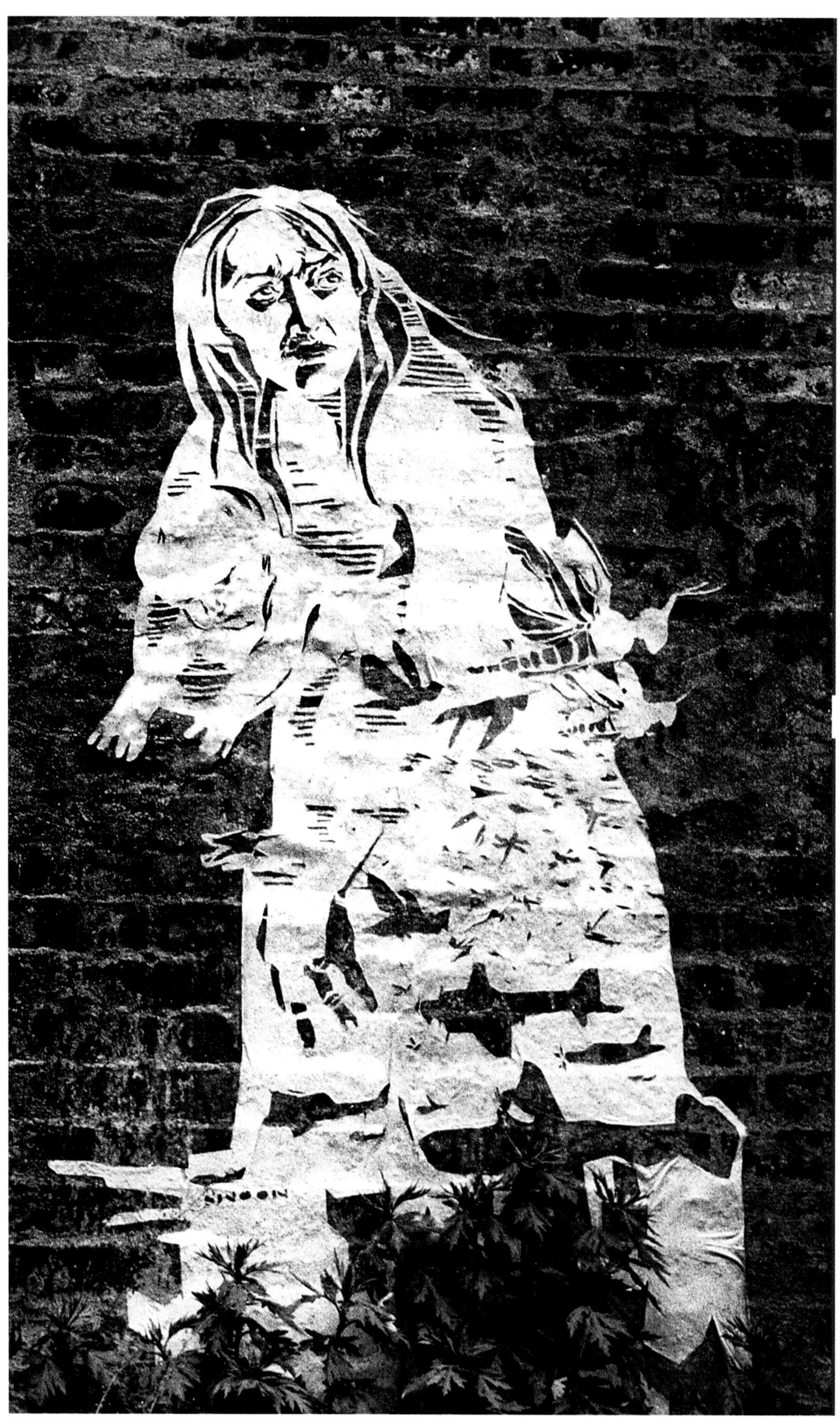
SWOON

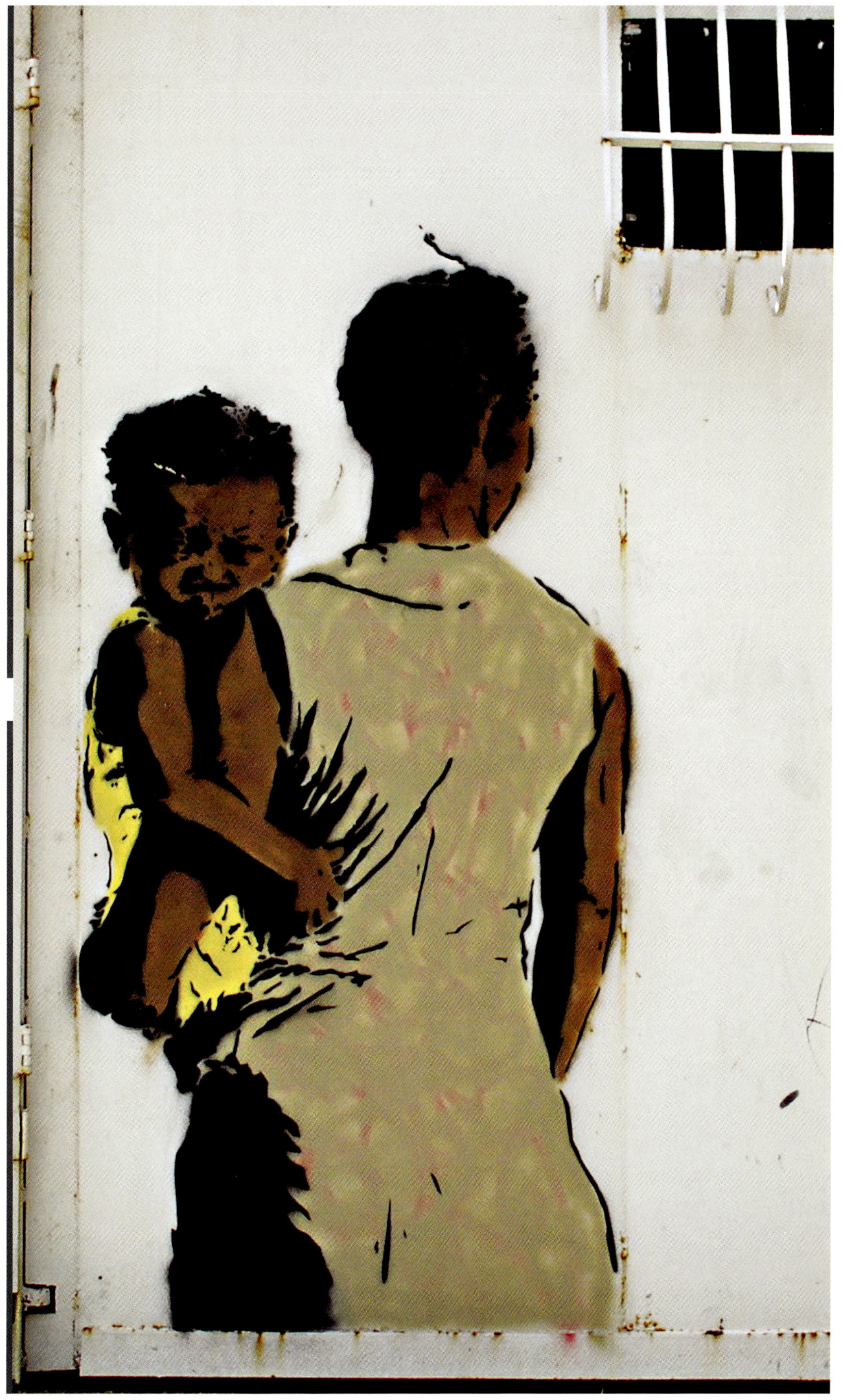

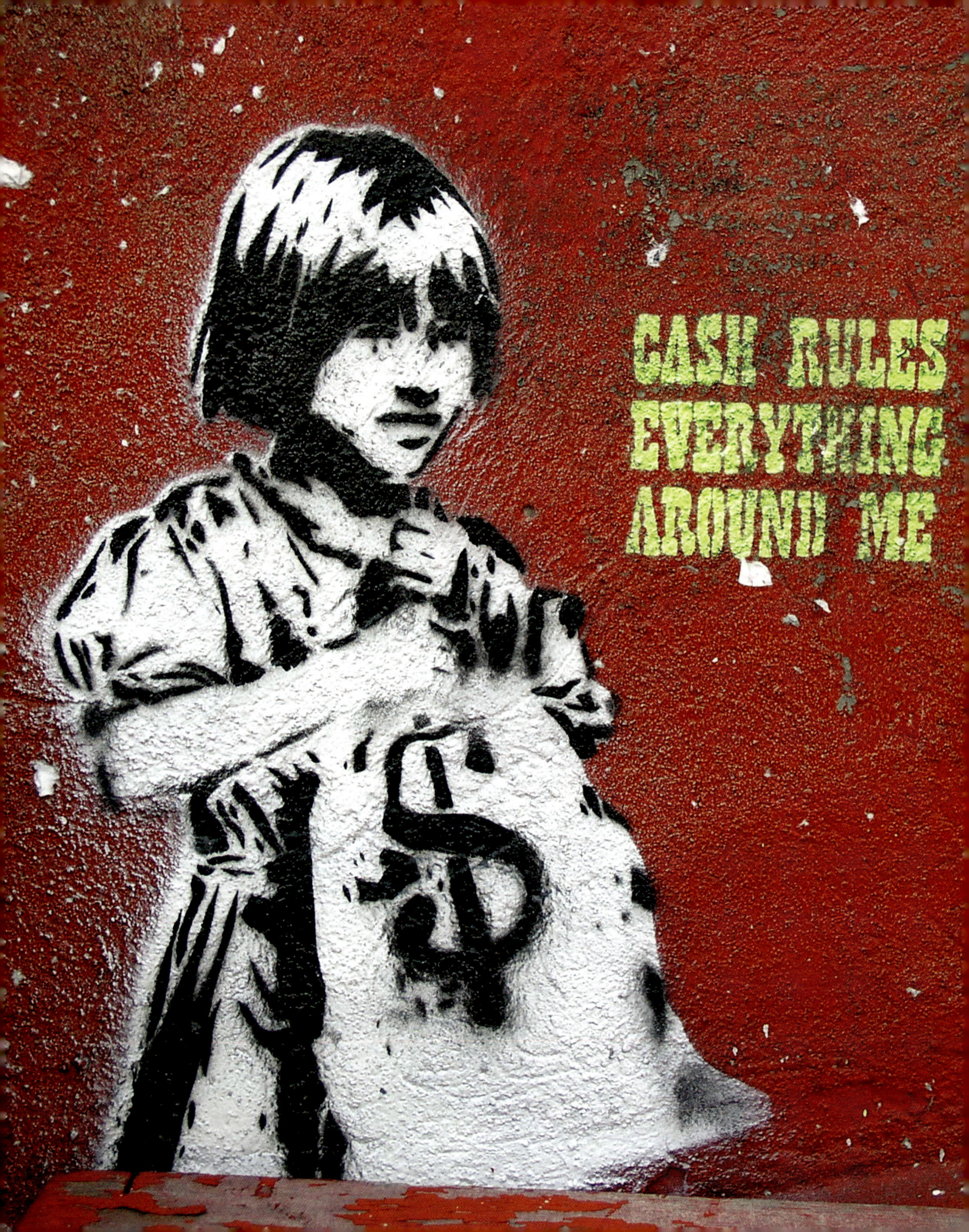
CASH RULES
EVERYTHING
AROUND ME

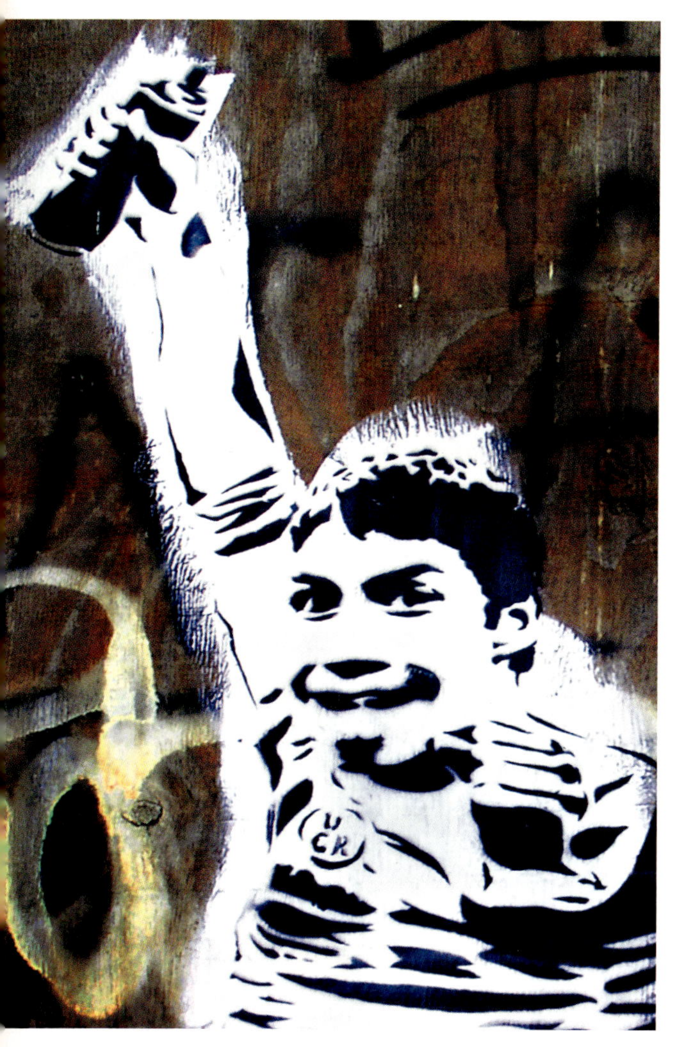

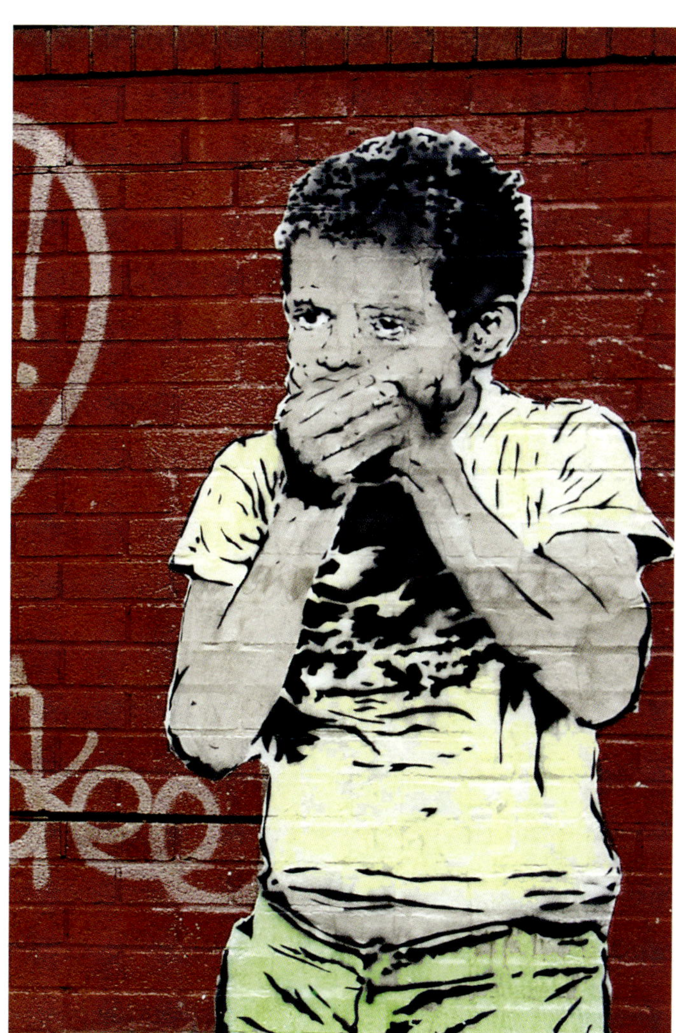

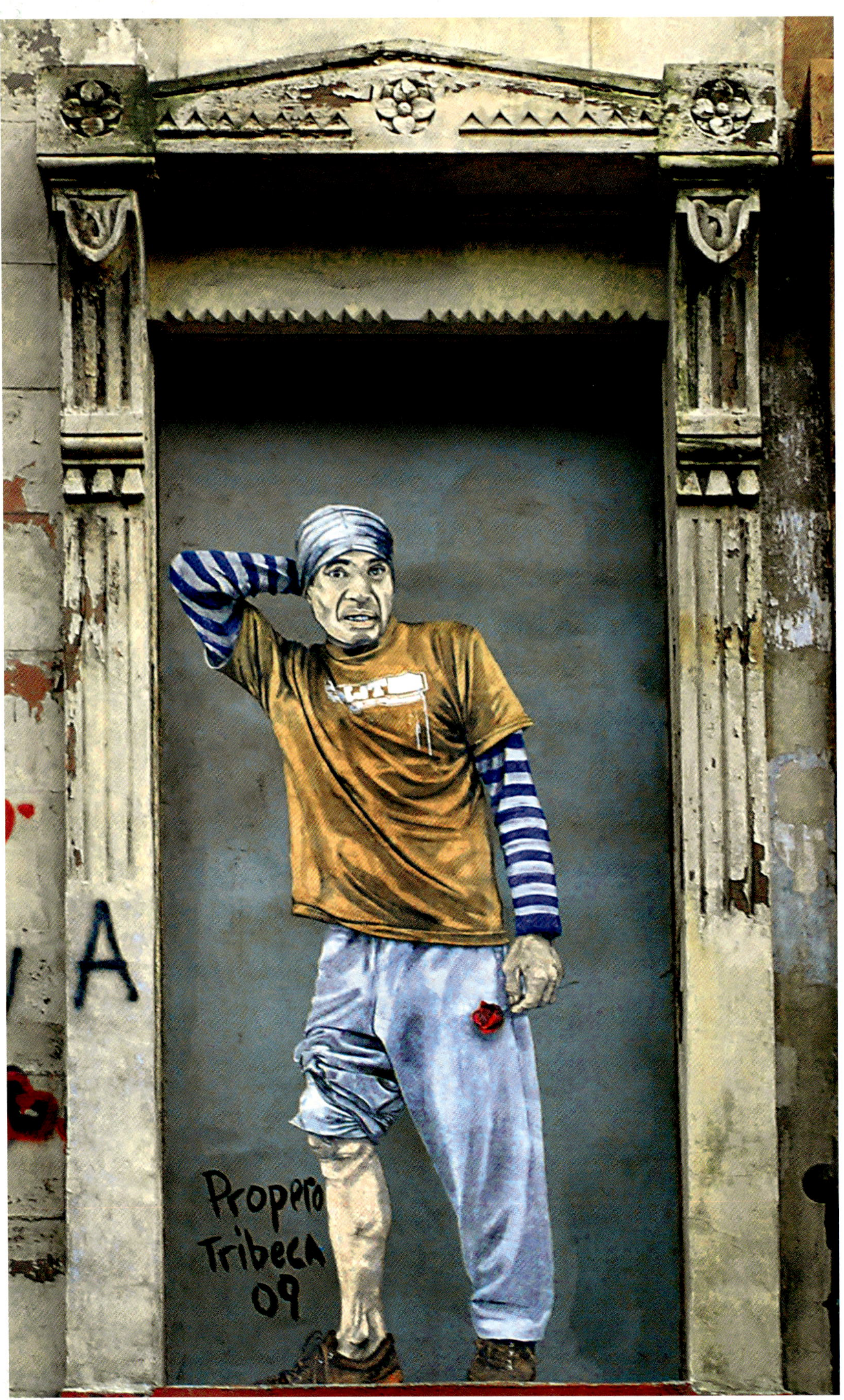
Propero
Tribeca
09

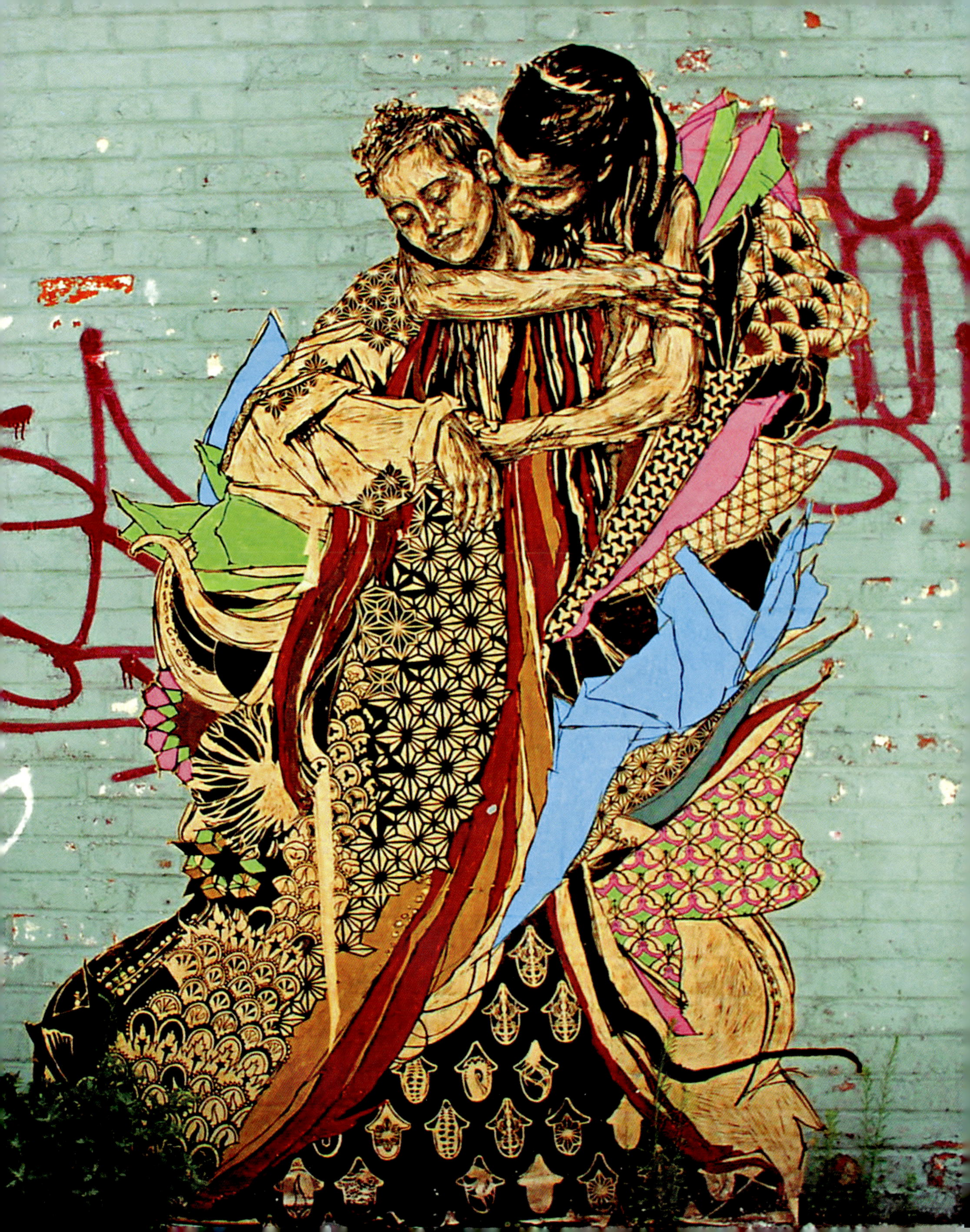

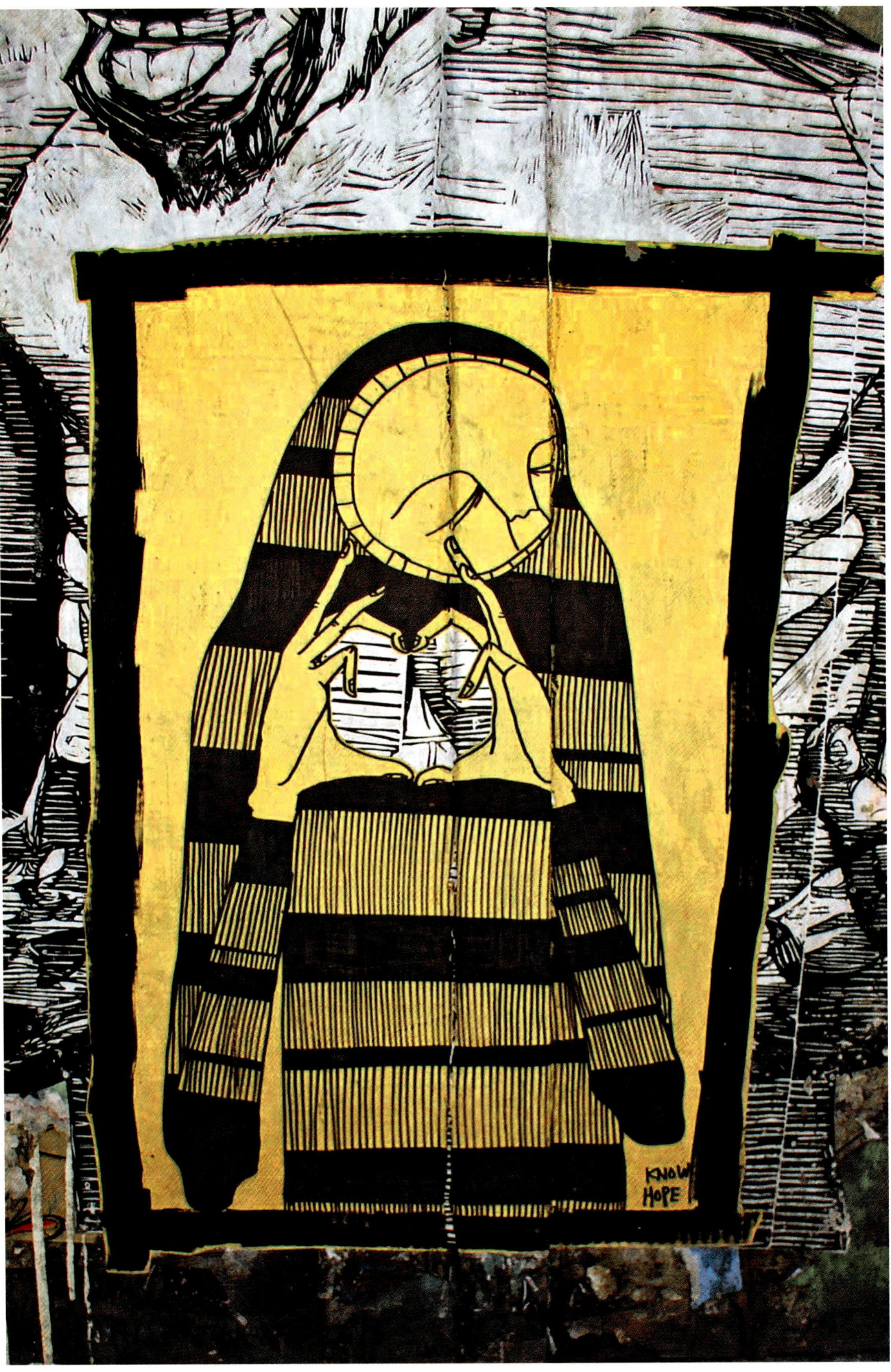
KNOW
HOPE

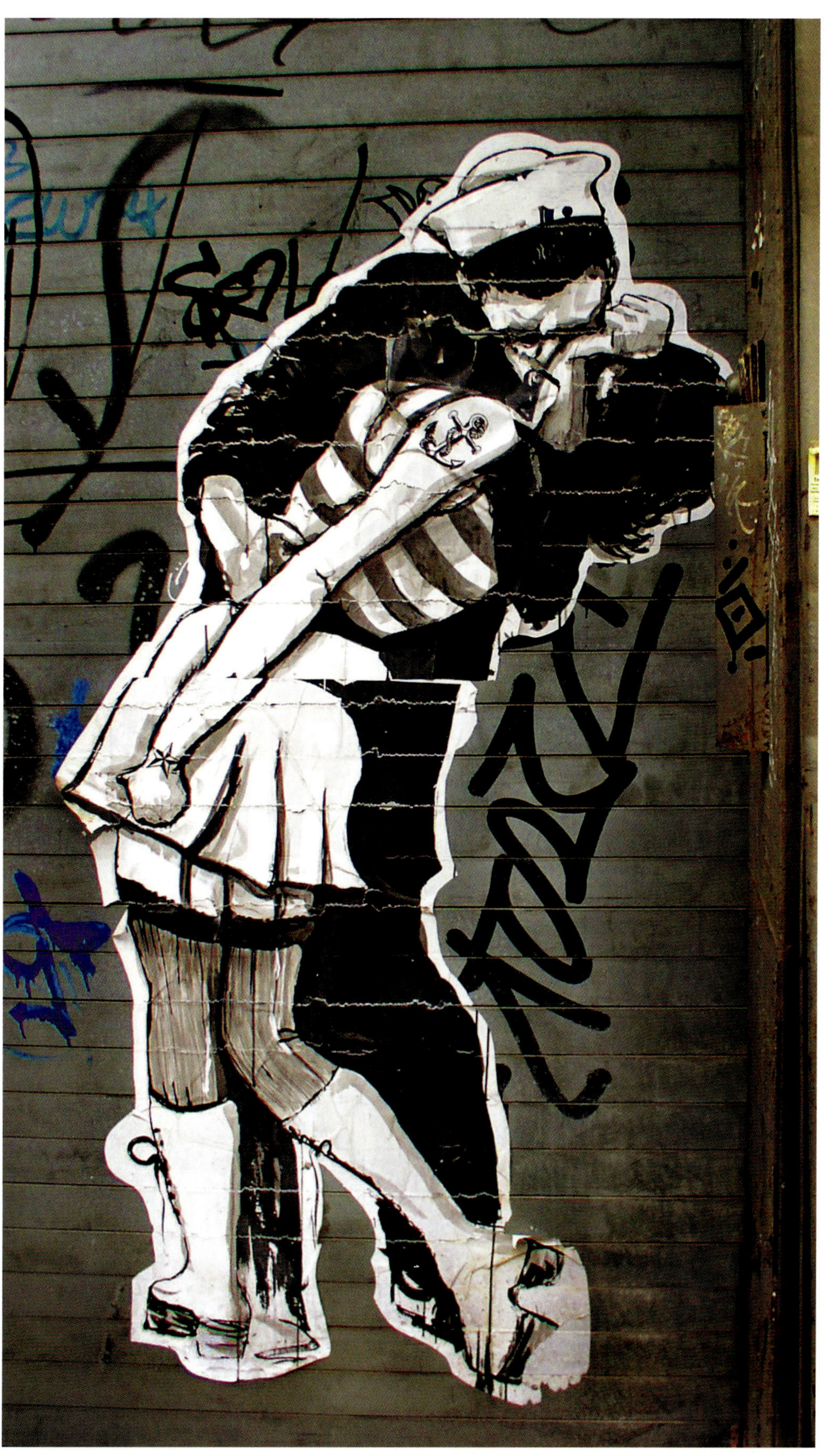

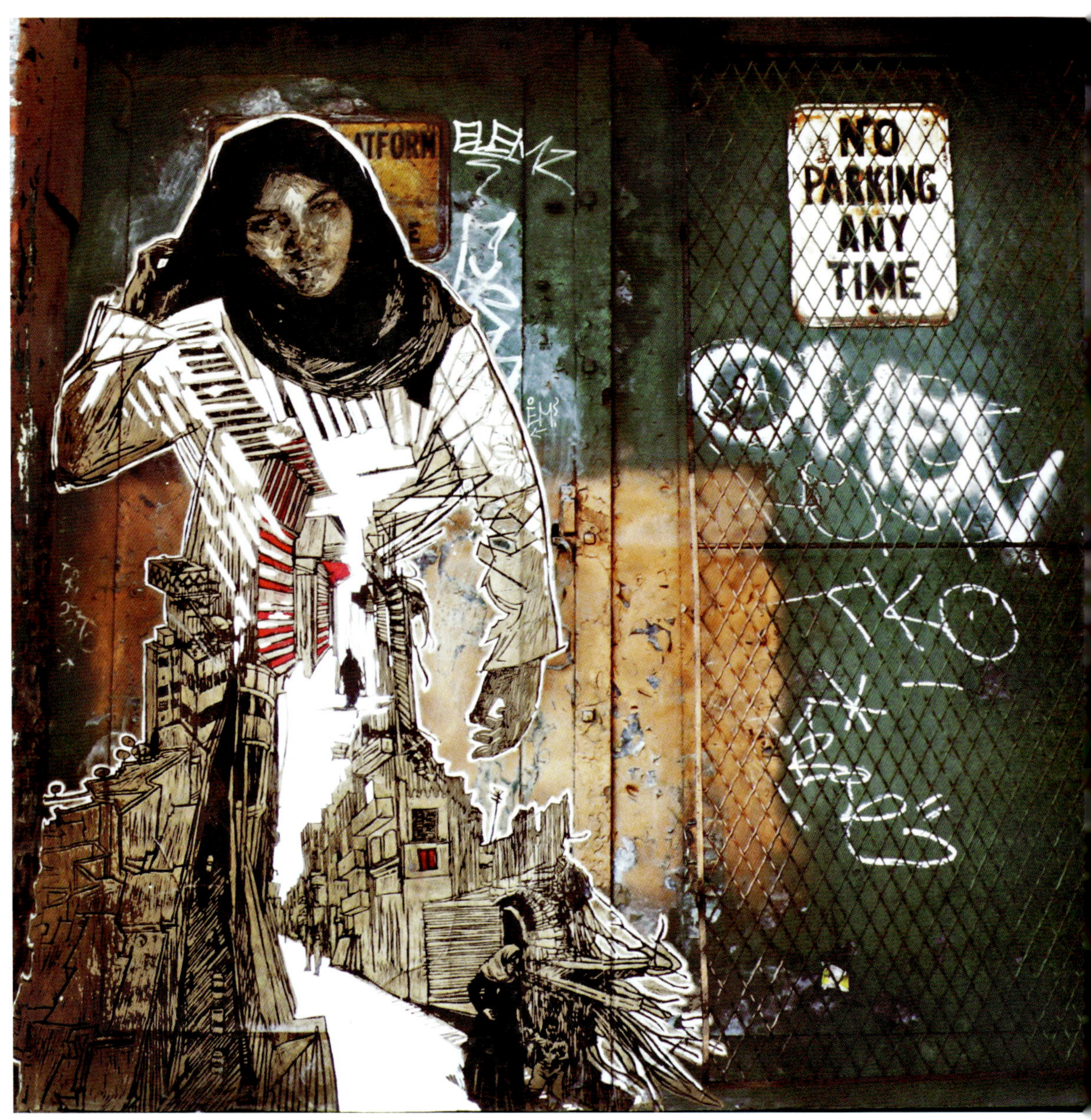
NO
PARKING
ANY
TIME

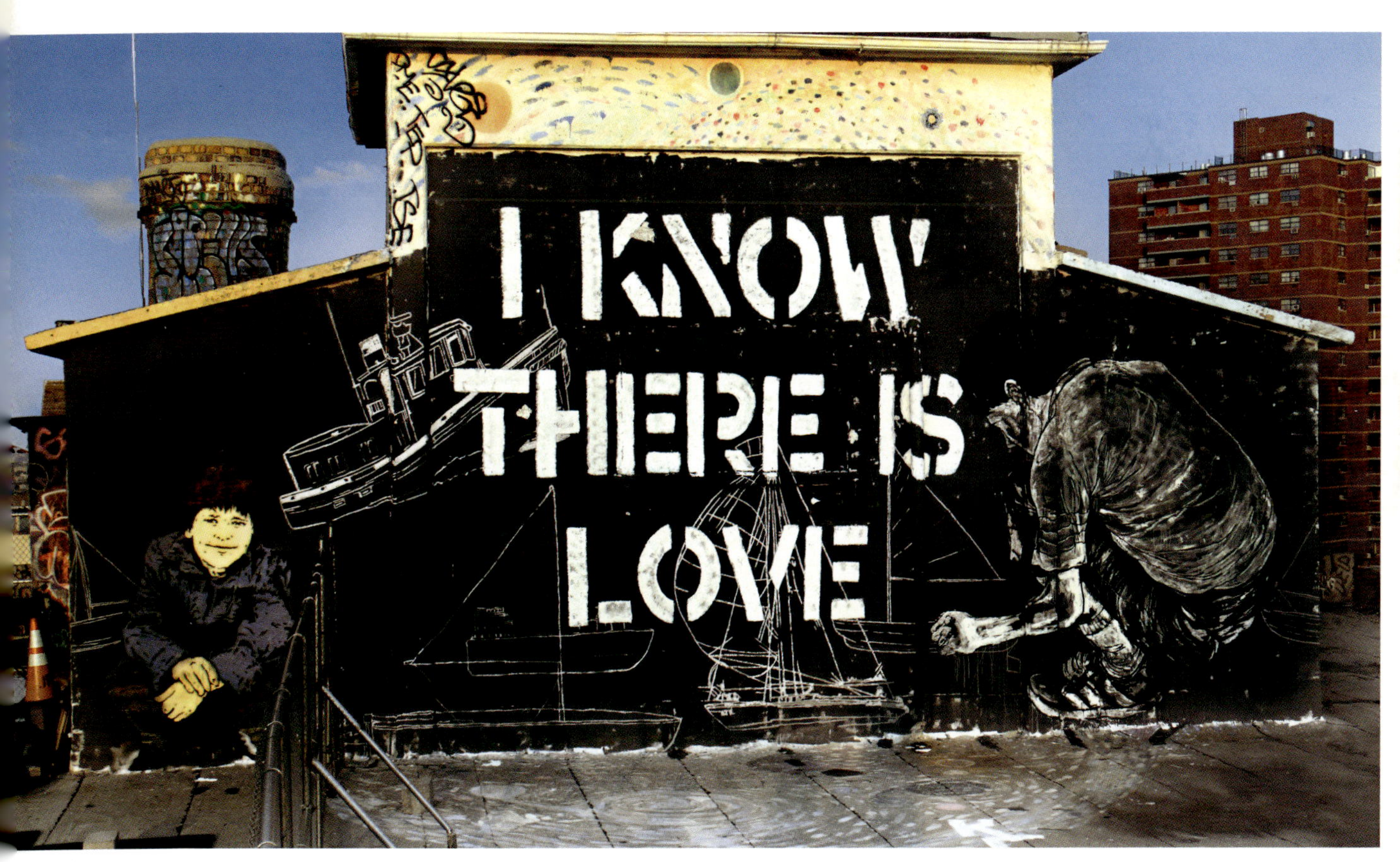
I KNOW
THERE IS
LOVE

INDEX

INDEX

Name	URL
Aakash Nihalani	aakashnihalani.com
Aiko	ladyaiko.com
Armsrock	armsrock.blogspot.com
Banksy	banksy.co.uk
Bast	bastny.com
Beast	beastrockstudio.com
Billi Kid	billikid.com
Bishop203	bishop203.com
Borf	myspace.com/borf_dc
Bortusk Leer	bortuskleer.com
Broken Crow	brokencrow.com
C.Damage	flickr.com/photos/c_damage
C215	myspace.com/c215
Cake	cakestreetart.com
Celso	elcelso.com
Cern	ymicrew.com
Chris (RWK)	robotswillkill.com
Chris Stain	chrisstain.com
Chris Uphues	chrisuphues.com
Conor Harrington	conorharrington.com
Creepy	creepy.headtank.com
D*Face	dface.co.uk
Dain	flickr.com/photos/22203131@N05
Damon Ginandes	damonginandes.com
Dan Witz	danwitzstreetart.com
DarkCloud	flickr.com/photos/dark-cloudsarchive
Dennis McNett	wolfbat.com
Deuce 7	deuce7art.com/ deuce7art.com/Deuce_7.html
Elbow-Toe	elbow-toe.com
Ethos	claudioethos.com
Fafi	fafi.net
Faile	faile.net
Fauxreel	fauxreel.ca
FKDL	fkdl.com/blog
Gaia	gaiastreetart.com
General Howe	generalhowe.com
GoreB	flickr.com/photos/goreb
Goons	flickr.com/photos/goons
Hellbent	hellbentart.com
Herakut	herakut.de
Hugh Leeman	hughleeman.com
Imminent Disaster	flickr.com/photos/disasterstrikes
Jef Aerosol	myspace.com/jefaerosol
JMR	jmrizzi.blogspot.com
Joe Black	mrjoeblack.com
Jon Burgerman	jonburgerman.com
Judith Supine	flickr.com/photos/judithsupine
Keely	keelybrandon.blogspot.com
Kid Acne	kidacne.com
Know Hope	flickr.com/photos/thisislimbo
Koralie	kogaylou.free.fr
Lister	anthonylister.com
Loafer Loafer	flickr.com/photos/loaferloafer
Logan Hicks	workhorsevisuals.com
Mark Carvalho	markcarvalhofineart.com
Matt Siren	mattsiren.com
Mr. Brainwash	mrbrainwash.com
Mike Marcus	mikemarcus.blogspot.com
Mint	mintandserf.com
Miss Bugs	missbugs.com
MOMO	momoshowpalace.com

WEBSITE

Name	URL
Mosstika	mosstika.com
Mr. Talion	flickr.com/photos/31192713@N03
Nick Walker	web.mac.com/nickwalkerz
Noah Sparkes	noahsparkes.com
NohJColey	nohjcoley.com
Os Gêmeos	12ozprophet.com/index.php/os_gemeos
Over Under	overunder.blogspot.com
Peru Ana Ana Peru	flickr.com/photos/peruanaanaperu
Peripheral Media Projects	peripheralmediaprojects.com
Pork	porknewyork.com
Poster Boy	flickr.com/photos/26296445@N05
Rene Gagnon	renegagnonfineart.com
ROA	fotolog.com/roabot
Royce Bannon	choiceroyce.tumblr.com
Senator	thebloodofpatriots.com
Serf	mintandserf.com
Shark Toof	sharktoof.com
Shepard Fairey	obeygiant.com
Skewville	skewville.org
Space Invader	space-invaders.com
Specter	specterart.com
Sweet Toof	flickr.com/photos/nolionsinengland/sets/72157611569302748
Swoon	swimmingcities.org
The Dude Company	flickr.com/photos/thedudecompany
Tian	tian.fr
Veng (RWK)	robotswillkill.com
WK Interact	wkinteract.com

For more information go to StreetArtNewYork.com

© Prestel Verlag, Munich · Berlin · London · New York, 2010
For design and layout, © by Steven P. Harrington, 2010
For photography, © by Jaime Rojo, 2010
For the text, © by Steven P. Harrington and Jaime Rojo, 2010

Prestel, a member of Verlagsgruppe Random House GmbH

Prestel Verlag
Königinstrasse 9
80539 Munich
Tel. +49 (0)89 24 29 08-300
Fax +49 (0)89 24 29 08-335

Prestel Publishing Ltd.
4 Bloomsbury Place
London WC1A 2QA
Tel. +44 (0)20 7323-5004
Fax +44 (0)20 7636-8004

Prestel Publishing
900 Broadway, Suite 603
New York, NY 10003
Tel. +1 (212) 995-2720
Fax +1 (212) 995-2733

www.prestel.com

Library of Congress Control Number: 2009942604

British Library Cataloguing-in-Publication Data: a catalogue record for this book is available from the British Library; Deutsche Nationalbibliothek holds a record of this publication in the Deutsche Nationalbibliografie; detailed bibliographical data can be found under: http://dnb.d-nb.de

Prestel books are available worldwide. Please contact your nearest bookseller or one of the above addresses for information concerning your local distributor.

Editorial direction: Christopher Lyon
Edited & Copyedited by: Ali Gitlow
Production: Nele Krüger
Design and layout: Steven P. Harrington, New York
Origination: Reproline Mediateam, Munich
Printing & Binding: C&C Printing
Verlagsgruppe Random House FSC-DEU-0100
The FSC-certified paper Chinese Golden Sun matt art is produced by
mill Yanzhou Tianzhang Paper Industry Co., Ltd., Shandong, PRC.

Printed in China.

ISBN 978-3-7913-4428-7

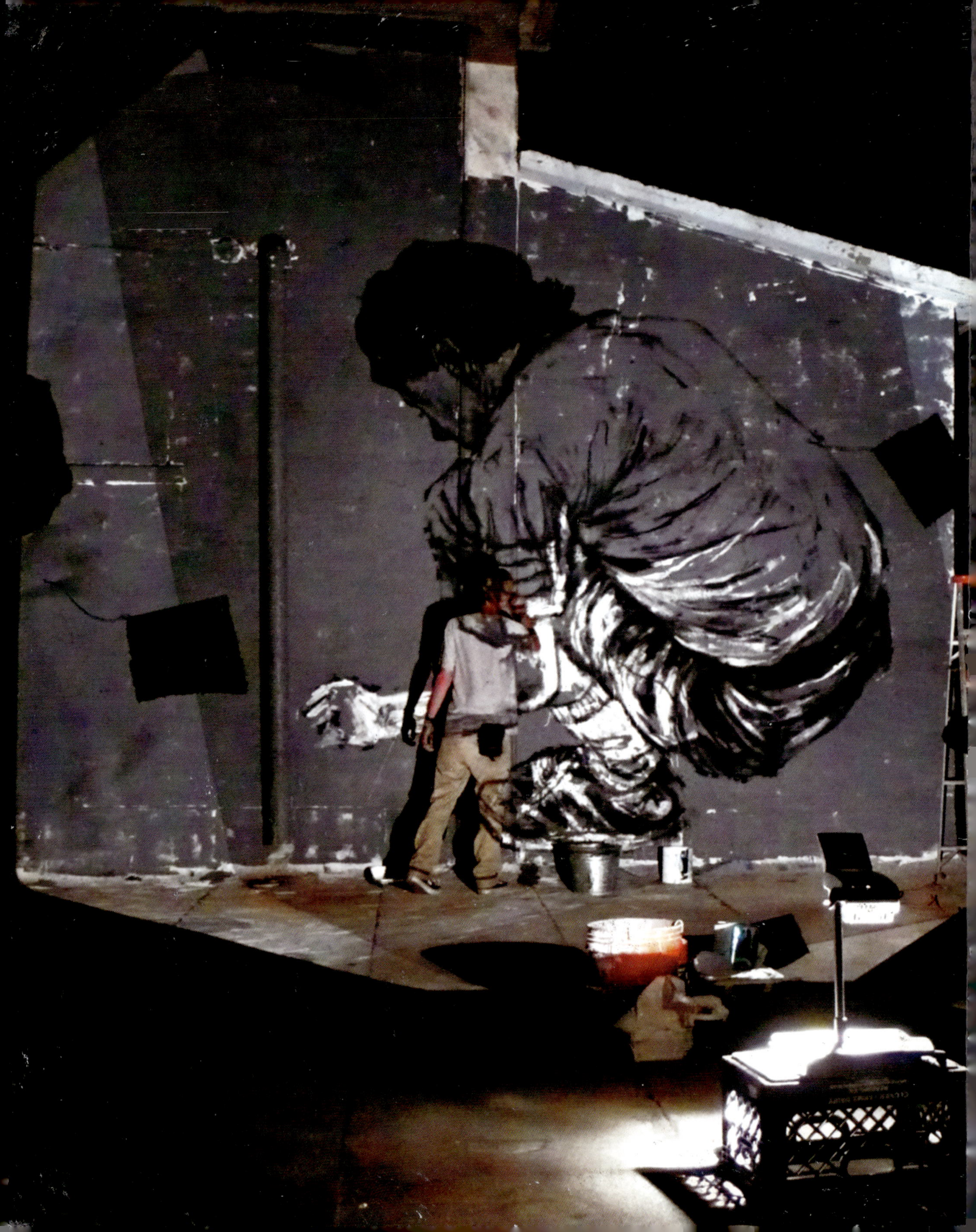